# Asian American Literature

*An Introduction to the Writings
and Their Social Context*

# Asian American Literature

*An Introduction to the Writings*

*and Their Social Context*

Elaine H. Kim

TEMPLE UNIVERSITY PRESS

PHILADELPHIA

Temple University Press, Philadelphia 19122
© 1982 by Temple University. All rights reserved
Published 1982
Printed in the United States of America

**Library of Congress Cataloging in Publication Data**

Kim, Elaine H.
  Asian American literature, an introduction to the writings and their social context.

  Bibliography: p.
  Includes index.
  1. American literature—Asian–American authors—History and criticism.   2. Asian Americans in literature.
  I. Title.
PS153.A84K55 1982      810′.9′895      82-5987
  ISBN 0-87722-260-6                       AACR2

To My Parents,
*Sae Sun Kim* and *Annie Lee Kim*
and My Son,
*Oliver*

# Contents

# Acknowledgments

I am inspired every day by the people of the Korean Community Center of the East Bay in Oakland, California, especially by community worker Kwang Woo Han, and by my students at the University of California at Berkeley. I am indebted to the staff and faculty of the University of California at Berkeley's Asian American Studies program as well: to Sucheng Chan for her comments and criticisms, to Ling Chi Wang for his encouraging support, to Janice Otani, who typed the manuscript and offered many useful suggestions, to Richard Komatsu and Elizabeth Megino, and to Wei Chi Poon and Kathy Hirooka of the Asian American Studies Library for making the task easier in innumerable ways.

I am also very grateful for the support and suggestions of Maxine Hong Kingston, the late Toshio Mori, Bienvenido N. Santos, Harold Hakwon Sunoo, Jere Takahashi, Ronald Takaki, Ronald Tanaka, and Hisaye Yamamoto DeSoto. I would like to thank Alan Covici, Spencer Nakasako, Alvin Planas, Sun-hae Song, and John Takakuwa for their technical assistance, Carey Pelton and Helen Hong for typing part of the manuscript, and my brother, Ronald Kim, for helping with the proofreading. The cover art is derived from an oil painting by Jong-Seung Moon. The artist's permission is gratefully acknowledged.

Parts of Chapter 1 were presented at the 1980 National Conference on Chinese American Studies as "Images of Chinese in Anglo-American Literature," to be published in *The Chinese American Experience* (San Francisco: Chinese Culture Center, 1982). The materials on Younghill Kang in Chapter 2 appeared as "Searching for a Door to America: Immigrant Writer, Younghill Kang," *Korea Journal*, April 1977. The materials on Maxine Hong Kingston in Chapter 6 appeared as "Visions and Fierce Dreams: A Commentary on the Works of Maxine Hong Kingston," *Amerasia Journal* 8, no. 2 (1981): 145–161.

# Preface

One of my students at Berkeley, a perceptive young man who had immigrated with his family from the People's Republic of China two years before, recently asked me why students form racial groups at schools and colleges in America. He was particularly puzzled that American-born Chinese who spoke little Chinese deliberately grouped themselves with immigrant Chinese, who spoke English haltingly. In Canton, he commented, a common language would have been a more important criterion for social compatibility than race. How could I have answered his question in a day? He had focused upon one contemporary manifestation of a fundamental problem, the roots of which are as deep as American history itself.

What I have attempted in this book is to trace the topography and rich textures of the Asian American experience as it is expressed in Asian American literature from the late nineteenth century to the present day. Although I have used my understanding of Asian American social history to interpret the literature, I have focused on the evolution of Asian American consciousness and self-image as expressed in the literature. For the purposes of this study, I have defined Asian American literature as published creative writings in English by Americans of Chinese, Japanese, Korean, and Filipino descent. This definition is problematical: it does not encompass writers in Asia or even writers expressing the American experience in Asian languages, although I have included some discussions of Japanese, Chinese, and Korean poetry about the Asian American experience that has been translated into English. This is not to say that writings in Asian languages are unimportant to a study of Asian American literature and experience: they are simply beyond the purview of this study, and I am confident that they will be presented elsewhere. Nor have I included in this book literature about Asia written by Asian Americans in English, except when it is revealing of the Asian American consciousness.

Calling this work a study of "Asian American" literature presents an enormous problem because, to begin with, the term Asian American is a controversial one. Like its predecessor, "Oriental," it was created in the West from the need to make racial categorizations in a racially divided or, at least, a racially diverse society. It has always been difficult for me to accept being called Oriental, since "Oriental" denotes east of somewhere, east of some other-defined center. Oriental is such an imprecise term: what is an Oriental flavor? an Oriental atmosphere or look? Asian American is a bit more precise. At least this term connotes an American identity for Asians, and it sounds more objective than Oriental. But Asian American and Asian Pacific American, while convenient for census count purposes, are also terms created and used to differentiate us from non-Asian and Pacific Americans. I would venture that the vast majority of persons of Chinese, Vietnamese, or Samoan ancestry would not, if asked, describe themselves as Asian and Pacific Americans but as Chinese, Vietnamese, or Samoan Americans, or indeed as Chinese, Vietnamese, and Samoans. To Asians all Orientals do not "look alike."[1] For instance, during the decades when Korea was colonized by Japan, enormous efforts were made by Korean Americans to clarify the distinctions between Koreans and Japanese, especially because the United States responded to that annexation by classifying Koreans in the United States with Japanese. No doubt many members of the Laotian, Cambodian, and Vietnamese communities in this country are confused when they are grouped together as Indochinese or as Southeast Asians. Distinctions among the various national groups sometimes do blur after a generation or two, when it is easier for us to see that we are bound together by the experiences we share as members of an American racial minority, but, when we do so, we are accepting an externally imposed label that is meant to define us by distinguishing us from other Americans primarily on the basis of race rather than culture.

That this book is about literature written in English by Asians from four different national groups means that I have accepted the externally imposed racial categorization of Asians in American society as an underlying assumption. Otherwise, I would have concentrated on a single ethnic group, such as Korean Americans, and I would have included literature written in Korean. Although I agree that the complexity of each group's American experience merits a separate study, I am myself interested in what Asians in America share and in how they can be compared within the context of their American experiences. I have noticed while studying this body of literature that, although it shares with most other literature thematic concerns such as love, desire for personal freedom and acceptance, and struggles against oppression and injustice, it is also shaped by other important particulars. American racism has been a critical factor in the Chinese, Japanese, Korean, and Filipino experience in the United States: it is no accident that literature by writers from those groups is often much concerned with this shared heritage. Racial policies and attitudes towards the different groups have often been quite similar, as have the responses to these policies and attitudes among them.

I believe that there is something to be gained from viewing the commonalities and differences among the four experiences as expressed in their literatures. I hope, for example, that my discussions of early Chinese, Japanese, Korean, and Filipino immigrant writers in Chapter 2 and of American-born and immigrant contemporary writers in Chapter 7 will vindicate my approach by demonstrating these commonalities and differences within the context of a shared American experience.

Whatever its origins, the racial classification of Asian Americans does in fact have its advantages for us. Our racial unity has been contributing to our strength, to our efforts to build community, and to the maintenance and development of a vital Asian American culture. This unity helps us function effectively in organizations and programs across the country: the Asian American Theatre Company in San Francisco, for example, showcases plays written, directed, and performed by persons of various Asian backgrounds and nativities and reflecting a wide range of perspectives and concerns; an Oakland Asian American language and employment training project offers programs for limited-English-speaking immigrants, who work closely with American-born and immigrant teachers of various national backgrounds; nearby bilingual Japanese, Filipino, Korean, and Chinese teachers provide childcare services for Korean, Chinese, Laotian, and Vietnamese pre-schoolers. Although most would agree that each nationality group should have its own identity and strengths, who would argue that pan-Asian American efforts should be cast aside?

While some readers may be bothered by the fact that this study focuses on four groups instead of one, others may criticize it for not encompassing all Asian Americans. I have included most of the literary figures from four or five generations of Asian Americans of Chinese, Japanese, Korean, and Filipino ancestry. But a reader of East Indian or Pakistani descent, for example, will search the book in vain for a discussion of his literature and culture in the United States. I can only beg the tolerance of my brothers and sisters from Southeast Asia and elsewhere by offering the argument that as yet there is relatively little literature in English expressing the sensibilities of very new population groups, such as Laotian, Cambodian, or Thai people, in the United States.

Some readers may fault me for including Korean American literature, which is hardly more plentiful than Vietnamese American writing at the moment, since the Korean American population is largely a new one too. Younghill Kang, however, emerged from among the handful of Koreans living in America long before the recent influx of immigrants and refugees from Asia began. Moreover, I could hardly resist including something about contemporary Korean immigrant writer Kichung Kim, whom I admire precisely because as a fellow Korean American I know he is poignantly expressing an experience shared by many people I know.

Since 1970, some Asian American literary history and criticism has been published, notably by Ronald Tanaka of Sacramento State University and Bruce Iwasaki of the Asian American Studies Center at UCLA.[2] Several anthologies of Asian American literature contain introductory essays of a general nature. The best known of these are in *Asian American Authors* (1972), edited by Kai-yu Hsu and Helen Palubinskas, and *Aiiieeeee! An Anthology of Asian-American Writers* (1974), edited by Frank Chin, Jeffery Paul Chan, Lawson Fusao Inada, and Shawn Hsu Wong.[3] As far as I know, however, mine is the first attempt to integrate the Asian American literary voice in one book-length study. I view this work as a beginning, a conversational gambit, and I trust that it will be complemented by many other studies that deal with issues I have not addressed.

Because the scope of this book is deliberately broad and detailed at the same time, it was difficult to decide how best to organize the materials contained here. I have been more concerned with breadth and variety than with classifications. I could have arranged the materials according to themes; I could have discussed writers of different nationalities separately instead of trying to weave them together; I could even have arranged the discussions around literary genre classifications, dealing first with poetry, then autobiographical writing, and finally with short stories and novels. What I did was to compromise: the arrangement is roughly chronological, beginning with early immigrant writings in English and ending with contemporary Asian American writers. The study is also organized—just as roughly—around themes, so I move from discussions of writing aimed at winning sympathy for Asian immigrants to writing that attempts to establish a self-defined cultural identity. Sometimes I group writers of different nationalities together, as in Chapters 2, 3, and 7, and at other times I discuss them separately, as in the chapters on Chinatown literature and on Japanese American family and community portrait literature, where I wanted to show how Chinese and Japanese American writers responded to the differences in their social experiences around the time of World War II. The problem I faced was that the body of literature did not lend itself to a single type of arrangement. Although it might have been desirable, for example, to discuss Chinese, Japanese, Korean, and Filipino community portraiture together in one chapter, the result would have been unbalanced, since there are many more examples of Japanese American community portrait literature, undoubtedly because the Japanese American community experienced a longer history as a family society and there has always been a larger proportion of American-born, English-speaking Japanese American writers, for reasons discussed in the book. Moreover, the two Filipino writers who could have been classified as portrayers of the Filipino American community, Carlos Bulosan and Bienvenido N. Santos, seemed more crucial to the chapters on early immigrant autobiography and on contemporary Asian American writing respectively. Since I found so few Filipino and Korean early immigrant writers, I decided to place them in Chapter 2 to show how early Asian immigrant autobiographical writing moves from Asia-orientation to expression of the immigrant's desire to find a place for himself in American life and culture. In order to organize the book in tidy thematic chapters, I would have had to resort to contrivance. I wanted the arrangement to be loose enough to reflect what I saw as the variety, diversity, and indeed the unevenness of the literature.

Traditionally, one of the problems facing Asian American and other racial minority writers in America has been that many readers insist on viewing their writing as sociological or anthropological statements about the group. Lately another view just as narrow has emerged—that critical focus be concentrated on how minority writers express themselves instead of on what they say. Certainly both of these perspectives are limited and attention should be paid to both "literary" and "content" concerns. For the purposes of this study, however, I have deliberately chosen to emphasize how the literature elucidates the social history of Asians in the United States. The problem of understanding Asian American literature within its sociohistorical and cultural contexts is important to me because, when these contexts are unfamiliar, the literature is likely to be misunderstood and unappreciated. But the fact that this book is not an attempt to appreciate the formal literary merit of Asian American literature does not mean that I see no value in formal and stylistic interpretations; it only means that such interpretations were not my intention here. I feel certain that there are many more competent than I who will continue to address this question.

One of the fundamental barriers to understanding and appreciating Asian American literary self-expression has been the existence of race stereotypes about Asians in American popular culture. Probably more Americans know Fu Manchu and Charlie Chan than know Asian or Asian American human beings. Even the elite culture shares the popular stereotypes. Contemporary Chinese American playwright Frank Chin notes that New York critics of his play, "Chickencoop Chinaman," complained in the early 1970s that his characters did not speak, dress, or act "like Orientals."

Certainly reviews of Asian American literature by Anglo-American writers reveal that the criteria used to judge the literary merit of Asian

American writing have not always been literary. Reviewers of Etsu Sugimoto's *A Daughter of the Samurai* (1925) praised the writer because she
"pleads no causes, asks no vexing questions" at a time when the controversial issue of Japanese exclusion was still being spiritedly discussed.
Critics of *East Goes West* (1937) lauded Younghill Kang for finding fault
with Koreans and Korean society, but they were disturbed by his comments on America and Americans. Promoters of Pardee Lowe's *Father and
Glorious Descendant* (1943) touted Lowe's enlistment in the U.S. Army
during World War II as evidence that he belonged to "one of America's
loyal minorities" and that the book might therefore be worth reading. In
more recent times, Daniel Okimoto's *American in Disguise* (1971) was
appreciated by critics for having been written with "restraint" during a
period of racial unrest, and Jeanne Wakatsuki Houston's *Farewell to
Manzanar* (1973) was praised for its "lack of bitterness, self-pity, or
solemnity" in portraying the internment of Japanese Americans during
World War II.[4]

Today, Maxine Hong Kingston complains that, although readers of
various ethnic and racial backgrounds have responded to *The Woman
Warrior* (1976) with profound understanding, she has also been very
much misunderstood. In *Publisher's Weekly*, for example, one critic
praised the book for its "myths rich and varied as Chinese brocade" and
for prose "that often achieves the delicacy and precision of porcelain."
According to this critic, "East meets West with . . . charming results" in
the book.[5] A closer look would have revealed that *The Woman Warrior* is
deliberately anti-exotic and anti-nostalgic. There is nothing "charming"
about the unexpected way Kingston satirically describes Chinese food,
which Chinatown tourists think they know so well:

> "Eat! Eat!" my mother would shout at our heads bent over bowls,
> the blood pudding awobble in the middle of the table. . . . We'd have
> to face four- and five-day old leftovers until we ate it all. The squid
> eye would keep appearing at breakfast and dinner until eaten.
> Sometimes brown masses sat on every dish. . . . I would live on
> plastic.[6]

Some reviewers call upon other non-literary—and also non-
sociological—aids to give them access to Kingston's writing. A New York
*Times* critic, for example, notes with approval that Kingston's name
indicates that she is married to an "American" (white), implying that she
herself is not "American" and that her marriage has some significance to
the book's approach to her Chinese American identity. In the *National
Observer*, one reviewer defends his interpretations of *The Woman Warrior*
by mentioning that his wife is Chinese Canadian.[7] Even the strengths of

*The Woman Warrior*, such as its portrayal of ambiguity as central to the Chinese American experience, are misconstrued by some critics. Michael Malloy complains that "[i]t's hard to tell where her fantasies end and reality begins"; he is confused by her depiction of some Chinese women as aggressive and others as docile, as if there can only be one type of Chinese woman. These confusions are "especially hard for a non-Chinese," he concludes, "and that's the troubling aspect of the book."[8]

According to Kingston, the most gratifying responses to *The Woman Warrior* have come from Chinese American women, whose appreciation of the book is not interrupted by the sense that it contains the "mystery of a stubbornly, utterly foreign sensibility" that haunts some Anglo reviewers.[9]

In response to her realization that the reading public was generally ignorant about Chinese Americans, Kingston deliberately filled in the history lessons in *China Men* (1980), even listing historical facts, such as items of anti-Chinese legislation. Kingston contends that she felt compelled to do this, even at the risk of spoiling the dramatic moments in the narration, because sacrificing historical background for the sake of story in *The Woman Warrior* had not worked: "The reviews of my first book made it clear that people didn't know the history—or that they thought I didn't. While I was writing *China Men*, I just couldn't take that tension any more."[10] Kingston meant *China Men* almost as a continuation of William Carlos Williams' *In the American Grain*, which she feels is "the right way to write about American history, . . . poetically and, it seems to me, truly." *China Men* picks up roughly where Williams' book left off, at about 1850. The problem is that, while American readers are familiar with Williams' characters, they do not necessarily know about Chinese Americans:

> The mainstream culture doesn't know the history of Chinese-Americans, which has been written and written well. The ignorance makes a tension for me, and in the new book I just couldn't take it anymore. So all of a sudden, right in the middle of the stories, plunk—there is an eight-page section of pure history. It starts with the Gold Rush and goes right through the various exclusion acts, year by year. There are no characters in it. It really affects the shape of the book and it might look quite clumsy.[11]

The challenge that Kingston and other Asian American writers face is how to preserve the artistic integrity of their writing and be understood at the same time by readers whose different cultural experiences might necessitate discourses and explanations that interfere with the art. According to Kingston, it may well be that, because of *China Men*, the road ahead will be easier, at least for some Chinese American fiction writers: "[M]aybe it will affect the shape of the novel in the future. Now maybe another Chinese-American writer won't have to write that history."[12]

In this book, as in *China Men*, there is movement between social history and literature—and for the same reason. The reader's familiarity with the sociohistorical context of Asian American literature cannot be assumed as it can in the case of Anglo-American literature. One is struck, for example, by the fact that even today most Asian American writing, whether in education, sociology, psychology, or literature, is usually prefaced by an explanatory overview of Asian American history. To those readers who are disconcerted by this book's movement between social history and literature and by my emphasis on sociohistorical rather than strictly formal concerns, I can only respond that I have found the knowledge of the social context of Asian American literature can mean the difference between understanding a work and completely misinterpreting it. In Louis Chu's *Eat a Bowl of Tea*, for example, the protagonist's sexual impotence must be viewed within the context of the Chinatown ghetto of aging bachelors, who are prevented by discriminatory laws and policies from establishing a tradition of normal family life. Without an understanding of this aspect of Chinese American history, one might conclude that the book is simply soft-core pornography and not a novel of manners. The bitterness and rage felt by John Okada's protagonist towards his mother in *No-No Boy* can be seen as an example of the generational conflicts that exist to some extent between all parents and children and also as an illustration of problems faced by the children of immigrant parents of many nationalities, but Ichiro's anguish cannot be fully understood apart from the context of the internment of Japanese Americans during World War II. The mother's attitudes towards Japan and the son's desire to be accepted as an American are key to understanding their relationship.

By studying Asian American literature, readers can learn about the Asian American experience from the point of view of those who have lived it. In this book, I trace Asian American self-images as they have evolved in response to changing social contexts. I also focus on ways in which individuals' self-images are related to attitudes towards Asia and America, to relationships within families, particularly between immigrant and American-born generations and between the sexes, and to the relationship between the individual and the ethnic community.

At the same time, it is important to remember that Asian Americans who write are not necessarily "typical" or "representative" of their nationality or racial group. No one expects John Steinbeck or Herman Melville to represent or typify all white Americans, or even all German Americans or Anglo-Americans, but because Asian Americans have been unfamiliar to most American readers, their visions and expressions are sometimes erroneously generalized. I recall the annoyance felt by a friend of mine when her non-Asian friends presented her with a copy of Maxine Hong Kingston's *The Woman Warrior*, saying, "Now I finally understand you." Maxine Hong Kingston is writing about *her* Chinese American experience and *the* Chinese American experience, but she has always stressed the need for many voices to speak out and express the diversity and variety of Chinese American life.

# Asian American Literature

*An Introduction to the Writings*

*and Their Social Context*

# 1

# Images of Asians in Anglo-American Literature

Caricatures of Asians have been part of American popular culture for generations. The power-hungry despot, the helpless heathen, the sensuous dragon lady, the comical loyal servant, and the pudgy, de-sexed detective who talks about Confucius are all part of the standard American image of the Asian. Anglo-American writers of some literary merit have used these popular stereotypes, although usually not as a focus for their work: Chinese caricatures can be found in the pages of Bret Harte, Jack London, John Steinbeck, Frank Norris, and other writers about the American West, and even in such unlikely places as Louisa May Alcott's books for children. But, for the most part, the enormous body of Anglo-American literature containing these caricatures, particularly those dealing primarily with Asians as a theme, are of much lesser stuff—pulp novels and dime romances of varying degrees of literary quality.

Many of these lesser works, though popularly read in their day, have by now been quite forgotten, but not before they contributed to national attitudes towards Asians. *Collier's Weekly* staff writer Wallace Irwin, creator of Hashimura Togo, the "Japanese" schoolboy whose "diaries" were serialized for the first twenty years in various magazines and syndicates of this century, was widely believed to be Japanese, or at least an authority on the Japanese; consequently, he was sent by the *Saturday Evening Post* to California in 1919 to investigate the "Japanese question." As a result of the investigation Irwin produced an anti-Japanese novel, *Seed of the Sun* (1921), which was hailed by New York *Times* reviewers as a book that everyone concerned about "the Japanese question" should read.[1] Another popular pulp novel, Peter B. Kyne's

3

*Pride of Palomar* (1921), which like *Seed of the Sun* depicts the Japanese as plotting to take over California land for the emperor of Japan, is credited with having inspired a symposium on the "yellow peril" that drew such participants as Edna Ferber, Rupert Hughes, the presidents of Yale and Harvard, and two state governors.

Some potboilers live on. John P. Marquand, winner of the Pulitzer Prize in 1938 for *The Late George Apley*, won fame and fortune from his hugely successful Mr. Moto novels of the late 1930s and early 1940s, many of which were the bases of Hollywood films. Marquand himself was "not even half-way serious" about the books, but he had become economically dependent upon them and was commissioned by publishers to continue producing them.[2] Sax Rohmer, creator of Fu Manchu, and Earl Derr Biggers, author of the Charlie Chan novels, were also widely read and acclaimed. Charlie Chan's lasting fame has surpassed his creator's, and Biggers profited handsomely from Hollywood's versions of his books. Rohmer's thirteen Fu Manchu novels have been translated into more than a dozen languages, including Braille. In fact, when the U.S. State Department received a crank threat from the "President of Si-Fan" in the late 1930s, the FBI sought information from Rohmer about that totally fictitious organization he had conjured up for his stories.[3] Probably Rohmer can be credited for having linked "Chinese" with "evil" in British and American minds for years to come.

Portrayals of Chinese are more numerous than for any other Asian group in Anglo-American literature. Although images of Japanese do have some unique dimensions, as will be discussed later, many of the depictions of Chinese have been generalized to Asians, particularly since Westerners traditionally found it difficult to distinguish among the East Asian nationalities.

There are two basic kinds of stereotypes of Asians in Anglo-American literature: the "bad" Asian and the "good" Asian. The "bad" Asians are the sinister villains and brute hordes, neither of which can be controlled by the Anglos and both of which must therefore be destroyed. The "good" Asians are the helpless heathens to be saved by Anglo heroes or the loyal and lovable allies, sidekicks, and servants. In both cases, the Anglo-American portrayal of the Asian serves primarily as a foil to describe the Anglo as "not-Asian": when the Asian is heartless and treacherous, the Anglo is shown indirectly as imbued with integrity and humanity; when the Asian is a cheerful and docile inferior, he projects the Anglo's benevolence and importance. The comical, cowardly servant placates a strong and intelligent white master; the helpless heathen is saved by a benevolent white savior; the clever Chinese detective solves mysteries for the benefit of his ethical white clients and colleagues. A common thread running through these portrayals is the establishment of and emphasis on permanent and irreconcilable differences between the

Chinese and the Anglo, differences that define the Anglo as superior physically, spiritually, and morally.

## Brute Hordes and Sinister Villains

The portrayal of "bad" Asians as faceless masses and diabolical geniuses provides us with an illustration of how these irreconcilable differences are depicted. An underlying theme of both views was often conquest of Western civilization: propaganda literature supporting Chinese exclusion during the last decades of the nineteenth century warns of the possible subsumption of the Anglo and of Western civilization itself by Asiatic hordes. In a poem by Daniel O'Connell, anthologized in the 1870s, a swarm of immigrant Chinese laborers threatens to pollute the country:

> We will make a second China by your pleasant Western seas;
> We will swarm like locusts that scourged the East of old;
> . . . We can do your women's labor at half a woman's rate . . .
> We'll monopolize and master every craft upon your shore,
> And we'll starve you out with fifty—aye, five hundred thousand
> more!

This is also the main theme of Atwell Whitney's *Almond-Eyed* (1878), which ends with a stream of heathen men and women "pouring in, filling the places which should be occupied by the Caucasian race, poisoning the moral atmosphere, tainting society, undermining the free institutions of the country, degrading labor."[4]

The two faces of the "bad" Asian are set forth in Irwin's *Seed of the Sun.* Here the Japanese farmers mercilessly exploit their stunted wives and children in field labor, living lives of Spartan sterility and working long hours on a handful of rice a day so that they can squeeze out the white farmers and take over the land for Japan. The farmers are carrying out the wishes of the Japanese emperor, who has charged them with the task of conquering the white race by acquiring the white man's lands and breeding with his women. According to an imperial epistle addressed to the Japanese settlers:

> If they build walls to wall themselves about and exclude us, we will tear down those walls or dig under them. In America we are already inside and we shall remain for glory of the Emperor. Small as we are in numbers here, let us see to it that our race shall increase. Seed of Yamato, germinate anew! Beget, beget, beget. . . . Prove your race quality in the blood of your children. Choose white women if you can. Where this is not practical, marry Negroes, Indians and

Hawaiians. Do not fear that our race shall be lost in such a mingling of blood. The blood of Japan is immortal. . . . Plant it where you will, Yamato's seed shall never die. Even unto the tenth generation, Japanese with blond skins and blue eyes will still be Japanese, quick with the one God-given virtue—loyalty to the empire and to the Emperor.[5]

Similarly, in Gene Stratton-Porter's *Her Father's Daughter* (1921), Japanese "students" are sent to infiltrate American schools to "absorb the things that we are taught, to learn our language, our government, our institutions, our ideals, our approximate strengths, and our only-too-apparent weaknesses" as part of a long-range scheme of world conquest.[6]

Many years after the Chinese had been effectively excluded from participation in the mainstream of American economic and social life and after all Asians had been excluded from immigration, naturalization, and the franchise in the United States, the image of them as brute hordes remained, repeated in the pages of adventure tales in which the individual members of these hordes are portrayed as "ridiculously clad, superstition-ridden, dishonest, crafty, cruel . . . marginal members of the human race who lack the courage, intelligence, skill, and the will to do anything about the oppressive conditions that surround them." There is a "yellow mask" on the face of the Asian brute, and his sunken eyes either register no feelings and no expression or, like "dull coals," "burn behind their slitlike eyeholes." Some have "wolfish fangs" and are described as "looking dumbly on . . . , stupid cattle, obeying blindly, with no conviction of right or wrong, stumbling, fighting on and on until the inevitable bullet cuts short their quest for women and a full belly."[7]

This Asian brute serves to demonstrate by starkest contrast the wholesome intelligence and heroism of his Anglo-Saxon counterpart. The white hero who saves the farms from Japanese control in *Seed of the Sun*, for example, has an "Anglo-Saxon look of health and well-being [that seems] to bring clean air into the poisoned atmosphere." Just as the rugged cowboy heroes in Western stories disposed of whole tribes of marauding Indians single-handedly, the virile protagonists of such pulp fiction make short work of the Asiatic hordes, who give them an opportunity to exhibit their heroic qualities. Among the many authors who employed the standard formula was Edgar Rice Burroughs, the creator of Tarzan. In *The Mucker* (1963), Burroughs' working-class Irish protagonist saves the aristocratic white heroine from hordes of little brown men whose ruler intends to make her his concubine. We see him through the woman's eyes:

He was wonderful! . . . Huge, muscular, alert, he towered above his pygmy antagonists, his gray eyes gleaming, a half-smile upon his strong lips. . . . He looked at the pile of bodies in the far end of the room and a broad grin cracked the dried blood about his mouth. "Wot we done to dem Chinks was sure aplenty, kiddo," he remarked to Miss Harding, [who] was looking at the man in wide-eyed amazement.

Similarly, in Jack London's *Star Rover* (1915), a shipwrecked British seafarer finds that the ignorance and sadism of the Korean people is matched only by their cowardice and ineptitude in battle:

> They went down like tenpins, fell over each other in heaps. . . . I made a mess of them and a muss and muck of their silks ere the multitude could return upon me. There were so many of them. They clogged my blows by the sheer numbers of them, those behind shoving the front ones upon me. And how I dropped them! Toward the end they were squirming three-deep under my feet.[8]

For the manly Anglo-Saxon, youth is no barrier to the vanquishing of the Asiatic horde. The teenaged American sailor in London's "In Yeddo Bay" (1922) wins the admiration and respect of a mob of bullying Japanese sampan men because they are awed by his "Anglo-Saxon . . . dislike of being imposed upon." They, like "the dark-skinned peoples, the world over, have learned to respect the white man's fist."[9] The young protagonist in "White and Yellow" in *Tales of the Fish Patrol* (1919) captures an evil-looking, pock-marked Chinese fisherman and reduces him and his "savage crew" to cringing and begging for mercy, with no weapons other than his manly spirit, confident voice, and commanding demeanor.

London's portrayals of the Asian are grotesque and unflattering evidence of his acceptance of white supremacy as both true and desirable:

> Don't talk to me about understanding the nigger. The white man's mission is to farm the world, and it's a big enough job cut out for him. There's one thing for sure, the white man has to run the nigger whether he understands them or not. It's inevitable. It's fate.

The Anglo-Saxon heroine of London's *Daughter of the Snows* (1902) wants to serve as an example to her race: "We are a race of doers and fighters, of globe-encirclers and zone-conquerors. . . . Will the Indian, the Negro, or the Mongol ever conquer the Teuton? Surely not!" According to London, the Chinese and the white man are "mental aliens," perhaps because their languages have made their thought processes "[radically] dissimilar."[10]

Even one brave Anglo teenager can subdue an entire horde of stupid, cowardly Asian brutes. But what of the evil Asian genius, the Oxford or Harvard graduate who speaks fluent English and uses his intellect and knowledge to dominate and destroy in a plot to conquer the Western world? How is he to be overcome and how is he to be explained? The image of the inhuman Asian was a common one. In his text to *Old Chinatown* (1913), Will Irwin senses something sinister when he surveys groups of Chinese businessmen: "[U]nderneath their essential courtesy, fruit of an old civilization, underneath their absolute commercial honor, runs a hard, wild streak of barbarism, an insensibility to cruelty, which, when roused, is as cold-blooded and unlovely a thing as we know." According to Jack London, the greatest threat to Western civilization was the possibility that brute hordes of blindly obedient Chinese and cruel, cunning Koreans might be harnessed under the leadership of the Japanese, who had learned to use technology devised by "Caucasian minds" and to "borrow [Caucasian] material achievement." The problem is that the racial inferiority of the Japanese makes it impossible for them to master the necessary complement of the Anglo-Saxon "soul stuff," which is "the product of an evolution which goes back to the raw beginnings of the race and not a coin to be pocketed by the first chance comer." The Anglo-Saxon is imbued with "a certain integrity, a sternness of conscience, a melancholy responsibility of life, a sympathy and comradeship and warm human feel, which is ours, indubitably ours, and which we cannot teach to the Orientals as we would teach logarithms or the trajectory of projectiles."[11]

The epitome of this stereotype is the famous Asian archvillain, the insidious Dr. Fu Manchu, who has mastered Western knowledge and science without comprehending Western compassion and ethics. Fu Manchu has a powerful intellect, but he has no physical or moral essence. Completely asexual, he is endowed with "an intellect so cold and exact, that the man in whose body it was set could sacrifice his own flesh and blood in the interests of his giant impersonal projects." Fu Manchu himself says that the brain, not the heart, is the seat of power, and it is lust for power that drives him. He will use any means to achieve his goal, which is the overthrow of the white race. He invents drugs that turn white men yellow and change dead men into zombies obedient to his will. With a pitiless smile, he can command rape and torture and the killing of both his enemies and his bungling followers. Fu Manchu is the diametrical opposite of the white hero: he is, in Rohmer's words, "not a normal man. He is superman, Satan materialized and equipped with knowledge which few had ever achieved; a cold, dominating intellect, untrammeled by fleshly ties, a great mind unbound by the laws of man." Ultimately, nothing can defeat the wholesome, warmly human British protagonists of the Fu Manchu novels—not superior intelligence, not ingenious weapons, not overwhelming numbers, not magic, because the battle is between good and primordial, Satanic, Chinese evil.[12]

## The Unassimilable Alien

In the portrayal of the Chinese villain, race is more significant than culture, and good and evil themselves are equated to race. Therefore, a Chinese who has been educated in the West can never be completely "civilized." In "Young Mr. Yan," as Wallace Irwin puts it:

Yu can take a Chink from 'is hop,
'is lanterns and gals and pigs and chop,
Yu can dress 'im up in yer Christian clo'es,
Put texts in 'is head and hymns in 'is nose,
But yu'll find, when he's actin' a dead straight part,
He's a Chinaman still in 'is yellow heart.[13]

The assumption that attitudes and behavior patterns are racially inherited is clearly seen in the many portrayals by Anglo-American writers of characters of mixed racial ancestry. When a Eurasian girl longs for freedom, she is "white at heart." When a mixed-blood boy is cruel to animals, it is because he has "inherited his callousness from his stoic Eastern blood." A war is waged in the blood of the Eurasian in Achmed Abdullah's short story, "A Simple Act of Piety": "The Chinese blood in her veins, shrewd, patient, scotched the violence of her passion, her American impulse to clamour loudly for right and justice and fairness." The Eurasian character in Irwin's *Seed of the Sun* is tortured by the feeling that "the dragon's tail of the Orient [is] fastened to the goat's head of Europe" in his being: "All the time the European in me is striving to butt forward, the dragon's tail is curling around some ancient tradition and pulling me back."[14]

Given the assumed biological incompatibility of the races, the dilemma of the Eurasian in Anglo-American literature is unresolvable. He must either accept life as it is, with its injustices and inequalities, or he must die. Most of the stories about Eurasians end with the death of the protagonist. The only real victory possible for him is mistaken identity. In Frank L. Packard's *The Dragon's Jaws* (1937), the heroine is assumed to be Chinese. Braver and more righteous than her Chinese companions, she leads a group of peasants to destroy a Chinese despot and is rewarded (after it is discovered that she is really white) with marriage to a handsome white hero. In Herbert G. Woodworth's *In the Shadow of Lantern Street* (1920), the hero grows up believing he is Chinese. Yet his superior intelligence, perceptiveness, courage, and integrity are explained only when his white father returns to claim him.

Rex Beach's *Son of the Gods* was one of the most successful books in this genre. Serialized in *Cosmopolitan* in 1928, it was published by Harper the following year and made into a successful film in 1930. Its hero, Sam

Lee, though tortured by inexplicable impulses towards rebellion and independence, tries to cultivate the Oriental restraint and forbearance that are "a fixed habit of thought, a tradition that had ruled 400 million yellow men for four thousand years." Instinctively, however, he is drawn to whites:

> There were times when he rebelled against all things Oriental and gagged at the Chinese flavor, times when a voice in him fairly shrieked that he was a white man in disguise. Like a soldier outside the lines he shouted "Friend! Friend!" and spoke the password, but nobody heard him. The inner voice clamoured so loudly and so insistently that he was amazed when others failed to hear it.[15]

As it turns out, of course, Sam Lee is a white orphan adopted by a Chinatown merchant, and the book ends with his paying homage to his dead foster father in a display of filial love and respect that would put most "real" Chinese sons to shame.

The theme of intermarriage between Asians and whites has fascinated the Anglo-American reading public, and is therefore delineated far more often than the actual incidence of such marriages would seem to warrant. It was admitted that intermarriage might improve the Asian; the offspring of intermarriages might be taller and handsomer. Yet there was the risk, stressed in many novels about intermarriage, that the yellow race would ultimately overwhelm and swallow up the white: "The Mongolian is a persistent type; and such mixed marriages as ours, through some inscrutable law of Nature, seem almost sure to perpetuate, and even to emphasize, one racial type and ignore the other."[16]

Sometimes the white partner is swallowed up by the Asian society. More often, the Asian partner "reverts," making it clear that race and biological predisposition will always win out over the trappings of culture. In Jack London's "Chun Ah Chun" (1912), a Chinese businessman in Hawaii has married a non-Chinese and fathered children who are sent to Harvard and Wellesley for their education. Despite his long sojourn in a Western milieu, he finds himself "harking back more and more to his own kind" and finally decides to move back to China, leaving his wife and children behind because "the culture of the West has passed him by. He was Asiatic to the last fibre, which meant that he was a heathen."[17]

Stock Chinese brutes and villains abound in a large body of short stories and novels set in the Chinatowns of the West from the latter part of the nineteenth century until the 1940s. Anglo-American writers like Frank Norris, Gertrude Atherton, and a host of lesser writers used Chinatown for local color and exotic effect, filling their tales with tong wars, opium dens, and sinister hatchetmen lurking in dark alleyways where mysterious trapdoors and underground passages led to torture chambers and slave quarters. The Anglo-American reader was led over "reeking sidewalks" along which glided "sphinx-eyed crafty yellow men" or "moon-eyed lepers," and peered into those greasy Chinese kitchens where "cackling cooks" prepared white mice and puppy dog stew. After shuddering at the poisonous scorpions, snakes, and spiders, they could then retire to the wholesome human normality of their own unequivocably "American" neighborhoods.

One of the most important characteristics of Chinatown as portrayed in Anglo-American literature is the absolute difference between Chinatown life—with its alien attitudes and ways—and so-called American life. In C. W. Doyle's *The Shadow of Quong Lung* (1900), for example, the Chinese villain sneers openly at the "laws of the White Devil" while he rules Chinatown according to his own concepts of law and order. In Lu Wheat's *Ah Moy* (1901), the villain is afraid that Western ideas of freedom and justice will contaminate Chinese youth and threaten the slave trade. Unlike Anglo-Americans, who can be forgiven for crimes of passion, the people of Chinatown are portrayed as admiring hired assassins precisely because they are dispassionate. Chinese fathers and husbands are depicted as so determined to save their face that they would sacrifice their wives and daughters in the process. The Chinese father in *Ah Moy* gives his daughter a dagger so that she can kill herself to avoid shaming him. Thomas Burke's Ah Fat, in the story "Big Boy Blue" (1921), poisons both cups when his daughter serves tea to a white policeman, so that the death of his enemy can be absolutely assured. In Achmed Abdullah's ironically titled "The Honorable Gentleman" (1919), a Harvard-educated Chinese in New York Chinatown kills his blind white wife when he learns that a surgeon might be able to restore her eyesight. He fears that she will leave him when she sees his "repulsive Mongol devil mask of a Chinese face," and her death is his way of preserving her love.

According to many Anglo-American writers, Chinese are not supposed to value their own lives. In Jack London's "Chinago" (1911), Ah Cho, scheduled to be executed for a crime he did not commit, tries meekly to protest, but finally accepts the mistake with typical "Oriental" stoicism. The other Chinese in the story, equally aware of his innocence, look on with mild curiosity. Another old Chinese in Hugh Wiley's "The Summons" (1926), similarly condemned and similarly innocent, thanks the judge and jury for cutting short his "waiting time on earth." Willing victims cannot be tragic figures. Lu Wheat's Ah Moy is "strangely indifferent to pain," a quality she has supposedly "inherited from uncounted generations of ancestors . . . reaching far back into the remotest night of forgotten time." Her "eastern soul" has given her a "splendid scorn of death."

## "Asian" English

The immigrant American's struggles with English have been a staple of American humor: the Italian organ-grinder, the Prussian martinet, the Jewish mother—all are found in the pages of American literature. In most cases, however, readers know from their own experiences with Jews, Italians, Germans, or Poles that examples they read about or see portrayed on the screen are nothing more than caricatures. For Asian Americans, the situation has been quite different. Only in California and Hawaii and a few urban centers were they present in sufficient numbers to engage the attention of the average Anglo-American, so the speech patterns attributed to persons of Asian descent were not counterbalanced by personal experience or by accurate representation in the media. Asians either spoke English badly because they were slow and unable to grasp Western ways, or they spoke it with a flowery, almost unnatural fluency that was humorous or sinister.

On the one hand was the archetypal Asian villain whose fluent command of English makes his cruelty all the more chilling. The "Manchu" leader in Van Wyck Mason's *The Hong Kong Airbase Murders* (1937) can quote Shakespeare and the ancient Chinese sages while committing unspeakable crimes against humanity. Beneath the polite formalities of educated speech, beneath the thin veneer of "civilization," lurks a monster of immorality only pretending to be human.

To generations of Americans, on the other hand, Chinese English meant "no tickee, no washee." A mainstay of popular American culture, the comic Chinese dialect is characterized by high-pitched, sing-song tones, tortured syntax, the confounding of *l*'s and *r*'s, the proliferation of *ee*-endings, and the random omission of articles and auxiliary verbs. Bret Harte's poem "Plain Language from Truthful James"—better known as "The Heathen Chinee" (1870)—provided the model for writings in this vein, which for two decades were epidemic in American newspapers and journals. Charles G. Leland's *Pidgin English Sing-Song* (1903), a collection of "songs and stories in the Chinese-American dialect," had remarkable success. The following excerpt is representative:

Ping-wing he pie-man son.
He velly worst chilo alló Can'tón.
He steal he mother piclum mice,
And thlowee cat in bilin' rice.
Hab chow-chow up, and "Now," talk he,
"my wonda' where he meeow cat be?"[18]

Leland and others asserted that their rendering of Chinese American dialect was accurate, however unlike it was to the actual pidgin English spoken by the Chinese of Hawaii and the Caribbean. But accuracy was of little importance to readers who chortled at the convolutions of "Eaty butter no have got" and "You of this what think?"

The inexact and inconsistent translations of Christian missionaries were responsible for many of the odd renderings attributed to the Chinese. They translated "see" as "look-see," "conversation" as "talk-a-talk," "weather" as "heaven's breath," and "America" as "land of Mei," presumably for precious or exotic effect.[19] In fact, America was to the Chinese no more "Mei country" than Thursday is "day of the god Thor" to the English. The ultimate absurdity is found in Fernald's *The Cat and the Cherub* (1896), in which a very young Chinese child speaks the "Chinese" English he could only have learned from the missionary in the story: "Missiolary men tekka me home mek good Chrisinjun boy."[20] Perhaps a biological propensity is involved here.

Japanese English as a source for humor was rendered most effectively and influentially by Wallace Irwin, whose popular serialized columns featuring a Japanese servant character employed by a white family were found in widely read American magazines for almost two decades. The humor lies in Hashimura Togo's inability to master English despite his most assiduous efforts, as well as in his inability to understand the culture and the people whose language he strives so comically to master. Togo invents words. He is verbose. He shares the supposed Chinese addiction to honorific speech. American life baffles him; his interpretations of its artifacts are as faulty as his understanding of the language: "What are this Hon. Vacuum, anyhows? Hon. Dictionary Book say 'Vacuum are Nothing.' How could Mr. Danl Webster speak such untruth by his Dictionary? Vacuum cannot be Nothing and yet make so much noises. This Intellectual Vacuum machinery resemble ostriches in what they eat."[21] The readers know, as Togo himself does not, that all his efforts to understand American life and to master English will be in vain, for as a Japanese he is an eternal alien to whom such an understanding is permanently beyond reach.

The comical Chinese servant, another stock image, made its first appearance in a number of popular plays and stories set in the American West in the latter half of the nineteenth century: cowardly, grotesquely dressed, speaking hilariously broken English, he had the virtue of intense loyalty to his virile and courageous white employer. Beginning in the middle of the nineteenth century, John Chinaman as played by Anglo actors appeared in popular melodramas such as Alonso Delano's *A Live Woman in the Mines; Or, Pike County Ahead* (1857), where he cries: "Indian come! He bang! bang! Bullet pop me! . . . Chinaman no fight; Chinaman good skin; keep him so. Mellican big devil—not hurty bullet him." Very Tart, the Chinese coolie in James J. McCloskey's *Across the Continent; Or, Scenes from New York Life and the Pacific Railroad* (1870), explains that

"Mellican man like fighteee. Chinaman like sleepee in box." For all his cowardice, however, the loyal Chinese servant is commonly ready to sacrifice his life for the sake of his Anglo master. In Gouverneur Morris' *Yellow Men and Gold* (1911), the Anglo hero and heroine are aided by the grinning members of a Chinese crew, so uniformly honest and kindly that it is difficult to tell them apart. One by one, they are dispatched by the enemy, until they become merely yellow faces "peaceful and mystical in death."[22]

Near the turn of the century, distinguished California historian Hubert Howe Bancroft pointed out why the view of the Chinese as engagingly comic curiosities was appealing:

It was quite amusing to see them here and there and everywhere and show them to strangers as one of the many unique features of which California could boast. It put one in quite good humor with one's self to watch them waddling under the springy poles sustaining at either end a huge and heavily laden basket; it made one feel quite one's superiority to see these queer little specimens of petrified progress, to listen to their high-keyed strains of feline conversation, and notice all their cunning curiosity and barbaric artlessness.

Apparently those not frightened by the Chinese found it difficult to view them without amusement:

[D]ecidedly it is hard to imagine a grave, great, and glorious Chinaman. There is something essentially ridiculous in all the pertainings of the outlandish creature. His tail is the sample and style of him; it stands for him in all things. Inside and out, he is altogether so droll as that, and that suffices to fill the measure of his funniness.[23]

## In Defense of the Asian American

Even Bret Harte, Mark Twain, and Ambrose Bierce, who are said to have portrayed the Chinese sympathetically, accepted most of the common stereotypes of the Chinese of their times and knew little or nothing of the reality of Chinese life in America. They tended to depict the Chinese as a helpless and pathetic or enigmatic people, and used Chinese characters primarily to expose the ignorance and follies of white men, who were their major concern.

Although Bret Harte was by no means an ardent defender of the Chinese, his "Plain Language from Truthful James" ("The Heathen Chinee") was not intended as an attack on the Chinese, but rather as a light-hearted exposé of white men's treachery against them. But Harte's readers chose to ignore the poem's ironic moral and to interpret it instead as corroboration of their own unfavorable opinions about the Chinese. The poem was extraordinarily popular: it was hawked in San Francisco streets; it was widely read in East Coast cities; it went through four editions in England in the year of its publication; it was, in fact, passed from mouth to mouth until it became common literary property. The poem was quoted many times on the floor of Congress during debates on the Chinese question.[24] Not the least effect of its enormous popularity was the prolonged interest it inspired in the pidgin English sing-song the Chinese were believed to speak.

Ambrose Bierce, who wrote briefly about the tribulations of the Chinese in a conscious effort to win more sympathetic treatment for them in "A Dampened Ardor," reported that Harte was greatly amused by the unfavorable meanings that so many read into "The Heathen Chinee," and Mark Twain commented that Harte was "quite concerned over achieving fame with a work which he considered of no importance." Even so, Fenn argues convincingly that Harte's handling of Chinese in subsequent stories seems almost an attempt to "make amends for the uncertainty of the sentiments expressed in that poem."[25] In any event, his treatment was never left ambiguous again. In "See Yup," the Chinese outwit the greedy white miners. In "An Episode in Fiddletown," there is an account of Chinese being harassed by ignorant whites. And in "Wan Lee the Pagan" an innocent Chinese boy is killed by a mob of white Christians.

Mark Twain, who admitted that he felt no particular affection for the Chinese,[26] viewed them as a pathetic people unable to defend themselves, and therefore a suitable vehicle for inveighing against the inhumanity of bigoted whites. In "John Chinaman in New York" (1899), the narrator pities the "friendless Mongol." In "Goldsmith's Friend Abroad Again" (1879), the details of the various injustices suffered by the Chinese at the hands of white Americans are told through "letters" written by Ah Song Hi, the ingenuous Chinese protagonist, to a friend in China. Despite his initial expressions of joy at America's democratic ideals and sympathy for the world's oppressed, Ah Song Hi is soon cheated by American labor contractors, ship captains, and employers and finally thrown into jail, where he is beaten by his fellow inmates and told he cannot testify against whites in court. It is clear that Twain was largely inspired by a sense of fair play: the Chinese subjects were convenient vehicles through which to attack the ignorance and violence of members of his own race. The play that Twain wrote in partnership with Bret Harte—*Two Men of Sandy Bar* (1876)—failed utterly to attract a public that had so cheerfully misinterpreted "The Heathen Chinee." As Fenn points out: "To make a play revolve around a . . . shrewd Chinaman, especially when he outwits his [white] associates with ease, is perhaps too much to ask—if not of the play, at least of the audience."[27] Ultimately, Twain and Harte turned their attention elsewhere.

Traditionally, the most ardent advocates of the salvageability of the Asian have been the Christian missionaries who worked with the people of China and Korea or within the Chinese and Japanese communities in the United States and Hawaii. In some cases, they were their only friends in the West. In addition to religious proselytizing, they provided English language instruction, recreational activities linked to Bible study, and scholarships for those who volunteered to study Christian theology. They argued that Asians who could be "brought up to the light" would reject their own culture and heritage, adopt Christian beliefs and practices, and thus become successfully integrated into American life. Because they were the Anglos who worked most closely and consistently with Asians, they were regarded by many other white Americans as authorities, and the information they disseminated was highly influential in shaping the public image of the Asian in America.

Eager to encourage financial contributions to their cause, however, they tended to emphasize the poverty and depravity of the Asians they were seeking to convert, and Asians themselves frequently complained that only the most negative aspects of their cultures were being presented.[28] In Swinehart's *Sarangie: A Child of Chosen* (1926), the Korean people are depicted as backward, impoverished, mercenary, ignorant, and superstitious, easy prey to the greedy aristocrats who rule them; even in such an environment it is perhaps a bit hard to believe that a Korean child would eagerly leave her mother after just one glimpse of the beautiful white face of a young Christian missionary. Charles B. Shepherd's *The Ways of Ah Sin* (1923) is set in San Francisco Chinatown, where "highbinders stalk their prey, [and] dainty slave girls bound in shackles by Ah Sin are forced to give themselves over to lives of shame . . . [as] the accursed juice of the poppy passes surreptitiously from hand to hand."[29] The Chinese girl is eventually saved from her "life of shame" by a good-hearted Christian missionary.

The realization that race prejudice can turn potential converts away from Christ is one theme in Maude Madden's *When the East Is in the West* (1923). This collection of short stories is organized around the supposed experiences of a Christian worker among the Japanese on the Pacific Coast. Kindness, Madden points out, may lead to conversion—the discarding of kimonos, chopsticks, Asian languages, non-Christian religions, and other undesirable practices and artifacts. Madden portrays Japanese girls saved from the clutches of unscrupulous Japanese gangsters by kindly missionaries; Japanese boys escaping lives of crime by embracing Christ; Japanese farmers achieving wealth and success after conversion to Christianity; and Japanese children who "innately" prefer the "decent homes" and "civilized white faces" of America to the "half-naked fishermen," "peculiar odors," and Buddhist idolatry of Japan.

Just as the portrayal of the helpless Asian heathen serves to illustrate the beneficence and strength of the white missionary, the docile and seductive Asian woman is a foil for the virility and attractiveness of the white male. Like the Christian missionary, this man is the key to her liberation from her own Asian culture, which is the source of her oppression and suffering. In Homer Lea's *The Vermilion Pencil* (1908), the Chinese woman is drawn to the white hero's blue eyes, fair skin, imposing stature, and physical strength. She will betray her husband and father for this demi-god; she will follow him to the ends of the earth; she will happily sacrifice her life for him. In Jack London's *The Star Rover* (1915), the British hero wins the most beautiful woman in Korea: "You are a man. . . . Not even in my sleep have I ever dreamed there was such a man as you on his two legs upstanding in the world," she cries. Even the daughter of Fu Manchu is attracted to her father's enemy, Nayland Smith, who is "the only man I could ever love."[30]

Not only is the white man desirable to the Asian woman in Anglo-American literature; in several romances and short stories, the Asian man is portrayed as dominated by desire for the unattainable white woman. In Carter Hixson's *The Foreign Devil* (1937), an aristocratic Chinese graduate of an American university returns to Asia to rule his people. Obsessed by his desire for white women, he eventually drags the unconscious heroine to a temple, accompanied by the beating of tom-toms. Before he can accomplish his intentions, however, he is stabbed in the back by his Chinese concubine, who turns the knife on herself after bowing low to his dead body. A virile white hero emerges from behind a screen to rescue the white heroine.

The Chinese man in Joan Conquest's *Forbidden* (1927), on the other hand, supposedly the richest and most powerful of all Chinese, Western-educated and "extraordinarily good-looking for a Mongolian," ignores the many Asian women available to him and pursues instead a white woman, who rejects him because he is Chinese. Another fabulously wealthy "Eastern" prince, in Paul Morand's *The Living Buddha* (1928), is diverted during his quest for spiritual enlightenment by an American girl who finds him exotic and interesting for a time. The white woman becomes an obsession for the prince: "[H]e was ready to give up everything, endure everything to keep her. Because the only image which did not leave him as he thought of her was her white skin." The prince even derives a perverse pleasure when the girl rejects him: "Before her, so tall and fair, he saw himself suddenly, a small yellow boy, with narrow shoulders, . . . a poor barbarian. But that humiliation pleased him."[31] The Asian man must learn to accept his inferiority. In Thomas Burke's "The Perfect Girl" (1921), an aging Chinatown bachelor advises the young Chinese men to conquer their desire for white women as he has: he finds a perfect, beautiful white woman who loves and cares for him in opium dreams.

## New Images of the "Good" Asian
## in Anglo-American Literature

"Sinister and wicked Chinese are old stuff," Earl Derr Biggers, creator of Charlie Chan, once said, "but an amiable Chinese on the side of the law and order has never been used." Between 1925 and 1932, Biggers wrote six Charlie Chan novels, all of them serialized in the *Saturday Evening Post* before being published in book form, some of them translated into as many as ten foreign languages. Forty-eight Charlie Chan films were produced in four studios, featuring six different non-Chinese actors in the lead role. John Stone, producer of the first Charlie Chan film, is reported to have suggested that the "character was deliberately decided upon partially as a refutation of the unfortunate Fu Manchu characterization of the Chinese, and partly as a demonstration of his own idea that any minority group could be sympathetically portrayed on the screen with the right story and approach."[32]

Why have Chinese Americans objected so strenuously to the production of a new Charlie Chan film in 1980? Charlie Chan emerges as a "wise, smiling, pudgy . . . symbol of the sagacity, kindliness, and charm of the Chinese people." His face is a placid mask; he stands like a statue, seemingly somnolent, with his beady eyes half-closed. He calls himself all manner of names—dull, stupid, old-womanish—an irony the public has been quick to appreciate, knowing that beneath his bovine exterior resides a shrewdness, attention to detail, and "Oriental" patience that, together with his perhaps racial "sixth sense," enable him to solve the most complicated murder mysteries. The bases for his popular appeal are simple enough. There is first the humor of incongruity: that an overweight Chinese should occupy such a totally unexpected position as that of police inspector. Second, there is the humor of his speech, which combines the inevitable "pidgin" with pseudo-Confucian aphorisms. Third, there are the mysterious and exotic Chinatown or international settings in which Chan operates. And, lastly, there is the public's familiarity with and approval of him as a non-threatening, non-competitive, asexual ally of the white man, usually contrasted with a parade of Asians in secondary roles as cowardly servants and vicious gangsters.

It has become fashionable since the 1940s to view Asians as a "model minority" (see Chapter 6). The "model minority" Asian, by never challenging white society, at once vindicates that society from the charge of racism and points up the folly of those less obliging minorities who are ill-advised enough to protest against inequality or take themselves "too seriously." As a permanent inferior, the "good" Asian can be assimilated into American life. All that is required from him is that he accept his assigned status cheerfully and reject whatever aspects of his racial and cultural background prove offensive to the dominant white society. And of course he must never speak for himself. Three examples of relatively recent attempts by Anglos to provide a sympathetic portrayal of Asian Americans through historical novels or biography are Vanya Oakes' *Footprints of the Dragon* (1949), Jerome Charyn's *American Scrapbook* (1969), and Vita Griggs' *Chinaman's Chance* (1969),

In Oakes' book, which is about Chinese railroad workers during the nineteenth century, the white railroad bosses are uniformly kindly and benevolent, while the Chinese workers are grateful for their high wages and exhilarated by the challenges their work provides. Oakes depicts their delight at being lowered over cliffs in baskets with explosives, that dangerous job commonly alloted to the despised Chinese, who had to trust that someone would hoist them back up quickly enough to prevent their being killed in the explosions.

*American Scrapbook* is about the internment of Japanese Americans at Manzanar during World War II. The most disruptive effects of that internment were felt by the older *issei* (first-generation) men, many of whom had passed the prime of their lives at the time of internment and were never able to recover the loss of everything they had worked for. Most tragic of all were the *issei* bachelors, who had been unable to marry because of a combination of factors including poverty and American laws that after 1924 prohibited both the sponsoring of wives from Japan and intermarriages with white women. In *American Scrapbook*, Charyn depicts the *issei* bachelors as comical old clowns. Afflicted with crooked backs, arthritic elbows, and weak hearts, they can still hobble forth to sputter "banzai!" at a picture of the Japanese emperor. They spend their time sitting on the open rows of toilets "like magpies." Their foremost concern is whether or not their Sears catalogue underwear order will be filled correctly. Charyn describes their living quarters:

> It's always a madhouse in there. The old men fight, pick their noses, show off their new pajamas, sing dirty songs. The stench is unbearable. You would need a gas mask to remain immune to the sweat, the farts, the sour breath emanating from every bed. There are no brothels at Manzanar, and the old men have to relieve themselves under the covers.

In striking contrast to Charyn's view, a young Japanese American prison camp inmate feels tears fill her eyes as she sees the *issei* standing patiently in the mess-hall lines at mealtimes:

> Residents in America for forty or fifty years, they pursued gigantic dreams and crossed an expansive ocean to America to live. The soil

they tilled was a mother to them, and their life was regulated by the sun. They were people who had worked with all they had, until on their foreheads wave-like furrows were harrowed.[33]

Vita Griggs' *Chinaman's Chance* is about the possibility of success implicit in the supposed Chinese virtues of patience, loyalty, adherence to Confucian ethics, and acceptance of the inevitable. This reworking of an old theme is based on the life story of Elmer Wok Wai, who was convicted of murder during the 1920s and spent seventeen years in San Quentin finding fulfillment in faithful domestic service to the family of a prison guard. In a "gesture of almost incredible devotion," Elmer Wok Wai "rises above his sad destiny" by choosing to continue his domestic duties rather than accept the parole that would have separated him from his adopted family. He is the quintessential Chinese servant, laughable for his bad English, lovable for his unstinting devotion, pitiable for the injustices that he has suffered, and approved of for the patience and resignation with which he can transcend them.

Elmer Wok Wai was Vita Griggs' house servant. Griggs said she followed him around with a pad and pencil while he washed her dishes and vacuumed her carpets. One can only conjecture as to how Elmer Wok Wai would have told his story, or how thousands of other servants, waiters, laundrymen, and, earlier, miners and railroad and agricultural workers would have told theirs. As it is, their real story is left to be reconstructed from poems carved on the walls of the Angel Island detention center, in pieces written by those close to them and, decades later, by their racial descendants who attempt to piece their story together with fragments of documents, legends, and their own powerful feelings.

Anglo-American literature does not tell us about Asians. It tells us about Anglos' opinions of themselves, in relation to their opinions of Asians. As such it is useful primarily in that it illustrates how racism impacts on culture. One attempt to transform the Asian into the Anglo image of him is seen in a satire published in the *New Yorker* in 1945. John J. Epsey, son of a pre-revolution missionary in China, describes how he and his sister attempted to force upon the Chinese their own notions of what a Chinese should be like:

As we got to thinking about it, there were so many things in Oo-zong's nature that weren't a bit Chinese. So we began to remold him into a member of his own race. There was his grin, for example. We had to explain to Oo-zong that the Chinese are an inscrutable people who rarely show joy or sorrow in public. He was to make his face, we told him, blandly intelligent. The effect, we added, would be heightened if he were to droop his eyelids a little. Then, when he was addressed, he was to tighten the corners of his mouth ever so slightly, which was as far, he should know, as any Chinese ever went in showing amiability. . . . It took hours of patient work in front of a mirror, but the result was the most Orientally bland face in all China. . . . The more I think of it, the more I realize how essentially responsible my sister and I were for making Oo-zong conscious of the habits of his own race, for making him, indeed, really Chinese.[34]

The best writers draw not only on their literary skills but also on their hard-won knowledge and experience, and especially on the empathy and understanding that permits them to enter into the lives and characters with whom they share a common humanity. Racist stereotypes have hindered the Western writer in his ability to understand and interpret the Asian. The narrator of Somerset Maugham's *On a Chinese Screen* (1922) struggles to free himself of what he recognizes are his own preconceptions, but in the end he must resign himself to the maddening enigma of China and the Chinese:

You cannot tell what are the lives of these thousands who surge about you. Upon your own people sympathy and knowledge gives you a hold; you can enter into their lives, at least imaginatively, and in a way really possess them. By the effort of your fancy you can make them after a fashion part of yourself. But these are as strange to you as you are strange to them. You have no clue to their mystery. For their likeness to you in so much does not help you; it serves rather to emphasize their difference. . . . [Y]ou might as well look at a brick wall. You have nothing to go upon, you do not know the first thing about them, and your imagination is baffled.[35]

Stereotypes of racial minorities are a record of prejudices; they are part of an attempt to justify various attitudes and practices. The function of stereotypes of Asians in Anglo-American literature has been to provide literary rituals through which myths of white racial supremacy might be continually reaffirmed, to the everlasting detriment of the Asian. Although changing the portrayals without changing the realities from which they emerge offers the mere illusion that the realities have been altered, a clear understanding of the stereotypes and their role in perpetuating illusions can contribute to the dynamic process of changing those realities.

Despite its questionable literary merit, the body of Anglo-American literature about Asians and Asian Americans is strikingly vast: it almost seems that, at least until the World War II era, all an Anglo writer had to do was pen a book about Chinatown or set a story in Asia to be accepted by a major publisher. One is particularly struck by the vast numerical superiority of books by Anglo-Americans about Asians to those written by Asian Americans themselves, whose own expressions found much less acceptance in a milieu where publishers, critics, and readers were better attuned to morbid or comical stereotypes created by Anglo-American writers.

Within the present context, it is not for white writers to define Asian humanity. Their task is rather to confront the varied aspects of their own humanity. For Asian American writers,[36] the task is to contribute to the total image and identity of America by depicting their own experiences and by defining their own humanity as part of the composite image of the American people.

# 2

# From Asian to Asian American

## Early Asian Immigrant Writers

Between 1840 and 1924, when the laws restricting Asian immigration were enacted, thousands of Chinese, Japanese, and Koreans migrated to the United States and Hawaii. In each case, immigration was prompted by active recruitment of labor for plantation, railroad, mining, or field work. And in each case, anti-Asian sentiment resulted ultimately in the passage of exclusion laws.[1] Filipinos were permitted to immigrate until 1934, when they too were barred by law from further entry.

The relatively small Asian population consisted largely of laborers without the means or, in some cases, the inclination to return to their homelands. Partly because their time was consumed in struggles for a livelihood, the Asian point of view on the immigrant experience is rarely presented in writings in English or even in Asian languages. Some unknown immigrants carved poems in Chinese into the walls of the barracks on Angel Island, where they were held before being allowed to enter the United States between 1910 and 1940.[2] Autobiographical information about a Japanese house servant and a Chinatown merchant was collected by Hamilton Holt, editor of *The Life Stories of Undistinguished Americans* (1906).[3] And Carlos Bulosan, a self-taught Filipino farmworker, was able only because of the mandatory rest required by his tuberculosis to write his account of the life of the Filipino migrants in the American West immediately prior to the Depression. But with these exceptions, Asian immigrant workers vanished without leaving behind much written account of their individual lives in America. Although some letters and diaries written in Asian languages have survived earthquake, fire, and Japanese relocation,[4] the general privation and loneliness of Asian immigrant life, sequestered as it was in field labor camps or urban ethnic enclaves, must have dampened the desire to communicate. In the face of pervasive American ignorance of and antipathy towards Asians, an Asian writer could hardly know where to begin and what audience to address. Moreover, since they were segregated from the mainstream of American social and economic life and prevented by law from becoming naturalized American citizens with voting and civil rights, many early immigrants did not learn English and did not consider the culture it represented as something that belonged to them or to which they could contribute.

Then, too, autobiographical writing and popular fiction were not in the tradition of the Asian cultures that produced the first immigrants. Even in the Philippines, where the American curricula and educational system had been instituted after the Spanish-American War, the majority of peasants had not the privilege of schooling, and most of the Filipino immigrants were illiterate. In fact, labor recruiters, in search of a docile labor force, preferred those who had little formal education. In China and Korea, writing and literature were the domain of the literati, who traditionally confined themselves to poetry and the classical essay. Autobiography as such was virtually unknown, since for a scholar to write a book about himself would have been deemed egotistical in the extreme. Fiction was considered frivolous. Farmers and peasants performed as storytellers, dramatic dancers, and singers, but rarely expressed themselves through the written word. And certainly they did not write autobiographies.

## Ambassadors of Goodwill

Quite understandably, then, the earliest Asian American writers were not representative of the general population of Asian Americans. Foreign students, scholars, and diplomats, who were, together with merchants, exempted from the Asian exclusion laws and who generally received better treatment in America than did Asian laboring people, comprise a disproportionately large part of the early Asian American literary voice. Their writing is characterized by efforts to bridge the gap between East and West and plead for tolerance by making usually highly euphemistic observations about the West on the one hand while explaining Asia in idealized terms on the other. Since many of these early Asian writers in English felt that they themselves understood two points of view and, in some cases, two epochs—to them the West stood for modernity and the East for tradition—they viewed themselves as straddling two worlds. Since they found that elements from two vastly different cultures could be combined within themselves, they concluded that there could be points of compatibility between other people of the two cultures. They saw themselves as ambassadors of goodwill to the West. Most of them, however, did not believe that social class distinctions could be bridged. Their writing is marked by dissociation from the Asian common people, whether in Asia or in the West, and even their pleas for racial tolerance are made primarily on behalf of members of their own privileged class. They tended to accept discrimination against the poor and uneducated members of their own race as reasonable, questioning instead the logic of discrimination against the educated elite. For this reason, their explanations of Asia to the West are usually focused on high culture, and the indignation they express at American race policies is often tentative and apologetic.

Since literate Asian immigrants were acutely aware of the common misconceptions in the West about Asia and Asians, much of their writing made a conscious attempt to win friends in the West for Asia through the dissemination of information about Asian traditions and high culture, particularly through autobiographical writing. Since these personalized descriptions of Asia were generally based on the life experiences of the members of the most privileged classes, the pictures they presented represent a very limited view of Asian society. Moreover, since the writers generally felt the need to challenge the negative views of Asia in the West, they deliberately sought to present as attractive a picture of Asian life as they could, a picture that they composed from elements of upper-class life. The result is that they concentrated their attentions on the charming superficialities of ceremonies and customs of food and dress, which they hoped would appeal to the benign curiosity of the Western reader.

At the turn of the century, a series of books by young men from various lands was solicited by the D. Lothrop Publishing Company. Lee Yan Phou's *When I Was a Boy in China* (1887) was one of the first of these, and New Il-Han's *When I Was a Boy in Korea* (1928) was one of the last. Lee was brought to this country at the age of thirteen as part of the Chinese Educational Mission, which through the Chinese government provided for the Western education of a small number of Chinese boys between 1872 and 1875. In *When I Was a Boy in China*, Lee includes discussions of his boyhood education and describes Chinese sports, games, food, clothing, folk tales, and ceremonies. He is profoundly aware of the stereotypes about China, and his book is a conscious attempt to correct these distortions, which he attributes to ignorance and which he believes can be rectified through the presentation of accurate information:

> I still continually find false ideas in America concerning Chinese customs, manners, and institutions. Small blame to the people at large, who have no means of learning the truth, except through newspapers or accounts of travellers who do not understand what they see in passing through our country. . . . What I tell . . . may often contradict general belief.[5]

*When I Was a Boy in Korea* is an almost anthropological account of manners and customs, including chapters on Korean holidays, sports, housing, food, and silkworm culture. New Il-Han had come to America as a child at the turn of the century through the offices of Christian missionaries in Korea. We know from the book's preface that New graduated from a Michigan college in business, married an American-born Chinese physician, and managed an Oriental food products store in Detroit, but the book itself contains nothing about his personal experiences in America but is instead a bid for sympathy and understanding of Korean traditional culture, from which he is now so far removed.

Similarly, Chiang Yee's *A Chinese Childhood* (1940) is a recollection of the beauty and warmth of Chiang's life in China. It was written in a small London apartment far from home, as if to comfort the writer in his lonely exile: "To me, living far from China, it has been sweet to recall these memories of my childhood in Kiulang."[6] Like Lee, Chiang wishes to correct the common Western misconceptions about Chinese life and of Chinese people as "superstitious, inscrutable fatalists" by depicting his own harmonious and happy family life. His account of Chinese customs, medicine, dress, sports, festivals, and ceremonies is augmented by idyllic illustrations. Chiang stresses the "humanity" of the Chinese people, whom he characterizes as law-abiding, peaceful lovers of nature and harmony whose troubles stem from contact with other nations.

Since most of the early Asian writers of autobiography are representatives of the highest social classes of Asia, they write from the vantage point of privilege. For example, Adet and Anor Lin (*Our Family,* 1939) long for the Chinese rickshaw and porter, for the sight of peddlers selling notions at the gate of the wealthy person's home, the "little services of the housemaids," the leisure around the stove talking and reading and eating melon seeds, picking flowers, walking along the seashore, and sitting in the rose garden. Anna Chennault (*A Thousand Springs,* 1962), Chinese widow of the American general of the Flying Tigers Division, which fought alongside Chiang Kai-shek before the Chinese Revolution, depicts China as a place where one rides in Yunnan rickshaws and is served tea and cakes by cheerful houseboys, indulged by Chinese carpets, jade, ivory, porcelain, yearly trips to Europe, and French finishing schools. Yet she characterizes herself simply as a "Chinese wife."

Perhaps the two best-known members of this group of writers were Etsu Sugimoto and Lin Yutang, both of whom are characterized by the extent to which they ignore the harsh realities of both Asian and American life.

### A Daughter of the Samurai

Etsu Sugimoto's *A Daughter of the Samurai* (1925) appeared only one year after the passage of laws prohibiting Japanese immigration to the United States. Herself the daughter of a *samurai* and therefore a member of the aristocratic upper classes of feudal Japan, Sugimoto was extensively educated in both the English language and Western culture. *A Daughter of the Samurai* is dedicated to Japan and America as Sugimoto's "two mothers, whose lives and environments were far apart, yet whose hearts met in mine."

While she admires America as the epitome of progress and modernity, Sugimoto, like many feudal aristocrats, regarded Japanese modernization with deep regret. Her personal account is laced with romantic Japanese legends, shimmering fairy tales, and lyrical descriptions of traditional customs and festivals, which were already being "lost in the mist of past years."[7] The Japan Sugimoto knows and loves symbolizes the beautiful and doomed past, and she stands between, a living bridge between two countries and two eras.

Sugimoto's aristocratic tact and consciousness of her diplomatic mission—she felt obliged not to "disgrace her nation"—makes for the subdued and gentle tone of her depictions of both Japanese and American society. She comments only tentatively on the wrongs rooted in the feudal social fabric of Japan, noting in passing that Japanese women's lives were "often little less than a useful sacrifice" and that the old order sometimes brought "inconvenience and humiliation . . . to blameless people." But the beauty of old Japan compensates for such occasional flaws. When describing her life in America, Sugimoto mentions with amusement that her American-born daughter is mortified that her newborn sister is "a Japanese baby" instead of a blonde, but she refrains from discussing the problems of racial discrimination or their effects. Nothing harsh or disagreeable is allowed to intrude in the narrative. For her the American people are a "race of giants" characterized by "generous purse, broad mind, strong heart, and free soul."[8]

Generally, American critics viewed *A Daughter of the Samurai* sympathetically as the "appealing narrative of a little daughter of old Japan." They found favor with it as an apologia for Japan and a hymn of praise to America by an endearing Japanese who has "no superiority complex, pleads no causes, asks no vexing questions" but instead "tells a tale with delicacy and taste."[9]

### My Country and My People

During four decades, Lin Yutang, the most famous self-styled Chinese cultural envoy to America, published a score of books on a variety of subjects from "the importance of living" to tracts against communism and notes on American culture and heritage. Best known as explicator of China to the West, Lin's writings include *My Country and My People* (1937), *The Vigil of a Nation* (1945), *Gay Genius: Life and Times of Su Tung Po* (1947), *Famous Chinese Short Stories Retold* (1952), *The Chinese Way of Life* (1959), *The Chinese Theory of Art* (1967), and *History of Press and Public Opinion in China* (1968).[10] He has been called a "critic of the Chinese and

American ways of life," "critic of life and interpreter of ancient wisdom," "interpreter of the Chinese to the West," who writes in "certainly the very best [English] any Chinese has ever written," whose "balanced outlook is accompanied by a welcome sense of humor," and who is a "genial world citizen."[11] Lin's enormous popularity in the West is attributable to three factors: he writes superficial, pithy pieces about China that are in perfect keeping with the American popular view; he is a bourgeois anti-Communist, the most popular political position for a Chinese in the United States; and he remains light, humorous, and not overly serious about himself or about China in his writings.

The book that brought Lin instant success was *My Country and My People*, in which he attempts to introduce to Americans the Chinese "people, character, mind, ideals of life, life, socio-politics, literature, art and daily life." In a series of humorous, chatty descriptions of Chinese characteristics, Lin tries to make the Chinese palatable to the American public and at the same time to demonstrate the urbanity and intellectual sophistication of which one educated Chinese is capable. Lin's popularity is based on his presentation of the "human side" of the Chinese without jeopardizing the reigning stereotypes. His description of the Chinese as backward, childlike, superstitious people, loveable but incapable of taking care of themselves, is in perfect keeping with the Western colonial view of them. Lin likens the Chinese "mind" to the "feminine mind," contending that both manifest a "lack of analytical thinking" and a "dislike of abstract terms." The Chinese, Lin writes, have always been willing to submit to tyranny, partly because of their "innate conservatism," which is a "sign of inward richness." According to Lin, Chinese do not want to be independent; they are contemptuous of material wealth, so they do not want to raise their standard of living. Chinese distrust civilization in favor of primitive habits; they glorify the idiot and the fool; and they possess a "farcical view of life."[12]

*My Country and My People* was an immensely popular book, read by millions of Americans. Written in 1935, it was revised in 1937 and again in 1939, and a new edition of it appeared in 1962. Part of the book's popularity can be attributed to its political stance. William Henry Chamberlain called its author a "brilliant anti-Communist": "[I]t is this rare ability to combine the philosophies and ideals of East and West that make his writings one of the strongest forces for international unity and understanding at work in the world of nuclear conflict."[13] Lin's writing is in the main amiable nonsense, passing for "Chinese" or "philosophy." His heavy-handed aphorisms are almost parodies, lacking even the wit of the fictional Charlie Chan:

> What is man, anyhow? Do we know the answer to that question better than man did a hundred years ago? . . . I would not bet yes and I would not bet no.

Uncertainty is bad because it makes a man nervous.

There is no difference but difference of degree between different degrees of difference and no difference.[14]

Lin's life as a self-styled "pagan loafer" who believed that the finest product of Chinese culture was a "romantic cultivation of the ideal life" made it possible for him to conjecture on the eternal submissiveness of the Chinese people to tyranny while they were engaged in fact in a bloody battle for national liberation. According to Chan Wing-Tsit:

> [W]hile the Chinese were dying by the millions, Lin had the heart to indulge in chitchat on the moon, rocks and gardens, dreams, smoke and incense, the art of growing old gracefully, and Confucius singing in the rain! No wonder many Chinese called his book "My Country and My Class" or resorting to a pun, called it "Mai Country and Mai People"—mai being the Chinese word for selling and betraying.

Chan contends that Lin was "out of tempo with the Chinese people": the typical Chinese is not a Taoist, as Lin would have him, and Chinese culture involves, according to Chan, "more than literature and art." It is clear that Americans never counted him as one of their own either. Although he is the only Asian included in *The Picture Book of Famous Immigrants* (1962), where he appears together with John Jacob Astor, Eleutherie Irenee Dupont, Andrew Carnegie, and Felix Frankfurter, the text describes him as "a combination of East and West, constantly smoking black cigars while he reads the philosophy of Confucius." Ironically, the compilers of the book were unaware of Lin's expressed dislike of Confucianism in favor of Taoism.[15]

### America through Asian Eyes

Views of the West through the eyes of an Asian narrator also held a certain appeal for Western readers, though more because of their solipsistic desire for novel views of themselves and for reinforcement of their ideas about Asians than because of interest in social criticism. One problem, of course, was that the American image of the Asian as inferior made it difficult for most readers to imagine an Asian capable of the kind of comment on American life that Europeans from Tocqueville to Trollope to Allistair Cooke were renowned for. In the preface to one Asian commentary on America, the American editor warns that because "the masses of Americans do not take the Chinaman seriously . . . [i]t will be difficult for the average American to conceive it possible that a cultivated Chinaman, of all persons, should have been honestly amused at our civilization." He warns readers not to expect the usual Chinese "pidgin English," because the writer had been educated in America and Europe. He encourages them instead to recognize that some of "our fads and foibles held up as strange gods . . . [do seem] grotesque when seen in this yellow light." The editor further warns the reader not to be affronted by the Chinese observer's attitudes towards America or his profound loyalty to China because these are the "hallmark of actual novelty [and] add to the interest of the recital."[16]

Several early Asian writers seeking publishers and readers in the English-speaking world attempted discussions of American life and customs. These writings do contain some succinct and intelligent social criticism and valuable cultural comparisons although they are characterized by a marked degree of inhibition, which may stem from a combination of genuine courtesy and tolerance and a fear of displeasing the reader. Occasionally, repressed rage against ignorance or discrimination emerges. Generally, though, if the writer does not simply praise America in rhapsodic terms, he apologizes profusely for even the most innocuous remarks about American habits and institutions. Otherwise, he strenuously attempts to dissociate himself from the majority of other Asians as a "cultivated exception" or chooses to remain completely anonymous.

Park No-Yong's *An Oriental View of American Civilization* (1934) is one attempt to view America through Asian eyes, as well as an effort to make basic cultural comparisons. Early in the book, Park observes that the notion of moderation and the "mean" exists in both ancient Greek and Chinese philosophies. In the essays, Park juxtaposes American speed, materialism, mass production, and orientation towards the future with Chinese stagnation and fatalism, concluding that the ideal way must be located somewhere between. Park's book contains only tactful and indirect criticisms of American society: he comments on fashion worship among American women and takes a few swipes at American imperialism and discrimination against the Chinese, which he feels have been carried "a little too far," but his social commentary never rises above the realm of cliche.

Wu Tingfang, who lived in the United States as a diplomat for almost a decade, comments in *America through the Spectacles of an Oriental Diplomat* (1914) that America "fairly approximates the high ideals of democracy" despite the existence of racism against Black people and discrimination against the Chinese. Since the ostensible purpose of the book is to encourage an understanding of the Chinese, particularly of the Chinese elite, Wu appeals to the rationality and common sense of the reader, arguing that whites cannot be racially superior to the Chinese, who are products of a rich and complex intellectual, moral, and artistic history. Wu even asserts that while Americans measure their lives by "accumulation," Chinese measure theirs by "morality" and are, as a result, a happier though simpler people.

Wu announces early in the book that he plans to write his "impartial and candid observations" of American life and hopes that

> American readers will forgive me if they find some opinions they cannot endure. I assure them they were not formed hastily or unkindly. Indeed, I should not be a sincere friend were I to picture their country as a perfect paradise, or were I to gloss over what seem to me to be their defects.

For the most part, however, Wu's criticisms of American society are politely muted, tangential, and innocuous. He wonders, at the book's close, how Westerners can engage in foxhunts and wear bird feathers in their hats while at the same time promoting a society for the prevention of cruelty to animals. The only concrete suggestion he can offer to American society from his Chinese vantage point is that American women follow the example of Chinese women in the selection of their clothing. Wu chides American women as given to frivolous and sometimes even "dangerous" dressing habits, citing a news story about a woman who died from blood poisoning after being stuck with a hatpin. Even this mild suggestion is offered apologetically:

> It would be bold, and indeed impertinent, on my part to suggest to my American friends that they should adopt the Chinese costume. It has much to recommend it, but I must candidly confess that it might be improved. . . . I have enough faith in the American people to believe that my humble suggestion will receive their favorable consideration.[17]

In general, the aristocratic Asian immigrant writers who focused their attention on the problems of the Chinese laborer attributed most of the blame for discrimination against them to the laborers themselves. White Americans usually view the Chinese in America as laundrymen and waiters because they were indeed primarily laundrymen and waiters. Little mention is made of the discriminatory practices that channelled the Chinese into these occupations. Without mentioning the effects of racially segregationist policies on the Chinese minority in America, Huie Kin (*Reminiscences*, 1932) chides them for maintaining those national customs which he says prompted anti-Chinese attitudes:

> As I now look back, I feel that we ourselves were partly to blame. . . . [O]ur people were too slow in adapting ourselves to the life of the people among whom we lived, moved and had our material well-being. We remained a clannish people, keeping our native dress, carrying vegetables on poles, making an "outlandish" sight and providing "grist" for the anti-Chinese propaganda.

Decades later, Betty Lee Sung, in *Mountain of Gold* (1967), regrets that the Chinese tended to gather in ethnic communities instead of dispersing themselves to "reduce the degree of visibility." Both Huie and Sung cling to the common notion that the Chinese brought discrimination upon themselves by looking different from other Americans and by "voluntarily" segregating themselves. Sung laments on the one hand that Chinese have been stereotyped as waiters and laundrymen while claiming on the other hand that Chinese youths' problems with the law stem from their refusal to accept low-paid jobs in restaurants and laundries. She also reproaches them for their faulty English without acknowledging the role of inadequate schooling and discriminatory employment practices in English language capability among Asian immigrants.[18]

In *Silent Traveler in New York* (1950), Chiang Yee also blames the Chinese ignorance of English for misunderstandings between Americans and Asians:

> The main obstacle to mutual understanding between people, is, I think, language. The first of my compatriots who left their fatherland for the West did not acquire much knowledge of the language of their new country. . . . As they lived according to their native customs, but could not talk about or explain these, they naturally aroused curiosity. If they had been able to explain themselves, China and the Chinese might have been spared many a misinterpretation.[19]

Such a view could only have been taken by an educated Asian aristocrat who had mastered the English language himself at an early age and who did not spend his life among other Asians in a basement laundry or laboring on a California farm.

## Younghill Kang: Searching for a Door to America

Many early Asian immigrant writers, including Lin Yutang and Etsu Sugimoto, viewed themselves as guests or visitors in America. They fully intended to return to their homelands at the end of a temporary sojourn in the West, to continue, perhaps, their attempts to improve communication and increase understanding between "East" and "West." The writings of Younghill Kang and Carlos Bulosan illustrate the transition from authors who view themselves as guests or visitors to those who want to find a place for themselves in American society. What we read now is, not the idealized commentary of a tour guide nor the polite account of an eloquent Asian diplomat, but a personal expression of the laboring immigrant's yearnings for a new life and the process of his education about the realities of American life. Because Kang and Bulosan took part in a personal transition from Korean to Korean American and from Filipino to Filipino American, they are representative of the genesis of Asian American literature. Moreover, the differences in interpretation of Asian American realities by Kang and Bulosan emblemize the diversity of perspectives in Asian American literature.

Elements of the "cultural ambassador" theme of Lin Yutang, Park No-Yong, and Etsu Sugimoto linger in the autobiographical works of a Korean immigrant writer, Younghill Kang (1903–1972). Like them, Kang was an educated Asian aristocrat. Like Lin and Park, he attempts to present in English the "Oriental Yankee's view of America." Like Sugimoto, he is convinced of "Eastern decay" and "Western rebirth." But Kang goes far beyond these writers, writing from the heart about his agonizing search for an entry into American life and therefore "in[to] the human affairs of his time."[20]

*The Grass Roof* (1931) describes Kang's life in Korea to the point of his departure for the West in 1921. *East Goes West* (1937) is a chronicle of his experiences in America. In both slightly fictionalized accounts, Kang is represented by the narrator, Chungpa Han. Kang himself considered the latter book the more important one, "more mature in style and technique" as well as more highly developed in content: "*The Grass Roof* may be said to have been written in the mood of the Everlasting Nay of Carlyle: *East Goes West* may be compared to the mood of the Everlasting Yea."[21] But it was the earlier book that won him accolades in America and Europe. *The Grass Roof* was translated into French, German, and other languages and won Le Prix Halperine Kaminsky in 1937. Even in his 1972 obituary in the New York *Times*, it was described as his "most important work."[22] Part of the reason lay in the book's novelty: it told a good deal about a country about which very little was known here. Kang was a unique figure for his time, the only Korean immigrant to have written book-length fiction in English, and autobiographical fiction at that. In this and in many other ways he was completely unrepresentative of his people, yet became something of a spokesman for Koreans in America almost by default.

That critics preferred Kang's descriptions of Korea to his discussions of his American experience is made clear in a review by Lady Hosie, author of *Portrait of a Chinese Lady*, who finds *The Grass Roof* rewarding because it stirs the nostalgia of the "lover of the East" and "explains scenes only half understood before." She is less enthusiastic about Kang's rendering of the West and of Westerners:

> Mr. Kang does not, I think, give a full account of American missionaries. Doubtless these are blundering human beings, just like the rest of us. He accuses them of lack of education, yet he longed ardently to come to their country for the kind of education they

receive. He was desperately eager to receive the benefit of their escort to America . . . and had no compunction when their religious meetings were used as a political cloak. . . . Mr. Kang is, however, on sure ground when he gives us Korea and Koreans. His book is a real contribution to literature and to our understanding of his countrymen and women.

Even those reviewers who praise *East Goes West* like it for what they saw as sustained optimism in the face of racism and discrimination in America. This optimism is called "instinct for self-preservation": one reviewer admires Kang's "good-natured naiveté," "curiosity," and "resourcefulness"; another comments on Kang's "humor and charm," calling *East Goes West* the description of a "successful search for the formula that was to make him an 'Oriental Yankee.'" Like the autobiographies by Pardee Lowe, Jade Snow Wong, Monica Sone, Jeanne Wakatsuki Houston, and Daniel Okimoto, which will be discussed in subsequent chapters, critics saw *East Goes West* as an example of how minorities should respond to American racism, that is, as another Asian American "success story."[23]

In fact, *The Grass Roof* is not a description of Korea and Koreans, and *East Goes West* is not a success story. *The Grass Roof* is a justification of Kang's departure from Korea, and its "contribution to our understanding" of Korea and Koreans must be accepted within this context. Kang's attitudes were highly unrepresentative of Koreans in his time. An aristocrat by birth, he is described as "one of the last immigrants to reach America before Oriental immigration was prohibited."[24] It is important to note that scarcely more than 13,000 Koreans had immigrated to America by 1924, the vast majority of them contract laborers for the sugar plantations of Hawaii. These laborers were brought here before Japan annexed Korea in 1909, at which time emigration from Korea was halted. Even those few Koreans who came to America as students and political refugees were generally not immigrants but sojourners on temporary visas, and they participated intensely, together with the contract laborers, in the overseas movement for Korean independence from Japan.

While in Korea, Kang's protagonist, Chungpa Han, did not join the national liberation movement that captured the imagination and hearts of thousands of others of his age who fought, wrote, and were imprisoned or killed by the Japanese militarists during the bitter years just prior to his departure for America. His brief imprisonment by the Japanese after his peripheral participation in the widespread Sam Il demonstrations only reinforces his desire to flee his country: "Now I could not . . . give my services [to the independence movement]. Besides I wished to escape death and torture if possible and come to America." Han decides against "mass movements" and "narrow nationalism" in favor of individual survival. His search for "universal truths" is inspired by his readings of

Shakespeare and by the philosophy of individualism and creativity prevalent in Western art since the rise of the bourgeoisie in Europe; these ideas help him justify his desire to escape from Korea:

> I began to realize that those who talk about others, others, others, all the time, and about doing service are usually like the worms that live off the life of another tree. Their ideas were not created by them, they give them no new application, they speak their enthusiasm by plagiarism and live it by mechanical process. Who are the people who really give service to humanity? Only those who can't help it, who give service as by-products of their own joy or anguish. Shakespeare worked for himself, not for others.[25]

Han has decided that Korea is lost. Korean culture is at its "dying gasp," and the narrow, antiquated world of his ancestors is suffocating and hopeless. Having described himself as a progressive, natural leader ("I can never remember a time when I did not consider myself more highly than most of my associates"), he flees from Korea as one flees a cripple or a corpse.[26] Kang has little of Sugimoto's romantic nostalgia: Han cannot return to Asia to await the advent of the "progressive American way," serving comfortably in the meanwhile as a cultural bridge. Disappointed by Confucian education as well as by his hard-won Japanese "Western" education in Korea, he decides that the world and real knowledge are attainable only outside Korea.

Life in Korea is too restrictive for an "energetic searcher after life" like himself. The Japanese conquest of Korea during his youth had transformed his country from a "small, provincial, old-fashioned Confucian nation" into a "planet of death":

> There life grew in manifold harmony, careless, free, simple and primitive. It had its curved lines, its brilliant colors, its haunting music, its own magic of being, but it was a "planet of lost time" where the heyday of life passed by. Gently at first. Its attraction of gravity, the grip on its creatures, maintained through its fervid bowels, its harmonious motion weakened. Then the air grew thin, cooler and cooler. At last, what had been good breathing to the old was only strangling pandemonium to the newer generations. . . . I know that as I grew up, I saw myself placed on a shivering pinnacle overlooking a wasteland that had no warmth, that was under an infernal twilight. I cried for the food for my growth, and there seemed no food. And I felt I was looking on death, the death of an ancient planet, a spiritual planet that had been my fathers' home. Until I thought to stay would be to try to live a plant on top of the Alps where the air is too cold, too stunting, and the wind too

brutally cruel. In loathing of death, I hurtled forward, out into space, toward a foreign body . . . and a younger culture drew me by natural gravity.

In old Korea, mobility is limited, and social networks of kinship and acquaintanceship are crucial to every aspect of an individual's life. In the immediate past, it would have been almost unthinkable for Han to refuse marriage with the girl chosen for him by his family. But now he asks: "[I]s she trained in the way I am? Can she read English? Can she talk Japanese and Chinese? As to all other kinds of training, making beds and making babies are not my requirements. I am not interested in that kind of education."[27]

Unlike his forebears and most of his contemporaries, Han is possessed of an alternative. Having learned "rebellion against nature and fatality" from the West, he can reject the decaying old order and seek the source of his new knowledge. He is, he feels, a "Faustian individual," original, rugged, imaginative, a lonely pioneer in a Brave New World:

> Between my father and little Aunt and me, there already seemed the barrier of an ocean, an ocean of time, since they and I lived in different eras. My grandmother died by the hand of a foreigner. The soul of my crazy-poet uncle was completely broken. My childhood friends I had grown away from and the friends of my first manhood were exiled in body or spirit. In my short eighteen years, I have seen the disintegration of one of the first nations of the Earth.

As he sets sail for America, he is exhilarated by the feeling of his uniqueness, noting that he is almost like a man with no nationality, "exiled from all humanity": "[I]t seems to me that the poet alone has no home, no national boundary, but is like a man in a ship. His nearest kin is the muse up in the clouds, and his patriotism goes to the ethereal kingdom."[28]

In America, Han would have ignored, if he could, his Korean past, his Korean identity, and perhaps his Korean compatriots. He is absorbed by the desire to find an individual place for himself in American society. The search is crucial to him because he knows that he cannot return to Korea. If he survives at all, he must survive in America.

Even in America, Han, a "rebellious individualist," cannot accept the revolutionary fervor of fellow Koreans. He describes "typical" Korean exiles with pity and condescension. Obsessed as they are by their desire to return one day to a liberated homeland, they remain exiled "in body, not in soul," like Pak, whom Han describes as "a most typical Korean":

> Western civilization had rolled over him as water over rock. . . . [H]e always sat in at Korean Christian services, because they had some-

times to do with nationalism.* With his hard-earned money, he supported all societies for Korean revolution against Japan. . . . For fifteen years, his single ambition had been to get back there and settle down. On Korean land, he wanted to raise 100 percent Korean children, who would be just as patriotic like himself. . . . But still he did not have enough money to travel back, get married, settle comfortably there. This made him rather suffering and gloomy, always looking on the dark side of things.[29]

Men like Pak often gave their life's savings to the independence movement. Intense desire for Korean independence from Japan characterized every class of Korean living in Hawaii and the United States for four decades. Farmers, waiters, and domestic servants by day became independence workers by night. Korean churches in America were meeting places for independence movement activities, and a group of Korean exiles even established a military academy in America for training fighters. Korean exiles in America were responsible for the political assassination of an American envoy to Japan.[30]

Han is unmoved by the patriotism almost all his acquaintances feel, and the result is his "loneliness and lack of nationalistic passion, my sense of uncomfortable exile even among my fellow countrymen." Unlike them, he feels he had escaped from ruin and decay by leaving Korea, and the idea of returning there is singularly unattractive to him: "If I went back to Korea, and returned to become a villager for always, was that any fun? Why should I keep on manufacturing babies for which there would be no future?"[31]

East Goes West is the chronicle of Han's continual search for the fictional America he had constructed within his own imagination: it is an idea, a "mental utopia," a place of regeneration, a dream full of magic and mastery, a "glorious vision" of enchantment and romance, a spiritual home.[32] The search is generally unsuccessful. Han's hopes and desires and his actual experiences are in continual conflict. Though sensitive and observant, he cannot understand why his expectations never seem to match the reality that he and his friends face year after discouraging year.

Though Han would no doubt have avoided the company of fellow Koreans, most of whom made him feel uncomfortable, he befriends two of the most acculturated of the exiles, the only two who are at all interested in Western literature. Jum, an unemployed cook who fancies himself a dapper New Yorker, is the boyfriend of a white call girl who dances in black body make-up at a Harlem night club. Having seen even

---

*Lacking clan or family associations or merchant guilds in America, Koreans grouped together in various Korean churches, which housed political activity for the independence movement and often had little to do with religion per se.

Korean nobles and court officials working as waiters and houseboys in America, Jum has rejected Korean culture as useless to material and psychological survival in the modern world. In Han's eyes, Jum belongs in America. He can flirt, neck, drink, and tell dirty jokes "like an American college boy." He seems self-assured and worldly-wise. Wherever he goes, "there was a chair waiting for him and a gay audience." But Jum's bubble bursts, and when his girlfriend finally casts him aside, he is forced to face the fact that he might indeed be only a "guest in the house." He marries a Korean American and settles down in Hawaii. Han receives a letter from him: "I have not failed, I have only not succeeded."[33]

The other Korean through whom Han searches for a door into American life is Kim, whom he meets in New York Chinatown. Kim, who has lived in the West for sixteen years, is supported by "Eastern bags of rice," money sent him by his wealthy landowning parents in Korea. He has benefited from "everything Asia had to offer": his family is wealthy; he is well schooled in classical Chinese poetry; his manner is princely; he is aristocratic and cosmopolitan:

> In the Far East he had wandered through the heart of the storms, amidst guns and fires, battles and revolutions. He had lived long in Europe, he had visited the Near East, even in Africa . . . one moment drinking the famous beer of Heidelberg, the next eating fetticini [*sic*] at Alfredo's in Rome; sauntering by the bookstalls in Paris, Shanghai, Tokyo; and now recalling everything over a glass of American gin in New York City.[34]

Surely, Han can learn a great deal from such a man. It turns out, however, that Kim's search for acceptance—in his case by the Western intellectual elite—has been no more successful than Jum's or his own. Kim can claim to belong to the same brotherhood as his hero T. S. Eliot, but his rootlessness and alienation are compounded by the color bar, which prevents him from ever being accepted as anything more than an "adopted child" by the Western literary establishment. He is always an observer, a taster, a hanger-on, never a participant:

> [S]hall I take my Korean silver cup-bowl and candlesticks to the sea? They might be rare down there, that realm knows no East or West. . . . No, I will not pack up my lofty objects. . . . I will give them to my old char woman, with my heavy German books by Spengler and Kant. . . . Has she any use for them, I wonder? Well, I have none, for I will enter the mermaid Universe. . . . One good in poetry would not be barren there, their muses have a swifter wing.[35]

Left stranded and penniless on a student passport when the family of the New England girl he loves separates them and his own family in Korea loses its fortune, Kim commits suicide. To Han, his death is a tragic waste, born of alienation from his own country and rejection by the country to which he wanted so desperately to belong.

Despite the sorry examples of his fellow exiles, Han is sure that he can succeed where they failed, and he embarks eagerly upon the task. He had not been daunted by his struggle in Seoul to find "universal truth," nor by the difficulties of his journey to America; he will "get to know the West" even if it takes him his entire lifetime. But even while he is "dreaming the Faustian dream," congratulating himself on having escaped "futile martyrdom" in his homeland, reality intrudes, as it does continually during the course of his account. How will he eat? Where will he sleep? That there might be a connection between race discrimination and his own dire circumstances never seems to occur to him. He is ever optimistic that if he keeps his thoughts "lofty," he will not become discouraged. Shakespeare's books become a talisman to him, a symbol of the elusive ideal of Western civilization. But hunger begins early to interfere with his attempts to study Shakespeare in his lonely, unheated room: "[I]n utter solitude and with a chilling heart, I feared pavement famine with plenty all around but in the end not even grass to chew. . . . [I]t was hard to concentrate. Even in the midst of Hamlet's subtlest soliloquies, I could think of nothing but food."[36]

Han seeks an opening into American life through scholarship and study. He attends college night school classes, hoping to find there "the whole Western hemisphere in one block" so that he can "feel its life in an unbroken stream pass through my heart-blood." But he is unable to find "unifying principles": "I could build no bridge from one classroom to another, just as I could build no bridge from New Hotel [where he works as a kitchen helper] into the mental utopia."

Naively, he tries to involve a bellhop in a literary discussion, ignorant that the boy is waiting for a tip. At another time, his books fall out of his suitcase in front of his vexed employer, who wonders if they have been contaminated by some Asiatic disease. He even stumbles over a volume, trampling his employer's garden flowers. Ultimately, he loses his job as house servant because he oversleeps, having read Shakespeare far into the night. Finally, what Han had wanted to gain through "the Kingdom of bookworms"—his dream of America and the West—has grown so dim that he can only turn inward, searching for the lost ideal through his own imagination:

> Thank God there were nights, long lonely hours to think, to become *me* again, to try to recapture the magic and mystery with which I had first dreamed of America. I could find it no longer in books, the books I have brought from college . . . , though I read them again and again.[37]

Han has been introduced to Western civilization through Shakespeare, but his true education comes in other ways. Having been denied a job at the Harlem YMCA, which is reserved for whites, he sleeps in nickel flophouses and mingles with the bums there. He wanders among the Korean exiles in New York Chinatown, "a ghostly world to be lost in, this town that was neither America nor China." He catches glimpses of American life from various vantage points. He works as a domestic servant for a white family who treat him "like a cat or a dog." He finds a job as a busboy in a Chinese restaurant, where the waiters with Ph.D.'s and medical degrees attend to customers who are call girls and shady characters. He peddles tea in Harlem, where he and his fellow Koreans are not "kicked around" as they are by those "pale people with steely eyes and ridged noses and superior shrewdness" uptown.[38]

Throughout all, he never ceases to hope that he will one day open the "closed book" of the true New Yorker and enter into a new and exciting world. When a missionary scholarship gives him the chance to mingle with non-Asians in a small theological college in British Canada, he seizes the opportunity, but his experiences at the college only reinforce his "essential isolation and misfit." He is made to feel "queer and alien" at the college. People speak to him as to a child. Once he is mistaken for a Chinese deaf mute. For the most part, he is treated with missionary kindness:

> [W]hen I look back, it seems as if everybody in Green Grove, with the exception of my enemy and his followers, was very kind to me, almost too kind. I belonged to no clique, I had no chum. I was inexorably unfamiliar. . . . Whenever anybody received a cake from home, no matter what others might be there, Chung-pa was always invited—then given two slices instead of one. I did not care much for cake, yet ate for politeness and gratitude. By and by I got sick. For me there was always special favor, special kindness, special protection . . . the white man's burden attitude toward dark colonies . . . kindness . . . brutal cruelty. . . . I weigh them in my mind, and it seemed to me better to miss the kindness and not to have the cruelty.[39]

But the cruelty persists. He is exploited by an American encyclopedia-peddling business, ridiculed and looked down upon by various employers, used by a religious charismatic leader to cheat believers. Finally, while employed as a clerk in the fake Oriental goods section of a department store, he sees salespeople compete ruthlessly with each other over pennies. He sees the trembling hands of an elderly widow who has wrapped dishes at the store for fourteen dollars a week her whole life. He overhears racist remarks. Little by little, he comes to view the department store as a microcosm of the world he inhabits:

This is American life, I said stubbornly. All day long the moving multitudes of humanity, with busy legs, constantly darting false smiles to cover their depressed facial expression, the worn-out machine bodies turning round in the aisles. . . . At last the dead-tired body moving from the cloakroom to breathe the [stale] street air. But where were all the enchantment and the romance, the glorious vision, which I had seen in my dreams of America as a boy?[40]

One possibility remains. Han makes a final attempt to belong in America through his desire for Trip, the young graduate of an exclusive northeastern girls' college, whom he meets through an old Quaker woman who has done relief work in China. Influenced by Kim's romance with an American girl, Han convinces himself that he is in love with Trip after hearing about her from someone. When he finally has a chance to meet her briefly,

my love for Trip seemed sublimely natural, inevitable, born with me, carried from Asia, since the far moment when I had set out to reach the West. . . . I had asked for a sign from America and it had come. . . . Even while fascinated and committed mind and soul to the Western learning, I had been dismayed and alone. But now all nature took on an instant face . . . and the moon and the stars seen from Asia, Europe, America, Africa, Antarctica, anywhere I might turn, shone and twinkled to tell me . . . Trip.[41]

Han is acutely aware that in Korea he would have had children by now. But he is fascinated by the idea of Western romantic love, and by the idea that if he participated in it, even unrequited, he would become that much more a part of Western civilization. The cultural barriers, however, are too obvious. As Han tries to entertain Trip with tales of his exotic background, we see (as he does not) that she is just trying to be polite.

"When I was born, it was a famine year," I paused, dramatically. "I never had a mother. She died. And I missed her so much."
However, Trip said, "*That* was probably a help. They don't seem to get on well with their mothers over here." And I was a little offended.[42]

Trip is interested in the idea of arranged marriages, not in Han, and she is thrilled at being stopped with Han in Chinatown by a plainclothesman checking to see if she is being abducted by a tong man. Later, Han considers telling her about Kim's death but decides against it because she "might shut me out" for speaking "all my thoughts."

During his sole evening at Trip's apartment, Han is "enchanted" by "the talk and the gaiety and the laughter." Tipsy with wine, he gives a recitation of Keats, Shelley, Browning, Ruskin, Shakespeare, while everyone applauds and laughs. He does not mind being funny to Trip's friends, since it gives him a sense of belonging to the group. Finally, flushed with "the joy of arriving in such a sweet world of eternal beauty and youth and delightful fellowship," he leaves among polite invitations to come back again: "The door of Paradise closed behind me." The reader knows that the American girls have no intention of befriending Han. His subsequent attempts to contact Trip fail: she never answers his carefully composed letters. When he finally returns to the apartment building, the girl and her roommates have vanished. His "love" for her is the same as his metaphysical dream of America—it is only an isolated idea in his hopeful imagination: "I did not forget her. Nor what I had come to America to find. I set out now inspired to seek the romance of America. . . . I became the man who must hunt and hunt for the spiritual home."[43]

Han has not found a doorway into American life. He is still groping, ever less hopefully, as the book ends. Contradictions—between economic survival and spiritual life, between the "ideal" of America and the actual experience of American life by an Asian immigrant, between Kim's hopeless romanticism and Jum's unconvincing, shallow buoyancy—are never resolved in the book. On his first night in America, Han had a dream: "A synod of ancestors seemed coming to visit me, watching me disapprovingly in that high Western bed, which had renounced plain earth so literally beneath. What can you hope to find here, they said. Life, I cried. We see no life, they said." *East Goes West* ends with a confirming nightmare. Han is separated from his childhood friends and a "paradise of wild and flowery magic" by his desire to find his money, contracts, business letters, and especially the key to his American car:

> And now as is the inconsequential way of dreams, I was running down the steps into a dark and cryptlike cellar, still looking for my money and my keys. The cellar seemed to be under the pavements of a vast city. Other men were in that cellar with me—some frightened-looking Negroes, I remember. Then looking back, I saw, through an iron grating into the upper air, men with clubs and knives. The cellar was being attacked. The Negroes were about to be mobbed. I shut the door and bolted it, and called to my frightened fellows to help me hold the door.
> "Fire, bring fire," called the red-faced men outside.
> And through the grating I saw the flaring torches being brought. And applied. Being shoved, crackling, through the gratings. I awoke like a phoenix out of a burst of flames.

I have remembered this dream because according to Oriental interpretation, it is a dream of good omen. To be killed in a dream means success, and in particular death by fire augurs good fortune. This is supposed to be so, because death symbolizes in Buddhistic philosophy growth and rebirth and a happier reincarnation.[44]

In every possible area of his American experience Han has met only disappointment, misunderstanding, loneliness, and alienation. Kim's suicide, Jum's "non-success," and an endless series of locked doors mock him as he faces at last the irreconcilable worlds of actuality and desire. Just as he had remained hopeful during the discouraging years of life in America, without objective reason for hope, he clings now to one comforting precept of Buddhist philosophy: he will live again, happily, in another time, another world. It is not the success he had hoped for when he left for America, so many years before, but it is the only dream left, the only one that will not be betrayed.

Although he remained unable to fully analyze the significance of his American odyssey, Kang's books remain valuable documents of an almost totally lost experience. He does not speak for Asians in America or even for most Korean immigrants at his own time. But his books contain a bit of the collective experience of the thousands of Asian men who worked as domestics, waiters, and cooks and who studied at American colleges or became objects of American missionary efforts. Chiefly, they give us the affecting testimony of one Korean's journey in search of the heart of America.

## Carlos Bulosan:
## A Filipino American Community Portrait

Carlos Bulosan was born in a small village in the Philippine Islands in the same year as Younghill Kang. Like Kang, he sought entry into American life and, like him, was often frustrated and disappointed. It was Kang's writings, as a matter of fact, that encouraged Bulosan to produce his own books:

. . . it was his indomitable courage that rekindled in me a fire of hope.

Why could not I succeed as Younghill Kang had? He had come from a family of scholars and had gone to an American university— but is he not an Oriental like myself? Was there an Oriental without education who had become a writer in America? If there was one, maybe I could do it too![45]

But the similarities between the two men are not nearly as important as the differences. Kang was an aristocrat of sorts, certainly a man of letters. Bulosan was from a poor peasant family. While Kang writes of his native Korea as an individual rebelling against a land offering little opportunity to the free spirit he considered himself to be, Bulosan remains keenly aware of what feudal and colonial practices—sharecropping, land seizure, and exploitation of peasants by church and absentee landlordism—have done to his motherland. For Kang, the homeland is the "planet of death" from which he must flee to survive; for Bulosan, memories of the Islands never cease to offer inspiration for a continued struggle for a better future. Where Kang speaks chiefly for himself and the members of his elite, Bulosan consciously strives to give voice to thousands of agricultural and menial laborers of Asian America:

What impelled me to write? The answer is—my grand dream of equality among men and freedom for all. To give literate voice to the voiceless one hundred thousand Filipinos in the United States, Hawaii, and Alaska. Above all and ultimately, to translate the desires and aspirations of the whole Filipino people in the Philippines and abroad in terms relevant to contemporary history.[46]

Bulosan shares with Kang a "gigantic dream to know all America." But Kang's desire is to gain personal admission into the existing charmed circle, while Bulosan wants to contribute towards the fulfillment of America's promise of democracy and equality. Therefore, while Kang's narrator moves ever farther away from his own exiled compatriots, Bulosan's faith in the working man and in justice for the exploited as the key to American fulfillment turns him towards fellow Filipinos, since true democracy in America would have to mean acceptance of Filipinos into the pattern of American life.

We must be united in the effort to make an America in which our people can find happiness. . . . We are all Americans that have toiled and suffered and known oppression and defeat, from the first Indian that offered peace in Manhattan to the last Filipino pea pickers. . . . America is in the hearts of men that died for freedom. . . . America is a prophecy of a new society of men. . . . America is also the nameless foreigner, the homeless refugee, the hungry boy begging for a job and the black body dangling on a tree. America is the illiterate immigrant who is ashamed that the world of books and intellectual opportunities is closed to him. . . . All of us, from the first Adams to the last Filipino, native born or alien, educated or illiterate—*we are America*!

There had been Filipino characters in the writings of Peter B. Kyne, Rupert Hughes, William Saroyan, and John Fante, although they were never as grotesquely omnipresent in American culture as Chinese and Japanese caricatures had been. Bulosan believed that he would be best able to portray "Filipinos as human beings."[47]

Bulosan became one of the best-known Filipinos in the Western world. A prolific writer, his published works include poetry, fiction, and essays. Within two years after his arrival in Seattle in 1930 at the age of sixteen, Bulosan had published several poems in poetry magazines. According to his brother Aurelio, as early as 1932 he was one of two Filipinos listed in *Who's Who*; the other was Carlos Romulo. By 1940, Bulosan had been published in journals such as *Poetry*, the *Lyric*, *Frontier and Midland*, the *Tramp*, and *Voices*. But it was during the war years that he attracted nationwide attention for his literary efforts: *Letter from America* (1942), *The Voice of Bataan* (1944), *Laughter of My Father* (1944; a collection of short stories first serialized in the *New Yorker*), *The Dark People* (1944), and *America Is in the Heart* (1946), the "autobiography" that has been considered his key work. Bulosan's book of stories about the Philippines, *Laughter of My Father*, was broadcast to the American armed forces around the world during the war in an attempt to encourage sympathy for American allies in the Pacific. His essay, "Freedom from Want," in the *Saturday Evening Post* (March 6, 1943), which had been inspired by President Franklin D. Roosevelt's January 1941 speech on the "Four Freedoms," was illustrated by Norman Rockwell and displayed in the examination room of the Federal Building in San Francisco as an example of an immigrant's faith in American democracy. *America Is in the Heart*, which emphasized the promise of democracy against fascism, was translated and sold in Sweden, Denmark, Italy, and Yugoslavia.

By 1947, Bulosan was recognized as one of the most prolific writers in America. His face appeared on covers of national magazines. *Look* hailed *America Is in the Heart* as one of the fifty most important American books ever published.

Bulosan's popularity waxed and waned with the political climate. Carey McWilliams notes that during the war, when Bulosan's reputation was at its apex, "this country was quite Philippine-conscious; the word 'Bataan' enjoyed a splendid resonance. . . . Most Americans seemed to be touched by the loyalty of the Filipinos who in turn, seemed to be grateful to us for helping them."[48] But the final decade of Bulosan's life was a decline into poverty, alcohol, loneliness, and obscurity. Too frail and weak to work at strenuous labor, he had undergone eleven operations, some for lung lesions and others for leg cancers, before he died in 1956. One kneecap had been removed, and he walked with great difficulty. He drank heavily, especially with the white woman who lived with him for five years and had left him before he died. Finally, he collapsed in a Seattle street and apparently died of exposure.

According to Norman Jayo, Bulosan was filled with a sense of foreboding and despair after the bombing of Hiroshima. He feared that the human race was entering a new, atomic, and nuclear era which he and his fellow travellers might be unable to "cope with."[49] Another factor that contributed to his decline was a plagiarism charge brought against him late in 1946 by Guido D'Agostino, who accused Bulosan of copying his "The Dream of Angelo Zara" (*Story* magazine and *The Best American Short Stories of 1945*) and publishing it in the *New Yorker* under the title "The End of the War" (1944). Although the case was settled out of court and he was posthumously vindicated by the *New Yorker* editors, the publicity aroused by the case was extremely damaging to Bulosan, who subsequently had difficulty finding anyone to publish his writings. Also disheartening to him was the adverse criticism he was subject to from intellectuals in the Philippines, many of whom gloated over the plagiarism case, red-baited him during the cold war period, and delighted in pointing out the various inconsistencies in his autobiography.[50] They assailed him for exaggeration, pointing out discrepancies between representations in the book and the actual facts of his life.

Because of *America Is in the Heart*, for example, Bulosan is believed to have been a menial laborer who arrived in America illiterate and who educated himself in a convalescent hospital. This is only partially true. Bulosan has been described as "an outstanding child-man," artistic, sensitive, and driven by loneliness and an intense desire "to make others happy":

> A tiny person with a limp, with an exquisite face, almost facially beautiful, with gleaming teeth and lovely brown eyes, shy, generous, terribly poor, terribly exiled in California, adoring Caucasian women, sartorially exquisite, always laughing through a face that masked tragedy. A Filipino patriot, a touch of the melodramatic about him, given to telling wildly improbable stories about himself, disappearing from Southern California for months at a time, probably to work in a Seattle or Alaska cannery, showing up finally at my home with some touching gift, a book of poems, a box of Filipino candy. . . . If I were a good Christian, I think I might label him a saint, for he radiated kindness and gentleness.[51]

The son of a small farmer in Central Luzon, Bulosan had almost completed secondary school in the Philippines before he accumulated enough money for the steerage passage to follow his brothers, Aurelio and Jose, who had left for America two years previously. Bulosan had already shown interest and ability in writing in high school, where he worked on the school literary journal. After he was admitted as a tuberculosis patient at Los Angeles County Hospital in 1936, he was befriended by two liberal young literary women, and, during the two years he spent convalescing, he read a book a day, he says, from among the various literature classics brought to him by Dorothy Babb. To this extent, he was self-educated.

Unlike the narrator of *America Is in the Heart*, Bulosan did not work for extended periods of time in the fields and canneries. From the beginning, his health was fragile, and one of his legs was two inches shorter than the other. Barred like other members of his race from all but the most menial labor and barred from that by his disability, Bulosan did undertake occasional work as a dishwasher or bakery employee, but he made his living largely from literary and union activities and was supported financially by friends and his brother Aurelio. When Bulosan met labor union leader Chris Mensalvas, who is represented in *America Is in the Heart* as Jose, and other Filipinos who were trying to organize Filipino cannery and packing-house workers during the Depression, Mensalvas encouraged Bulosan to write for the union papers. For a time, he edited a cannery workers' union publication. Bulosan helped found the UCAPAWA (United Cannery and Packing House Workers of America) between 1934 and 1938, but he was a writer rather than a cannery or packing-house worker. Mensalavas had arranged to have him hired as a UCAPAWA yearbook editor in 1952, and Bulosan lived on that income until he died four years later.

Bulosan addressed his writing to an American audience in an attempt to win better treatment for his compatriots: "[I]t has always been my desire to make [lots of people] cry anyway, and to make them feel the very depth of our sorrow and loneliness in America. I have always wanted to show them our capacities for love, our deep spiritual qualities, and our humanity."[52] *America Is in the Heart* is in many ways part of that inclusive and characteristically Asian American genre of autobiography or personal history dedicated to the task of promoting cultural goodwill and understanding. Many Filipino writers felt that they should address an American readership, because of the unintelligibility of the forty-odd Filipino languages, because publishing facilities are thought to be better in America, and because many Filipino writers felt in the past that "the most effective way to put our nation on the cultural map of the world is to have excellent works of Filipino writers published in America . . . the cultural center of the world."[53] Similar arguments held for the writing of personal histories. In most of Bulosan's short stories about Filipino American life there is a first-person narrator that could represent Bulosan himself, and though *America Is in the Heart* describes Filipino American life in California in a general way, it is presented as personal history so that its veracity and impact might be strengthened and so that it might have more market appeal. In fact, P. C. Morantte recalls that Louis Adamic recommended to Bulosan that he write the book as an auto-biography or personal history because it would sell best that way.[54]

Most American critics and readers valued *America Is in the Heart* primarily as a personalized social document. Max Gissen classified the book with "the growing literature of protest coming from dark-skinned peoples all over the world." Another reviewer asserted that the book is important because it is "the kind of 'life history' document which pro-vides the flesh for the bones of social theory"; that it is "life history" makes it credible. A third critic wrote that since the conditions described in the book are "so degrading" that they are "almost incredible," the reader is tempted to put down the book but for the compassion he feels for the narrator and his "touching determination to rise above the sur-rounding brutality." The presence of the narrator is critical: Bulosan is "an appealing little waif who could arouse the compassion of any good-hearted American" long enough to finish the book.[55]

During his union organizing assignments, Bulosan witnessed, heard about, and in some cases experienced some of the events and incidents so vividly described in his "autobiography" and in his short stories. According to his brother Aurelio, Bulosan "used to mingle with the ordinary Filipinos, talk with them, and act like them. But they didn't know that Carlos was gathering materials from them. You see, when you write something about the people you have to be among them. You must feel every word you write."[56] What seems quite clear is that Bulosan, like the narrator in "The Thief," viewed his life and his spirit as being essen-tially at one with the life and spirit of the compatriots who people his autobiography and his stories:

> He started to tell me about his life, and for the first time I began to understand him. I tried to piece the fragments together, and sud-denly I discovered that I was also piecing the fragments of my life together. I was then beginning to write, and I felt like writing the complete story of his life.[57]

Bulosan was primarily a fiction writer, and *America Is in the Heart* is both less and more than a personal history: it is a composite portrait of the Filipino American community, a social document from the point of view of a participant in that experience. According to Ruben R. Alcantra, all students of the Filipino experience in America should "start with the assumption that Carlos Bulosan's *America Is in the Heart* is a required text. In that concrete and sensitively written account of what it meant to be a Filipino in America before 1946, Bulosan set forth the primary themes in the Filipino-American experience." Another Filipino American scholar,

Epifanio San Juan, Jr., asserts that the book "has become an identity-defining primer" for a million Filipinos in the United States. According to Carey McWilliams:

> One may doubt that Bulosan personally experienced each and every one of the manifold brutalities and indecencies so vividly described in this book. It can be fairly said . . . that some Filipino was indeed the victim of each of these or similar incidents. For this reason alone, *America Is in the Heart* is a social classic. It reflects the collective life of thousands of Filipino immigrants. . . . It is the first and best account in English of just what it was like to be a Filipino in California and its sister states in the period, say, from 1930 to 1941.[58]

The saga of the Filipino American experience during the 1930s is governed by a profound compulsion to belong to the new land. It begins, in both *America Is in the Heart* and Bulosan's short stories, with an innocent youth, filled with bright hopes for the future. The youth is driven by poverty and desperation from his native land. Having heard about American democracy and equality, he is stunned when he finds himself excluded and victimized by American racism. As Bulosan had written in a letter:

> Western people are brought up to regard Orientals or colored peoples as inferior, but the mockery of it all is that Filipinos are taught to regard Americans as our equals. Adhering to American ideals, living American life, these are contributory to our feeling of equality. The terrible truth in America shatters the Filipinos' dream of fraternity.
>
> I was completely disillusioned when I came to know this American attitude. If I had not . . . studied about American institutions and racial equality in the Philippines I should never have minded so much the horrible impact of white chauvinism. I shall never forget what I have suffered in this country because of racial prejudice.
>
> Do you know what a Filipino feels in America? . . . He is the loneliest thing on earth. There is much to be appreciated all about him, beauty, wealth, power, grandeur. But is he part of these luxuries? He looks, poor man, through the fingers of his eyes. He is enchained, damnably, to his race, his heritage.[59]

The newly arrived Filipino wants to become American, to participate in the beautiful country he has learned about in his homeland. In "My Education," Bulosan says his journey to America was a torturous search for roots in a new world:

[I]n America I felt a vague desire to see what I had not seen in my country. I did not know how I would approach America. I only knew that here must be a common denominator which every immigrant or native American should look for in order to understand her, and be of service to her people.

The narrator of *America Is in the Heart* arrives in Seattle filled with hope. "Everything seemed familiar to me. . . . With a sudden surge of joy, I knew that I must find a home in this new land." Even after he and his companions have been cheated out of their money and suitcases and tricked into a season's cannery labor in Alaska, he clings to his dreams of America: "Surely the destitute and vicious people of Seattle were merely a small part of it. Where would I begin the pilgrimage, this search for a door into America? . . . I wanted to know Americans, and to be a part of their life. I wondered what I had in common with them."[60]

The episodes described in *America Is in the Heart*, as well as in "I Would Remember" and other short stories, convey the fear, the poverty, and the decadence to which Filipino laborers in California had been condemned. The narrator of *America Is in the Heart* moves among the drunks and criminals, among the members of other exploited minorities—Blacks, American Indians, Mexicans, Koreans—witnessing murders, lynchings, assaults, and merciless violence, increasingly appalled by the degraded life he shares with them. His own brothers and friends become thieves and hustlers, and he himself drifts into petty crime, stealing bedsheets from transient hotels, cheating at cards, succumbing to the "planless, hopeless, directionless" life to which he and his compatriots have been condemned. He begins to live like a hunted animal, sleeping with a knife under his pillow, carrying a gun, watching in horror his own descent into despair and depravity:

> When I came face to face with brutality, I was afraid of what I would do to myself and to others. I was terribly afraid of myself, for it was the beast, the monster, the murderer of love and kindness that would raise its dark head to defy all that was good and beautiful in life.

Yet:

> As time went by I became as ruthless as the worst of them, and I became afraid that I would never feel like a human being again. Yet no matter what bestiality encompasses my life, I felt sure that somewhere, sometimes, I would break free. This faith kept me from completely succumbing to the degradation into which many of my countrymen had fallen.

Bulosan discerns the bitter distrust that has driven Filipinos together to hide "cynically behind our mounting fears, hating the broad white universe at our door," "narrowing . . . our life into an island, into a filthy segment of American society." And yet he discerns always, both in Filipinos and in other Americans, "a seed of trust, that ached to grow to fruition." Filipinos were both brutal and tender, cheating and betraying at one moment and risking their lives for one another the next. America too was a paradox of kindness and cruelty: Jose, whose feet had been amputated during his attempt to escape the white railroad detectives, is well treated by the white hospital staff. The narrator wonders why the police beat him brutally for no reason other than the "crime of being Filipino," and again why a dying white girl helps him escape death at the hands of anti-union goons: "I almost cried. What was the matter with this land? Just a moment ago I was being beaten by white men. But here was another white person, a woman, giving me food."[61]

Bulosan was convinced that the social evils that plagued the Filipino in America rose not out of man's nature but from the environmental factors that had been created and could therefore be changed by human beings. The urge for good, for the ideal, was lodged permanently in the human heart. The America in his heart is the unrealized potential, the unfulfilled dream of a democratic America, which could come into being through the labor of Filipino immigrants and other Americans:

> [M]y faith in America . . . was something that had grown out of my defeats and successes, something shaped by my struggles for a place in this vast land . . . something that grew out of the sacrifices and loneliness of my friends, of my brothers in America and my family in the Philippines—something that grew out of our desire to know America, and to become a part of her great tradition, and to contribute something toward her final fulfillment.[62]

It is often a white woman who symbolizes the America to which Bulosan's Filipinos want to belong. In his letters, Bulosan reveals his fascination for the subject of the relationships between white women and Filipino men:

> [A] Pinoy's feelings for a white woman, beautiful and necessary in many ways, but at the same time cruel and hard in a way that the primitive-minded Pinoy does not understand and refuses to understand. . . . There is really a need for a novel covering the ideal courtship and marriage of a Pinoy and an American white woman.[63]

In "Silence," the unknown white woman becomes the Filipino protagonist's reason for existing. Having lived alone for years, he had been writing in his lonely room, working simply to "run away from the silence" all around him, until one day he notices a white girl on the college lawn across the street from his room. Every day from then on he watches her from his window, and the sight of her makes it possible for him to go on living and working:

> [S]omething changed inside him. It was as if the void in his being had caved in and a flood of sunlight flowed warmly in its place. . . . Now the silence that had followed him everywhere was drowned by the riot of color in his room. She was alive in his room, in his mind and heart. She was the living music of his days and nights. . . . She was his own discovery and creation, and so long as she was in his mind the silences would be quieted.

In "The Romance of Magno Rubio," the tragicomic Filipino peapicker is in love with a white woman he has seen only in a photograph:

> Magno Rubio, Filipino boy. Four-foot six inches tall, dark as a coconut. Head small on a body like a turtle. Magno Rubio. Picking peas on a California hillside for twenty-five cents an hour. Filipino boy. In love with a girl he had never seen. A girl twice his size sideward and upward.

Rubio "works like a carabao and lives like a dog," burrowing in the mud "like a brown beetle" with other migrant workers. Even though the girl is only interested in cheating him of some money, loving her makes him "a human being again," gives him "somebody to work for," makes him feel "clean in his soul."[64]

The white woman is a dream, an ideal. She symbolizes the contradiction between what is brutal in America and what is kind and beautiful. Concretely, the Filipino man's interest in white women did not stem merely from sexual desire, powerful though that impulse might have been. Marrying a white woman would free him from sexual oppression and emasculation, give him the possibility of a stable family life and at least a partial entry into the mainstream of American life.

Bulosan struggles quite consciously against his tendency to idealize women. No one knows better than Bulosan that he cannot write realistically about women: "Throughout my life, from my farthest childhood until now, I was never really close enough to a woman to know what kind of animal she is. And this is why when writing, when talking, my thoughts of women are too idealized." In *America Is in the Heart*, Marian, the woman who rescues the narrator after his beating, is "the song of my dark hour," the one who proved to him that there was love and kindness in America. Mary, a girl who lived platonically with him and other Filipinos, has "milk-white skin" and "deep blue, frightened eyes"; her mere presence enraptures the men:

> She became the delicate object of our affections. She was an angel molded into purity by the cleanliness of our thoughts. When a stranger came into our household and looked at her longingly, I could see some of my companions doubling their fists. This platonic relationship among us was healthy and clean and in a way it gave me a new faith in myself.

Mary symbolizes not merely the good and pure, but also the unattainable. She simply disappears one day, a fleeting dream, probably unaware of the special meaning she had come to have for a lonely group of homeless men.[65]

The combination of books and white women is particularly fascinating to the narrator of *America Is in the Heart*, dating back to a boyhood meeting with a kindly white librarian who seems to personify opportunity through education to the boy in the Philippines. Much later, when a young store clerk invites him to her apartment and shows him around, he is attracted by both her and her books: "I followed her slowly, drinking in her grace, the lovely way she moved her body. In the living room, piled along the wall, were books of many sizes and colors. Books! I was enchanted when I saw them. They drew me irresistibly to them." In America, the narrator is befriended by two sisters who give him books. There is a "disturbing sensuousness" about Alice Odell, and a kind of "maternal solicitude" about Eileen; in her, he finds again "the good of my youth": "I yearned for her and the world she represented. . . . She was undeniably the *America* I had wanted to find in those frantic days of fear and flight, in those acute hours of hunger and loneliness. This America was human, good, and real."[66]

Besides white women, books and book knowledge hold out the abstract promise of equality for Bulosan. Like Kang, Bulosan's narrator dreams of belonging to the "domain of the universal intellectual discoveries of man." While hospitalized, he reads Russian, Spanish, French, and American writers:

> [F]rom day to day I read, and reading widened my mental horizon, creating a spiritual kindship with other men who had pondered over the miseries of their countries. . . . I, too, reacted to my time. I promised myself that I would read ten thousand books when I got well. I plunged into books, boring through the earth's core, leveling all seas and oceans, swimming in the constellation.

American literature, he hopes, might give him access to American society:

> There was something definitely American, something positively vital in all of them [the American poets]. . . . I could follow the path of these poets, continue their tradition and [perhaps] I could arrive at a positive understanding of America. . . . I had been looking for this side of America; surely this was the real side of living America.

For a time, books provide Bulosan's narrator with a sense of belonging to America that he could not derive from any other source. He begins to wonder if there was "a happy situation in the world outside of books," and turns for a time to fables and fairy tales. Finally, he resists the temptation to try to escape from reality through books:

> Reading only made me live the acute pain of the past. When I came upon a scene that recalled my own experiences, I could not go on. But mostly I felt that other writers had lied about life, that they were afraid to depict it as it really was in their environment.

Bulosan finally concludes that it is "disastrous to know and live and work and struggle only with intellectuals." They are too often dreamers "incapable of working [a dynamic social idea] out to the end."[67]

Carlos Bulosan hoped that he might contribute to the fulfillment of the American promise by integrating the Filipinos' struggle for freedom and equality in America with his writing, which would become a weapon in that struggle:

> I only want to expose what terror and ugliness I have seen, what shame and horror I have experienced, so that in my work, however limited in scope and penetration, others will find a reason for a deeper grievance against social injustice and a higher dream of human perfection.

For the narrator of *America Is in the Heart*, writing is a kind of therapy for loneliness and a sense of futility. It lifts him above the limitations and ugliness of his narrow world, gives him a voice for his longing and sorrow, and puts him in touch with the currents of his time: "[W]hen I came home to our apartment, sitting alone in the midst of drab walls and ugly furniture, I felt like striking at my invisible foe. Then I began to write. . . . I had something to live for now, and to fight the world with."[68]

It was socialist thought and the labor movement that finally made Bulosan feel he had become American. He is like the protagonist of "Be American": Consorcio arrives in America a native, innocent peasant boy from the Philippines, full of hope that he can become a "real American," only to slip into the wandering life of the itinerant Filipino menial worker. Consorcio becomes an American through his union organizing activities, by dedicating his quality for "our America":

> Socialist thinking was spreading among the workers, professionals, and intellectuals. . . . To most of us it was a revelation—and a new morning in America. Here was a collective faith dynamic enough to release the creative spirit that was long thwarted in America. My personal predicaments seemed to vanish and for the first time I could feel myself growing and becoming a living part of America.[69]

Writing for the union magazine *New Tide*, participating in organizing activities among Filipino peapickers and cannery workers, made Bulosan feel that he was part of a vast and vital movement based on a common faith in the working man of every nationality. He felt the exhilaration of working for a cause that would become "part of history." The Filipino Communist movement on the West Coast gave Bulosan's narrator the "inspiration and courage to withstand the confusion and futility of my own life." Alone, he could never hope to "blast away the walls that imprisoned the American soul." Fighting alongside others who believed, as he did, that ideas had to be integrated with actions, he had found his own answer to nihilism, fear, and despair. Writing for the labor movement would be his weapon against injustice and his key to American life:

> I . . . became convinced that it was the duty of the artist to trace the origin of the disease that was festering American life. . . . Labor demanded the active collaboration of writers. In the course of eight years, I had relived the whole course of American history. I drew inspiration from my active participation in the workers' movement. The most decisive move that the writer could make was to take his stand with the workers.[70]

Through women, through art, through the labor movement, Carlos Bulosan sought an end to his lonely life as a social and psychological exile and a way to plant roots in American life. Finally Bulosan realizes that his search for roots in the new world end in loneliness because loneliness and rootlessness are part of a shared American identity: "It was a discovery of America and myself. . . . I began to recognize the forces that had driven many Americans to other countries and had made those who stayed at home homeless." As the years separate him from his homeland, he concludes that roots cannot be defined in terms of places or persons, but only in terms of ideals:

I knew, then, that I would be as rootless in the Philippines as I was in America, because these roots are not physical things but the quality of faith deeply felt and clearly understood and integrated in one's life. The roots I was looking for were not physical but intellectual and spiritual things. I was looking for a common faith to believe in and of which I could be a growing part.[71]

As is characteristic of many immigrants, for many Filipinos the years of exclusion from participation in American life is strangely accompanied by a feeling of separation from a homeland to which they could no longer return. Nevertheless, Bulosan's memories of home grew more vivid with time, feeding his longing for freedom in America:

I seem to remember my world as a little boy in Binalonan vividly as if I were an artist. I think I could paint the whole town and village where I grew up. . . . I always write about that life beautifully, but when I take another background like the U.S., I become bitter and angry and cruel.[72]

Bulosan's writing about the Philippines is shaped by the controlling vision of hindsight. Both *Laughter of My Father* and the first section of *America Is in the Heart*, which takes place in the islands, are evenly paced and written with almost pictorial clarity and vividness. The sections of *America Is in the Heart* that are set in this country suffer from a rapid, fluctuating pace that almost amounts to imbalance and undisciplined movement. It is also subject to disconcerting solemnity mixed with what Carey McWilliams has called "minor histrionics."

Bulosan himself was far from satisfied with the book. It had been poured out in haste, out of a sense of personal urgency and to satisfy impatient publishers:

*America Is in the Heart* . . . is important in that it reveals, for the first time, our plight in America, and also in the islands. I could have written a great and wonderful book, but I worked too fast and the company was in a hurry to bring it out; so that what we have now is imperfect and fragmentary; but perhaps I will write a sequel someday.

Having been told by his doctors that he had not long to live, Bulosan says that he wrote six hundred pages of *America Is in the Heart* in twenty-eight days because he felt that he was "racing with death." This might explain the unevenness of the narrative. The humorlessness of this "undisciplined outpouring," he says, was deliberate. When *Laughter of My Father* was published two years earlier, critics had hailed Bulosan as the "manifestation of the pure Comic Spirit." Horrified, Bulosan replied that the book had been meant as a satirical indictment against an economic system that sealed off the possibility of development for the peasant and that he did not think his father's life, or the life of the other peasants of the Philippines, was funny in the slightest; on the contrary, the book had been written in tears. Anger at the thought of this misinterpretation of *Laughter of My Father* compelled Bulosan to write *America Is in the Heart* completely without humor:

> I made a little table in the backyard and started writing about my anger and how it grew inside me like a scimitar. But I found out that in writing about it, I was really writing my autobiography. "What a life," I said to myself. . . . "Now they will know that I am not a laughing man."[73]

Although he had originally addressed his writing to an American audience on behalf of Filipinos in America, in the tradition of earlier Asian goodwill ambassador writers, towards the end of his life Bulosan turned his attention towards the Philippines and a Filipino audience. Perhaps he did so in part because he felt that he might be better understood by Filipinos. Even while American critics misinterpreted *Laughter of My Father*, Bulosan's belief that in the book "for the first time the Filipino people are depicted as human beings" was underscored by letters from Filipinos who said he had written "about them and their times": "I felt that I would be ineffectual if I did not return to my own people."[74] When he died in 1956, Bulosan was working as a writer for the UCAPAWA in Seattle. He was working on a novel about Philippine national hero Jose Rizal, a work he considered his "gift and last will . . . to the Filipino people." Late in 1949, Bulosan mentioned wanting to write "a long novel covering thirty-five years of Philippine history" because "I owe it to the Filipino people."[75]

Carlos Bulosan's writing is the "testament of one who longed to become part of America." At the same time, it is more than that: it is the chronicle of loneliness and compassion by a member of an oppressed and exploited minority on behalf of all the oppressed who might hope to contribute to "a better society and a more enlightened mankind."[76] Younghill Kang and Carlos Bulosan share with the Asian goodwill ambassador writers a sustaining desire to win American acceptance. But unlike the Chinese sojourner intellectuals, Younghill Kang sought opportunities to set down roots in American life. Carlos Bulosan identified himself with the poor and disenfranchised of both Asia and America and dreamed fervently of a future world of social and racial equality where all men could be brothers.

# 3

# Sacrifice for Success
*Second-Generation Self-Portrait*

No matter how excluded from American society the first-generation Asian immigrants felt, they knew that they should not have to reject their racial identity in order to be acceptable in America. Such a rejection would have been tantamount to self-negation. Cultural ambassador writers like Park and Sugimoto maintained their intellectual bases in Asia, to which they ultimately returned as cultural "go-betweens," Younghill Kang continually searched for a thread that would connect his Korean ancestry to the America he was aspiring after, and Carlos Bulosan's desire for fulfillment of the "America of the heart" was fired by cherished memories of his life in the Philippines. But second-generation writers, when confronted with racial barriers, could not so easily identify with Asia, since they had been born, raised, and educated in the United States. Their autobiographical writings therefore reflect the conflicts caused in their personal lives by race discrimination and popular misconceptions about the relationships between race and culture.

For the American-born Asian, the "choice" between Asia and America was false because it was in reality a choice between yellow and white. When "Asia" was chosen, it was because "American," or white, doors seemed closed. Even the superficially practical solution to this externally imposed cultural conflict, suggested frequently by social psychologists—the "happy marriage of East and West" within the individual Asian American psyche—was a false one because it assumes permanent and immutable inferiority to whites on the basis of race. Since an American-born Asian's racial characteristics could not be sloughed off, as Vita Sommers puts it,[1] there could never be a complete solution to the "identity dilemma" of the Chinese or Japanese American. Therefore, the optimal avenue for the second-generation Asian in America was to study Asia, Asians, and East-West relations, often from "American" sources, sometimes subject to distortions and omissions, with an eye towards making himself into a living bridge between the two cultures.

Until recently, published Asian American writers presented the Asian American experience lightly and euphemistically, even humorously, without significant expression of concern about the manifestations of social injustice.[2] Bitterness against Asian cultures and values, and Asian American values and life styles, were far better tolerated by publishers and a predominantly white readership, which has been traditionally more receptive to expressions of self-contempt and self-negation on the part of members of racial minorities than to criticisms of problems in American society. Limited as they were by such a climate, and often by their own ignorance as well, it should not be surprising that those early Asian American autobiographers who did publish accepted the "cultural bridge" role while at the same time expressing their ardent desire for acceptance in American society by any means necessary, and under almost any conditions.

## Life among the "Loyal Minority": Second-Generation Chinese American Autobiography

Pardee Lowe's *Father and Glorious Descendant* (1943) is the first published book-length literary piece by an American-born Chinese in English. Jade Snow Wong's *Fifth Chinese Daughter* (1945 and 1950) is the best known and most financially successful book by a Chinese American. Both books emerged during a period when the American public was more sympathetic to China and more aware of Chinese Americans than it had ever been. The popular image of the sinister Chinese opium eater had changed by the 1930s, as Palmer observes, so that it became now "important to see behind the mask and realize, after all, how genuinely likeable, how overwhelmingly human the Oriental is."[3]

In particular, Americans were becoming aware of the distinctions between Chinese and Japanese. Stereotypes for each group had often been interchangeable. Even after the Chinese were excluded from immigrating, vestiges of the anti-Chinese movement were on hand to greet the newly arriving Japanese and Koreans and, later, the Filipinos. But the international political situation during World War II affected American public opinion with regard to Asians. While the view of the Japanese as enemies hardened, the view of other Asians, our allies, underwent a re-evaluation, and their image improved considerably. According to a 1943 public opinion poll, only 3 percent thought Chinese were cruel, while 56 percent thought of the Japanese as such; only 4 percent thought of Chinese as treacherous, while 73 percent thought Japanese were.[4] The editors of *Aiieeeee! An Anthology of Asian-American Writers* (1974) suggest that some of the early writings by Chinese Americans served as anti-Japanese propaganda: Chinese, they contend, were "cast in the role of good guy in order to make [Japanese Americans] look bad."[5] Thus, the social and intellectual climate between 1940 and 1950 was favorable to Chinese American writers like Lowe and Wong, though only at the expense of the tragic situation faced by Japanese Americans during this period.

In 1943, *Father and Glorious Descendant* was touted as the worthy work of one of America's "loyal minorities." The publishers were quick to celebrate this "loyalty" by indicating on the book jacket that its author had enlisted in the United States Army, equating Lowe's "patriotism" rather obliquely with literary merit. The value of the book for reviewers seems to have been Lowe's love for America coupled with respect for his "Oriental roots," resulting in an "excellent blending of the two cultures [that] will contribute greatly toward better understanding of one of our *loyal* minorities."[6]

In 1950, *Fifth Chinese Daughter*, helped popularize the notion that American racial minorities have only themselves to blame for lack of success in American life. Wong herself writes that members of racial minorities who try to blame social conditions for their difficulties are merely lazy. Like Lowe, Wong sings the praises of American opportunities and life, and attributes to her own individual effort her success here. Such a view, especially as expressed by a member of a racial minority group, was important in the post-war era, when charges of racial discrimination in the United States were circulating in developing countries, which, having recently been freed from colonial rule, were questioning the validity of American world leadership. The U.S. State Department, having already negotiated for the rights to publish *Fifth Chinese Daughter* into a number of Asian languages, arranged for Jade Snow Wong to be sent on a speaking tour in 1952 to forty-five Asian locales from Tokyo to Karachi, where she was to speak about the benefits of American democracy from the perspective of a Chinese American.[7] The book has been translated into many languages, and the publishers estimate that there had been a quarter of a million readers by 1975. *Fifth Chinese Daughter* is still widely used in junior high school and high school literature classes in California as the best example of Chinese American literature, and Jade Snow Wong was selected in 1976 as the person best representing Asian Americans for a PBS documentary about American racial minorities.

What *Father and Glorious Descendant* and *Fifth Chinese Daughter* have in common, then, is more than their co-existence as autobiographies of American-born Chinese. They function as political statements reaching far beyond the realm of Chinese American experience itself, statements in fact about American society and the American role in international affairs. Both writers express accommodation to rather than challenge of distortions about Chinese Americans and, by placing the blame for whatever difficulties they faced upon themselves, their families, their communities, or their race, promote the image of Chinese Americans as the model minority. Lowe and Wong were viewed as representative of their entire group, even though they were both rather exceptional: Lowe's father was a successful dry goods merchant and Wong's was the owner of a Chinatown sweatshop.

What Lowe's and Wong's autobiographies have further in common is their expression of ardent desire for acceptance by other Americans. In Lowe, this desire takes the form of contempt for things Chinese alternating with repeated apology for Chinese or Chinese American culture and values and praise of everything "American." A significant portion of *Father and Glorious Descendant* is devoted to evidencing Lowe's "American" identity, or the kinship between his values and behavior and those of American whites. Lowe places himself as narrator at the side of the imagined white American reader. Together they view the absurdities and exotic quaintness of Chinese American life, as outsiders looking on in amusement or chagrin. Jade Snow Wong's bid for acceptance is made differently: she assumes the role of the anthropological informant taking the reader on a guided tour of Chinese American society. Chinese food and holidays are boasted as attractive and fascinating, while Wong exhibits her value as cook of Chinese food, maker of Chinese-style pottery, and portrayer of Chinese American family and community life. While Lowe's book is a plea for his acceptance as a fellow American with some superficial if immutable Chinese characteristics, Wong's book asks for a place for her as a "special" American, one who can do more tricks, speak more languages, and serve up more exotic and appealing dishes than "ordinary" Americans. Insistence on the acceptance of the reality of one's Asian American identity would have been tantamount to a challenge hurled in the face of white complacency and ignorance. Neither Wong nor Lowe was ready to launch such an assault, which might help explain why their books were the only works of second-generation Chinese American literature published until 1960.

### Father and Glorious Descendant

Critics called *Father and Glorious Descendant* a "solid" and "significant . . . study . . . by one of the few qualified to make it," an "amusing and often illuminating" book that helps "explain" the Chinese of San Francisco by portraying well "a people and a problem."[8] The critics failed to note that in order to demonstrate his loyalty to and love for America and his own acceptability as a fellow American, Lowe felt it necessary to derogate everything Chinese or Chinese American. What reviewers took to be an explanation of the quaint Chinese American customs and life is, in fact, a lightly disguised document of self-contempt and repressed anguish. The book title hints at the stereotype of Chinese filial piety: Lowe dedicates the book to his father, and concludes it with praise of the wisdom of his father, who said, "Among our people, children are begotten and nurtured for one purpose—to provide for and glorify their parents."[9] But the book is really about the "glorious descendant": it glorifies the son, even to the point of rejecting the father. Embedded in the narrative is Lowe's aversion to the "typical Chinese," whom he feels are "certainly peculiar in their dark ways and vain tricks"; his refusal to go to China to study and his eventual rejection of Chinese language study; and ultimately his secret marriage to a white woman, which he mentions almost only in passing, against his father's wishes.

The characteristics Lowe admires in his father are those that set him apart as more "American" than other Chinese in the eyes of whites, who like him because he is tall, speaks English, and does not dress "like the average Oriental." On a ferry, Lowe is proud that he and his father do not fit into the white passengers' conception of Chinese as coolies infesting America with slavery, concubinage, prostitution, opium, and leprosy. He feels glad that his father has no queue, folds his Chinese daily the way white commuters do, and wears Western clothing, so that the white brakemen and cable car conductors recognize him apart from other Chinese travelers "as an individual worthy of special notice." He is proud that his father is accepted by "Americans" for "the very un-Chinese quality of his business and social gatherings" and that his father wants his children to "rub shoulders with Americans." Conflict arises because his father does in fact inhabit a biracial world: his "American ways are not American enough" and "his Chinese habits and ideas . . . are queer, unreasonable, and humiliating." The father's reluctance to buy a "modern home" to which Lowe and his brothers and sisters can comfortably invite their "American" friends occasions a bitter argument that results in two years' passing during which father and son do not engage in more than monosyllabic conversation. The supreme moment of reconciliation comes when Lowe is "lecturing" to tourists whom he guides through the Golden Gate International Exposition in San Francisco, and a Kansas tourist asks Lowe's father if he knows "that other Oriental . . . who could use the English language so fluently and so effectively." Telling the "American" that "that other Oriental" is his own son and being congratulated gives him "all the satisfaction and contentment humanly possible," the younger Lowe surmises. Ultimately, everything, even the final reconciliation between father and glorious descendant, is weighed against white acceptance.[10]

Lowe's book is laced with popular stereotypes of Chinese Americans: there is a tour through the singsong houses, a description of the *hwangap* ceremony (sixtieth birthday celebration), complete with bird's nest soup and an exotic menu list, and recounting of Chinese holidays, with detailed descriptions of particular celebrations into which the narrative finally degenerates. Chinese American family life, according to Lowe, consists primarily of silence, "polite Oriental salutations and formal bowing and scrapings," of meditations upon the classics.[11]

Chinatown is portrayed as a place where Chinese can be left alone by "Americans" as long as they pay their taxes, do not molest others, and mind their own business. It is also a place, however, where "vicious Chinese elements" take advantage of this "live-and-let-live policy." Thus, the popular notion that Chinese take care of their own is combined with the other popular idea that Chinatown is a den of vice and crime, and that Chinese people are incapable of effective self-government. The political and economic ghettoization of the Chinese is overlooked, and Lowe depicts Chinatown residents as cheerfully working twelve hours a day, seven days a week, without objection or thought of doing otherwise. He celebrates his father's penchant for order and compromise, even if it means exploitation: "Better a dog in peace . . . than a man in anarchy!" is his motto.

Lowe sees Chinatown as a "beehive" and its inhabitants as "drones." Chinese sailors congregate there in "cackling groups," and Chinese conversation is "jabbering." Lowe is disgusted by the sight of Chinese dressed in "typical Chinese garments" or wearing queues "coiled up like a rattlesnake in their hat." He calls Chinese singsong girls "creatures" and their procuresses "reptilian." Chinese music is "totally alien," Chinese tongs are sinister, Chinese school is an "unmitigated nuisance," the Chinese language tutor is an "Oriental Ichabod Crane" who proves, like the language he teaches, useless to the modern world. China itself is "backward, with no redeeming features," a place where ringworm and disease prevail. To Lowe, Chinese family life is boring and suffocating, Chinese religion "old junk," Chinese people "emotionless automations," and Chinese customs "strange." Lowe views Chinese undocumented workers with the amused disdain of an immigration officer, blaming the Chinese themselves for the problem, even though he suspects his own father and mother of having participated in illegal immigration dealings.[12]

While things Chinese are repulsive and unacceptable to Lowe, things American are irresistibly attractive. China is the symbol of backwardness, but America is the epitome of modernity, "god's own country" where there are free schools and libraries, bathtubs, toilets, and railroad trains. At Chinese school, Lowe had hidden Western novels and magazines behind his Chinese textbooks. In American public school, he felt "free to indulge in my own most un-Chinese inclinations." While he hated as a child the "endless columns of queer-shaped [Chinese] characters which bore not the slightest resemblance to English," his "inner spirit" was "wrestling victoriously with the details of the battle of Bunker

Hill, Custer's Last Stand, or the tussle between the *Monitor* and the *Merrimac*." Lowe finds tong men cannot compare with the grandeur of "American heroes":

> Even though at the age of nine I was already an inveterate reader of the blood and thunder tales glorifying such fearless men as Buffalo Bill and Wild Bill Hitchcock, I found the stories with their plots and counterplots, armed nests, the oddness of the hatchetmen—such as "Big Queue," "Midget Pete," "Handsome Boy," and "Hot Stuff"— extremely sinister; they did not possess the flesh and blood qualities of my American heroes.[13]

Lowe writes that it is difficult to be a filial Chinese son and a good American citizen at the same time. Actually, his choice has been made. There is no conflict other than the problem of being accepted by other "Americans." His final victory is the total Americanization of his father, who had left China for good, cut off his queue, named his children after American statesmen, and crusaded for a home in a white neighborhood, away from the Chinese community. But what was only begun by the father is finished by the son. It is the son's intermarriage that makes his father a real American: "By virtue of our elopement, father's modernity [and therefore his Americanness] culminated in the acquisition of an American [white] daughter-in-law. Father was truly an American."[14] Indeed, Lowe cannot be satisfied that his father is really Americanized until his is buried in Western clothing in an American cemetery.

Paradoxically, Lowe's youthful intolerance for his Chinese roots and his differences with his father are tempered because the white world he desperately seeks channels him back to them. Upon graduation from Stanford and Harvard, he can find work only in the role American society allows him—as "China expert" or interpreter of Chinese and China to the West. Although he rejected Chinese language education as a child, Lowe's interest is kindled by a Stanford professor who had been a missionary in China. Through another Stanford professor, he is hired to assist in a "sociological investigation" of San Francisco Chinatown. Soon he is writing articles for *Asia* magazine and other journals on Chinese American life. Lowe joins the China war relief movement, telling his father that the movement must have an American direction and a national base. Although the leaders of Chinatown do not like this idea, they are forced to accept it when influential white Americans are enlisted in the cause.

The book ends with Lowe working for the International Secretariat of the Institute of Pacific Relations, giving guided lecture tours to "American" tourists at the Golden Gate International Exposition during World War II. Still concerned that non-Chinese readers not identify him overmuch with the Chinese customs and life he is describing, Lowe explains that his youthful intolerance of his stepmother's religious practices was changed by his "iconoclastic American college education," because of which he was able to study comparative religion and understand the universality of religion. At the close of the book, his "return" to Chinese American culture through the graces of American education is still described in terms of being, like the reader, an outside observer, a lecturer or informant on Chinese and Chinese Americans rather than a participant:

> [S]he mumbled her simple, informal prayers, while I stood at one side, not actually participating, and yet worshipping with her in spirit. My calm acceptance of Stepmother's rituals amazed me. . . . Barbaric it might have appeared in form and details to alien eyes. But not to mine that morning. . . . [It] will forever symbolize for me the deeply religious heart whose prayers are grounded in universal humanity.[15]

When viewed from a contemporary vantage point, Pardee Lowe's autobiography is important today not for the portrait it paints of the Chinese American community and culture but for its record of the psychological responses of one American-born Chinese to race discrimination. That Lowe's critics and reviewers were uninterested in or unable to perceive this primary dimension and valued the book instead for what they took to be objective description of the Chinese American people as a whole is something for which Lowe himself cannot be blamed. Lowe was born in America in 1905 and lived, during his youth, in East Belleville, California, far from the Chinese American community. Unlike other young Chinese Americans of his time, he spoke only pidgin Chinese. Moreover, since there were so few American-born Chinese living in this country during his time, Lowe's course was uncharted and his case unique. In light of this uniqueness, it is not surprising that he sought escape from Chinese American society and immersion in white American life. His book can only reflect the limitations he faced and thus his urgent desire to disappear as a Chinese American.

Although sincere, *Father and Glorious Descendant* is a humiliating book. A pioneer in Chinese American letters of sorts, Lowe felt an ambivalence over Chinese and American culture not unlike that felt by many marginal persons. Today it is easy to see his attempts to become assimilated into the dominant culture as accommodation to racism. Modern Asian American readers, more secure in their identities and numbers, might wish that it had not been *Father and Glorious Descendant* that first broke Chinese American "silence."

*Fifth Chinese Daughter*

Jade Snow Wong was only twenty-four years old when she wrote her autobiography. Many of the chapters in *Fifth Chinese Daughter* were revisions of essays she had written while she was a college student. It should not be surprising, then, that the two most striking features of the book are its documentation of her often enraged struggle to attain individual definition apart from her family and her acceptance of attitudes popularly ascribed to the Chinese American minority during her era.

Although efforts at individual autonomy and independence from family control are common to young adults, Wong's particular situation as an American-born Chinese meant that she was also pressed to reconcile the apparent differences between her own racial identity and the antipathetic non-Chinese world beyond what she perceived as the narrow confines of her ethnic culture. Wong's solution is to utilize her familiarity as an American-born Chinese with the non-Chinese world to gain status and strength in the eyes of her Chinese family and community while at the same time using her Chinese background in such a way as to win as much acceptance as possible from non-Chinese Americans.

The objective social and economic inferiority of Chinese in America during Wong's time effectively limited the degree to which she could actually integrate those two identities: the inequality of the two backgrounds was at the root of the inherent power and leverage she could gain over the Chinese American community through contact with white society in the first place. Moreover, her social acceptance had always to be measured according to standards ultimately set by the objectively stronger society, meaning that judgments of her Chinese background were made from a white frame of reference. Therefore, Wong's assertion of her Chinese identity was restricted to identification with whatever was acceptable about it to white society, and the Chinese identity that Wong defined involved whatever was most exotic, interesting, and nonthreatening to the white society that was her reference point. This explains why Wong's self-definition has so much to do with Chinese food, for example, and why whatever rage she did feel against what she calls "injustice" or "prejudice" is directed against her own Chinese family and community.

The demands of editors and the reading public during the World War II era were based on a new receptivity to the Chinese American minority, but they were also conditioned by expectations rooted in long-established images of the Chinese as a group. New interest in the "real family lives" of Chinese American people still had about it an element of curiosity about exotic customs, people, and food. Like Lowe, Wong uses her Chinese American life to entertain and enlighten non-Chinese readers. Unlike Lowe, who attempts to identify himself with the non-Chinese reader, Wong assumes the role of an anthropologist's key informant: rice-washing, shopping for Chinese groceries, cooking Chinese food, the Chinese garment factory, and her family's childrearing practices are elaborated in meticulous detail.

Unlike Pardee Lowe, Jade Snow Wong was born and raised in the Chinese American ghetto in San Francisco Chinatown. Chinese was her first language. She was not encouraged by her family to "rub shoulders with Americans." Instead, she was taught by her father to read and write classical Chinese and by her mother to cook Chinese food. Nevertheless, the "culture conflicts" experienced by Lowe were familiar to her. The first of these occur when she attends public school and experiences both the unaccustomed demonstrativeness of the non-Chinese teachers and the racial taunts of a non-Chinese classmate. Since her public school was located in Chinatown, she only obtains a close look at "Americans" when she begins working as a teenaged servant in the homes of white Americans. Comparisons between her own family and these families make her "uncomfortable," she says.

Sympathetic to but not uncritical of Chinese life, Wong establishes early in the book that her own family life was frugal, restrained, and disciplined. She feels the lack of affection and praise. Her world contrasts negatively with the world outside Chinatown, where affection, creativity, and personal feelings are welcomed and encouraged rather than stifled. Wong's attitude towards white society is an expression of her desperate desire to escape from the strictures of her family and community to a world where curiosity can be satisfied, questions answered, and youth and women treated as equals of elders and men.

Rather than evaluating whether or not the negative aspects of her family and community are particular to her own family or conditioned by the social and economic restrictions that shaped the Chinese American community, Wong attributes them to Chinese culture and tradition. Her father's lack of affection and sobriety are equated with Chinese tradition. His distrust of originality, individuality, and emotional expression are "Chinese attitudes." Meanwhile, she does not question the contradiction of her own position as servant without individual democratic rights. She is grateful even to have parity with her employer's pets: working as a servant in the dean's home, she notes that everyone, "including a pair of cocker spaniels . . . Pupuli and Papaia, and a black cat named Bessie, and Jade Snow, were recipients of the Dean's kindness and consideration." At Mills, she says, people are accepted as equals no matter how much or how little money they have; in the next paragraph, she describes the residence hall as "a large, colonial structure" with a "kitchen staff [that] was entirely Chinese, some of them descendants of the first Chinese kitchen help who worked for the founders of the college." Apparently, she sees no contradictions here either. Life at Mills College becomes a striking alternative to the restrictions she resents at home, a place where she could experience "democratic living in the truest sense."[16]

Wong rationalizes her position as servant by seeking refuge in her cultural identity as a Chinese. She works stoically, aware that she is to her employers "merely another kitchen fixture." Employed as a kitchen servant for a wealthy white woman, she is humiliated by the uniform she is forced to wear and resentful that she must "slave like a shadow" in the hot kitchen while the guests and their hosts relax in a cool garden. When the meringue cake falls and she is ordered to make another, Wong attributes her difficulties to cultural differences and channels her anguish into a desire to show off her ability to cook Chinese food:

> That afternoon was a torturous nightmare and a fever of activity—to manage another meringue cake, to get rolls mixed, salad greens cleaned and crisped, vegetables cut, meat broiled, the table set, and all the other details of a "company" dinner attended to. By the time she was at last washing the dishes and tidying the dining room she felt strangely vague. She hadn't taken time to eat her dinner: she was too tired anyway. How she wished that she had been asked to cook a Chinese dinner instead of this interminable American meal.[17]

Ironically, Wong's new-found freedoms from the limitations of her Chinese family are based on certain aspects of her Chinese identity, particularly those involving Chinese food. Her contacts with white society show her that this is her "point of distinction," as she calls it, in the eyes of non-Chinese. Wong had early learned that "her grades were consistently higher when she wrote about Chinatown and the people she had known all her life." Her most victorious achievements—being class valedictorian and being chosen to christen a ship as a reward for an essay written about absenteeism—are crowned by her family's treating her teachers and the chauffeur to an authentic Chinatown dinner. While at Mills College, Wong begins cooking Chinese food for her college classmates when she discovers that "the girls were perpetually curious about her Chinese background and Chinese ideologies." A moment of triumph occurs when she cooks a Chinese meal for the dean's musician guests at the dean's request and is delighted to find that through Chinese food she can win attention and recognition; exultant, she recalls:

> For the first time Jade Snow felt an important participant in the role of hostess. Because of everyone's interest in the kitchen preparations, she soon lost her shyness in the presence of celebrities and acted naturally. There was no talk about music, only about Chinese food.[18]

The autobiography even contains recipes for tomato beef and egg foo yung, complete with exact measurements and instructions, for the edification of the interested reader.

She feels more like a participant and less like a spectator in college life when she wins praise for a paper on *Chin Ping Mei*, which is chosen to be read at a literature conference by her instructor. Her essays on Chinatown and her father had been printed in the Mills College journal, and her college English teachers encouraged her to send some of her articles to magazines. The penultimate chapters in her autobiography are based on these efforts. They detail her "rediscovery" of Chinatown and include tours of a shoe repair shop, the Chinese opera, and a Chinese herb store, and she includes a humorous anecdote about her parents' attempts to arrange her marriage—all part of her effort to humanize the Chinese for the benefit of Western readers.

Unlike Pardee Lowe, Wong does not roundly reject her Chinese identity. Instead, she accepts the role of interpreter of the "life and heart of the Chinese people" in order to "contribute in bringing better understanding of the Chinese people, so that in the Western world they would be recognized for their achievements."[19] Through this role, she feels able to win recognition and acceptance from her Chinese family and at the same time "enlightening" "Westerners." Certainly not a few Asian Americans have been encouraged by parents and educators to respond to abuse by seeking secret comfort in the superiority of their cultural heritage. According to a specialist on American ethnicity, Gerald Haslam, the Chinese in America were sustained through their travails by this notion: "the knowledge that their ancestors had created a great and complex civilization when the inhabitants of the British Isles still painted their fannies blue" enabled them to rationalize and endure rejection without significant anger or injury.[20]

When Jade Snow Wong is taunted by a young white boy calling "yellow Chinaman, Chinky, Chink, no tickee, no washee, no shirtee," she describes herself as having felt "astonished." Having "considered the situation and decided to say nothing," she walks placidly away, eyes straight ahead of her, thinking of the boy as "tiresome and ignorant":

> Everybody knew that the Chinese people had a superior culture. Her ancestors had created a great art heritage and had made inventions important to world civilization—the compass, gunpowder [*sic*], paper, and a host of other essentials. She knew, too, that Richard's grades couldn't compare with her own, and his home training was obviously amiss.

Upon reflection, Wong decides to "forgive" the boy for being "unwise in the ways of human nature," and reckons that whites in general are inferior to Chinese in this regard: "They probably could not help their own insensitivity. Mama said they hadn't even learned how to peel a clove of garlic the way the Chinese did."[21]

As even a glance at the American public school textbooks from 1900 to 1970 reveals, the "superior culture" so comforting to those who experienced race prejudice was clearly considered a thing of the past. Wong's defensive reaction to anti-Chinese attitudes is in fact merely an acceptance of the illusion of superiority, an "inner resource" that represents withdrawal from conflict rather than militant challenge. The popular acceptance by whites of the idea of Asians as foreigners or sojourners both divides them from non-Asians in America permanently and serves to justify discriminatory practices against them on the grounds that they do not really wish to participate in American society. Asians, on the other hand, typically responded to exclusion from American society by identifying more intensely with Asia. According to Younghill Kang, Korean exiles in America became more fiercely patriotic to Korea while in America, and in the short stories of Bienvenido N. Santos misery and alienation among Filipinos in America intensify their love and longing for their homeland. Chinese laundrymen, Korean waiters, and Filipino farmworkers often donated their life savings to independence movement activities sponsored in their homelands. No one knows how many Asian "sojourners" in America would have dreamed of retirement to Asia or contributed so handsomely to independence movement activities had they believed they were welcome in the United States.[22]

Unlike Pardee Lowe, who strenuously attempted to assert this American identity, Jade Snow Wong tries to be acceptably Chinese. Like him, however, she discovers that the ever more attractive features of the world outside the Chinese American community can be attained only through re-definition and assertion of certain "positive" aspects of her Chinese identity. The avenue into American life for both Lowe and Wong is the presentation of these as offerings to the non-Chinese world. The critical point missed by Lowe and Wong, however, was that they were limited from the start by the non-Chinese point of reference they continually had to address. They could not be fully integrated as equals into American society and were thus obliged to use their ethnicity as their "point of distinction" in order to win even conditional membership in that society.

Jade Snow Wong is another, and major, proponent of the notion that Asian Americans are a unique blend of "Asian" and "American" cultures. For Park No-Yong the conciliation was perfectly embodied in the doctrine of the mean, a notion that could be found in both Western (ancient Greek) and Chinese philosophy. For Wong it lies in "personal balance": "Each Chinese American like me has the opportunity to assess his talents, define his individual stature, and choose his personal balance of old and new, Chinese and Western ways, hopefully including the best of both."[23] Paradoxically, a combination of the fundamental aspects of the "best" of both means Western civilization—thought, social relations, creative thinking, mental work, way of life—combined with far less critical and pivotal aspects of Chinese civilization, such as food and holiday celebrations.

Ultimately, through the blending of the "Chinese" and "American" qualities, Wong becomes a mere curiosity to both cultures. She admits that after attending college she feels more like a spectator than a participant in her own community. When she invites her economics class to her father's sewing factory, she feels "suddenly estranged" from "observing the scene with two pair of eyes."[24] When she establishes her pottery business in Chinatown, her wares are purchased and appreciated only by whites; the Chinese buy not one single piece. Both whites and Chinese talk about her while she works as if she were a blind deaf mute, as though she were not even present. In a taped interview twenty-five years after the publication of *Fifth Chinese Daughter*, she admitted that she still felt "unaccepted in Chinatown" because of "lack of understanding" on the part of the Chinese there.[25]

In the end, Wong's response to her particular dilemma as an American-born Chinese was to work harder, to seek comfort in certain aspects of her Chinese identity, and to refuse to admit the existence of discrimination. According to Wong, there is no escape from race prejudice; one must simply decide "how much to accept and utilize."[26] This response marked her as a Chinese American success story.

Wong was encouraged to write *Fifth Chinese Daughter* by English teachers and publishing house editors, who were largely responsible for the final version of the book. The editor who asked her to write the book, Elizabeth Lawrence, cut out two-thirds of the manuscript, and the teacher, Alice Cooper, helped "bind it together again." When asked in an interview whether or not she was satisfied with the final results, Wong replied that she was willing to accept the better judgment of her editors: "Some of the things are missing that I would have wanted in. Then, you know, it's like selling to Gump's or sending to a museum. Everybody has a purpose in mind in what they're carrying out. So, you know, you kind of have to work with them." When asked what had been left out, Wong replied that aspects that were "too personal" had been eliminated by the editors, adding, "I was what, twenty-six then? And you know, it takes maturity to be objective about one's self."[27]

Whether because of the editors or not, the emotional life that Jade Snow Wong might have expressed in her autobiography never fully emerges. We know that she was driven by a "desire for recognition as an individual," a desire she felt was thwarted by her family. We also know that she was almost vengefully anxious to "show everyone" that she could succeed in becoming a model of social propriety. She felt lost in a "sea of neglect and prejudice" at home. But in the end these sporadic glimpses into her emotional life are subordinated to descriptions of Moon Festivals and egg foo yung recipes. The submergence of the self so contradictory to her insistence on individuality is epitomized by her reference to herself in the third person singular throughout the book.

The sparks of inner life that lay submerged in *Fifth Chinese Daughter* despite Wong and her editors are extinguished in her most recent book, *No Chinese Stranger* (1975), which she says she wrote because so many people wanted to know what had happened to her during the thirty years that followed the publication of her autobiography. *No Chinese Stranger* is little more than a lifeless summary of Wong's childhood joined to travel notes. The book represents a continuation of Wong in her role as transmitter of Chinese "culture" to non-Chinese, complete with directions for writing Chinese characters, making Chinese kites and kite paste, Chinese squab, tomato beef, and roast chicken. Moreover, it is written in a pedestrian, uninspired prose style: "The Chinese were cheerful, grateful, softspoken, dignified, purposeful, courteous, confident, efficient. . . . They are the ones who remained to dike, canal, bridge, till, move, build, plant, think, innovate, learn and work, sacrificing and serving their country as its goals were set, changed, and expanded."[28]

*Fifth Chinese Daughter* is valuable as a document of Asian American social history. The preoccupation of Lowe and Wong with their Asian American identities is worked out in different ways. But it was imposed upon both of them by a society which would not accept them for what they were—Americans of Asian descent. As second-generation Asian Americans, they were psychologically vulnerable to the unspoken question, "Why don't you go back to where you came from?" Since they only belonged conditionally in American society, their bid for acceptance required heavy sacrifices. They were both unique as educated young Chinese Americans. Within the context of the ignorance and lack of tolerance engulfing them, their desire for personal success through acquiescence is understandable, although, in light of today's changing attitudes, rather pathetic.[29]

## Success and Sacrifice:
## Second-Generation Japanese American Autobiography

I have no face—
This is a face
(Nisei! Nisei!)
My face of astigmatic eyes,
Other eyes.

. . . Where is the heart to scour this enemy mask
Nailed on my flesh and artifact of my veins?

Where is the judge of the infernal poll
Where they vote round eyes honest and mine knave?

This is a dream,
These eyes, this face
(Nisei! Nisei!)
Clutched on my twitching plasm like a monstrous growth,
A twining cyst of hair, of pulp, of teeth . . .
Tell me this is no face,
This face of mine—

It is the face of Angloid eyes who hate.[30]


The conditions faced by the Japanese in America were qualitatively different from those faced by Chinese Americans, and these differences help account for important differences in their writing. Japanese Americans have written more prolifically in English than any other Asian American group, for a variety of complex reasons; among them is the fact that Japanese were more inclined than the Chinese to settle in America because they had few clan or family obligations in Asia, and they could not so easily return to their rapidly industrializing homeland as other Asians could return to their impoverished ones.[31] Moreover, largely because of the relative political strength of Japan in world affairs, the U.S. government signed an agreement with Japan in 1909 that permitted Japanese men to invite wives to join them in America. As a direct result of the 1907 Gentleman's Agreement,[32] Japanese immigrants were able to start families in America long before the Chinese, who had started immigrating to this country a generation earlier. Consequently, English-speaking, American-born *nisei* appeared in relatively large numbers earlier than second-generation Chinese Americans.

Since the 1920s and 1930s, a substantial amount of Japanese American *nisei* writing has been produced. Most of this was published in Japanese American community newspapers and journals where writing in English did not have to concentrate on battling the ignorance and misconceptions of non-Asians. On the other hand, whenever *nisei* writers addressed themselves primarily to whites, they faced the same problems as writers discussed earlier. Like *Father and Glorious Descendant* and *Fifth Chinese Daughter*, certain Japanese American autobiographies have been paraded as melting pot "success stories." During World War II, however, Chinese American loyalty and success were carefully distinguished from Japanese American perfidy and disloyalty, and Japanese American writing was suppressed or confined to the "underground"— internment camp—journals; Toshio Mori's *Yokahama California*, which was scheduled for publication in 1941, did not appear until almost a decade later. By the mid-1950s, however, long after the West Coast Japanese had been released from the concentration camps and were more scattered across the country than they had been before the war, some Japanese American writing had begun to appear outside the Japanese American "newsprint ghetto." One of the most successful of the books was Monica Sone's *Nisei Daughter* (1953).

### Nisei Daughter

At first glance, Sone's book seems modeled after Jade Snow Wong's "success story" autobiography, as an exemplification of the "plucky perseverance" of Asian American minorities. *Nisei Daughter* (1953) seems to be evidence of how Japanese Americans can survive internment and discrimination with almost incredible resilience, fortitude, and cheerfulness. Upon closer examination within the context of Japanese American social history, however, the autobiography appears as an account of the gradual suffocation by racial discrimination of everything that is creative, spirited, or pugnacious in one *nisei* woman.

No published Japanese American autobiographer responded to American racism as did Jade Snow Wong. They hardly had the choice: because of Japan's position in international affairs, the Japanese in America simply could not be "acceptably Japanese" as Wong had been "acceptably Chinese." The assertion of one's Japanese identity in America was viewed as a hostile gesture before and directly after World War II.[33] *Nisei* autobiographers expended much energy trying to clarify the differences between Japanese and Japanese American or between "Japanese" and "American." American racism required that they prove that they were not "Japanese" in order to prove that they were "American." That task occasioned much anguish and sorrow, for in the extreme it entailed the rejection of one's heritage, one's own Japanese parents, and even one's physical characteristics. In his *Issei and Nisei*, Kitagawa describes how many *nisei* responded to their impossible dilemma:

> The younger generation often look askance at the peculiar habits and customs of the parents, even ridiculing the traditional Japanese manner and etiquette . . . or mocking the . . . the Japanese way of expression. . . . The young Japanese are prone to be ashamed of their race and their homes, to which they will not take their American [*sic*] friends. Their one desire is to lose their racial, national, or linguistic identities, and to become an integral part of the American people as soon as possible.[34]

*Nisei Daughter* is a testimony of the sacrifices exacted from Japanese Americans by American racism. The first half of the book is devoted to clarification of the distinctions between what is Japanese and what is Japanese American; Kazuko (the narrator) makes clear her rejection of the former and her option for the latter. The last half records the attacks on Japanese American identity and Kazuko's gradual realization that the choice was not a viable one. During the course of the book, we see Kazuko being forced to sacrifice not only the "Japanese" identity she detests but also the Japanese American one that she loved in order to bid for acceptance as what she is—an American. She is allowed neither, nor is she permitted acceptance into white society. The testimony is made lightly, with good-natured humor and plenty of self-mockery, and it ends hopefully with what sounds like a high school civics class speech. But the reader is left with a terrible uneasiness.

Japanese culture and identity is epitomized in *Nisei Daughter* by Japanese school, where *nisei* children learned Japanese etiquette and Japanese language. *Issei* parents, aware of the prejudice and discrimination awaiting their children in American society, wanted to prepare them for eventual return to Japan or at least for "Japanese jobs" requiring bilingual ability.[35] But *nisei* children found Japanese school bothersome and sometimes distasteful. Student life was regimented and restrictive: pupils worked "with clenched teeth and perspiring hands" under their teacher's "vigilant eyes," like "convicts at hard labor." The teacher, who wore a "facial expression cemented into perfect samurai control," looked "as if he had just bitten into a green persimmon." The model pupil is a *kibei*—an American-born Japanese schooled in Japan—who is detested by the other *nisei* children. To Kazuko, the Japanese "traditions" promoted at *nihon gakko* had little applicability to her life in the Seattle slums:

> As far as I was concerned, Mr. Ohashi's superior standard boiled down to one thing. The model child is one with deep *rigor mortis*— no noise, no trouble, no backtalk. . . . They made little headway, for I was too much the child of Skidrow. As far as I was concerned, Nihon Gakko was a total loss. I could not use my Japanese on the people at the hotel [that my parents operated]. Bowing was practical only at Nihon Gakko. If I were to bow to the hotel patrons, they would have laughed in my face. Therefore promptly at five-thirty every day, I shed Nihon Gakko and returned with relief to an environment which was the only real one to me.[36]

Whatever the value of Japanese etiquette and formality in Japan, Kazuko concludes that it is totally inappropriate in America. Mrs. Kato is described as creating a bottleneck at a crowded streetcar stop in downtown Seattle, bowing politely trying to let Mrs. Itoi proceed in front of her, while the irate fellow travelers turn and stare at them. To Kazuko, there seems to be something false and unnatural about Japanese etiquette anyway, something almost opposed to important social virtues. Her own mother, whom she thinks of as warm and affectionate, had come to America "at the wrong age" as "an energetic and curious seventeen-year-old on whom the cement of Japanese culture had not yet been set."[37] Despite the fact that she tried hard to cultivate the proper Japanese mannerisms—the "gentle and soft-spoken manner" expected of a Japanese woman and the "poker face" demanded by particular occasions—she "rattled the sensibilities" of the more proper Japanese women of the neighborhood.

Mrs. Matsui, an older woman who has mastered the superficial aspects of Japanese etiquette, is depicted as hawklike, repressive, and haughty. Her daughter, who is delicate and polite on the surface, is as vicious and hypocritical as her mother. In Kazuko's view, persons molded, stifled, and "cemented" by Japanese etiquette become warped so that a veneer of polite socialization coats the surface of very unsociable, ill-tempered, and even vindictive instincts:

> Yaeko [Mrs. Matsui's daughter] would sit quietly beside her mother, knees together, dress pulled down modestly over the ankles, hands folded demurely in her lap, and eyes fixed dully on the floor. Whenever Mother gave her a magazine to look at, Yaeko would bow graciously. "*Arigato gozai masu.*" And she would stare politely at one picture for a long, long time, turn a page so slowly and quietly that I felt like tearing into her and rattling the paper for her. But whenever we were given permission to play outside, Yaeko became a different person. She would look at me scornfully, "Let's not play jacks again! It's baby stuff. Don't you have some good magazines to read . . . like *True Love?*" I did not have *True Love* magazines. So we played an ill-tempered game of jacks at which time she would cheat, pinch and jab my elbows whenever she felt I was taking too long.[38]

Kazuko dislikes visiting other Japanese homes. It is difficult to remember all the things well-bred Japanese children are not supposed to do: "We must not laugh out loud and show our teeth, or chatter in front of guests, or interrupt adult conversation, or cross our knees while seated, or ask for a piece of candy, or squirm in our seats." The children are expected to "eat quietly like meek little ghosts and politely refuse all second helpings," refusing also proffered "sodawata" and sipping instead "scalding tea out of tiny burning teacups without handles and [nibbling] at brittle rice wafers." When a visit is over, Kazuko feels enormous relief:

> I staggered out at last into the frosty night, feeling tight as a drum and emotionally shaken from being too polite for too long. I hoped

on our next call our hostess would worry less about being hospitable and more about her guests' comfort, but that was an impudent thought for a Japanese girl.[39]

Kazuko's rebellion becomes more energetic when she visits Japan, where everyone is puzzled by her Japanese-American appearance and behavior. She does not know how to bow; people stare at her foreign clothing; and it is uncomfortable to sit "like a pretzel" on the floor. Her self-consciousness becomes anger eventually, and when the Japanese boys attack her brother, she shocks them by biting and scratching them as no proper little Japanese girl would ever dream of doing. One night, she slaps her arrogant cousin and is surprised that Yoshiye collapses weeping instead of fighting back: "It was like striking a sack of flour. There had been no resistance or angry response, only a quiet crumbling away."[40]

Especially since she portrays the Japanese traits she abhors humorously and at the expense of Japanese culture, it might seem that Sone shares the early missionaries' depiction of Japanese American rejection of their cultural heritage in order to become bona fide Americans. But Sone's contempt for the hypocrisy and superficiality of Japanese etiquette implies no praise of American culture. It is instead part of an effort to reject self-contempt. In *Nisei Daughter*, white bigotry is as repulsive as Japanese *rigor mortis*. Both represent what is inimical to Japanese American life, which is painted as full of excitement, urgency, and color in the Seattle waterfront neighborhood's "compact little world" of Japanese families and "fading, balding, watery-eyed little men," soapbox orators, and hot dog stands. But while her youthful responses to Japanese inhibition and white prejudice are equally critical, she begins to vacillate between feelings of rage and self-blame as she grows older and begins to mix in the "white world." The same little girl who longed for a "rip-roaring fight which would lift the roof right off the house and make the neighbors hang out of their windows" and who has to fight the urge to kick every white policeman she sees in the shins becomes quieter and less sure of herself as she comes into contact with the world outside her Japanese American ghetto: in the end it is not Japanese school but her experiences in the Seattle school system that transform her from a "jumping, screaming, roustabout Yankee" into "a polished piece of inarticulateness," which she somehow connects to her "Japanese blood":

Although I had opinions, I was so overcome with self-consciousness I would not bring myself to speak.

Some people had explained this as an acute case of adolescence, but I knew it was also because I was Japanese. Almost all the students of Japanese blood sat like rocks during the discussion period. Something compellingly Japanese made us feel it was better to seem stupid in a quiet way rather than to make boners out loud. I began to think of the Japanese as the Silent People, and I envied my fellow students who clamored to be heard. What they said was not always profound or even relevant, but they didn't seem worried about it. Only after a long agonizing struggle was I able to deliver the simplest statement in class without flaming like a red tomato.[41]

When she sees cartoons caricaturing Japanese, she feels her "pride bruised." Years of drawing careful distinctions between Japanese and Japanese American have been spent in vain, since to the bigots they are the same. Kazuko is made aware of the hatred against Japanese when people stare coldly at her on the streets or refuse to wait on her in department stores. In the end, she is overwhelmed by this racial rejection and begins to internalize the rebuff and blame herself. While she could resist the inhibitive and repressive aspects of the Japanese American community, she is not equipped to handle the pervasiveness and virulence of white American repudiation based on race.

Upon hearing Roosevelt's declaration of war, Kazuko, like many other *nisei,* "writhed involuntarily." Though it was perfectly clear to her that she was neither Japanese nor to blame for Pearl Harbor, her shame is aroused by the white American prejudiced classifications of her as being Japanese and therefore one of the enemy: "I could no more have escaped the stab of self-consciousness than I could have changed my Oriental features." When she hears the executive order for evacuation, Kazuko thinks of herself as a "despised, pathetic, two-headed freak, a Japanese and an American, neither of which seemed to do me any good."[42] It becomes evident that the dual identity had been thrust upon her. She had been careful all her life to make clear distinctions, but now suddenly there was no such thing as Japanese American. She was Japanese in the eyes of other Americans.

Kazuko's childhood spirit is now interfaced with shame. Even as she works with her family gathering the Japanese objects in the house for burning when rumors of FBI investigations spread through the Japanese community, she is overcome by despair and a sense of guilt rather than outrage:

I gathered together my well-worn Japanese language schoolbooks which I had been saving over a period of ten years with the thought that they might come in handy when I wanted to teach Japanese to my own children. I threw them into the fire and watched them flame and shrivel into black ashes. . . . It was past midnight when we finally climbed upstairs to bed. Wearily we closed our eyes, filled with an indescribable sense of guilt for having destroyed the things we loved. This night of ravage was to haunt us for years.

Closed in on all sides by "the wall of prejudice," Kazuko and other *nisei* who have rejected the possibility of going to Japan as unrealistic, are hemmed in by the limitation of choices: "Even with all the mental anguish and struggle, an elemental instinct bound us to this soil. Here we were born; here we wanted to live. . . . It was too late, much too late for us to turn back." It is shame that triumphs, and her spirit is broken by the timidity born of shame: "In the privacy of our hearts, we had raged, we had cried out against the injustices, but in the end, we had swallowed our pride and learned to endure."[43]

Kazuko's "endurance" has its roots not only in Japanese *bushido* (as recent sociologists and anthropologists contend) but also in the limitation of options brought about by American racism. Even the quality of the prose style mirrors this deterioration towards the end of the book: what had begun as a sparkling and witty prose degenerates into a halting and stilted style culminating in a pitiful civics class polemic on "democracy." From the moment that the evacuation order is received, her timidity redoubles. She worries about having a "respectable hairdo" on evacuation day; she feels embarrassed when white farmers' families stare at her and the other evacuees as they perspire in their baggy clothes. After having been "arrested," she expects to have her plate whisked away on the train, and when her family gets together with another family to leave the camp and go into a town on a pass, they are careful not to be offensive, "hoping . . . not [to] attract too much attention" and "trying to blend into the wallpaper design." When she finally leaves the camp, she has to "creep" into Chicago, because she had been warned by fellow prisoners to behave "as inconspicuously as possible so as not to offend the sensitive public eye."[44]

In this dilemma, the only answer readily available to the *nisei* in *Nisei Daughter* seems to be the disintegration of the Japanese American community and individual integration among the whites. The compact little world of Kazuko's childhood had been pleasant and warm; it had been a Japanese American world in which the family could have ham and eggs on lunar New Year's and attend picnics where both hot dogs and pickled plums were served. Kazuko's cultural background enabled her to feel sympathy and compassion for both *issei* and *kibei* as well as fellow *nisei*. And it equipped her to appreciate her parents, who are depicted with affection. But when the community in Seattle had been forcibly disrupted and the Japanese had been moved into a camp, where they remained isolated and remote from the rest of the world, what had been vital and thriving in Japanese American life began to die, so that among friends "even our core of conversation died out with the monotony of our lives." Japanese America and the *issei* generation were made to seem part of the distant and useless past; just as Kang had seen Korea as a place where everything was dying, isolated and remote from both reality and modernity, and had escaped to America as the place where there was life, Kazuko is forced to leave Japanese America behind. The only way she can re-establish herself in the world outside the camps is by striking out alone, going to a midwestern city and getting a job as a domestic. She must leave her disintegrated family and community behind in order to survive in America as a "whole person instead of a sadly split personality," working in America's "main stream, still with my Oriental eyes."[45]

When Kazuko goes back to visit her old parents in the camp, she finds it "quiet and ghostly": her father had been ill, and her parents were heartsick about "being your Japanese parents." They, like so many other *issei*, had been forced to step down from their position in their families and communities but had been allowed no new place in the scheme of things. They are condemned to live out the remainder of their lives as "perpetual foreigners," dying vestiges of the past: "As I looked out of the window, I saw them standing patiently, wrapped in heavy dark winter clothes, Father in his old navy pea jacket, Mother in black wool slacks and a black coat. . . . They looked like wistful immigrants." Just like her Japanese American community, Kazuko's beloved parents must be sacrificed. She must leave them behind barbed wire, wondering "when they would be able to leave their no-man's land, pass through the legal barrier, and become naturalized citizens." The closing pages of *Nisei Daughter* contain a hopeful speech about American democracy, but the mood that dominates is a mood of wondering—wondering "if we must beat our heads against the wall of prejudice all our lives" and wondering when the *issei* would ever "pass through the legal barrier" and be released from camps.[46]

The book is much more than it appears. It is not a chronicle of self-contempt; it is not an outraged protest book. But neither is it a cheerfully ingratiating document of Japanese American success through ability to "endure." It is rather the subtly documented story of the sacrifices demanded of the *nisei* by the racial exclusivity of American society, of a soul's journey from rage to shame, from self-assurance to uncertainty. At the end, Sone writes that the "Japanese and American parts of me were now blended into one," but somehow the statement remains unconvincing because the blend seems externally imposed, and everything, including the answers to Kazuko's unspoken questions, is left in limbo.

During the 1960s, Japanese American "success" was widely acclaimed as irrefutable evidence of the existence of equal opportunities for nonwhite people in America.[47] The Japanese Americans were "out-whiting the whites," having high incomes, high median years of schooling, high rates of intermarriage (if rate of intermarriage is a measure of success), and relatively few crimes or cases of mental illness in the group.[48] In the 1970s, Japanese American autobiographical writing that was appropriate to the high demand for timely accounts written by successful minority informants began to appear. Japanese American "success stories" had come to be regarded as examples for Blacks and other minorities to follow, just as thirty years earlier Chinese American "success stories" had been favorably compared with Japanese American problems. In both cases, the comparisons served to de-emphasize the critical role of individual and institutional racism as it affected the American minority experience in general. The Japanese American autobiography in the 1970s has, consequently, much in common with the Chinese American autobiography of the 1940s.

## Japanese American Autobiographies in the 1970s

Several Japanese American autobiographies were published by major American publishing companies during the late 1960s and early 1970s. Among these are Daniel Inouye and Lawrence Elliot's *Journey to Washington* (1967), Daniel Okimoto's *American in Disguise* (1971), Jim Yoshida and Bill Hosokawa's *The Two Worlds of Jim Yoshida* (1972), and Jeanne Wakatsuki Houston and James D. Houston's *Farewell to Manzanar* (1973).[49] These books were the first Japanese American autobiographical narratives addressed primarily to non-Japanese audiences since *Nisei Daughter* appeared in 1953.

Instead of providing evidence of how far the Japanese American minority had progressed during the recent decades towards becoming well-adjusted, successful, and self-confident Americans, as no doubt they were meant to show, contemporary Japanese American autobiographies reveal that the process of self-negation documented in *Nisei Daughter* had been continuing at an accelerated and relentless pace for twenty years. The result, in *American in Disguise* and *Farewell to Manzanar*, is the almost complete disappearance of the self. The more complete the process of self-negation, the more likely that the autobiography will be hailed as a "success story." No doubt this is because the distinction between "success" and "disappearance" or "assimilation" has not been made any clearer than the distinction between cultural pluralism and "melting pot" notions.

Okimoto's *American in Disguise* and the Houstons' *Farewell to Manzanar* were favorably received by critics, but for reasons that suggest that the criteria used to judge their quality are related to the arguments used by sociologists and social psychologists in their attempts to explain the differences between Asian Americans and Afro-Americans. Phoebe Adams noted about Okimoto's *American in Disguise* that its "provacative ideas are expressed with such scholarly restraint that they may go unread in the current racial uproar"; another reviewer praised it for talking of "the Negro problem sympathetically and yet not without the racial pride of one from a subculture which always worked hard and had a devotion to education as a spur to achievement."[50] Similarly, reviewers praised *Farewell to Manzanar* for being "remarkably lacking in either self-pity or solemnity" and for being "told without bitterness."[51] We are reminded of the reviewers' reaction to Sugimoto's *Daughter of the Samurai* fifty years earlier.

But like *Father and Glorious Descendant, Fifth Chinese Daughter*, and *Nisei Daughter, American in Disguise* and *Farewell to Manzanar* are at the same time much more and much less than their reviewers think. These modern Japanese American "success stories" are in fact records of sacrifice, self-negation, and the repression of anger and outrage.

*American in Disguise* reads like a travelogue. It has the apparent candor of a personal account, yet it lacks the honesty of tone found in *Farewell to Manzanar*. The narrator's inability to face himself is revealed as his self-contempt becomes apparent to everyone but himself. Under the veneer of sophistication and finesse of an "Ivy League Nisei," as he calls himself, a turbulent battle is raging.

The central contradiction is that the narrator thinks of America as the land of opportunity and freedom, and yet "society" has instilled in him a "sense of shame, . . . self-pity and self-hatred" by "turning racial ethnicity into a poisonous source of self-contempt." He believes that in America he has the freedom to "define to my satisfaction just how willing I was to acknowledge the Asian background in me," but he has to go to Japan in search of his true racial identity. There, finding himself culturally American, not accepted as a Japanese but as a Japanese American, he is able, he says, to "acknowledge the Japaneseness in me without embarrassment or apology." American racism has created Okimoto's need for the "therapeutic experience" of Japan, and for him, it has necessitated a process of double self-negation.[52]

The key reference point in the book is white America. The narrator's early experiences with white prejudice influence him deeply. Like Lowe, he is even introduced to Japanese culture and history by a white professor at Princeton. His discussions of the comparisons between Japanese and American society are addressed to white people: they are academic, anthropological, explanatory, like Jade Snow Wong's discussions of Chinese American life. Okimoto finds that white girls appeal to him "personally as well as physically," especially since they have the "seductive attraction" that might give him "crowning evidence of having made it." He finds Japanese women dull or mercenary and Japanese society stifling, narrow, and inbred. Feeling that he must choose between Japanese society and American society and between Japanese women and "American" women, he chooses "American." He finally conquers the fear that he likes white girls for the "wrong reasons" by marrying one in Japan, calling intermarriage the "key to final assimilation."[53]

Okimoto insists that "although feelings of profound ambivalence will probably never be permanently settled," he is now comfortable with his new-found Japanese American identity: "[I]t was not until I accepted my ethnic heritage that I could reply without hesitation to the question 'What are you?'—I am Japanese American, not someone in disguise." But the book ends with the writer's reference to his children, for whom, "[p]hysically, at least, half the disguise I have worn will be lost." Even in the end, the narrator, who has supposedly come to terms with his Japanese American identity, still views his Asian face as an unfortunate "disguise."[54]

The real disguise in the book is worn by self-contempt, which is masquerading as self-knowledge and pride. According to Okimoto, the crucial problem facing the Japanese American minority is the mentality stemming from an "excess of success." It does not occur to him that the mindless conformity and lack of creativity he attributes to Japanese Americans might indicate that their "success" has not been excessive. This may explain why the narrator does not perceive his own self-negation. He indirectly declares himself lacking in creativity when he condemns Japanese American literary potential to extinction:

[I]t appears unlikely that literary figures of comparable stature to those of minorities like Jews and blacks will emerge to articulate the *nisei* soul. Japanese Americans will be forced to borrow the voices of James Michener, Jerome Charyn, and other sympathetic novelists to distill their own experience. Even if a *nisei* of Bernard Malamud's or James Baldwin's talents did appear, he would no doubt have little to say that John O'Hara has not already said.[55]

Paradoxically, again, Okimoto suggests that Japanese Americans "borrow the voice" of James Michener, who wrote the "Foreword" to *American in Disguise*. The basis for Michener's authority comes from the fact that he had to introduce his Japanese American wife to Japan ("My wife never became as Japanese as I," he writes) and that both he and Okimoto are engaged in interracial marriages. Michener feels that Okimoto "brood[s] a little too much upon the grievances of his youth"; he acknowledges that Okimoto might have had some "irritations," but they are all the more evidence of how far Japanese Americans have come:

If Okimoto needs to feel that at Pasadena he was grievously mal-treated, and if from this conviction he gets strength to persevere to Princeton and to Harvard and to Tokyo University . . . then he has put his Pasadena experience to good account. And if an accumula-tion of irritations led him to write the book then that is a very good use to which to put irritations.[56]

Though, to Michener, Okimoto is a perfect example of how a minority person can overcome obstacles without "too much bitterness" by trying harder, if he were to write the book himself it would be titled, according to his wife's "joke," *America through Slanted Eyes*. In short, neither Michener nor Okimoto takes the book seriously.

Like *American in Disguise, Farewell to Manzanar* illustrates one *nisei*'s response to racism—a desire to be assimilated or to disappear. But Jeanne Wakatsuki Houston is conscious of the impulse. *Farewell to Manzanar* is an account of her confrontation with her past, with childhood internment at Manzanar relocation center and with her adolescence in southern California. In retrospect, she discerns that her past was governed by what she calls a "dual impulse"—the desire to disappear completely and the urge to fight invisibility. Upon closer inspection, however, it becomes clear that the impulse is not a dual one after all: the method of fighting disappearance turns out to be an attempt to assimilate, which is in effect the same as disappearing.

Like Okimoto's book, *Farewell to Manzanar* is addressed primarily to the white reader. The book was written with the help of a University of California–Santa Cruz grant, and in the hopes of educating "middle class America" about Asian Americans: "Each book, each film is chipping away at the unfamiliarity and ignorance. We have to educate them, we have to get our foot in the door. We aren't the ones needing education about Asian Americans; middle class America needs to learn." The Houstons were careful not to let the book become rhetorical, "guilt-producing, or self-pitying," because "we can't afford to get the whites uptight. . . . [W]e didn't want to turn them off." The book's assimilationist image and the authors' sensitivity to their potential white audience's expectations might be responsible for the book's subdued tones and hence some of its popularity.[57]

The gentle tone, the lack of bitterness so appreciated by the book's critics, may also be traced in part to Jeanne Houston's feelings of unworthiness. *Farewell to Manzanar* was actually written out by James D. Houston, who taped hours' worth of his wife's recollections and thoughts. Much of what she said was "tearful gibberish," so the husband would have to select and write, pursuing particular aspects that he thought might be valuable, and later the wife would read what he had written to correct and amplify. Often, he would insist on pursuing items she did not deem important or worthy: when her husband kept asking her to elaborate, "I kept saying, 'Who'd be interested in that?' . . . feeling unworthy and feeling that my experience was unworthy."[58]

What is crucial about *Farewell to Manzanar* as a work of Asian American literature is not the story of the internment so much as the story of a *nisei* woman's response to racism.[59] As Lee Ruttle notes in the *Pacific*

*Citizen*, Japanese internment has finally become an acceptable item of discussion after twenty-five years of relative neglect: "Now that publishers' doors have been opened to this subject (and they do follow trends), one can almost hear the typewriters clacking from coast-to-coast, aspiring writers itching to tell *their* version of the story." The Houstons chose to write a family story about evacuation after being advised by a New York agent that historical and political writing about the internment would not sell because it would be too "issue-oriented." Aware of the renewal of anti-Japanese sentiments emblemized by the citizens' boycott of Japanese products in 1972–1973, they decided that a personal, family experience story would be more palatable because it would be "believable, to reach that universal core of humanness." Part of their reason for choosing to write about one family's experience was also that "no one can argue" with a personal account: "I didn't go into what caused the evacuation; people can't argue with me about whether it was right or not. It's just about the effects of evacuation on one family as I know them. No one can argue with that."[60]

Jeanne Houston was only seven years old at the time she was interned. Recalling her experiences at Manzanar twenty-five years later, she must piece together the account from yearbook photographs and other people's recollections. The view of the internment experience is far removed from the source, re-created and told indirectly not by those who lived through it as adults but by someone who was only a child at the time and written by someone who did not share the experience at all. Perhaps, this too explains why the "bitterness" is gone.

*Farewell to Manzanar* gives the impression that the writers were trying to re-shape the family's experience to suit what they found in sociology studies or history books. For example, the "steady crumbling away of family life" and the "emasculation" and despondency of the *issei* men are frequently discussed in books about internment. Jeanne Houston contends that the book is her father's story "more than her own"; that is, it is the story of her father's "sense of loss and collapse" into historical context.[61] Even though the "fall" of the *issei* man because of internment is a vital and tragic aspect of the Japanese American experience, Houston seems to be hiding behind the dashing, colorful, and historically significant figure of her father. She seems unsure of the validity and quality of her own experiences as a Japanese American, so she tries to legitimize them through a generalized experience that is becoming acceptable to discuss and write about.

The device used to join the father's life, internment, and Japanese American history is the image of "intersection" at Manzanar, where the father's life "ends" and the daughter's "begins." But actually, the lives of father and daughter intersect when the girl rejects her father and concentrates on acceptance by whites, and the father ultimately becomes just a "Japanese father to frighten my [white] boyfriends." Like her Japanese face, he is only something to "thwart my social goals," which were to have irrefutable evidence of acceptability as an American.[62] Of course, internment at Manzanar is the brutal embodiment of the racism that prompts the narrator's desperate desire to be acceptable to the very people who incarcerated her. The book records the girl's varied efforts to deal with this racial rejection, which includes the loss of respect for her father, rather than the erosion of her father's masculinity *per se.*

One of her childhood responses is "fear of Oriental faces." The sight in camp of a woman who powdered her face with rice flour in the traditional Japanese manner was "ghastly" to her, and she thought the woman "diseased." The sight of two white-faced, white-clad Japanese nurses made up in the Japanese manner reminds her of cobras: "they are a pair of reptilian kabuki creatures at loose," but she is attracted to their "negatives"—two white nuns dressed in black habits who had come to live at the camp. She becomes involved with these nuns to the point of wanting to be baptized Catholic, which her father will not permit. In a response to oppression not uncommon among subject women, she is fascinated by stories of female saints' sacrifices: "[W]hat kept me coming back, once I started, were the tales of the unfortunate women like Saint Agatha, whose breasts were cut off when she refused to renounce her faith. . . . I was fascinated with the miseries of women who had suffered and borne such afflictions."[63] She imagines herself among them while carrying a heavy load one blistering day, and faints from sunstroke.

The narrator is plagued, both in camp and after release, by the idea that she deserves hatred. In camp, she dreads the "humiliation" she will have to face on the "outside"—"that continuous, unnamed ache I had been living with. . . . Call it the foretaste of being hated. I knew ahead of time that if someone looked at me with hate, I would have to allow it, to swallow it, because something in me, something about me deserved it." As she grows older, her response to the camp experience is a consistent sense of self-blame and unworthiness. When she finally leaves the camps and enters a sixth-grade class, a classmate innocently exclaims over her ability to speak English. The realization that she would be "seen as someone foreign, or as someone other than American, or perhaps not seen at all, . . . brought . . . the first buds of true shame" and she decided that, since she was going to be invisible anyway, she would prefer to "completely disappear." When her white girlfriend defends her against hostile stares, she is "always amazed. . . . I would much rather have ignored those looks than challenged them." When faced with rejection, she accepts and internalizes the blame: "If refused by someone's parents, I would never say, 'Go to hell!' or 'I'll find other friends,' or 'Who wants to come to your house anyway?' I would see it as my fault, the result of my failings, I was imposing a burden on *them.*"[64]

While she is plagued by a sense of unworthiness and fascinated by the idea of silent sacrifice, self-blame, and even martyrdom, she also longs for acceptance, a kind of "disappearance" as Japanese American. Like the *nisei* veterans in Okada's *No-No Boy* (1957), who wear their wounds as badges of their identity as Americans, not Japanese Americans, the narrator attempts to assimilate through roles that help obscure her Japanese American identity. As a young girl, she wants to be confirmed as Roman Catholic because she would be able to wear a white lace dress like a princess' at the confirmation. Throughout her life, she is fascinated by princesses and queens. Her "post-Manzanar ambitions" are prompted by the same impulses that bring to her a recurrent dream of looking through a window at a blond, blue-eyed high school queen she can never be:

> Watching, I am simply emptied, and in the dream I want to cry out, because she is something I can never be, some possibility in my life that can never be fulfilled.
> It is a schoolgirl's dream, one I tell my waking self I've long since outgrown. Yet it persists. Once or twice a year she will be there, the boyfriend-surrounded queen who passed me by.[65]

The queen arouses neither envy nor malice in her, only despair and a sense of hopelessness.

As a young girl, she learns to twirl a baton and becomes a majorette. Twirling a baton to the tune of a John Philip Sousa march is "thoroughly, unmistakably American." Moreover, when she twirls a baton for the Boy Scouts band, the Navy men and their sons enjoy watching her in her satin outfit with the short skirt. Houston notes in retrospect that the use of Asian "femininity" as a "resource" is both a degrading and an exhilarating bid for acceptance.[66]

Wearing a braided costume with boots draws attention away from her Japanese American identity. Fastening on clothes and roles—as majorette, as carnival queen, as nun, as confirmation "princess"—is part of the desire to be invisible and acceptable at the same time, just as U.S. Army uniforms have made men from minority groups feel more "American" and less Asian, Black, or Chicano. Through clothes and roles, invisibility can become acceptability, since attention is drawn not to the person but to the image in the braided uniform or white gown. In order to become a high school carnival queen, the narrator pays special attention to the clothing she will wear on the day she is to "walk out for inspection by the assembled student body." Knowing that she can't "beat the other contestants at their own game" as a bobbysoxer or look "too Japanesy," she decides to "go exotic" to suite the "positive" stereotype of the Oriental woman. She wears a sarong and a hibiscus flower and wins the contest. When she appears at the coronation in a high-necked, ruffled white dress and walks the "make-believe carpet to its plywood finale," the dream that came true turns sour. The role, her identity, people's expectations of her, all become confounded, and the dress she is wearing takes on symbolic significance:

> Suddenly it was too hot out there. I imagined that they were all murmuring about my dress. They saw the girls behind me staring at it. . . . [T]he dress was stifling me. I had never before worn such an outfit. It was not at all what I should have worn. I wanted my sarong. But then I thought, NO. That would have been worse. Papa had been right about the sarong. Maybe he was right about everything. What was I doing out there anyway, trying to be a carnival queen? . . . It wasn't the girl in the old-fashioned dress they had voted for. But if not her, who *had* they voted for? Somebody I wanted to be. And wasn't. Who was I then?[67]

Released, during the passing decades, from the need to prove her loyalty and "Americanness," a need that tyrannized or influenced other *nisei* writers like Okada and even Sone, Houston is able to probe freely her adolescent responses to being a Japanese American woman. The book is important for this reason. According to her, the writing of the book had an intensely therapeutic effect: "Writing it has been a way of coming to terms with the impact these years [before and following the war] had on my entire life." Forcing herself to confront her sense of unworthiness, she writes, led to her eventual "farewell" to the state of mind that caused her "Manzanar mentality:"

> Much more than a remembered place it [Manzanar] had become a state of mind. Now, having seen it, I no longer wanted to lose it or to have those years erased. Having found it, I could say what you can only say when you've truly come to know a place: Farewell.

She admits, however, that the "shame and the guilt and the sense of unworthiness" that characterized her "Manzanar" state of mind remains "like a needle" that had shrunk, over the years, to a "tiny sliver of suspicion about the very person I was."[68]

It is this "tiny sliver of suspicion" that may explain the curious incongruity between the book's tone, which is tough and resilient, and its content, which is characterized everywhere by diffidence. In an interview, Jeanne Houston stated: "I never considered myself a writer. I couldn't have written it without him [James]. . . . The voice is mine, the viewpoint is mine. The technique and the craft is James'."[69] The diffidence and sense of unworthiness that remain as a "tiny sliver" in *Farewell to Manzanar* may explain why Jeanne Houston's story had to be told by someone else. In every case where one person tells another's story, some elements are lost and others gained. Elmer Wok Wai was transformed by Vita Griggs, and though Jeanne Houston could oversee her husband's work, his vision no doubt shaped the portrayal of her experiences.

Sone's, Okimoto's, and Houston's Japanese American autobiographies are not stories of the virtues and rewards of Japanese American patience and obedience. Rather, they give evidence of the limitations forced upon Japanese American *nisei*: not allowed to be either American or Japanese American, they were relegated to a kind of limbo somewhere between invisibility and conditional acceptability. And they chronicle the sacrifices and repression of anger necessitated by these imposed limitations.

Autobiographical writing by second-generation Asian Americans such as Pardee Lowe, Jade Snow Wong, and Monica Sone are important documents of individual responses to the social contexts of all Asian Americans and of individual attempts to win acceptance and understanding of certain segments of the group. It would be misleading to conclude, however, that the self-contempt and euphemization that generally characterizes them were in fact the most typical responses among Asians in the United States to social segregation and race discrimination. Even among American-born Chinese, rejection of the Chinese American community, romanticization of their Chinese heritage, and the desire to "disappear" by being fully assimilated into white society have always been complemented by an attitude of rebellion against oppression and expression of a need for preservation of cultural integrity within the American context.[70] By far the most common response among American-born Asians to the discrepancy between their aspirations and the realities that confronted them was intensified identification with their own ethnic communities in the United States. Only there could they find sympathy, understanding, and psychic sustenance. In some cases, they banded together not merely to protest against Anglo discrimination or to assert their validity as Asian Americans, but also to form a united front against their parents' generation. Social clubs ranged from those like the "Haole Haters" and the "Never-Give-A-Damn-Club" in Honolulu to those that aimed consciously at "changing what is not satisfactory." Smith notes the tendency among Chinese Americans in Hawaii during the 1920s to pay less and less attention to white opinion or acceptance:

They are no longer satisfied with being nobodies in the American [*sic*] group when they may be men of importance on their own. . . . A considerable number of American-born Chinese, after meeting the rebuffs and going through a process of disillusionment, returned to their own group and became the most enthusiastic protagonists for their own organizations.

Mears describes in detail the feeling of one American-born Japanese girl:

> The experiences I've had with the Americans [sic] make me feel like avoiding them as much as possible. . . . I always pity the newly-arrived immigrant for I know that he will have to undergo harsher and harder situations than I. I can picture him ridiculed, insulted, and physically harmed at the hands of Americans [sic]. Since they are here, I always try to sympathize with them, make them feel at ease, and try to make them understand the situation; as long as they belong to the same race as I, we have a friendly feeling toward each other, but not so with the Americans [sic]. . . . Since I am Japanese in blood, I always want to stay so and remain and go with my own group.[71]

# 4

# Portraits of Chinatown

Asian immigrants' autobiographical writing can provide important insights into the social history of particular groups as well as apt portrayals of community life. The autobiographical writing of Younghill Kang and Carlos Bulosan offers readers a vivid understanding of the writers' self-image within the social context of the Korean and Filipino American experience. But *East Goes West* and *America Is in the Heart* are more than mirrors of their creators; they are windows into Korean and Filipino immigrant community life. Second-generation Asian American autobiographers, preoccupied as they seem to be with trying to win individual acceptance in American society, often present a much less complete view. Their efforts to win acceptance are perhaps more desperate because they cannot take comfort in the possibility of finding a place in any society but America's. The negative attitudes towards the Chinese American community expressed in Lowe's *Father and Glorious Descendant* and the exoticized depiction of Chinatown life presented in Wong's *Fifth Chinese Daughter* present only a partial picture of community life. Both Lowe and Wong are primarily concerned with the issues facing American-born Chinese, particularly within the context of their immigrant families, and this orientation represents but a fraction of the concerns within the Chinese American community at large. Even during the times described in the two books, the vast majority of Chinese in America were single men or "married bachelors"—men separated by miles and years from their wives and families in China. Chinatown life was largely organized around the needs of these womanless, childless men who had been segregated from participation in the mainstream of American life by race discrimination.

The omnipresent Chinatown bachelors are featured in vignettes of Chinese "uncles"[1] in Lowe, Wong, and Virginia Lee (*The House That Tai Ming Built*, 1960). In *Father and Glorious Descendant*, the bachelor is "Uncle" Jack, the illiterate gambler and itinerant actor who plays cards and shoots pool in an interracial underworld inhabited by other social deviants. While Lowe admires the character's worldly ways and refusal to conform to the dictates of "Confucian propriety," the figure is more clown than hero. Uncle Jack's rebellion against the strictures of Chinese American life, which Lowe himself resents so roundly, is never explained, and the character's moment of triumph occurs when he is billed as "China's Most Outstanding Troubador" and appears on stage in a Chinese costume to sing American popular songs.

Virginia Lee's Chinatown bachelor is an impoverished opium addict who inhabits a filthy and foul-smelling hovel. The protagonist, Bo-lin, visits this "uncle" as a child to hear his tales of were-tigers and the Eight Immortals and to learn the sayings of the sages. The aging addict tells her that he is unable to return to China because of his poverty, but eventually he is deported by narcotics agents. To Bo-lin, who has no understanding of his circumstances, his deportation is simply the tragic loss of a source of enchanting information about an exoticized China where poetry, philosophy, art, and ancient legends come together over Chinese tea and oranges.

Jade Snow Wong gives us a fleeting glimpse of the Chinatown bachelor in *Fifth Chinese Daughter*. In a chapter about "Uncle" Kwok, a worker in her father's garment factory, little Jade Snow, noting that Uncle Kwok seems eccentric and strange, asks her mother why he is so "queer." The older woman explains that Uncle Kwok is poor and works part-time as a janitor, sustaining himself on the dream of someday becoming a tutor or a great scholar. Having spent many years studying the Confucian classics, Uncle Kwok carries his books, which are his only possessions, about with him in a worn satchel. His studying has been of little use to him in America. Uncle Kwok is presented as a hopeless dreamer and a pathetic fool, a mysterious part of the Chinatown scene about whom Wong is only a little curious.

Although these three figures are memorable, their portraits are sketchy and incomplete. They are not integrated into the other elements in the autobiographies or stories, as if their creators were aware of their presence but had little interest in their real lives. Certainly most second-generation Chinese Americans met such persons every day. But Lowe, Wong, and Lee express little interest in them beyond their value as interesting character sketches to be appended to descriptions of customs, festivals, and artifacts that make up the Chinese American community they present for the reader's edification.

## Popular Attitudes towards
## Chinese American Communities

As we saw in Chapter 1, early "Chinatown" literature in the United States served as propaganda for Chinese exclusion. Chinatown vice and poverty were set forth as evidence that the Chinese were unsuitable as immigrants, and as warnings that if immigration should continue, unacceptable Chinese habits and practices would flourish here unabated, posing a grave threat to the "sweetness and purity of our national waters."[2] According to Robert McClellan:

> No important area of Chinese life eluded the scrutiny of free lance writers, crusaders for moral justice, would-be authors, and others who fed the insatiable appetite of the Sunday supplements and cheap magazines. Few were the homes which escaped unscathed from the onslaught of feature articles, poems, and cartoons depicting the Chinese in barbarian posture. A clandestine visit to Chinatown at midnight arranged through a privileged contact with the local police and guided by a detective who "knew the secrets necessary to gain admission" won for the adventurer the right to speak with authority on all oriental problems. On Sunday and during the week the American version of Chinese sin and shame in all its glory paraded through the front parlors of the nation's homes.[3]

Long-lived interest in Chinatown crime was recently revived when youth problems consequent to the arrival of Chinese immigrant families since 1965 was linked to old Chinese tong wars. Even though the Hong Kong-born youth had no affiliation with the old South China secret societies, and even though Chinese youth crime bears at least as much resemblance to youth crime in urban Black and white communities as to old tong wars, stereotypes of Chinese warlords and hired killers lurking in shadows have been brought into the contemporary investigation of Chinatown youth problems. In 1973, California Attorney General Evelle Younger's office issued a pamplet in which Chinatown youth crime was linked to both tongs and a Chinese Communist plot.[4]

Interest in Chinatown as a nest of opium-sodden yellow slaves is complemented by fascination with what is viewed as exotic quaintness, which attracts millions of tourists each year to the glittering Chinese ghettoes of New York and San Francisco. No other ethnic community has added so many tourist dollars to its city's coffers. Tourists themselves seem oblivious to the real lives of those who live and work in the Chinatown community. In 1978, when film reporters interviewed tourists in New York Chinatown about their impressions of the community and its people, the tourists commented enthusiastically about the inexpensive food and the bizarre sights but seemed luxuriously unaware of the inhabitants and workers there:

> *Interviewer*: Why did you come to Chinatown?
> *Tourist*: Because I'm starving and can't wait to eat. . . .
> *Interviewer*: What do you think about the life of the people who work here, like the waiters and cooks?
> *Tourist*: They're anonymous. They just seem to all do their jobs. They're not very involved in what they're doing. It's just like being paper mâché dolls.[5]

Anglo-American literary portrayals of Chinatown and its inhabitants have served to reinforce widespread popular misconceptions about the Chinese in America and to strengthen the popular prejudices against them. The extent and tenacity of these images even among persons who have had no contact with Chinese Americans and who are not consciously anti-Chinese can be seen in the results of attitude surveys among American children and adults. Bruno Lasker's *Race Attitudes in Children* (1929) reproduces (in their own spelling) youngsters' answers to a questionnaire about race administered by a choir school teacher in a church "known throughout the country as a center of liberal Christianity in a cosmopolitan city":

> The Chinese . . . are a stealing and distrustful people.
>
> I do not like the Chinese because they are so sly and I am afraid they will plunge a knife into me when my back is turned.
>
> I dislike [the Chinese]. Because they have such a bad reputation.
>
> I don't like they thats all.
>
> . . . their bringom into our country opium.
>
> [I don't like] Chinese. Because I do not like to be knifed. Chinese—they kill.
>
> [I don't like] Chinese—to crafty.
>
> I don't like Chinese because they stab you with knives.
>
> . . . Chinese do a lot of underhand work.
>
> I do not like the Chinese because of the looks of the slant eyes gives me a chill.
>
> Chinese you can never tell what they are going to do next.

I do not like the Chinese because they have a certain air about them, a sneaking, slimy air.

I do not like the Chinese because they are so backward and refuse to be helped—and have such an aversion to help from foreigners.

The teacher conjectures about the origins of these children's attitudes: "The answers suggest that the boys have been reading stories of the Chinese which were bloodthirsty. There is no other known source for such ideas."[6]

Although images of Chinese are often specific, vivid, and fully developed, they are rarely based on actual contact with Chinatown and the Chinese people, as the results of extensive interviews conducted in 1935 by Paul C. P. Siu of non-Chinese about their opinions of Chinese laundrymen indicate. One respondent emphasized the laundryman's "criminal appearance," which "seemed to convey the idea that he gladly would have slit a few . . . throats." Other responses follow:

. . . My first experience with a Chinese laundryman came when I was nine years old. My mother sent me to the laundry. . . . Now I had heard all sorts of weird stories about "Chinaman" [*sic*] and was rather afraid. I had heard that they chased boys with a red hot iron and did all kinds of mysterious and sinister things in their back rooms.

. . . as a child, I had been given the impression that he was the "kidnapper" of bad little boys, placing them in his bag and carrying them away to unknown places. Many were the times that I watched the bag intently from a distance in order to see some "squirm" or move, or hear some muffled groan of his victim in his fat bag. . . . I began to look for evidence of "dead rats" . . . for we [boys] . . . discussed . . . their love of "dead rats" just as we craved chicken, candy, sweet potatoes, etcetera.

I was scared to go in to the Chinese store though I did not know why. . . . I thought I would be killed if I didn't get out quickly. I remember the tingling feeling I had in my back as I left; I thought they would stab me or something. . . .

R.S. . . . had no contact . . . with any . . . Chinese . . . but she had a preconceived notion of Chinese as violent, mysterious people with an unwholesome habit of snatching their enemies from obscure alleys into still darker back rooms through sliding panels, and there disposing of them efficiently and silently by thrusting knives into their backs.[7]

None of those interviewed for the study could pinpoint exactly the source of their impressions.

According to Siu's study, even those who had established regular contact with Chinese laundrymen tended to view them as "washing machines" and "not really persons." Although they seemed "creepy" and a bit fearsome, they were taken for granted by the community at large as "a sort of public utility" whom one does not attempt to understand or get to know as a fellow human being.

## Chinatown Community Life before 1949

To understand the Chinese American portrayal of Chinatown and to counterbalance both the stereotype of the Chinatown resident as a crafty villain and the view of him as a "non-person," it is necessary to view some of the factors that have shaped Chinese American community life. Most of the Chinese who immigrated to the United States before 1949 originated from the villages of southeast China, predominantly from four Szeyup districts (Sunwei, Toishan, Hoiping, and Yanping) from which a pattern of young male emigration to Southeast Asia had been established for centuries before the large-scale movement to the New World began in the mid-1800s. The tradition of emigration to foreign lands for the purpose of earning money to support families in China had been firmly established among the people of these villages long before American labor recruiters began their search for Chinese laborers.[8] The pattern of Chinese labor recruitment makes it apparent that even employers of Chinese labor never intended the Chinese to become permanent residents in the United States. Instead, they were expected to fulfill their contract commitments and return to their homeland.

The anti-Chinese movement, which was most virulent in California and the American West, where the largest Chinese populations have been concentrated, resulted in the segregation and containment of the Chinese communities in the United States. Besides mob violence and incidences of hangings and murder, Chinese were subjected to discriminatory legislation that limited their participation in the economic and cultural mainstream of American life. In 1882, along with lunatics, idiots, and criminals, Chinese were the first immigrants to be excluded by federal law from entry into the United States on the basis of nationality. From 1924 to 1943, no China-born person could immigrate to the United States unless he could prove that his father was an American citizen. Alien Chinese were declared ineligible for naturalization, no matter how long they resided here. No alien or citizen Chinese could sponsor his China-born wife, and any female American citizen who married a Chinese alien would automatically lose her U.S. citizenship. After 1932, white women who had divorced their Chinese husbands were eligible to regain their citizenship, but American-born Chinese women could not be naturalized because of their race, which made them ineligible. It was not until 1952 that Chinese could become naturalized U.S. citizens.

Intermarriage between Chinese or "Mongolians" and whites was prohibited in the fourteen states where most Chinese lived.[9] Intermarriage was deemed a "gross misdemeanor" in Nevada, subject to a $500 fine or one year in prison. In Maryland, it was an "infamous crime" subject to ten years' imprisonment. Anti-miscegenation legislation remained on the books in California until 1967.

The scarcity of women in the Chinese American community also created social problems for the Chinese: the ratio of men to women in the Chinese communities here was 19:1 in 1860, 27:1 in 1880, 14:1 in 1910, 7:1 in 1920, and 3:1 in 1940.[10] Coupled with the anti-miscegenation legislation and immigration, the shortage of women served to limit the growth of the Chinese population on the American mainland as well as their opportunities to set down roots through the establishment of a normal family life in their adopted land; in 1920, only 20 percent of the Chinese in America had been born in the United States. This situation led to the flourishing of gambling, drug abuse, and prostitution among the familyless Chinese men as well as the intensification of feelings among them that they must consider their time in America as a temporary sojourn necessitated by economic need and sustain themselves with dreams of ultimate triumphant return to China.

### The Bachelor Society

Between 1908 and 1943, almost twice as many Chinese left the United States as arrived. Between 1880 and 1920, the Chinese population here actually decreased by about 40 percent. A number of the Chinese who did arrive were traveling back and forth between China and the United States, since a pattern had been established according to which a man would labor here for a decade or more, return home to visit his family, deplete his savings, hopefully father a son, and return to America to work for another decade or two.

The majority of Chinese in the United States before 1949 were "married bachelors" who had wives in China whom they saw once every ten or twenty years if they were fortunate. They labored to send regular remittances to support their families in the villages, where sometimes as many as 80 percent of the inhabitants relied on overseas men for their income.[11] The overseas Chinese were commonly viewed as benefactors by those in their home villages, who had very little idea of the hardships and social isolation endured by most Chinese in America. Laundrymen and waiters were pressured by requests for money, gifts, sponsorships, and requests that they return to China as wealthy men.

Many overseas Chinese, prevented as they were from participation in American life and dependent on their home villages for their sense of social significance and status, concentrated their energies and attention on working towards triumphant return to their villages as wealthy men. Most regarded their life in America as a prison term that had to be endured in order to obtain freedom. According to one laundryman, Chinese might have thought differently had they been allowed to live normal lives in America:

> I have no other hope but to get money and get back to China. What is the use of staying here; you can't be an American here. We Chinese are not even allowed to become citizens. If we were allowed, that might be a different story. In that case, I think many of us Chinese would not think so much of going back home.[12]

But most overseas Chinese could not travel back to China easily. Only citizens and legally admitted aliens could obtain return permits, and many Chinese feared that they would be barred from re-entry if they left. Moreover, the trip was costly, not only in terms of passage fare but also because each returning Chinese was expected to distribute gifts and money in the villages. Otherwise, he might appear to have been a failure in America.[13]

During his stay in the village, the returning Chinese was sometimes able to father a child, who would be raised in the village after the father set out again for America. Usually, the father did not see the child again until he had fully grown, and then they might meet as strangers, either in the village or in America. Chinese fathers in America were usually eager to bring their sons to work with them, not only because they needed assistance but also because the more family members a man had with him in America the stronger his social and economic influence would be, both in the village and in the Chinese American community. The return of the overseas Chinese to the villages with money to spend helped reinforce a chain migration of sons and "paper sons."[14]

Leong Gor Yun reports that, in 1936, 75 to 80 percent of Chinese in the United States were laundrymen or restaurant workers. Anti-Chinese activities had resulted in the gradual relegation of the Chinese population on the American mainland to non-competitive or ethnic enterprises in urban ghettoes. Driven from the mines by the Foreign Miners' Taxes in California, they had been prevented from fishing on the West Coast by laws prohibiting the use of Chinese fishing nets and vessels. White workers protested the employment of Chinese in factories and on farms. Even after Chinese immigration and naturalization had been prohibited,

Chinese employment was retricted by regulations preventing those ineligible for citizenship from various occupations. For example, it was reported in 1946 that those ineligible for citizenship were prohibited in New York City from twenty-seven occupations from undertaking to dentistry and teaching.[15]

Chinese were employed in the vice industry, in grocery and supply stores, in garment work and in domestic service, as well as in restaurants and laundries. By 1950 the majority of Chinese in America were concentrated in half a dozen occupations, laundry work being seventy-four times as numerous as any other occupation. Siu's interviews of white workers indicate that Chinese laundry work, which has been a strictly American phenomenon, was permitted because whites did not want to do laundry work themselves and because it was clearly acceptable as menial work for a despised people:

> My opinion of him is quite natural so long as he remains only a laundryman. . . . [H]e is all right as long as he stays in his place and does not try to do too much. . . . One thing I like about them is that they keep their place and don't try to mix with the white people.

> The Chinks are all right if they remain in their place. I don't mind their working in the laundry business, but they should not go higher than that. After all, there aren't enough jobs for us whites, without them butting in.[16]

The average Chinese restaurant worker's day extended from eleven o'clock in the morning to one o'clock the next morning, while laundrymen labored seventeen hours a day, or an average of more than twice as long as the average American worker.[17] Despite economic hardships, the primary source of dissatisfaction among Chinese workers was social rather than economic. Not only did many of the Chinese men view their life and work here as temporary; since they had lost their individuality and were blocked from a normal sex and family life, many lived in a state of suspended despair as they marked the passage of their lonely years. Some reminded themselves that if they were to be doomed to poverty, it might have been better to be poor at home: "It is awful. Although one can earn little in China, he can se his wife and children in the morning and his parents in the evening." "Being a laundryman is no life at all. I am not an old man yet, but I feel old."[18]

In many cases, lack of acceptance and hardships served to intensify the overseas Chinese men's longing for their homeland. Acutely aware that their inferior status was directly linked to China's international position, overseas Chinese who believed that their own road to freedom and equality lay in the strength and independence of the Chinese nation contributed their lives' savings to Sun Yat-sen's movement for national liberation. Between 1931 and 1932, war funds were cabled directly to battlefronts in Asia. During the war with Japan, the average laundryman contributed $12.50 to $18.50 bi-monthly, not including special contributions, for several years to support the Chinese resistance.[19]

### Social Life in the Bachelor Society

Chinese residents of San Francisco and New York Chinatown were virtually sealed within the physical boundaries of their enclaves, not only by housing restrictions but also because those who ventured beyond those boundaries were susceptible to attack by white hoodlums. Chinese men found their social activities limited and circumscribed by the invisible walls around the ethnic ghettoes within which they were contained.

In some cases, men fearful that life would pass them by determined instead to live for the present, exacting small social pleasures whenever they could be found. Unable to understand or enjoy themselves even at the American movies, the married bachelor would "stroll down the street with a lonely heart and a desire to get excitement after a week of strenuous labor" with few ideas as to where to obtain it. Many men turned to eating, gambling, and bought love; according to one Chinatown laborer:

> Right now my heart is gone. All I care is to take life as it is. When I have money I would buy something good to eat and there is a girl [a prostitute] I can find, I go and see her. . . . I am getting old too soon. I must enjoy myself before I am too old. So long as I have a place to sleep and something to eat and I can manage to send a few hundred dollars home—I take life as it is. I can't expect a life better than this and it is no use to try.[20]

Even after the tragic trade in Chinese women declined, white, Black, and mixed-blood prostitutes continued to ply their trade in Chinatown. Armed with the knowledge that these were lonely and womanless men despised in American society, free-lance prostitutes of all races frequented single-man Chinese laundries in the early mornings and at noon and solicited waiters in cheap Chinese restaurants. Those who did not avail themselves of opportunities presented to them on the streets or by visitors to their work sites could always visit brothels. Some Chinese said they visited brothels merely because they had nothing else to do on their days off. Chinese men in the East and Midwest frequented dance halls, where they paid ten cents for a minute's chance to hold a woman in their arms. Some men even attended church-sponsored English classes primarily because the teachers were female and they were hungry even for kind looks and words from members of the opposite sex. Calendars with pictures of nude girls were imported from Shanghai expressly for the "Chinese American" trade; in China they had little sale value. Laundrymen sometimes amused themselves with smutty picture books and magazines, which they would look at in their back bedrooms after fifteen hours' laundry work. Venereal disease and the mental disorders associated with it were found to be "quite high" among Chinese in America.[21]

In general, seeking out prostitutes would have been condemned in the villages, but the Chinese community in America condoned it as "natural and inevitable for sojourners separated for long years from home and family," as long as it did not interfere with remittance payments to families in the villages. Moreover, oldtimers actively introduced newcomers to these vices and the men of Chinatown passed the women's names around among themselves. Young Chinese men who had been sponsored as sons or paper sons were quickly assimilated into the established Chinese American life patterns, for there was no other alternative in a hostile society:

[T]hey . . . go to work in a laundry or store as soon as they land. They are rarely given an opportunity to learn English, and since money is more important, they make no effort to learn. They pick up enough English from their relatives and cousins to get along: the numbers from one to ten and directions to Chinatown.[22]

Gambling was one of the few recreations available to the Chinatown bachelors. For many, it was the only social outlet that offered the possibility of economic freedom. Gambling was a major feature of all Chinatown communities. In 1936, there were fifty gambling houses with a weekly business of at least $100,000 in New York Chinatown, where only 30,000 Chinese lived with an average weekly income of $20 or $25. Portland's 2,000 Chinese were served by no fewer than thirty gambling houses; the 1,500 Chinese of Philadelphia were supplied with three lotteries and six fantan houses. Pittsburgh boasted six houses for only five hundred Chinese, while Detroit's half-block Chinatown contained no fewer than five gambling establishments.[23] The nucleus of the gamblers consisted of waiters, busboys, and laundrymen, who

wagered their meager salaries at tables established near their places of work. Laborers from distant areas returned to Chinatown when their work was done and gambled part of their wages on the chance that they might win enough to end their lonely sojourn in America. . . . Some men made a killing, . . . others continued to play day after day, year after year. As the time for return to China stretched into an ever-receding future, gambling became a ritual, hope diminished but did not die, and the daily routine still included a trip to the gambling parlor. . . . By the 1950's in Chinatowns all across the United States aged bachelors could be seen at certain appointed times wending their way slowly from lonely rooms above the neon-lit avenue to the tiny parlors where the games of chance still offered a tiny ray of hope.[24]

### The Importance of the Community Network

One of the direct results of discrimination against and neglect of the Chinese minority in the United States was the development of an organizational network that functioned as a substitute for normal family life. Chinese in America depended on this network more and more as their sojourn extended into decades. According to Ching Wah Lee, "one factor which bound the Chinese together in the early days was a certain loneliness. They felt that the [American] people were not too interested in them, except as curiosities."[25] Since their isolation was not entirely voluntary, it seems unfair to accuse them of clannish self-segregation. It seems reasonable to conclude that they turned to internal community regulation and direction because they received few benefits, rights, or privileges under American law and social structures.

Chinese American community regulation was based on moral rather than strictly legal obligations. Bound together by their social status as a despised minority, tied by tradition and common beliefs and interests, the Chinese immigrants constructed a world based on social solidarity between families and clans to protect themselves in a cold or hostile environment. This social network provided them with a sense of belonging that they could derive nowhere else. To Americans in general, they were only things or stereotypes. To fellow Chinese, a Chinese American was a human being deserving of sympathy, appreciation, and understanding. When visiting Chinatown, he could be "recognized as a person" and enjoy a life of primary relations where sentiments and attitudes were warm, intimate, and spontaneous.[26] A laundryman's shop, however poor, was his home, where he entertained members of his social circle. Chinatown, however limited, was his social center. In the company of other laundrymen and waiters, the Chinese in America could feel free of race consciousness. Chinatown bachelors could play mahjong and practice the lively Chinese art of storytelling and verbal debate in each other's laundries and basement rooms.

Chinatown's self-regulating community structure had its roots in traditional China, although it was organized around the particular needs and interests of the overseas Chinese. Traditionally, an individual's first loyalty was to his kinsmen. Chinese family relationships dominated political and economic activities and served as a primary tool for social control. An individual's reputation was his family's reputation and one's personal affairs could not be strictly one's own. In America, clan or family surname associations provided mutual aid, and clan leaders served *in loco parentis* because of the problems of mutilated or grafted family life. Regulation of commercial competition was organized through clan memberships as well.[27]

### The Emergence of a Family Society

Chinatown's community structure was organized around making more tolerable what almost everyone had believed was but an extended and temporary sojourn in America: personal relationships, mutual aid, and self-government in the Chinese bachelor society existed well outside the realm of American society. Far from the Chinese villages where lived the families they supported, the aging Chinese bachelors had constructed an increasingly ingrown community where healthy development was effectively blocked by racial segregation and socioeconomic barriers. Their Chinatown life existed "in spite of, rather than in cooperation with, the Americans among whom they breathe[d] and somehow [found] their being." The Chinese bachelors became more dependent on their ghetto social structure for psychological sustenance as their sojourn extended into lonely decades, seeking companionship and mutual support from one another as a substitute for the family life they had been denied. But their community was subject to atrophy and inner decay as a consequence of its isolation from both China and American society. Moreover, while a few prospered as merchants and entrepreneurs and gained political and social power within the ghetto, according to Stanford Lyman,

> by far the majority remained hopeless and trapped, too impoverished to return to China and too oppressed to enter fully into American society. Sojourners without wives to provide them with a home and children, they could not even procreate a second generation of substantial size in America. For two decades their numbers declined in America, and some thought the Chinese would eventually die out, remaining but a memory in America's history.[28]

Changes were forced on the fossilizing patterns of Chinatown life with the advent of the Chinese Revolution, which for many Chinese in America sealed off the possibility of ever returning to China to retire. Both the confiscation of property they had been trying to accumulate in China through their remittances and the uncertainty of their political and economic futures in a new China forced many to surrender the dream of return, however real or practical, that had sustained them during many long years of labor in America. At the same time, new legislation in America permitted the entry of a limited number of China-born wives and children after 1943. Chinese American family life can be said to have begun in earnest after 1949.

## Chinese American Portraits of Chinatown

There is precious little Chinese American literature about Chinatown community life. Much of the existing literature serves to reinforce
popular stereotypes. Two China-born aristocrats who wrote fictional
pieces about Chinatown life are Lin Yutang and Chin Yang Lee. Their
novels, *Chinatown Family* (1948) and *Flower Drum Song* (1957), are among
the more widely read works of Chinese American literature. *Flower Drum
Song* was adapted into a highly successful Broadway musical and later
into a popular Hollywood film.

### Chinatown Family

*Chinatown Family* is set in New York Chinatown. Its main characters
are the members of a laundryman's family who have journeyed to America to join the father at his laundry. Their life is portrayed as a uncompli-
cated passage upward from a basement laundry to a first-floor restaurant.
Although mention is made of cultural adjustment problems, such as
relations between American-born and foreign-born Chinese, in general
the story has a soap-opera quality. The characters are modeled after
familiar stereotypes of docile, grateful Chinese who can accept brutality,
injustice, and hardship cheerfully. Tom Fong Senior has toiled for decades in his basement laundry, viewing only the "legs of men, women,
and children passing by on the sidewalk at street level." It becomes his
son's task to deliver finished laundry to white women, who invite him to
pick up their soiled lingerie from their bedroom floors. When the younger
Fong asks his father why he chose laundry work, the older man replies:
"Those American men! They could not cook and they allowed us to cook
and wash. Now we wash America and cook America because we wash
better and cook better." The senior Fong's method of "washing better,"
particularly during the Depression, consists of lowering his prices and
working longer hours: "he stood on his legs and sweated until 11:00 at
night, thanking heaven that there was no law against that." Although he
admits that he has suffered certain forms of ill treatment, Tom Fong
accepts his condition, rationalizing his difficulties by seeking refuge in
the philosophy of Lao-Tse, which he had to know by instinct, since he
was illiterate: "Tom Fong had been so used to being called a Chink that it
did not really hurt. He had not himself read Lao-tse's statement 'who
receives unto himself the calumny of the world is the preserver of the
state.' But it was in his blood." By avoiding conflict and "seeking the low
places," uncontending and unnoticed as the common sparrow which
multiplies and flourishes unharmed by men, Tom Fong tells his son, the
Chinese race will one day emerge victorious: "[w]hen you looked at his

face, there was no record to tell what he had gone through. . . . That downward-curved upper lip concealed a whole load of emotions seldom expressed. It also expressed patience and endurance as if it was saying, "We shall see who has the last laugh."[29]

Lin Yutang was himself attracted to Taosim and the writings of Lao-Tse because of his interest in the preservation of the status quo through rationalization as opposed to resistance or opposition. "Conquer the mosquito by conquering the itch," aristocratic China-born Elsie tells the laundryman's son. A victim of injustice can transcend his oppressors by seeking refuge in the knowledge that those who occupy lowly places can never be overthrown.

Removed as he was from the real-life experiences of the Chinese laborers, whether in America or in China, Lin depicts a fortuitous blend of feudal Chinese and American capitalist cultures as bringing success and happiness to the laundryman's family. All of the characters in *Chinatown Family* call America "a good country" where opportunities abound and where one can do whatever one pleases without government interference. Even the one old Chinatown bachelor Lin depicts in *Chinatown Family*, Uncle Tuck, who has been beaten and almost killed by American racists and has only one eye left, feels "as rich as Rockefeller." He has been relegated to live out his life of poverty in the back room of a temple, supported by the family association, but he advises young Tom Fong that America is a wonderful country where anyone can do whatever he wants to. Having worked in the laundry for over thirty years, Fong plans to go on working indefinitely because "every minute . . . spent at the large ironing board meant more nickels. It was just like picking nickels up from the street. There was no limit to what they could earn except sheer physical exhaustion."[30]

Ironically, Lin has to engineer the Fong family's reward for their docility and hard work through Tom Fong's death, without which their upward move from the laundry to the restaurant would not be possible. Fong dies a "typically American death," lying in a pool of blood after having been accidentally struck down by a car. The driver's mother, overwhelmed by guilt, apologizes and gives the dead man's family $2,000, which reinforces his widow's faith in both Taoism and America. By doing nothing but dying, Tom Fong has enriched his family. Fong's widow marvels at the "kindheartedness" of Americans, who freely help those in trouble. "It's a good country, America, don't you think?" she exults.

*Chinatown Family* is a highly idealized portrait in which the familiar stereotypes of Chinese abound. Conflict is absent from the story because Lin does not really consider a laundryman's life significant enough to be dealt with seriously. His apparent boredom with the subject explains why the portrait is broken by narrations and lectures on the Chinese rotating credit system, American jazz, and traditional Chinese philosophy. Even the dialogue between the laundryman's son and the Chinese refugee are but recitations of classical Chinese verses.

Lin's formula for Chinese American success requires manipulation and a great deal of luck. Just as the timely miracle of the laundryman's death affords the family their upward mobility in American society, a young Chinese in America can be spared the life of a sexless celibate gathering up dirty lingerie or the ludicrous existence as a Chinese American bebopper by being introduced to a beautiful, chaste, Mandarin-speaking new immigrant whose jade bracelet, "instinctive" modesty, and simple Chinese gown can stir the Chinese American's almost-forgotten cultural "consciousness."

### Flower Drum Song

Like *Chinatown Family*, *Flower Drum Song* presents a highly euphemized portrait of Chinatown life, but in this case the portrait is meant to be a comedy. Though he is an accomplished humorist, Chin Yang Lee is unable to bring the potential satire to life in the novel because it is difficult to distinguish between what is intended and what is unintentional, or the extent to which Lee is himself accepting or satirizing popular misconceptions about the Chinese. The Chinese in the book are rich sojourners, too arrogant and complacent to learn English beyond what is necessary to count to ten thousand dollars. Chinese American problems—the problems of the shortage of women, race discrimination, and generation conflict—are made to appear comical. Chinatown life is shown as quaint, bizarre, and exotic. The English language is comically mangled.

The main characters are wealthy refugees from Taiwan, living in San Francisco Chinatown, although few Mandarin-speaking immigrants ever settled in that predominantly Cantonese-speaking community of laundrymen and waiters.[31] Although San Francisco Chinatown is an impoverished ghetto, wealthy exile Wang Chi-Yang lives there voluntarily, because he speaks only Chinese (the Hunan dialect) and eats only Chinese food, governing his personal and family life and furnishing his unlikely spacious home and garden as he would have done in China. Wang converts his hundreds of thousands of dollars into American bills, which he thinks of as "play money." Naturally, he does not work, so he spends his days resting, contemplating, counting his money, and walking to the herb doctor's shop a few yards from his home.

Wang's son, Wang Ta, finds that he faces problems confronting other Chinese of a lower social class: the problem of the shortage of women and the problem of job discrimination. Wang Ta's friend Chang humorously attributes "all the tragedies of Chinatown" to the shortage of women. In China, he explains, attractive women are "a dime a dozen," but in Chinatown, where there are not enough women, men will kill each other over a pretty girl. Ultimately, Chang marries a dark-haired non-Chinese who is cheerful, hard-working, and affectionate, while Wang Ta is saved from eternal bachelorhood by the magical appearance of a new immigrant from mainland China who can reminisce with him about his lively old home in China with its flowers, bees, butterflies, and young bamboo.

While the problem of marriage and the shortage of women is magically dispensed with for the two men, the problem of unemployment remains. This too is easily dispatched when Wang Ta decides to attend medical school and Chang, a forty-year old grocery clerk with a Ph.D., learns how to "accept reality" cheerfully: "[I]t's a matter of adjustment. . . . By compromising, by being more objective, by trying to adjust yourself, you will find there is somethng nice about everything."[32] After having thoroughly discussed their problems, the two friends go off to lunch on medicine pigtail soup and smoked duck feet with pork.

The problem of generation conflict is also solved without excessive difficulty. Old Wang Chi Yang finds it hard to accept the fact that his youngest son likes to play ball instead of studying Confucius, that he chews bubble gum and tries to make sandwiches out of Chinese dishes. Certainly there are comical aspects like these in the misunderstandings between the immigrant generation and the youngsters raised and educated in this country. But conflicts based on such banalities are rare. Old Wang's sons want their father to face the fact that they are living in America and not in China. The problem is finally solved when old Wang compromises by going to the Chinese hospital where Western medicine is practiced instead of to the herb doctor.

In *Flower Drum Song*, Chinese are portrayed as comical, unmanly, and unreasonable. Chinatown is depicted as a playground for wealthy exiles. Chinese life in America consists of problems relating to marriage and cultural adjustment set against a backdrop of quaint and often bizarre customs, exotic foods, and strange medicines. It would be unfair to condemn the portrayal because it treats Chinese American life humorously. Certainly humor is a dimension that should be vital in Asian American literature. The problem arises from the question of audience. In light of the vast body of existing stereotypes about Chinese, among which are euphemisms that discredit their experience and dehumanize their lives, in light of the vast misunderstanding of Asian American life, one more book that perpetuates stereotypes has not been welcomed by Asian Americans seeking to break through the legacy of ignorance.

Contemporary Chinese American writers Frank Chin, Jeffery Chan, and Shawn Hsu Wong have condemend *Flower Drum Song* as insulting to and distortive of Chinese American life for the purpose of being acceptable or entertaining to the non-Chinese, to whom Chin Yang Lee addresses himself. The book is dedicated to the Yale University Drama School staff. According to Chin *et. al.*, *Flower Drum Song* is an "imported apothecary of ginseng and tuberculosis" that capitalizes on the "chow-mein–spaghetti" formula of the Chinatown books for "bucks and popularity."[33]

Some mention should be made of Chin Yang Lee's psuedo-historical *The Days of the Tong Wars* (1974), which consists of a group of "historical sketches" based on research about the early experiences of the Chinese in California. The colorful characters include Little Pete, the Chinese gangster; Ah Toy, the prostitute; slave girls, laundrymen, hired assassins, and "jabbering laborers" with their queues "coiled like snakes." Their troubles are made light of, since they bring them upon themselves. The 1871 Los Angeles massacre, in which dozens of Chinese men, women, and children were hanged and shot by a white mob, was supposedly brought about because of a lovesick tong man. Though their work was difficult and hazardous, the grateful "Chinaboys, believing in fate, carried on and braved all disasters philosophically." The faithful Chinese servant's "only unhappiness" in America is the food: he hates potatoes, and "cheese was his worst enemy." Wah Lee, the Chinese laundryman, asks, "You dirty? Me wash belly clean."[34]

Lee's shallow and comical portrayal of Chinese American history, complete with pidgin English, is especially disappointing because there is little enough recorded Chinese American history and Lee has the ability to do original research in Chinese and to write skillfully in English. However, he is apparently more interested in amusing and entertaining his readers by perpetuating their prejudices and ignorance than in the authentic presentation desired by the descendants of the figures at whose expense he writes.

Neither Lin Yutang nor Chin Yang Lee were representative of the Chinese population in America. Although *Chinatown Family* is a portrait of a laundryman's family, such a life could hardly have been further from Lin's own experience. An ardently anti-Communist aristocrat, Lin continually sang the praises of America as the golden land of freedom and opportunities that most Chinese laundrymen never tasted. Chin Yang Lee, himelf a "stranded Chinese" from Taiwan, might have been equipped to portray these exiled aristocrats with authenticity and deft satire; yet he felt obliged to use Chinatown, where the Taiwan refugees rarely settle, as the exotic setting of his story. Neither Lin nor Lee could speak with authority or truth about Chinatown life, partly because they were themselves never part of that life. Their own orientation made it difficult for them to distinguish between reality and stereotype.

### And China Has Hands

A completely different point of view on Chinatown life is presented by H. T. Tsiang in *And China Has Hands* (1936), which tells the story of a New York laundryman named Wong Wan Lee. Although the book is roughly written, it is the first fictional rendition of the bachelor society in English by a Chinese immigrant.[35] The laundryman's daily life and his experiences in American society are described in realistic and sympathetic detail. We see the Chinatown tourists from the laundryman's point of view and the underside of American society as experienced by the waiters and laundrymen who comprised the majority of Chinese in the United States before 1950.

Having purchased a basement laundry with his savings from his retaurant labor, Wong settles quickly into a life of washing, handling, ironing, sorting, and packaging laundry, greeting customers, and feeling isolated and homesick. Lonely for the company of women, Wong is unable to derive satisfaction from white prostitutes and taxi dancers who call him "Chinky," and he feels sorry for Chinese prostitutes because he sees them as futilely trying to save enough money in tips to pay their owners thousands of dollars as the price for their freedom. During the course of the story, Wong's laundry is visited by burglars, hoodlums, taunting children and youths, dance hall managers advertising their businesses, Black and white prostitutes plying their trade, white housing inspectors in search of illegal payoffs, and Chinese doctoral candidates selling fancy overcoats on installment plans. Wong vaguely hopes to save enough money to return to China to join the Chinese resistance movement. Unable to pay the bribe demanded by the housing inspector, he tries his hand at gambling and loses everything. Finally, he is forced to close the laundry and become a busboy again. Eventually, he is killed while participating in a picket line with strikers protesting unfair working conditions at a Chinese-owned cafeteria.

### Eat a Bowl of Tea

In contrast to Lin Yutang and Chin Yang Lee, Louis Chu was himself a Chinatown product. Born in Toishan, Chu immigrated with his family to Newark, New Jersey, in 1924, when he was only nine years old.[36] Chu maintained his interest in and understanding of the conditions of life in the Chinatown bachelor society throughout his life. He was bilingual in Chinese and English, and his American experiences enabled him to sympathize with both the older and the younger members of the immigrant generation. He was particularly sensitive to the effects on the

Chinese American community brought about by its transformation from a bachelor society to a family society after 1949.

*Eat a Bowl of Tea* (1961) portrays the Chinatown community on the threshhold of change, from China-orientation to America-orientation, from a community of aging bachelors to a community of young families. The novel's theme is the theme of revelation and discovery. Illusions are shattered and old patterns, which have become empty rituals, are challenged, until the self-deceptions and hypocrisies of ghetto life are exposed, one by one, until what remains is the stark reality of what has been most vital and resilient in their lives. The real strength of the Chinese American community is found not in the old men's fantasies but in their human relationships, which have made possible their psychic survival amidst danger, poverty, and hostility. It is upon this foundation, which they must learn to value with a critical eye, that they will build their new future life in America.

*Eat a Bowl of Tea* presents a compassionate portrait of daily life, manners, attitudes, and problems in the Chinese community from the viewpoint of the laundrymen and waiters. Because it is not an idealized euphemization, neither the weaknesses nor the inherent strengths of the community are overlooked.

The community being portrayed consists not of glittering curio shops filled with dynastic art objects or exotic menu items but of dingy basement rooms inhabited by aging Chinese men who have spent their lives laboring in laundries and restaurants. Their contacts with American society are limited to harassment by police and immigration officials and brief encounters with prostitutes. Their life's pattern is an alienating cycle from restaurant to laundry and back to restaurant again.

Wah Gay's life in America has been toilsome, difficult, and lonely. Only after decades of restaurant labor has he finally managed to establish himself in semi-retirement as the proprietor of a mahjong room frequented by other lonely Chinatown bachelors. Wah Gay lives in the basement mahjong room, a "shut-in dingy place" like a "prison cubicle" with a dank and chilly smell. All of the men of Chu's Chinatown share the common world, going from the basement rooms they inhabit to basement work and meeting places. Lee Gong, having returned home early one day, returns to his room:

> It was strange to find himself in his room at this time of day. He should be at Wah Gay's club house playing mah-jong, which was what he had planned to do after his cup of coffee. He stared absently at the coal stove with its blackened chimney sticking into the wall.
>
> He had lived in this room for more than twenty years. Twenty years was a long time. Maybe this room was unlucky. . . . look what

happened to his roommate Lee Sam . . . still at the hospital somewhere on Long Island.

Sam was working in a laundry when one night two men came in
to beat and rob him . . . after that he was never the same. . . . [H]e
kept saying that someone was after him . . . someone was looking
through the plate glass at him with a butcher knife . . . finally they
had come to take him away. . . . Maybe this room brings bad luck.

At the end of each day, the old bachelors, alone in their rooms, console
themselves reading over letters from home and fantasizing about eventual reunions with wives they have not seen for twenty-five years:

[In the evenings, Wah Gay] lay alone and pensive on his folding
bed, only an arm's reach from the old-fashioned sink that stood
against the wall near the doorway. Privacy from the rest of the room
was afforded by a wooden partition which reached to the ceiling. A
small oblong table stood at the foot of his bed. The mah-jong players
had gone. He was all alone now. Each time he had received a letter
from his wife he began to relive the past. He knew it was not right to
let the old woman stay in the village by herself. He often wondered,
during lonely moments, if perhaps some day he and Lau Shee
would have a joyous reunion. His mind began to wander in the
clouds.[37]

The legacy of the oldtimers is bequeathed to the newcomers: when
Wah Gay's son, Ben Loy, emigrates from the home village to New York to
join his father, the alienating cycle of life is passed on to him. Ben Loy
thinks his father's place is a dungeon. "Only an old man like his father
could stand a shut-in dingy place like this," he tells himself. But Ben Loy
himself fares little better. Wah Gay sends him to a Chinese restaurant in
Connecticut to work, where the waiters share a dormitory room owned
by the restauranteur. Because they only slept there, the dormitory was
never a home to them:

The room was sparsely furnished. No sofa, No chair. When they
sat, they sat on the bed. It was not necessary for the boss to furnish
these rooms with any degree of luxury. It was a place to sleep, a
dormitory. It was unusual for roommates to meet and talk in their
room; their hours of work prevented it.[38]

Ironically, Wah Gay has sent his son away because he knows he
cannot guide him properly. Having left China twenty-five years before,
the old man has not met his son again until his arrival in New York as a

grown man. Himself a former frequenter of brothels and now the operator of a mahjong club, Wah Gay knows he has not set a good example for
his son to follow and fears his son's scrutiny of his failures: "The proprietor of a mah-jong shop would hardly be the type to teach the wisdom
of Kung-fu-tze to the young ones. No one realized that more poignantly
than Wah Gay himself. That was why he had asked Chuck Ting to give
his son a job in Stanton."[39]

One snowy night, the restaurant having closed for lack of customers, Ben Loy and an older fellow waiter find themselves in the dormitory
with the sudden prospect of long leisure hours. Restless and eager for
excitement and pleasure, the older man suggests that they go to New
York to find some prostitutes. Faced with the prospect of being left all
alone in the dormitory with "only the four walls to talk to," Ben Loy
decides to accompany his friend. Thus Ben Loy the newcomer is initiated
into the life's pattern of many men before him, including his father. Ben
Loy begins to seek the company of prostitutes regularly.

Wah Gay is plagued by guilt for having left his wife behind to cling
only to his empty promises. Lau Shee's letters are a constant reminder to
her husband of these promises: "Dearly beloved husband. . . . More than
twenty springs have passed since you left the village. Those who go
overseas tend to forget home and remain abroad forever. I hope my
husband is not one of these." When pressured, Wah Gay mentions
nothing of his bachelor life but offers instead the urgency of business as
an excuse for not returning home. As the chasm between himself and his
aging wife widens over the years, Wah Gay entertains occasional
thoughts of "a brief reunion": "But there was always tomorrow. . . .
Maybe next year, maybe the year after next. And the dutiful wife waited
and hoped. She faithfully went to the market place every Sunday and
prayed for her husband's return."[40]

Although he comforts himself with the thought that his wife feels no
bitterness but "only sympathy and understanding," Wah Gay secretly
knows that he has neglected her. He arranges a marriage between their
son, Ben Loy, and Mei Oi, the daughter of his old Chinatown friend, Lee
Gong, who is also plagued by intermittent feelings of guilt for his failure
to be a real husband and father to his family in China. Mei Oi lives in the
village, and Wah Gay at first plans the marriage so that she can remain
there to keep his wife company until she passes away. He hopes that the
new daughter-in-law can give the old woman some comfort in compensa-
tion for his own neglect, so that "in the remaining years which marked
the late evening of Lau Shee's life, she might find her loneliness more
bearable with a daughter-in-law to share her tribulations." Thus Wah
Gay will not feel pressured himself to return to his wife and will be
absolved of responsibility for her "tribulations."[41]

However, the old man does not want his son to inherit his own life pattern. Because Lee Gong also wants to assuage his guilt, the two men decide that Ben Loy should bring his bride to America to live instead of spending the years separated from her as his father had been separated from his own wife. Not only do they want to utilize their children to mend their relationships with their wives, but both old men also look forward to the advent of grandchildren to comfort them in their old age and give them status as grandfathers. Grandchildren would invest their empty lives and their letters home with new meaning and content:

[Wah Gay looked forward to] the pleasant task of writing to his wife Lau Shee, informing her that Ah Sow was at last with child. This, he assumed, [would be] the first of such missives. For indeed, in America, with the best possible nutrition, babies would come as regularly as the harvest. Lau Shee would announce proudly to their cousins in the village: Our Ben Loy has another son. And then there would be celebrations. Tiny feet and tiny voices would come to see Grandpa.[42]

Wah Gay lives in a world of fantasy that his unlived life and unfulfilled responsibilities can be lived through his son. Lamenting frequently that "nowadays women are not to be trusted," he is thrilled at the prospect of a beautiful and virtuous village girl as a daughter-in-law. The village marriage ceremony is like a fairy tale union, with Ben Loy and Mei Oi "like characters out of story books: the gold prospector from the Golden Mountain, the school girl, the educated girl in the long dress." Mei Oi's mother has blessed the marriage because she believes that, unlike her own life, her daughter's would be an enchanted dream, in which she would see her husband "in the morning and at night."[43] Mei Oi dreams of a happy life in New York, "the greatest and most beautiful city in all the world": "[S]he would be happy, very happy. A whole new panorama of fertile fields lay before her. Youth. Dreams. The future. All that a girl from New Peace Village in Sunwei could ever hope for."[44] Instead, she finds a corrupt community of decrepit old men, a community in which she as a young women cannot fully participate. Unlike her village, where there was "a oneness, a togetherness, a sense of belonging, a proud identity," New York Chinatown is a hostile and lonely environment where old men play mahjong and joke about sex. Ben Loy, having been bequeathed the curse of his father's bachelor life patterns, reflects the old man's inability to be a real husband to his wife. Riddled by guilt for his past habits, he is "like a man who had a new house with a key" when he brings his bride to New York. The naive and inexperienced Mei Oi, on the other hand, feels lonely and unloved and is eventually seduced by a predatory old bachelor, Ah Song. Instead of fulfilling the expectations of her father and her father-in-law, she becomes an adulteress, pregnant with the child of a man who is not her husband.

Mei Oi becomes the primary agent for change in the Chinatown community of *Eat a Bowl of Tea*. She visits upon the old men the collective revenge of all their neglected wives by exposing to them their own hypocrisy and self-deception, revealing that what seems to be a carefree bachelor life is, in fact, lonely and predatory. What the old men's wives in the villages imagine about America is but the illusion framed by letters and hearsay. The village girl they idealize turns out to be a flesh-and-blood woman with needs and thoughts of her own. The fathers, while purporting to have sacrificed themselves for their children's sake, are manufacturers of fantasy, unable to give guidance and support to their children except in appearance. The moribund community structure is organized around the saving of reputations rather than giving real aid and support to its members.

Mei Oi's presence changes the cycle that had been set in motion generations before. The Confucian relationships are exposed as illusory: the relations between fathers and sons and wives and husbands are only abstractions. In reality, elders have deprived youth of guidance, and friends are predatory and self-serving. The distance between Wah Gay and his son is aggravated by the fact that the young man has lived most of his adult life apart from his father and that the father, anxious to avoid his son's knowing of his own failure, sends him to live in another town. Ben Loy, in turn, tries to escape meeting his father, knowing that "when a Chinese father and son get together, it is frequently a one-way bawling out."[45] The father-son relationship is reduced to mutual avoidance. Whether or not the ideal Confucian father-son relationship could be maintained in China, there is little room for its development within the sterile and limited confines of the Chinatown bachelor society.

Although the old men tell themselves that their outrage over Mei Oi's infidelity is caused by their concern for their children's welfare, in fact they are furious because both of them had been intending to utilize the young people to compensate for their own failure as husbands and men and the adultery brings scandal upon them. Likewise, the head of the family association is annoyed because it will affect the clan: "If one were disgraced and lost face, the other would be similiarly affected. The scandal had broken upon one, as it had upon the other." Ben Loy worries more about the community gossip than about the problem itself: "The discovery of an act is even more humiliating than the act itself. . . . [W]hen it becomes public property, it is mortifying. Ben Loy was most concerned about any publicity over the cause of his wife's infidelity."[46]

Almost all the Chinatown inhabitants are acutely aware of their dependence on the community structure. The two deviants—Mei Oi and her seducer, Ah Song—are the two who derive the least protection and support from that structure. Mei Oi has received neither guidance nor support from her father. When she meets her father for the first time at Idlewild Airport, she scans his face trying to find some resemblance between the stranger who stands before her and the old photographs her mother kept in the village. Later, when Lee Gong confronts her, having heard her name linked with scandal, she is unable to confide in him, for he is a complete stranger to her: "How could she confess such a face-less thing to her own father? It might have been easier if she had known him all her life."[47] There are few women to turn to, and she feels lonely and isolated in a male-dominated world. There is no Jo family association, not even any Jo family members in New York to protect or pressure Ah Song, which helps explain his socially unacceptable behavior.

The clan associations and the community structure are substitutes for families for the old bachelors. They provide a limited arena in which courage and manliness can be exhibited. The reality of their daily lives continually intrudes upon these exhibits, so that, after Lee Gong writes his aggressive and threatening notes to Ah Song, he must return, shoulders sagging and aching with rheumatism, to his cold and lonely room. Slightly bent and rapidly graying, Wang Foo Ming, having presided importantly over the clan association meeting, hurries back to his corner grocery store.

In the Chinatown world, relations between friends and relatives are corrupted by the absence of women and a normal family life. In-laws meet at gaming tables, where men entertain lustful thoughts about their friends' wives and daughters. Ah Song had been a frequenter of the mahjong room operated by the father-in-law of the woman he seduces. Chin Yuen's gesture of friendship to Ben Loy is to introduce him to prostitutes in New York. In this predatory atmosphere, even precious friendships are threatened. Though Chin Yuen is Ben Loy's "good and loyal friend," he is tempted to try to seduce his friend's wife, his dreams mixed with thoughts of the family life he has missed:

> If someone was going to steal his best friend's wife why not Chin Yuen? . . . *Don't trust anybody, not even your best friend. . . . Fatty water should not be allowed to flow into another's rice paddy.* Why should a stranger be permitted to ravish the beauty of Mei Oi? . . . If he could in some way take Mei Oi's affection away from this outsider, he could be doing Ben Loy a favor.[48]

But despite its apparent weaknesses and decay, there is no escape from the Chinatown ghetto. Even newcomer Mei Oi recognizes the invisible boundaries circumscribing her: "[W]here can one escape from a big city like New York City? It would not be New York City she would be running away from, but New York's Chinatown." When Wah Gay momentarily contemplates escaping his shame by disappearing far from his fellow Chinese and from New York Chinatown, he relinquishes the scheme because of his psychological and physical dependence on the community:

> If he hadn't sunk such deep roots in New York, Wah Gay would find it easier to pull up his stakes and disappear. After more than forty years in the community, a sudden uprooting would be bound to have repercussions. If he were to go anywhere, say Boston or Washington D.C., he had many friends there too. How could he face them? . . . His type of business demanded a large enough city to have a number of mah-jong players.[49]

It is community mores, not American law, that bring about the administration of justice in Chinatown. Ah Song drops his charges against Wah Gay for cutting off his ear because he is condemned by the community at large to five years' exile from New York Chinatown as a public menace and a traitor to the friendship of his fellow Chinatown residents. One community leader proclaims:

> Did not Ah Song take advantage of Wah Gay's hospitality? Did you not visit him at the basement club-house every day? Drink his coffee? Drink his tea? Wang Wah Gay treated him like a brother. Even better than a brother. And how did he repay him? He made love to his best friend's daughter-in-law! Is this the kind of people we want in our community?[50]

Ah Song, himself socially and economically dependent on Chinatown, can only accept the decision and drop the charges.

Important too are the inherent strengths of the community, which sustain its residents by providing them, whether they care to admit it or not, with the real meaning of their lives. Even as they console themselves with fantasies of returning to China and illusions of family life, their most important moments are spent with each other in Chinatown, where they can feel the sympathy, understanding, and appreciation not available to them anywhere else. It is the warmth and profundity of their friendships that have sustained them during years of lonely sojourn. After executing his violent act of revenge on Ah Song, Wah Gay seeks refuge in the tiny slum laundry of his old friend, and the depth of friendships in the Chinatown bachelor community can be felt in the touching moment when Wah Gay and Lee Gong part near the end of the novel:

[T]he two in-laws ate silently. There was so much to be said that neither of them could find words for their thoughts. When they had finished eating, Lee Gong permitted Wah Gay to pay for the dinner.

Out in front of the restaurant, they paused and looked at each other, speechless. They were choking with emotion. Finally, Wah Gay stuck out his hand.

"See you again, grandpa!" he said.

Lee Gong heard himself called grandpa for the first time in his life. Astonished and taken aback, he quickly recovered sufficiently to grab the extended hand.

"See you again, grandpa!"

They set out in opposite directions and, when they were a few feet apart, each whirled and called out, "You have my address?"

They nodded to each other and continued down the street. With bowed head, unknown to each other, each took out a handkerchief and dabbed at his eyes. In their hearts was the grim thought: in all probability, we will never see each other again.[51]

The novel ends on a note of optimism because of the compromises made by the young, who are prepared to alter the course of Chinese American community life in the future. Ben Loy and Mei Oi have been deceived. But they can avoid being destroyed by the same illusions that cursed their predecessors, both in America and in China, by recognizing and accepting reality in place of the fantasy and self-deception to which their fathers have been clinging. The presence of Mei Oi has irrevocably removed the mask over the hypocrisy of the old men's lives. Ben Loy must drink a bitter bowl of tea: he must make amends for the excesses of the bachelor legacy. He must accept his own mistakes, his wife's mistakes, and the child who, although illegitimate, will be his own. Ben Loy will be the father and husband Wah Gay was not, because he has chosen to face reality.

A change is due, but it will mean continual compromise. Although the curse of his father's life has touched him, it has not destroyed him. The cycle of bachelor life ends with Ben Loy. At the beginning of the story, we are told that "marriage opened a new vista of life for him. The apartment became a home, his and Mei Oi's. Not just a place to hang his hat. . . . A husband and wife relationship. It gave him a feeling of dignity."[52] Ben Loy is determined not to live the way his parents did, "separated by oceans and continents." He has left China behind. But he will remain a Chinese and his community will be Chinatown. By moving to San Francisco, he has merely exchanged one Chinatown address for another, but he has compromised by asserting his independence from his father while at the same time acknowledging his need for the Chinese

American community. Ben Loy will not mix Chinese herbs with Western medicine. It is the Chinese remedy that cures him, bitter though it is. Ben Loy is a "good boy" who "still has Chinese culture," unlike the *jook sing* who simply say "To hell with you." In a desperate moment, he envies and admires the outspoken freedom of American sons in their relationship with their parents, but ultimately he dismisses their outspokenness as "animal behaviorism."[53]

While she also wants the support of the community and the clan, it is Mei Oi, to whom present-day Chinatown and its bachelors have little to offer, who heralds a new way of life for Chinese America. Mei Oi knows that girls are as "well-liked" as boys in America. She has the resilience to fight without quitting, and she has already decided that she will raise her children differently from the traditional Chinese way, without the cold formality of her father and without the repressiveness she notes in her cousin:

> She disapproved of the way Eng Shee had called her children: *Dead boy this and dead boy that.* . . . In the villages one would expect children to be called *dead boy bitches or dead girl bitches* by their aroused parents, but in America one would think that a parent, be it father or mother, would feel more affectionate toward his offspring.[54]

Perhaps Mei Oi's children will be more like the *jook sings* Wah Gay detests than like his "sympathetic" and "understanding" wife across the ocean—but there will be ties of affection and a closeness between parents and children that had not existed before among Chinese in America. A family community will supplant the bachelor society.

Because they insist on clinging to their illusions, Lee Gong and Wah Gay have had to compromise also: Wah Gay must leave New York and return to the drudgery of restaurant labor, while Lee Gong, having nowhere to go after the mahjong club is closed down, leaves New York to go to work at his cousin's poultry market. Both men are tragically and unnecessarily disrupted, quite out of proportion to their follies, but they are promised through Ben Loy's regained strength the eventual status of grandfather. Although Ben Loy and Mei Oi have moved to San Francisco Chinatown, leaving behind parental supervision for a life of relative independence, they will invite their fathers to their second baby's haircutting party. The book ends with the promise of reunion and reconciliation. A new community will be built around the acceptance of realities and new orientation that arise from the possibility of setting down healthier Chinese roots in America.

*Eat a Bowl of Tea* provides us with an optimistic portrait of the Chinatown community told from the viewpoint of the laundrymen and waiters and devoid of stereotypes and cliches; the book's humor is not based on notions of white supremacy nor does its interest lie in lectures on Chinese art and high culture. While the flaws in Chinatown life are mercilessly revealed and the writer identifies with the new Chinese community coming into being, the old men are compassionately portrayed. Without an understanding of the social forces that shaped those men's lives, *Eat a Bowl of Tea* might seem to be merely a quasipornographical Chinese American novel. But Ben Loy's sexual impotence symbolizes the social impotence of generations of Chinatown bachelors constricted by genocidal American laws and policies.

The moving and vital quality of Chu's portrayal of Chinatown life and attitudes can be attributed in part to his ability to appreciate the Chinese spoken around him by a people to whom verbal skill and witty exchanges are valued as a social art. Instead of the "pidgin English" invented for comic effects by Anglo-American writers, Chu translates the idioms and images directly in all their colorful and vibrant forms from Cantonese dialects. Wah Gay shouts to his son: "You think because you can open and shut your eyelids, you're a human being?" Instead of delivering explanatory lectures on Chinese American attitudes and values, Chu transcribes Szeyup colloquialisms in dialogues in such an integrated way that they vividly reveal those attitudes as well as the relationships among the people of the Chinatown community:

> "Everybody's interested in sex," cut in Ah Song, who had kept quiet up to now.
> "Everybody but you, you dead boy. You're dead," said Ah Mow pleasantly to his employee.
> ". . . Chong Loo is all right," said Ah Song. ". . . Maybe he is a many-mouthed bird, but he works for a living. . . . Wow your mother, Wah Gay, do you think he's like you, never worked in your life?"
> They both chuckled. "You dead boy," said Wah Gay. "You're still young yet [he is in his forties]. Why don't you go to work?"
> "Who me? I've worked more than you ever hope to work, you sonavabitch. . . ."
> "When did you ever work?" replied Wah Gay. "I've known you for almost twenty years." He pointed his finger at Ah Song. "You sonavabitch, if you ever worked at all, you must have worked when you were a mere boy. Ever since I've known you, you haven't done a single day's work."
> "Shut up your mouth. Do I have to tell you when I go to work?"[55]

The skillfully crafted dialogues also reveal the relations between the young and the old. While informality and earthiness are permitted among peers, the dialogues between relatives of different ages are formal and inhibited. When Ben Loy visits his uncle, his agitation remains hidden under an outward calm demonstrated in the ritual interchange. The young man remains politely uncommunicative, while the uncle, on the other hand, has the privilege of giving fatherly lectures that reinforce the proper distance between him and the younger man. Chuck Ting knows that Ben Loy's wife is unfaithful to him, but the younger man cannot be certain of what his uncle means by asking about her. The indirectness of the exchange reveals little to either participant about the true feelings of the other:

> "How is Ah Sow [Mei Oi]?"
> "Hao," replied Ben Loy, wondering what the old man was up to. The slowness of the unfolding made him nervous and irritable, but he assumed an outward calm.
> "How is business at the restaurant?" Chuck Ting asked casually. He lit a cigarette, puffed on it, and tilting his head, blew smoke into the air.
> "Fair," Ben Loy said flatly. He had always seen him smoking cigars.
> "Are you making a little money where you are now?" Uncle Chuck Ting smiled broadly. His casualness was disarming.
> "Some," replied Ben Loy, a little annoyed at such a personal question. Then he added, "But not enough to get rich on."
> . . . "How is Ah Sow?" he asked again.
> "She is fine," replied Ben Loy, impatiently. "You have a kind heart."
> "Does she like New York? I gues she has been here for almost two years now."
> "She likes New York very much." But to himself. He certainly didn't ask me here to ask me this.[56]

*Eat a Bowl of Tea* never achieved the popularity or financial success of Chin Yan Lee's *Flower Drum Song*. Chu died in relative obscurity in 1970, before the limited first edition of his first and only novel had sold out. Nor was it as widely read as Jade Snow Wong's *Fifth Chinese Daughter* and Pardee Lowe's *Father and Glorious Descendant*. It is indeed ironic that the stylized depictions of quaint, exotic lifestyles or lurid fantasies about Chinese sin and vice created by Anglo-American writers about Chinatown were the ones that gained relative prominence.

In recent years, renewed interest on the part of many Asian Americans in their buried history has resulted in research, the collection and translation of oral histories, and the search for early writings by Asian

Americans that attracted little attention in earlier decades. *Eat a Bowl of Tea* was rediscovered in the early 1970s, and nine years after Chu's death the book was reprinted by the University of Washington Press, largely through the efforts of young Chinese Americans who valued the book for its dramatic documentation and uneuphemized, unexoticized portrait of Chinese American community life, not from the viewpoint of an aristocratic outsider but from the perspective of one of those who lived it.

# 5

# Japanese American Family and Community Portraits

Like the Chinese Americans, Japanese Americans have been affected by the fluctuating relationship between their country of origin and their new land. Anti-Japanese activities, culminating in the mass internment of almost the entire Japanese American minority on the West Coast after the declaration of war against Japan, profoundly influenced the social and economic status of the Japanese in America, the development and shape of their communities, and the attitudes and behavior of individual Japanese Americans. By the eve of World War II the Japanese communities in the United States had evolved a pattern of economic and social life that paralleled but existed outside the mainstream of American society. Unlike the Chinese community, which had become predominantly urban by the end of the nineteenth century and which was comprised primarily of foreign-born men living in America as bachelors, about half of the Japanese Americans were living in rural areas clustered around small Japanese towns, or *nihonmachis*, all through the western United States. Moreover, the American-born Japanese, or *nisei*, had outnumbered the immigrants, or *issei*, by 1930.

Because of Japan's status as a rising power in the Pacific, the absence of foreign occupation or direct intervention, and the country's rapid industrial modernization, fueled by unimpeded Japanese colonization of Korea and Formosa, conditions of Japanese immigration more closely paralleled European than other Asian immigration. While it is true that the majority of Japanese who came to America between 1885 and 1907 were single young men, they were not the most impoverished persons in their homeland and were also relatively well educated,[1] especially about American life and customs. They had had opportunities to become familiar with the currents of Western thought and modern Western life: in the cities especially, information about important social, political, economic, and cultural world trends was readily available. Many Japanese immigrants had become interested in going to America after reading books about the United States that were circulating in the urban centers.[2] Moreover, the Japanese government not only screened immigrants carefully to make sure that they would properly represent their motherland abroad but also gave an official briefing for each immigrant, during which he could become acquainted with some of the rudiments of American life. For the most part, the *issei* had a highly positive attitude towards America when they left Japan. The typical *issei* "regarded America as his land of opportunity, where he could finally make a man of himself. He came to America filled with dreams. He was fully prepared to undergo any degree of hardship and to discard Japanese customs and manners if that would help him realize his dreams."[3]

The dreams were for the most part unfulfilled. For one thing, the Japanese in California inherited the anti-Chinese sentiments of earlier days; like the Chinese before them, they were accused of lowering the wages and living standards of white workers. But it was the alleged arrogance of the Japanese immigrants' demands for equal pay and treatment that angered white workers the most. Japanese were criticized for "aping their betters" and compared unfavorably to the now excluded Chinese, who were characterized as "knowing their place." According to Charles Marden, people saw "the Chinese in terms of stereotype A, the inferior, humble, ignorant who could be condescendingly tolerated; [and] the Japanese . . . in terms of stereotype B, the aggressive, cunning, and conspiratorial requiring more active dominant efforts to keep them in their place."[4]

As we saw in Chapter 1, anti-Japanese agitators argued that the Japanese were unassimilable because they were fanatically devoted to the Japanese empire and were even participating actively in schemes for Japanese conquest of the West Coast, possibly through land acquisition. Almost every item of anti-Japanese legislation in the United States was followed by renewed interest among Japanese immigrants in Japan, in Buddhism, and in Japanese language schools for American-born children, whom the *issei* feared would be unable to establish a tolerable life in America because of race prejudice. *Issei* parents who heard about the debates in Congress over whether or not American-born Asians should be deprived of American citizenship feared that their children would have no future here and urged them to prepare for the eventuality of working and living in Japan. But the thought of returning to Japan was unrealistic, even for most *issei*. It served primarily to comfort the immigrant and sustain him through his difficulties. One *issei* comments that his longing for Japan was directly related to his feelings that he was not welcome in America:

I still feel a longing to go back to Japan. Here in this country, I am an alien because I have no citizenship, and my world feels small because it is restricted at certain points. When I walk around among the Americans, I have a feeling that I don't belong here.[5]

The West coast white laborers' vociferous call for Japanese exclusion caused problems for President Theodore Roosevelt, who was concerned about diplomatic crises that might result from a Japanese exclusion policy. While he supported continued exclusion of the Chinese, Roosevelt pointed out that the people of Japan were virile, accomplished, and "civilized." In an attempt to avoid provoking Japanese imperial anger, he effected a compromise with the California white politicians. According to the Gentleman's Agreement of 1907, Japanese immigrants were able to bring in wives as non-laborers and to establish families in America, as their Chinese predecessors had been unable to do, but Japanese laborers were excluded from immigration. By 1924, when all Japanese immigration was finally halted by law, over 14,000 Japanese women had come, mostly as "picture brides," to join husbands they had seen only in photographs.

While early Chinese immigrants were shackled by their passage debts, many Japanese immigrants had free passage to Hawaii. Thousands of Japanese were brought to Hawaii between 1885 and 1894 through Robert Irwin, who had arranged for the passage fares to be paid by the Hawaiian government and sugar planters. Moreover, many of the Japanese immigrants were second and third sons who, because of the Japanese custom of primogeniture, could not inherit family lands and enterprises in Japan and therefore sought other avenues of economic opportunity. The fact that they did not receive inheritances also freed them from the responsibilities of supporting families back home that encumbered the Chinese immigrants. The Japanese immigrants were therefore better able to invest in farmland, even though it did not produce immediate returns or the regular cash flow that wages could. Moreover, the arrival of the picture brides helped encourage Japanese men to set down roots in American society, and the presence of women and, later, children allowed them to consider family-operated farms and small enterprises. Japanese were highly successful in agriculture in the American West, introducing many crops that had not been successfully grown before. Japanese farm families utilized their collective labor to reclaim land, to irrigate, and to cultivate intensively many varieties of fruits and vegetables. By 1940, almost half of the working Japanese in California were in farming. American-born Japanese college graduates, unable to find work in other areas, returned to their families' farms and fruitstands. Many other Japanese Americans worked in produce stands and seed stores, although some entered domestic service or became fishermen. Those who did not work in agriculture, fishing, or domestic service usually engaged in small-scale enterprises catering to Japanese farmers and fishermen.

Part of the relative success of the Japanese immigrant agricultural and related enterprises can be attributed to the collective behavior of the group. Trades, for example, were established and regulated through provincial organizations called *kenjinkai*. Immigrants tended to give first consideration in business to those belonging to the same prefectural organization. Like the Chinese, Japanese pooled their money in rotating credit associations.[6] Moreover, Japanese tended to cooperate in business with members of their own race, to whom they gave better and faster service. At a time when anti-Japanese violence threatened them, they worked through their ethnic association, the Japanese Association in America, or *nihonjinkai*, for group protection.

One of the attitudes that set early Japanese immigrants apart from the Chinese was their active interest in adopting the clothing, mannerisms, and customs of Anglo-Americans. The early Chinese, required under penalty of death to maintain their queues as signs of their obeisance to Manchu rule and concerned with eventual return to their villages in China, did not generally adopt Western-style clothing. The Japanese, on the other hand, had their hair cut in modern European styles and attempted to dress like Americans as much as possible. Japanese picture brides told of being whisked from the ships by their new husbands directly to the dressmaker's, where they would be outfitted in Western clothing, including hats, corsets, high-necked ruffled blouses, long skirts with bustles, high-laced shoes, and, for the first time in their lives, brassieres and hip pads.[7] Some Japanese immigrants converted to Christianity and tried to learn English. The Japanese Association, charged with providing newcomers' services, instructed the immigrants how to behave in public—for example, to refrain from public breastfeeding, a common practice in Japan. Community leaders admonished immigrants to learn American customs and recall always that they should behave as "guests" in their new country.

Although the *issei* lived socially apart from the American people, they admired and tried to emulate Americans. Very few felt hostile or resentful:

No amount of discrimination discouraged them from trying to win acceptance. The individual Japanese concluded that it was not unnatural, not even unjust, for Americans to reject him as long as he was not like them. How he wished, for example, to be able to speak English perfectly, without any Japanese accent! How he wished that he had been taller and better built or of lighter complexion, so that they could not so easily tell that he was a Japanese! Without knowing it, he was a victim of . . . self-hate.[8]

Many Japanese immigrants early made a case for citizenship because they wanted to live permanently in the United States. (In 1922, however, the Supreme Court ruled that Takao Ozawa, an English-speaking, Christian *issei* who had graduated from Berkeley High School and who attended the University of California before applying for U.S. citizenship in 1914, was ineligible because of his race.) Aristocratic Etsu Sugimoto, who never intended to settle in America herself, referred to the United States as one of her two "mothers"; she said she was almost equally fond of America and Japan. According to Daisuke Kitagawa, most *issei* regarded Japan as their "mother" and the United States as their "mother-in-law." Just as the Japanese daughter bids farewell to the home of her childhood and cleaves to her in-laws' home when she marries, the Japanese immigrant felt he must cleave to his adopted land and endure whatever abuse or hardship he encountered. At the same time, like the Japanese bride, he could never stop loving and longing for the childhood home that had been left behind.

Some Japanese Americans responded to rejection and discrimination by trying to modify their own behavior.[9] Many *issei* even accepted racial discrimination as a price they had to pay in order to be fully Westernized. The reverse face was their concomitant sense of superiority to other nonwhites, such as Chinese, Koreans, Filipinos, and Blacks: "I may not be as good as the white man, but thank God I am not half as bad as these others."[10] At times, Japanese Americans resented being classified with Chinese and feared that, if they associated with Blacks, their own status would be lowered in the eyes of whites. The outcome of such acceptance of white racism as part of American life was servility in front of the powerful on the one hand and disdain for the less powerful on the other. In *Hawaii: The End of the Rainbow* 1964), Kazuo Miyamoto describes the frame of mind of the *issei* leaders who had been selected for imprisonment in Honolulu after the bombing of Pearl Harbor. Humiliated and feeling apologetic, many *issei* inmates developed a "prisoner complex," deriving an almost perverse pleasure from the knowledge that someone, even a prison guard, was watching over them. The book ends with the grateful internees sailing back to Hawaii from a mainland prison camp on a ship: they decide to clean the ship's toilets to show their deliverers the diligence and cleanliness of the Japanese people.

This is not to say that all Japanese Americans were passive and afflicted with self-contempt. There were many instances in which *issei* and *nisei* stepped forth to defend themselves and others and from injustice. For example, Hawaii *nisei* Kiyoshi Okamoto organized a committee of one at Heart Mountain (Wyoming) prison camp in 1943 to protest that it would be unpatriotic and undemocratic to submit without challenge to imprisonment, substandard living and working conditions, and discriminatory treatment. Okamoto was joined by dozens of other Japanese Americans, although the predominantly *nisei* Japanese American Citizens' League attacked Okamoto's Fair Play Committee, arguing that *nisei* rights had only been restricted and that if the Supreme Court ruled internment constitutional, their rights would not have been abridged after all.

It cannot be concluded that this tendency towards conformity and lack of critical thought is merely a Japanese cultural survival on American soil: it might have been a village tendency in feudal Japan that, when transplanted in America, flourished and was reinforced by segregation and relegation to marginal social status. The Japanese community became increasingly narrow as its members associated almost exclusively with one another. The community was a haven for its vulnerable and isolated members. But while the experience of social segregation strengthened the group's sense of social solidarity and gave its members their most meaningful social identity, the boundaries that circumscribed it also allowed the tyranny of conformity and mutual exploitation to flourish unchecked, under the guise of regulation of deviant behavior for the good of the group.

Social censorship of individual actions proved to be a powerful force in controlling attitudes and behavior. Sensitive to criticisms by anti-Japanese agitators at the turn of the century, the Seattle Japanese American community undertook steps to rid itself of gambling and prostitution. The prevalent attitude was that the behavior of any Japanese could be either a credit to or a blot upon the reputation of the entire community. Sons were warned that their actions would reflect upon their families as well as on the entire Japanese race. It was frequently said that "a Japanese deliquent harms us all." Behavior was reinforced or punished through gossip, whether spoken or written in Japanese newsletters and the Japanese language newspapers. An economic boycott was a tool for pressuring deviants and nonconformists. Few dared to criticize the tyranny of the social structures that shaped their behavior and their relationships, for to do so would have threatened the only psychological security they could rely on in a hostile environment. It was impossible for an individual to hide in his community, but neither could he dream of finding solace or acceptance elsewhere. Denied the possibility of other options, individuals clung to patterns of *ken* loyalties long after prefectural associations had ceased to be important in Japan. All the social groups emphasized the solidarity of their particular inner circles to the exclusion of out-groups. Real unity among the Japanese Americans existed only when the groups were united against anti-Japanese agitation; otherwise, the *nihonjinkai* had less importance than smaller organizations. Individuals ostracized by the ethnic community, unable to gain acceptance in the anti-Japanese host community, often found life so intolerable that they went back to Japan. By the eve of World War II the Japanese American community had become stale and ingrown:

> [T]he total frame of reference of the immigrant Japanese in America had . . . been reduced to his own tight little community. As a result, the Japanese community was . . . extremely static—like a bear cooped up in a cage . . . it had . . . a great deal of energy that it had little opportunity to expand.[11]

## Issei and Nisei

The *issei's* dream of returning to Japan someday faded as the years passed. But because they were in America but not of it, they remained in perpetual limbo, suspended between two worlds, neither of which they could claim as their own. Lacking contact with other Americans, most *issei* spoke but little English. Their hopes for their future in America were channelled into their American-born, American-educated *nisei* children, especially after the exclusion legislation of 1924 eliminated continual contact with Japan through new immigration. As the years passed, the immigrant Japanese relied increasingly on his children to vindicate him, to prove that his sacrifice and his decision to leave Japan had been worthwhile after all:

> [T]he Nisei gave positive meaning to the Issei's life. The Issei parents lived simply to see their Nisei sons and daughters grow up into first-rate Americans, so that they could shout from the housetops to all the world, "See, we knew it all the time!" To achieve that, they did not mind paying any conceivable price.
>
> To the Issei, the Nisei was an incarnation of America that had broken through the barriers and had come to live in the midst of the segregated Japanese community. "Flesh of his flesh, bone of his bone," the Nisei was *his* beyond dispute, and yet he was an American, too. The Nisei was there already! The gulf had been bridged. The wall of the partition had begun to crumble. The goal of the Issei's long pilgrimage was now in sight. That which was unreachable had come to him. Indeed, he had not hoped in vain.[12]

Having been themselves deprived of formal education opportunities, *issei* parents eagerly sent their children to public kindergartens, on which they depended for their children's training in American ways of life according to the "American mode of instruction." The *issei* trusted the

American teachers, continually reminding their children that the teacher was always right and that the perfect pupil was well-behaved and diligent. The entire community network was mobilized to pressure the *nisei* to perform successfully in school. In gossip and in community newspapers, the failures and successes of *nisei* pupils were publicly announced and carefully weighed: "The Nisei child knew no one who did not think he should do well in school. On top of this, he was always being compared with other Japanese children."[13]

Through watchful community judgment of individual performance and actions, the *nisei* were guided by a sense of collective obligation. Parental emphasis on duty and responsibility and the use of shame, guilt, and gossip pushed the *nisei* towards academic achievement. Appeals were made on the basis of ethnic pride: children were exhorted not to fail or misbehave, lest they reflect negatively on the entire group. Parents continually reminded their children of the sacrifices they had made for their education's sake and demanded that the children show their gratitude by making the most of their opportunities.[14]

### The *Nisei* Dilemma

As an American-born and American-educated person with a Japanese face and heritage, the *nisei* was faced with a difficult dilemma. He was caught between the America of his parents' dreams and the realities of the color bar, which denied him real access to American society. His dilemma was incomparably worse than his parents' because he was rejected by his own country. By law, he was an American citizen; he had no sense of belonging to another country. While his parents place their hopes of finding an entry into American society in him, whom they considered an American, he was treated by American society as an undesirable alien. Only the *nisei* knew what they really were—Americans of Japanese descent.

Moreover, despite the fact that the *issei* had encouraged their children's Americanization, even they could not help viewing that Americanization process with mixed emotions, since the schools were gradually educating their children away from them:

They were proud that their offspring took so naturally to a language that they themselves were incapable of mastering. They knew their children must absorb the American culture, must be Americans, to make their way in the land of their birth. But they were also disturbed that the Nisei were ignoring, and in some cases rejecting, their Japanese heritage. The gradual change from Japanese-language-orientation to English-language orientation was evidence of this change; how could one understand Japanese when one could not even speak the language.[15]

One inescapable fact that influenced both *issei* and *nisei* attitudes towards learning English was the fact that it was the langauge of social power in American society, while the Japanese language might even be viewed as a social deficit. Understanding their parents' unspoken feeling that ability to speak English somehow made them superior, and having been educated in American schools, many *nisei* children "acquired the typical attitude that the English language was superior to all other languages." Many *nisei* children resisted their parents' attempts to send them to Japanese language schools. The *nisei* knew that fluent speakers of English had superior economic status, and many concluded that there was no need to speak Japanese, "a language that might classify them with the 'Chinks' and the 'Japs.'"[16]

*Nisei* and *issei* tended to see each other through a haze of broken English and Japanese.

> *Mr. Siegel*: You can talk Japanese with your parents?
>
> *James Sakamoto* (age 17): Simple language—broken English. They have been here quite long, but they have not had the chance to talk English.
>
> *Siegel*: You get along pretty well with them?
>
> *Sakamoto*: Sure, they are my father and mother. . . . Well, I can understand them, but that is about all.
>
> *Siegel*: How can they manage to get along with you if you cannot speak the language well?
>
> *Sakamoto*: They can just about guess what I am trying to say to them.

Knowing that they might appear as ridiculous to their children when speaking broken English as their children appeared to them when trying to speak Japanese, *issei* parents often addressed the children in Japanese, while the *nisei* responded in English. In *Pineapple White* (1972), Jon Shirota portrays the old immigrant father speaking as follows to his white daughter-in-law:

> "Toilet funny kind," he said.
> The girl looked at him.
> "Make sure havo dime when go toilet," he advised.
> The girl blushed.
> He rubbed his eyes again. "Burn like hell."
> "It's smog," she said.
> "Huh?"
> "Air pollution."
> He still did not understand.

Monica Sone describes her discomfort as she listens to her mother's conversation with her American teacher:

> "You seem so young, Mrs. Itoi, you look more like her sister."
> "Yes, I am, thank you." Mother smiled back, more intent on being gracious at the moment than on the subject matter. . . .
> "Did KaZOOko tell you we're having a special program for the May Festival soon?"
> "Oh, yes, it was very nice. I enjoyed the program so much." Mother nodded enthusiastically. I curled inside.
> ". . . My what a wonderful seamstress you are, Mrs. Itoi. And I love that color! It's as lovely as can be."
> "Oh no, it's not so good," Mother said modestly. She could have said "thank you" at this moment, but I was content that Mother was talking about the same thing as Miss Powers. All of a sudden Mother burst out, "It's too red, but my daughter, she likes red. I think it's *lousy!*"
> A tense silence followed. Miss Powers was struggling to keep a straight face. I felt as if I was standing outside a furnace. I managed to tug at Mother's elbow and whisper, "*Kairo*, Mama, let's go home."[17]

Profound communication problems sometimes resulted. According to one *nisei*:

> I feel that I cannot go to my parents for advice when I have a problem to face because there is a language barrier between us and I am unable to make them understand me, neither can they make me understand them. I learned the Japanese language at home but not so that I could speak very fluently. Most of the time I use English at home, but mother cannot use it at all. Because of this difficulty in communication I have to work out my problems myself.[18]

Part of the communication problem stems from ambivalence on the part of the *issei* themselves about whether or not they should have encouraged their children's absolute fluency in Japanese:

> "Odd, isn't it? he mused. "Our own children almost strangers. . . . We sacrifice everything for them. . . , then discover we don't even understand them."
> "We should have taught them more Japanese," she declared.
> "My wife and I tried," he said. "But the moment the boy stepped out of the house he forgot he was Nihon-jin."

"Exactly what happened to my daughter," Aiko-san said, head going down.

"Sure wish I could speak English," he reflected. . . .

"Speak Japanese," she suggested.

"You speak Japanese to your grandchildren?"

"All the time."

"They understand?"

"Sometimes."

"What do they call you?"

"Grandma, most of the time," she said, "Obaa-chan when they want something really bad."[19]

*Issei* parents, meanwhile, commiserated over their children's lack of familiarity with even the most basic tenets of Japanese etiquette, watching with dismay as their broadly smiling children swaggered, arms akimbo, and spoke boisterously. "*Nisei* are not good," they often agreed:

[T]here was a general trend among Issei to brand the younger generation as upstarts. . . .

"Nisei? Bah! This younger generation is bad—no manners, no ability, no spirit, no good," the Issei cried worriedly.

"They're our disgrace," lamented others. "All they look for is good times! Go shows, ride nice cars, take out girls to dances, wear good clothes. . . . [N]othing but pleasures all the time. Nisei are no good!"[20]

By the 1930s, the proportion of young *nisei* was growing, but the *issei* still held the purse strings, established the standards of behavior, planned the routine of community life, and ruled their families. Prevented by race discrimination from finding employment outside the Japanese American community even after graduation from high school and college, *nisei* architecture graduates, for example, found work as valets, import company clerks, or ukelele teachers. According to John Modell, the vast majority of Los Angeles *nisei* were economically dependent on *issei* enterprises as of 1940. The fruitstand had become a bitter symbol of the *nisei*'s dependence on his family and community as well as of the color bar he could not overcome:

I am a fruitstand worker. It is not a very attractive nor distinguished occupation, and most certainly unappealing in print. I would much rather it were doctor or lawyer—but my aspirations of development into such [were] frustrated long ago by circumstances [and] I am only what I am, a professional carrot washer.[21]

Economically dependent as they were on the *issei*-dominated Japanese American subculture and economy, the *nisei* were fully cognizant of the extent to which the *issei* depended upon them as their own stepping stone into American life. Many *issei* had been forced by the Alien Land Laws in California and other states to register their lands in their American-born children's names.[22] *Nisei* status was based at least in part on their legal position as owners of land on which their parents were legally tenants or employees.

By the late 1930s, many *nisei* appeared to be expending most of their energies trying to convince themselves and the American public that despite their physical appearance and their parents they were really Americans. To do that, it became necessary for them to prove as conclusively as possible that they were not at all Japanese:

> The Nisei sought to show that they could indeed be assimilated culturally, and in their zeal many made it a point of [*sic*] rejecting their Japanese heritage, asserting with pride that they spoke no Japanese and knew nothing about Japan. Many years were to pass before Nisei, from a position of security, could take pride in their ancestral culture.[23]

### The Internment Experience

The dilemma of the *nisei* was greatly exacerbated by the internment experience, which forced all Japanese Americans to consider what their racial identity really meant. The *issei* were faced with what they saw as conclusive proof that they would never be accepted into American society. Many *issei* felt that they were to blame for the internment of their American-born children: after all, if they had not been Japanese, perhaps the decision to relocate the entire group might never have been made. The *kibei* raged, reasoning that what they had been taught in Japan had been true after all—that the United States was a racist country to which they owed no allegiance. The *nisei* were likewise torn. Some, outraged by the travesty of the ideals of justice that they had learned about in public schools questioned the existence of democracy in America. Others, anxious to prove their loyalty and worth as American citizens, responded by doing whatever they could to cooperate with the War Relocation Authority, which had been established to supervise the relocation centers.

Scholars and students of American history have conjectured about the reasons for internment as well as about its effects on the Japanese American minority. Some have even argued that the relocation experience had positive effects on the group, providing them with their first real opportunity to prove their loyalty to the United States and forcing dispersal and integration of the population that had previously been impossible.[24] In 1963, Congressman Barrett O'Hara of Illinois marvelled that the Japanese Americans had emerged from internment "without scars or resentment."[25] Recently, Japanese American scholars have pointed out that the forced fragmentation of the Japanese American family and community was a painful price to pay for this dispersal.

Japanese American communities were broken up by the relocation. Family farms and businesses had to be sold, either at the time of removal or during the internment, since internees were usually unable to pay even the taxes on their lands and businesses while they were interned. Even when the camps were closed after the war, most Japanese American families were unable to regain their properties and homes, and were scattered instead across the country as wage laborers. Nor could Japanese language and culture easily survive the experience: on the eve of evacuation, many Japanese Americans burned their kimonos, diaries, Japanese language books, letters, photographs, and even their phonograph records and magazines in a panicked effort to destroy whatever might be construed as evidence of their links to Japan in the minds of their oppressors.[26] Many Japanese language schools were closed, never to be re-opened. Few Japanese Americans wanted to be marked by the cultural identity they felt had made them suspect in the first place.

Family life was also disrupted permanently. Although the internees had been brought together in the camps by their sense of being confronted by the same unfortunate destiny, family members drifted apart in the camp environment. The relocation centers were built in isolated regions, such as deserts, far from towns and major population centers. Each family was assigned a ten-by-twenty-foot "apartment" in a block barrack. These units were crowded and inadequate, and, since privacy was lacking, family members tended to separate, meeting only at meals and at bedtime. Parents felt unable to guide and discipline their children, whom they did not see all day and whom they hesitated to scold within earshot of the neighbors beyond their paper-thin walls. Finally, *nisei* children stopped meeting their parents even at the mess halls, gathering instead with persons of their own age group. Made tense and anxious by their insecure situation and their uncertainty about their futures, internees fought with each other over food and scrap lumber. Persons settled in a particular camp were sometimes hostile and wary towards newcomers. Wild rumors about camp authorities stealing supplies and food or about authorities' plans to exterminate the group spread from one end of each camp to the other. Tensions were worsened by the external structures imposed on the camps by the War Relocation Authority, which encouraged inmates to inform on each other in the name of patriotism.[27]

The War Relocation Authority established governing bodies within the camps that reversed the traditional Japanese community structure and pattern of leadership. Since *issei* were classified as enemy aliens and *kibei* were systematically singled out as suspect and arrested whenever there was a disturbance,[28] *nisei* were chosen as the only persons eligible to be representatives from each block to the community councils. All representatives had to be U.S. citizens and had to speak fluent English. Although the councils had little power, the WRA encouraged *nisei* representatives to inform on the *issei* and the *kibei*. Rifts between the *nisei* and their *issei* parents or *kibei* brothers were the inevitable result of these policies.

Some *issei* and *kibei* argued that the camp authorities hated all Japanese and were horrified when *nisei* members of the Japanese American Citizens League volunteered to serve as an official link to the FBI and Naval Intelligence offices or to aid camp authorities in searching for contraband in the barracks. These searches were particularly enraging to many of the immigrants, who, having been deprived of their freedom and livelihood, found it difficult to endure the destruction and confiscation of their personal belongings just because they were Japanese goods.[29]

Probably the group most adversely affected by internment were the *issei* men, who felt useless and frustrated, particularly as their wives and children lost confidence in them: "The men looked as if they had suddenly aged ten years. They lost the capacity to plan for their own futures, let alone those of their sons and daughters." According to Harry Kitano, by the end of three years' imprisonment, formerly enterprising, energetic *issei* men had become obsessed with feelings of hopelessness, insecurity, and inertia. Charles Kikuchi notes that his father spent all day simply lying on his cot.[30] The average *issei* man was fifty-five years old at the time of internment. His means of livelihood had been cut off indefinitely, and many *issei* fathers became despondent over the thought that they had lost everything they had worked for in America and were now too old to start over. They were painfully cognizant of the fact that they could not protect their families, who were no longer dependent upon them. Until the internment, they had reigned unchallenged as the supreme authorities in family and community life. Now they were as much wards of the U.S. government as their wives and children were, and it was the government, not the *issei* father, who put food on the table and organized the children's lives.

What made matters worse was that the *nisei* youths and young adults could earn higher wages than their fathers in the same camps, since the WRA salary scales, which ranged from twelve to nineteen dollars a month, and job categories, which included teaching and medicine as well as menial labor, were based on ability to speak English and on citizenship status. Older *nisei* who had been trained as dentists or teachers found work in their professions for the first time behind barbed wire. Younger *nisei* could be class presidents, yearbook editors, and pompon girls; for the first time in their lives, they were able to participate in school life as student leaders. They practiced baseball and baton twirling and attended camp high school dances, much to the chagrin of their conservative parents. They were offered such recreation programs as camp-sponsored Hollywood films about American heroes fighting "Japs" in the Pacific. These activities tended to draw the *nisei* ever further away from their parents.

The community was torn apart by the administration of the "loyalty questionnaire" by the camp authorities in 1944. The two most controversial questions asked were whether or not the internee would be willing to serve in the American armed forces and whether or not he or she would forswear his allegiance to Japan and pledge his loyalty to the United States. The questionnaire itself was ambiguous: it had been intended as a means of segregating "loyal" from "disloyal" internees, but it was called "Application for Leave of Clearance." Explanations of how the results of the survey would be used were vague. Many families feared that some members would be released while others would still be held, or that some would be sent to other camps and that their families would remain separated indefinitely. *Issei* parents sometimes pressed their children to answer the questions as they did so that the families would not be separated. Many *issei* feared that since they were not permitted to become American citizens, to answer "yes" would leave them stateless. Moreover, if they replied that they would forswear allegiance to Japan, it might be concluded that they had been saboteurs in the past. For many *issei*, furthermore, loyalty to Japan did not preclude loyalty to the United States; to forswear loyalty to Japan meant to have never been Japanese, an impossible denial of one's roots and culture. Despite the many ambiguities of the loyalty registration questionnaire, however, the vast majority of internees, both *issei* and *nisei*, answered "yes" to both questions.

To the horror and chagrin of *issei* parents, many of whom believed that the U.S. government intended to confiscate permanently their means of livelihood, render them stateless, and then exterminate their sons on the battlefield by using them as buffers for white soldiers, many *nisei* responded to the U.S. Army's call for recruits into a segregated *nisei* combat unit as an opportunity to prove their patriotism in blood. *Issei* parents begged their children not to volunteer, but the U.S. government had ruled that any attempt to prevent men from joining the armed forces was an act of treason. A number of *nisei* left secretly without their parents' permission.

By 1944, one-third of the *nisei* from the camps had left to join the army, take jobs, or attend schools outside the relocation centers. The demoralized elderly came to regard the camps as an asylum in a hostile society, and tight-knit groups of *kibei* calling for repatriation to Japan harassed and threatened those who were not pro-Japan at the segregated "disloyals" camp at Tule Lake. By the end of the war, only a small core of older *issei* and young children were left in the camps, standing patiently in the mess hall lines, since mealtime had become the center of their camp lives. According to one *nisei*: "Everytime I see these oldsters with re-signed, peaceful expressions meekly eating what is offered them, I feel my eyes become warm."[31]

What were the lasting effects of internment? The *issei* faded away, superseded by youthful and inexperienced *nisei* who had no interest in living the way they had in the past. Japanese communities were dislo-cated, and scars on the relationships among individuals and groups in the community were deep. According to *nisei* playwright Wakako Yamauchi, third generation Japanese Americans, or *sansei*, have accused the *nisei* of not wanting to talk about the evacuation experience. *Nisei* silence, she contends, stems partly from the fact that many *nisei* were "overwhelmed by a current of events we could neither understand nor stem" and partly from an attitude of "self-defense," since perhaps "deep inside something tells us we could have been braver, or stronger, and what has happened is past history and what good does it do to bring back those events that might prove that we could have, should have, behaved more courageously."[32]

## Japanese American Experience in Japanese American Literature

Traditionally, Japanese from all levels of society expressed them-selves in *tanka*, *haiku*, or *senryu*, formally structured poetic forms orga-nized according to the number of syllables within a certain number of lines. Japanese language newspapers in America actively solicited poems commemorating particular community events, sometimes even tragic accidents or deaths, from among the *issei* immigrant readers. Partly because many of the Japanese language diaries and journals kept by the immigrants were destroyed on the eve of the war by families fearful that these artifacts might bring into further question their loyalty to the United States, relatively few literary records of the immigrant experience remain. Those poems that have been preserved through the Japanese language newspapers express the varied thoughts and sentiments of the *issei* about their life in America. *Issei* wrote *senryu* that reveal their feelings about the evacuation:

Thirty years
in America
become a dream
(Sasabune)

As one
of the Japanese
I gather my belongings
(Keiho)

I leave behind
not only you,
my California
(Shocho)

Loyalty, disloyalty
if one should ask
I cannot answer
(Toshu)[33]

When she discovered that there were hundreds of Japanese house-wives, gardeners, maids, farmers, and businessmen all across the United States who wrote poetry as a hobby, Lucille M. Nixon worked with Tomoe Tama to collect and translate some of the poems written in poetry circles. These are published in a book titled *Sounds from the Unknown* (1963). Longing for Japan and desire for a place in American society are expressed in many of the verses:

Drying persimmons each year,
My mother waited,
Longingly for me to return.
And now it is three years
Since my mother passed away.
(Kuni Okutara, Honolulu, p. 4)

As many clouds
Rise up around Izumo,
So at Mt. Ranier,
And for fifty years this reminder
Has made my heart ache for my homeland.
(Genji Mihara, Seattle, p. 91)

I am possessed
By this metropolitan phantom,
And have become as familiar
With New York in twenty years
As with a well beloved elderly wife.
(Kisaburo Kinoshima, New York City, p. 90)

Standing in front
Of the officer
At the immigration hearing,
With all my heart wishing to remain here,
I steadily continued my prayers.
      (Kyoko Sakakura, San Francisco, p. 53)

Going steadily to study English,
Even through the rain at night,
   I thus attain,
   Late in life,
American citizenship.
      (Kyoko Nieda, San Leandro, California, p. 49)[34]

Kazuo Ito included translations of Japanese immigrants' poetry in *Issei: A History of Japanese Immigrants in North America*, which was translated in 1973:

Used to loneliness
I celebrate a New Year's
Alone in a far land.
      (Hideko, p. 762)

These faithful flowers—
My tenderest sentiment
Goes to them always.
Like my life in this strange land,
They bloom in spite of trampling.
      (Katsuko Hirata, p. 695)

Still unaccustomed
To the language of this land,
I often guess wrong.
      (Hosui, p. 619)

When did I decide?
(Now, I cannot remember.)
But here I returned,
To the soil of this wide land,
To bring up all my children.
      (Takeko Ujimoto, p. 695)

Gold carp from Japan
Carried all the way abroad
To Canada, and here
In this new world of water.
(Toyoshi Hiramatsu, p. 724)

The *issei* attitude towards the *nisei* generation is revealed in the following lines:

Lives of devotion.
Issei laid the cornerstones
And built foundations
Upon which the Nisei now
Live and prosper.
(Kimiko Ono, p. 892)

All those Issei hopes
Now fulfilled in succession
By Nisei and Sansei.
(Ichiyo, p. 762)

I'm writing letters
To my children in English
It is something like
Scratching at an itchy place
Through your shoes.
(Yukari Tomita, p. 626)[35]

### *Nisei* Writing

A far more detailed and extensive account of the Japanese American experience has come to us through the English-speaking, American-born *nisei* generation, whose writing provides us with insights into the *issei* through their children's eyes as well as into *nisei* thoughts and feelings about what it has meant to be an American-born Japanese.

By 1930, more than half of the quarter of a million Japanese in America were *nisei*, who were more fluent in English than in Japanese. Almost two decades before Pearl Harbor, Japanese American writing in English had already established itself, at first in English language sections of Japanese community newspapers such as *Hokubei Mainichi* and the *Nichibei Times*. *Nisei* addressed each other in letters and essays printed in the *Kashu Mainichi*, and Hisaye Yamamoto wrote essays for special literary supplements in the *Rafu Shimpo* holiday issues. Eventually, *nisei* were writing in their own publications, such as the Japanese American Citizens

League English language newspaper, *Pacific Citizen,* where several of Toshio Mori's short stories were first published. *Nisei*-operated literary magazines, such as *Reimei* and *Leaves,* flourished in the 1930s, containing mostly romantic short stories and sketches of *nisei* life as well as translations of contemporary Japanese literature. During internment, *nisei* organized and wrote for camp journals, newsletters, and literary magazines such as the Poston *Chronicle,* the Topaz *Times, Trek* (Topaz), and *All Aboard* (Topaz). Most of this *nisei* writing never found wide circulation outside what Frank Chin has called their "newsprint ghetto." Toshio Mori recalled "thirty to fifty" aspiring *nisei* writers who are now "lost," having given up their literary efforts in discouragement after the dispersal of the population during the post-war years.[36]

Ironically, it was the segregation of the *nisei* that first encouraged their literary attempts. Among themselves, they did not need to fear being misconstrued according to some distorting stereotype or worry about having to preface each poem, story, or essay with an explanation of who they were, why they were writing in English, or how they differed from prevailing images of Japanese Americans. The existence of a small but concrete, palpable, and known audience of fellow *nisei* gave many writers a feeling of confidence. According to Toshio Mori, although everyone knew that having a work published in the community newspapers or magazines was no special accomplishment, since these papers tended to accept everything, many *nisei* felt encouraged just by seeing their work in print.[37]

Many early *nisei* writers commiserated with one another about the discrimination and intolerance they all felt or debated about the meaning of democracy from their particular vantage point as descendants of Japanese immigrants and as members of a racial minority group. But some of the most important *nisei* fiction has to do with conflicts within the family that were exacerbated by cultural differences between them and their parents and by external pressures exerted on the family and community.

Racial discrimination and Japanese American family and community life had been dialectically related from the start. The confluence of pressures from both sources on the *nisei* is clearly seen in Taro Katayama's "Haru" (1933). The central character is a sensitive young *nisei* girl who, having grown up on an isolated West Coast farm in the most abject poverty, has been "fired by the romantic notions that even the most rural of high schools will instill in the young of every race." Haru rebels inwardly "against the inexorable, stifling realities of her existence," dreaming abstractly of some vaguely beautiful future she secretly knows is impossible. At times, when her dreams fail her, she feels only "a dull and painful emptiness." Haru's parents, desperate to save her from a life of deprivation and themselves from the burden of having to support her indefinitely, are delighted when an unctuous go-between notifies them that a wealthy Japanese potato farmer's *kibei* son is searching for a suitable wife. Three men—Haru's father, the potato farmer, and the go-between—enthusiastically plan the match, never dreaming that Haru might object. Ordinarily pensive and silent, Haru rebels: "It's not fair to me. . . . I won't marry anyone that I don't know anything about . . . and . . . haven't seen. . . . It isn't civilized, it's cruel and savage! . . . They don't do things like that in America." But dread of endless poverty and the terrifying prospect of being left alone when her parents die render Haru's "romantic ideals and notions . . . strange and immeasurably distant," so she acquiesces to a meeting with the young man.[38]

The shrewd and grasping Takahashi proves repulsive in every aspect:

> Young Takahashi loomed before her, large and stout, with a red, broad-nosed face and dull, sensual eyes. She noticed a large mole at the side of his nose and his wide-set teeth, revealed by his somewhat supercilious smile of greeting. . . . She secretly watched young Takahashi eat enormously of everything on the table. She was repelled by his perspiring face, by the working of his powerful jaws, and by his huge, fat hands that reached ponderously for the various dishes.[39]

Revolted by the thought of marriage and intimacy with Takahashi, Haru at first contemplates writing a simple letter of refusal to the go-between, but she knows that he probably does not understand much English and she cannot write in Japanese. The thought of living on under the reproachful eyes of her parents and subject to the "sneers, contempt, and the malicious conjectures" of the Japanese community forces her to consider the marriage. For a moment, she reflects that a *nisei* need not "pay attention to the opinions of the small world to which her parents belonged," but she realizes that she has no other alternatives. Fellow *nisei* live too scattered and distant for her to have had any friends among them, and she had never become close to her American classmates, who avoided her outside the classroom. From her American neighbors, although polite and friendly, she senses "something of pity or condescension in their attitude toward her and her parents." Haru is prevented by color bars from a social or economic life independent of her family and community: "She could do nothing to earn a living in the world beyond the farm. At the thought of walking about in strange places, looking for work and food and shelter, a cold shudder ran through her. . . . She had no escape." Pressed by Japanese family tradition on the one hand and segregation from American life on the other, Haru is presented with only two options: she can commit suicide, or she can marry the man who makes her feel "cold and hollow" within. She finally chooses marriage.[40]

The double tyranny of community traditions and race discrimination is the subject of much *nisei* writing. At times, Japanese values and traditions are depicted as sustaining and valuable, but in the view of many *nisei*, Japanese "virtues" are secondary because they serve primarily to justify and perpetuate both the authoritarian aspects of the community structure and the injustices existing outside the community. Since the tyranny of the *issei*-dominated community is closer at hand, some *nisei* writers concentrated their efforts on exposing what they thought was a mask of hypocrisy and self-deception among the *issei*.

A powerful criticism of authoritarianism and tyranny in the Japanese American community from the *nisei* perspective is found in Milton Murayama's *All I Asking for Is My Body* (1975). The central character is the first-born *nisei* son of sugar plantation workers in Hawaii. Toshio Oyama is seen through the eyes of another *nisei*—the narrator, his younger brother Kiyoshi. The two brothers represent two contrasting but also overlapping *nisei* responses to the problems of the Japanese family system before World War II.

The *issei*, "cut off from the world ever since they left their farming villages in Japan," have transplanted in Hawaii almost intact the feudal Japanese family, which constitutes a rigidly hierarchical pecking order that almost everyone in the Japanese American community supports. The Oyamas live on Pigpen Avenue next to an open sewage ditch, condemned to field labor to repay an enormous inherited debt. Just as the older Oyama sacrificed himself and his family, taking comfort in the belief that he was being filial, he expects his oldest son to accept responsibility for the as yet unpaid debt when his turn comes. Toshio is admonished that he must be a "good filial son"—patient, dutiful, hard-working, and mindful of his obligations to his parents. He is told stories of heroic young *samurai* in old Japan who sacrificed themselves for their parents, who suffered in silence even when falsely accused, and exhibited courage instead of selfishness by adhering to the traditional Japanese virtues of *gaman* (patience), *enryo* (restraint), and *yamato damashii* (Japanese spirit). Toshio, however, challenges the community's blind acceptance of these mores and values, which he contends serve only to justify the imprisonment of the individual within a self-perpetuating and exploitative hierarchy: "Hard work, patience, holding back, waiting your turn, all that crap, they all fit together to keep you down." When reminded that his father slaved for his grandfather's sake and that other first-born sons work willingly for their parents' benefit, Toshio argues that everyone has acquiesced to tyranny by deceiving themselves about the real nature of their situation:

"Every child must repay his parents."

"How much? How long?"

"Your father helped grandfather for twelve years without one word of complaint."

"Grandfather is a thief. . . . You Japanese are really blind! . . . It's there in front of your eyes and you say, it's a lie! You just can't see! You don't see what's out there, you only see what's inside your head. Like grandfather. He asks your money, you say you gave it to him. Even when you begged him to leave you enough to live on for a month. You even gave that to him. Black is white and white is black. Inside your head he's like a god. But by his actions, he's a thief."[41]

It is not only his own family but all the Japanese families in Pepelau who participate in their own oppressions, according to Toshio. Having been themselves squeezed by their own fathers, fathers pass on their oppression to their sons when they rise in the hierarchy:

"Papa, he been do his big thing already, he was a filial number one son, so now he figure his turn to sit back and catch the gravy. I doan think it bother him if we all die on the plantation so long as we filial and give him lotsa face."[42]

The family hierarchy is only a small part of the "system," which is the "bloodsucking bully":

"It's not only papa. Every family like that."

"Thass what I mean. The whole system is upside down. You pay and pay and pay and you never pay enough. And they treat me like *I* was the bad guy. They want me to be a nice guy so they can bury me alive. . . . The more you shut up, the better they look."

"You see the dumb Bulaheads, they like it for their sons to be dumb. They like them to obey. They consider you a better man if you said yes all the time."

"The plantation the same way," I said.

"Yeah, we gotta fight two battles all the time."[43]

Indeed, the fictional company town of Pepelau where the Oyamas live is structured exactly like a pyramid: the plantation boss's house is built on the top of the hill: next are the houses of the Portuguese, Spanish, and *nisei* lunas (plantation foremen). Below these are the identical wood frame houses of Japanese Camp, and at the bottom of the hill are the run-down shacks of Filipino Camp. The toilet pipes and outhouse drainage ditches run downhill to the lower boundary of the camp.

Toshio rants and raves, but in the end he has internalized the values, however oppressive, of the family and community. He must continually express his frustration, as if to convince himself of the validity of his position: "Shit, all I asking for is my body. I doan wanna die on the plantation like those other dumb dodos. Sometimes I get so mad I wanna kill the, you know what I mean? . . . I look like the aggressor . . . but I not. I fighting for my life."[44] He continues working for his parents. He tries to become a professional boxer, hoping to get out of plantation life and bring in a money prize for his family at the same time. Finally, he marries and begins to settle down to a life not patterned much differently from his parents'.

Ostensibly, Toshio has been the rebel risk-taker, the complainer filled with fury against whatever threatens his self-determination. Kiyoshi has been the conformist, the peacemaker, always trying to apologize for his parents and mollify his irascible older brother at the same time. In the end, however, it is Kiyoshi who pays off the family debt, through a sheer stroke of luck, and it is Kiyoshi who opts for his own freedom and moves away from Pepelau. He has been inspired by his older brother's struggles and moved by the words of one haole teacher Toshio suspects of being a "commie or a queer," since "nice haoles are always after something else." The teacher has been important to Kiyoshi:

> The others ignored your questions or what they saw out there, or tried to make you see only the things they wanted you to see. He talked of freedom, while everybody else talked of duty and obligation. It was like we were born in a cage and Snooky was coaxing us to fly off, not run away, but be on our own and taste the freedom and danger of the open space. . . . Snooky gave me a glimpse of what it could be. I would have to get out and be on my own even if the old man was successful and he was doing me favors, even if the plantation made me its highest *luna*. Freedom was freedom from other people's shit, and shit was shit no matter how lovingly it was dished, how high or low it came from.[45]

The catalyst for Kiyoshi's escape from the imprisoning confines of the "icky shit-hole" of his community is the Japanese attack on Pearl Harbor, which rips the mask from the face of the entire Japanese American community. It causes Kiyoshi to ponder the suppression of individual freedom in the name of collective identity that he had traditionally accepted:

> It just didn't make sense, I kept thinking. Here they worried you to death, made you a nervous wreck, don't do this, don't do that, don't do anything that'd bring shame to the Japanese race, don't be a

rotten apple and spoil the whole barrel. What chance have I got, me, a single apple getting slammed by a barrel full of rottenness? Even if I tried deliberately, every day of my life, I wouldn't be able to produce one-thousandth of the massive shame of Pearl Harbor.

Kiyoshi seeks out his Japanese language teacher in a desperate effort to reconcile what he has been taught with the shame he feels because of Pearl Harbor, which he feels "was like watching your older brother whom you believed in and loved now running wild committing murders":

"You know, you've always said, 'Be proud you're Japanese.' 'Never bring shame to the Japanese race.' What if they, all of them, bring shame to me? What about me? I feel ashamed I'm Japanese. I feel a shame I can never erase, and here I haven't done a single bad thing."

The teacher has no satisfactory answers, and Kiyoshi concludes that he must never again subordinate his individual identity to that of any group, for in the end, despite all the individual's effort in support of the group, the group might destroy him, as Japan's actions threatened to destroy Kiyoshi. Kiyoshi concludes that the commitment to "face," which has been exacted by his family and community, must be relinquished, because to save face means to pretend and hide so much that "you ended up covering for those above you, even defending their wrongs as rights," within the family, within the community, within the plantation system, and even with regard to Japan.[46]

Kiyoshi's revelations precipitate his decision to leave Pepelau to join the army, where he can "earn the right to complain and participate, . . . a right to the future." Indeed his decision is fortuitous, since on his first night away from home he wins enough at craps to pay off the family debt. This winning constitutes for him his "bail money out of this prison of filial piety and family unity."[47]

*All I Asking for Is My Body* is a rejection of the oppressive aspects of the Japanese family system and the plantation system that nurtured it, in favor of the freedom of the individual. Unquestioning adherence to inherited conventions is condemned as hypocritical self-service parading as virtue. There is little of value in the Japanese family or community in *All I Asking for Is My Body*, except perhaps for the relationship between the two *nisei* brothers, who complement each other and whose ideas and identities are developed during their dialogues. But even as an advocate of self-determination and human freedom, Toshio is not without his faults: at times he is stridently self-righteous and pigheaded. By contrast, his more conventional and sensitive younger brother's sympathy shifts across the generations between his parents and his brother.

As if in anticipation of being criticized for a negative depiction of the Japanese American family and community, Murayama has written:

When you're dealing with two conflicting cultures, you face a problem. Are you going to be pro-one, pro-the-other, or impartial. If impartial, how? What I worked out was simple: I will use the same yardstick of honesty for both, I will criticize the Japanese family system with the same candor I criticize the plantation system. But what about the priority of values? What is number one? Here again the key was simple: Whatever promotes freedom is good, whatever suppresses it is not good. . . . Freedom was freeing oneself from group loyalties and collective myths and stereotypes. Freedom was finally freedom of mind.

Murayama has said that he wanted to "expose an authoritarian system from inside, from underneath," "to set the record straight" even if the picture presented was not attractive: "I want this history remembered, not lost—like it is, with love, with all the warts showing."[48]

### The Internment Experience

The cathartic effect on the Japanese American minority of the war between Japan and the United States is reflected in almost all *nisei* writing. Certainly no other single event had more profound and far-reaching impact on each individual and on the community of which they were all part. In *All I Asking for Is My Body*, Kiyoshi observed that at the time of Pearl Harbor he felt "[e]verything was exploding in the rest of the world while we were like some prehistoric monster frozen in ice." For the most part, the Japanese American response both in Hawaii and on the mainland to the bombing of Pearl Harbor is depicted in *nisei* writing as horrified disbelief followed by shame. In Shelley Ota's *Upon Their Shoulders* (1951), the *issei* and *nisei* alike condemn the Japanese attack as "ridiculous . . . braggadocio":

"The *baka*," he said under his breath. . . . "Do you know what this makes us! . . . Enemy aliens!" . . . Over and over the words ran in his mind. He bit his lips—he who had prided himself on being an American. . . . [H]e would be classed with those plotting fiends who had planned this attack. He was defeated. He saw himself imprisoned for the duration of the war, . . . his property confiscated, . . . all the years of work destroyed—years working toward a dream of personal and economic freedom. Like a child he wept, his tears running down his pale cheeks.[49]

Regarded by many Americans as foreigners, *nisei* responded by feeling somehow personally responsible for Japanese military actions.

Hisaye Yamamoto recalls as a child "feeling that I was somehow responsible when the subject was brought up in class, esepcially when the
teacher-principle assigned a composition on the topic, 'What will I do if
war breaks out between the United States and Japan.'" In Toshio Mori's
"The Slant-Eyed Americans," the *nisei* are filled with shame upon hearing the news of Pearl Harbor on the radio: "Sometimes I feel all right. You
are an American, I tell myself. Devote your energy and life to the American way of life. . . . Then I got sick again thinking that Japan was the
country that attacked the United States. I wanted to bury myself for
shame." Upon hearing Roosevelt's declaration of war, Monica Sone, like
many other *nisei*, "writhed involuntarily."[50]

Because few Japanese Americans could escape from the implications of the war and the internment of the mainland Japanese Americans,
many works of Japanese American literature are linked to the internment
experience. Several of Toshio Mori's stories take place at Topaz. Hisaye
Yamamoto's "The Legend of Miss Sasagawara" is set in Poston. Sections
of Monica Sone's *Nisei Daughter* are devoted to camp life. Contemporary
writers like Jeanne Wakatsuki Houston, Janice Mirikitani, Momoko Iko,
Lonnie Kaneko, Lawson Inada, and James Mitsui, themselves too young
at the time of incarceration to recall the experience clearly, have reconstructed it in stories, plays, novels, and poems set in the camps or have
investigated its significance from a contemporary vantage point.

Unquestionably, internment propelled to crisis dimensions the conflicts and tensions already existing in the Japanese American family and
community. But no Japanese American literary work depicts the frag-
menting effects of internment on the family and community more vividly
or poignantly than John Okada's *No-No Boy* (1957).[51] The novel is set in
Seattle just after the end of the war, when the disfiguring effects of the
internment and the racial hysteria that made it possible were discernible
in Japanese American communities all along the West Coast. Like *All I
Asking for Is My Body*, *No-No Boy* is about the *nisei*'s rebellion against the
*issei* generation, about the *nisei*'s desire for an identity separate from his
parents'. Clearly, the *nisei*'s rejection of his parents is linked to his
desperate desire for acceptance in American society, which the *nisei*
believes is made impossible by his Japanese heritage. The *nisei*'s unfulfilled longing to participate in American society causes the fragmentation
and disfiguration of both his family and his community.

*No-No Boy* is replete with contradictions and unanswered questions:
whether the self-deluded *issei* who are still waiting for a final Japanese
victory are fanatical fools or the hopeless victims of a racist society in
search of temporary comfort; whether the *nisei* veterans who fought in
the American army are brave and heroic, or self-hating martyrs; whether
the Japanese American community is a comforting haven or destructive
to the individual Japanese American. The question that underlies all the

others is whether America is in fact the desirable land of democracy and freedom or a racist, predatory society.

The *nisei* of John Okada's novel are driven almost to self-destruction by their desperate desire to belong in America. In the *nisei* world, there is hardly a sacrifice too great for the prize of acceptance. War veteran Kenji loses his leg and eventually his life, while the people of the community think of him as an enviable hero. Ichiro's "mistake," the mistake of refusing the draft, is serious enough for him to be totally ostracized by the community. Another "no-no boy," Freddie, is killed by someone whose hatred of him makes him feel important among his peers. Brothers betray brothers, children turn against their parents, who become alcoholic or commit suicide; husbands desert wives, and wives commit adultery. The community is torn apart by the almost hysterical desire of its members to be accepted as genuine Americans, no matter what the cost.

Like the world of *Eat a Bowl of Tea* and *All I Asking for Is My Body*, Okada's community has been sustained by self-deception that must now come to an end. Like Ben Loy and Mei Oi, like Tosh and Kiyo, Ichiro has been deceived. His mother's fanatical loyalty to Japan has led him to imprisonment for refusing the draft and then to the hatred of his fellow *nisei*, who are themselves desperate to prove their loyalty through their collective reputation. Ichiro's mother's fanaticism culminates, after her stubborn refusal to admit Japan's defeat, in her insanity and eventual suicide.

Ichiro's mother, "dried and toughened" through the many years of hardship in America, is unable to "accept a country which repeatedly refused to accept her or her sons" and turns all her hopes toward Japan. She walks twenty-six blocks to save 35 cents on ten loaves of day-old bread from a bread factory, saving her pennies for what she dreams will be her eventual triumphant return to Japan. Ashida-san works the night shift at a hotel, "grinning and bowing for dimes and quarters from rich Americans who he detested, and couldn't afford to take his family on a bus," but always comforted by the thought of ships on their way to conquer America. Although Ichiro understands that these *issei* are the victims, not the originators, of the hatred that destroys their rationality, he cannot forgive them, because they have allowed their stubbornness and weakness to make them irrational and resistant to truth or change. He blames them for refusing to face the fact that they were never going to return to Japan, that their real future was in America. Even though "growing families and growing bills and misfortunes and illness and low wages and just plain hard luck were constant obstacles to the realization of their dreams," they should have tried to learn English, to integrate themselves into white society, to buy homes and make long-term commitments to an American future. They should have "exchanged hope for reality" and reconciled themselves, instead of clinging to illusions and rationalizations. But what makes Ichiro bitterest is that the *issei*'s inability to face reality is passed on to their children.[52]

When his mother dies, Ichiro feels no regret. He has suspected her of an "incurable strain of insanity," which he hints might be a "Japanese" insanity that might spread through the family to him. The affliction is "Japanese" to the extent that it revolves around loyalty to Japan and reminds Ichiro of Japanese fascism and militarism. Just as many *issei* are susceptible to false hopes and illusions, many *nisei* are also weak and vulnerable. Ichiro asks himself:

> Was it she [Ichiro's mother] who was wrong and crazy not to have found in herself the capacity to accept a country which repeatedly refused to accept her or her sons . . . or was it the others who were being deluded, the ones . . . who believed and fought and even gave their lives to protect this country where they could still not rate as first-class citizens because of the unseen walls?[53]

While some *issei* are subject to unrealistic hopes of being saved by Japanese ships from humiliation and drudgery, many *nisei* are afflicted by stifling, narrow-minded thoughtlessness caused by their feelings of inferiority and insecurity. Ichiro's mother is a "rock of hatred," whose "curse" has sent him into prison and shame, but his former friend, a *nisei*, spits on him for being a "no-no boy" and the other *nisei* assume the roles of moral judges on his deviant actions. Their desperation to prove themselves as Americans drives them to idolize and accept those who wear war wounds as proof of their loyalty and despise those who refused the draft. Ichiro feels forced to escape from the diner and the tortured young *nisei* working there who "had to wear a discharge button on his shirt to prove to everyone who came in that he was a top-flight American."[54]

Because of their desperation to be "Americans," hatred of "no-no boys" is prevalent among the *nisei*. Bull threatens Ichiro and Freddie at a night club just to win approval from the crowd. Emi's husband re-enlists in the army because his brother had refused the draft and he feels he must prove his own loyalty again and again. Even Ichiro's younger brother, Taro, betrays Ichiro by leading him into an ambush so that Taro can win acceptance from his peers.

The fragmented and warped Japanese American community in *No-No Boy* almost disintegrates during the course of the novel. Ichiro himself is characterized as incomplete and fragmented. He and his brother Taro are two halves of the same person, joined by a common weakness. Ichiro thinks he refused to join the army because he was too cowardly or too unimaginative to go against his mother's wishes. Taro joins the army and betrays his brother because he too is cowardly. Taro rejects Ichiro because he hates "that thing in his elder brother which had prevented him from thinking for himself," and yet Taro is also unable to think for himself. According to Ichiro, what differentiates the two brothers is only time and circumstance:

> Taro, my brother who is not my brother, you are no better than I. You are only more fortunate that the war years found you too young to carry a gun. . . . And you are fortunate because the weakness which was mine made the same weakness in you the strength to turn your back on Ma and Pa and makes it so frighteningly urgent for you to get into uniform to prove that you are not a part of me.[55]

Just as Ichiro fears that his mother's insanity has contaminated him, he finds his father's weakness in himself and in his brother. The old man is described as a "fat, grinning, spineless nobody" who is afraid to challenge his wife's delusions even in crisis. In fact, none of the characters in *No-No Boy* can be healthy and complete. Ichiro and Kenji, a returned *nisei* veteran, are also two parts of an incomplete whole. But while Ichiro is despised and outcast from the *nisei* community because he has refused the opportunity to prove his loyalty in battle, Kenji is the veteran whose gangrenous amputated leg serves as an immediate and indisputable sign of his "manliness." The fusion of the two men takes place when Kenji "procures" Emi for Ichiro:

> "She needs you," said Kenji, "No, I should say she needs some-one. Just like you need someone. Just like I need someone some-times. I won't apologize for her because then I'd have to apologize for myself. . . . I'm only half a man, Ichiro, and when my leg starts aching, even that half is no good."
> The hot color rose to his face as he lashed out at Kenji angrily. "So you're sending in a substitute, is that it?"[56]

The interchangeability or the complementary nature of the two men is brought out clearly when they ask each other if they would ever change places: Ichiro, the detested, and Kenji, the dying. In the topsy-turvy world where Japanese American men are required and require each other to risk their lives and their manhood, to sacrifice their families and their wives, to prove their loyalty to America, Ichiro would change places with his dying friend if he could:

> I'll change with you, Kenji, he thought. Give me the stump which gives you the right to hold your head high. Give me the eleven inches which are beginning to hurt again and bring ever closer the fear of approaching death, and give me with it the fullness of yourself which is also yours because you were man enough to wish

the thing which destroyed your leg and, perhaps, you with it but, at the same time, made it so that you can put your one good foot in the dirt of America and know that the wet coolness of it is yours beyond a single doubt.

But Kenji, mutilated and slowly dying, would not change places with Ichiro. The measure of manliness and loyalty becomes all the more ironic and bizarre when it begins to be considered in terms of inches of amputation. As pieces of Kenji's leg are chopped away, as the stump comes closer to his body and his "manhood," the two men wonder how many inches of leg is worth the sacrifice and whose problem is worse:

> "We've both got problems, bigger than most people. That ought to mean something."
> . . . "I was thinking all the time we were silent that I decided that, were it possible, I might very well trade with you."
> "For eleven inches, or for the seven or eight that'll be left after the next time?"
> "Even for two inches. . . ."
> "Mine is bigger than yours in a way, and then again, yours is bigger than mine."[57]

In Ichiro's world, nothing can be complete. Kenji is losing inches of his body little by little. Ichiro describes himself as "half a man" and his mother as a withered, stunted adolescent. The individuals in the Japanese American community described in *No-No Boy* are stunted and incomplete because their options are limited. Faced with a choice between the army and the concentration camp, between America and Japan, between his country and his parents, Ichiro chose prison, saying no to both impossible options, and is outcast for his choice. Kenji is forced to choose between his wife and his country. Taro chooses between his brother and his country. Virtually all the *nisei* in the novel are subjected to a choice between Japan, which represents their race and their parentage as much as it does militarism or fascism, and America, which represents the realities of racial bigotry as well as the dream of democracy. Faced with such choices, individuals felt cut in half, as Ichiro does:

> There was a time when I was your son. . . . Then there came a time when I was only half Japanese because one is not born in America and raised in America and taught in America without becoming partly American. . . . But it is not enough to be American only in the eyes of the law and it is not enough to be only half an American and know that it is an empty half. I am not your son and I am not Japanese and I am not American. I can go someplace and tell people

that I've got an inverted stomach and that I am an American, true and blue and Hail Columbia, but the army wouldn't have me because of the stomach. . . . I wish with all my heart that I were Japanese or that I were American. . . . I do not understand you who were the half of me that is no more and . . . I do not understand what it was about that half that made me destroy the half of me which was American and the half which might have become the whole of me if I had said yes I will go and fight in your army because that is what I believe and want and cherish and love.

Ichiro describes the torment of being torn between desire to belong and knowledge of rejection: "[I]t is not an easy thing to discover that being American is a terribly incomplete thing if one's face is not white and one's parents are Japanese of the country Japan which attacked America. It is like being pulled asunder by a whirling tornado."[58]

Like the characters and community, the America in *No-No Boy* is not yet whole and complete. Kenji notices Japanese discriminating against blacks and concludes that race hatred is eroding the Japanese American community and the world beyond it:

The Negro who was always being mistaken for a white man becomes a white man and he becomes hated by the Negroes with whom he once hated on the same side. And the young Japanese hates the not-so-young Japanese who is more Japanese than himself, and the not-so-young, in turn, hates the old Japanese who is Japanese and, therefore, even more Japanese than he. . . .

And Kenji thought about these things and tried to organize them in his mind so that the pattern could be seen and studied. . . . And there was no answer because there was no pattern and all he could feel was that the world was full of hatred.

What Ichiro detests in his mother is her irrational absolutism, which allows her to equate good and evil with nationality. She gloats over the death of her friend's son, who has joined the American army. To Ichiro, tragedy makes "no distinction as to what was wrong and what was right and who was Japanese and who was not."[59]

Ichiro detests no less the race prejudice that allows the internment of the Japanese Americans because of their nationality alone. He longs to be accepted for "what he is," not as a Japanese or an American or a Japanese American: "If Smith would do the same for Eng and Sato would do the same for Wotynski and Faverghetti would do likewise for whoever happened by. Eng for Eng, Jap for Jap, Pole for Pole, and like for like meant classes and distinctions and hatred and prejudice and wars and misery." Kenji hates the ghetto, hoping that there will be no "Jackson Street wherever I'm going to." He concludes that racism can be ended only when communities are broken up and scattered and distinct national and racial groups can no longer be identified. He advises Ichiro to leave the Japanese American community and try to find anonymity somewhere far away: "Marry a white girl or a Negro or an Italian or even a Chinese. Anything but a Japanese. After a few generations, you've got the thing beat." But Ichiro wants to belong to the *nisei* community and to be a part of America at the same time. Before the war, poverty and segregation had been tolerable to him because at least his peers faced similar problems. What obsesses him now is that he might have forfeited his chance to move with other *nisei*, his chance to attain the American dream that had become possible for the *nisei* who had volunteered to fight in the U.S. Army. Ichiro is acutely aware of the furniture, rugs, and phonographic equipment in Kenji's family's house, which to him symbolize belonging in America:

> Ichiro looked out at the houses, the big, roomy houses of brick and glass which belonged in magazines and were of that world which was no longer his to dream about. Kenji could still hope. A leg more or less wasn't important when compared with himself, Ichiro who was strong and perfect but only an empty shell. He would have given both legs to change places with Kenji.

Ichiro's desire for material comfort is part of his desire to be acceptable, an average all-American. Ichiro hopes that someday there will be a place for him in America's "vastness and goodness and fairness and plenitude" and that in time he too will "buy a home and love my family and . . . [be] walking down the street holding my son's hand and people will stop and talk with us about the weather and the ball games and the elections," just like in the movies and magazines.[60]

Throughout the novel, Ichiro has hovered between hope and despair, between bitter anger and almost pathetic gratitude for a kind word from a white man. What he finally comes to understand is that the contradictions within himself and within his community also prevail in America. The same America that is abundant, beautiful, and desirable is also an America where racial hatred and injustice flourish. Ichiro realizes that he is not alone after all, not even when he is on the outside looking in, but that almost everyone else is probably on the outside too. Perhaps, he concludes, there is no "in" after all. What had seemed to be individual alienation might be common to all, and it might be causing people to commit acts of hatred towards each other:

[W]hat about the young kid on Burnside who was in the army and found out it wasn't enough so that he has to keep proving to everyone who comes in for a cup of coffee that he was fighting for his country like the button on his shirt says he did because the army didn't do anything about his face to make him look more American? And what about the poor niggers on Jackson Street who can't find anything better to do than spit on the sidewalk and show me the way to Tokyo? They're on the outside looking in, just like that kid and just like me and just like everybody else I've ever seen or known. . . . Maybe the answer is that there is no in. Maybe the whole damned country is pushing and shoving and screaming to get into someplace that doesn't exist, because they don't know that the outside could be the inside if only they would stop all this pushing and shoving and screaming, and they haven't got enough sense to realize that. . . . And then he thought about Kenji in the hospital and of Emi in bed with a stranger who reminded her of her husband and of his mother waiting for the ship from Japan and there was no answer.[61]

Ichiro's final affirmation comes when he understands the connections between himself and other human beings. He has felt totally alone and ostracized as a "no-no boy," misunderstood and hated by everyone. His search has been a search for wholeness, for completion and connections. The connection emerges as compassionate love that has the potential to combat the damage done to America's potential, to the *issei*, to the diseased *nisei* community. This love is a "good sharp knife" that cuts out the tumors. Ichiro's painful compassion for and understanding of the fellow *nisei* who hate him because they are also on the outside looking in even helps him understand the *issei* he once hated and resented.

In a transparent bid for attention and approval from his peers, Bull causes a "no-no boy" to die in an accident. Ichiro is overcome by compassion for his friend's killer when he looks into his "frightened, lonely eyes" peering through a film of tears and begging for solace. Ichiro and his friend's killer are together in sorrow and struggle, victimized by racism and the feelings of inferiority that drive them to make terrible and self-destructive mistakes. He decides that he should not "disappear," should not leave his community, his roots, and his past:

A man does not start totally anew because he is already old by virtue of having lived and laughed and cried for twenty or thirty or fifty years and there is no way to destroy them without destroying life itself. That he understood. He also understood that the past had been shared with a mother and father and, whatever they were, he too was a part of them and they a part of him and one did not say this is as far as we go together, I am stepping out of your lives, without rendering himself only part of a man. If he was to find his way back to that point of wholeness and belonging, he must do so in the place where he had begun to lose it.

*No-No Boy* ends with the hope that the America in Ichiro's heart will one day become a reality: "He walked along, thinking, searching, thinking and probing and, in the darkness of the alley of the community that was a tiny bit of America, he chased that faint and elusive insinuation of promise as it continued to take shape in mind and in heart."[62]

*No-No Boy* was not welcomed by the American public, much less by the Japanese American community, at the time it was first published. According to Charles Tuttle, the Japan-based publishers: "At the time we published it, the very people whom we thought would be enthusiastic about it, mainly the Japanese-American community in the U.S., were not only disinterested but actually rejected the book."[63] No doubt the Japanese American community was protecting itself from being revealed in such an unflattering light, even a decade after internment. The Japanese Americans in *No-No Boy* are not the patient, law-abiding, hard-working, docile model minority: they are tormented, uncertain, and incapacitated by self-hatred. The community described in the novel has been violently distorted by racism. Nor is American society portrayed in a very favorable light. What is desirable does not yet exist.

Most of Okada's characters are not fully developed. The fragmentation and disintegrating influence of American racism on the Japanese American community and its members are depicted through the incompleteness of each individual character: Ichiro is filled out by Kenji, Taro, Freddie, and Bull. *No-No Boy* explores creatively the effects of racism on the Japanese American community and on the individual Japanese American psyche. It is an important book not only because it is a pioneer effort but also because it is a moving and contemporaneous expression told by an insider of an experience heretofore largely ignored in American culture.

### Community Portraits

Some *nisei* writing focuses on the conflicts between the immigrant and American-born Japanese, potentially growth-producing conflicts rendered debilitating and noxious by the context of race hatred and oppression. But not all *nisei* writers have seen the relationship between the generations as an adversary one. And some who created portraits of the Japanese American community emphasized the way people lived and interacted in a variety of settings and situations without ever addressing the problems of race prejudice directly. Indeed, such a view represents in a more balanced and authentic way the total life of the community, particularly prior to internment: although the *nisei* might have raged against discrimination, they had other concerns as well, and although everyone was affected by prejudice and discrimination, they were also preoccupied with their economic and social lives, the relationships between parents and children and between men and women, their friendships and their urges towards freedom and creativity. These concerns were not completely determined by external forces. Without a doubt, life in the Japanese American community was not always satisfactory, but community life had its strengths as well. What Hisaye Yamamoto writes about Toshio Mori's stories might also have been said about her own:

And what of the prejudice that all of us have borne the brunt of, to some degree or the other? . . . [I]t is the white who is marginal, only incidentally mentioned if he impinges on our daily lives, but in some of these pieces, we are made aware that he has been out there all the time, writing the rules of the game. Anti-Japanese discrimination in California is a fact of life which Toshio has accepted and taken in stride long since; within the shelter of the Japanese community, dignity has been possible.[64]

### Hisaye Yamamoto: A Woman's View

Hisaye Yamamoto has chronicled Japanese American social history in her short stories.[65] In "The Brown House" (1951), "Seventeen Syllables" (1949), and "Yoneko's Earthquake" (1951), we are introduced to Japanese American rural life, *issei-nisei* relationships, Japanese American attitudes towards Filipinos, Chinese, Mexicans, and Blacks, and the position of *issei* women in the community. "Las Vegas Charley" (1961) traces the life of an *issei* widower from Japan to the California farms to the internment camps to Las Vegas, where he works as a dishwasher and gambles his wages away until he dies. In "The Legend of Miss Sasagawara" (1950), Yamamoto records part of the Japanese American internment experience. The story is set in a desert camp. We catch glimpses of how families lived and interacted as well as of how internment affected their behavior. The bizarre actions and appearance of Miss Sasagawara, a social deviant in the Japanese American community, is seized upon by her fellow inmates, who use her to help relieve their tension, boredom, and sense of insecurity.

When asked about her motivation to write, Yamamoto has said:

I guess I write (aside from compulsion) to reaffirm certain basic truths which seem to get lost in the shuffle from generation to generation, so that we seem destined to go on making the same mistakes over and over again. If the reader is entertained, wonderful. If he learns something, that's a bonus.[66]

Most of Yamamoto's stories have something to say about the relationship between the *issei* and *nisei* generations, who are brought together in stories essentially addressed to fellow *nisei* almost as a warning to them not to lose the experiences of their parents, which they (and she) can only partially understand. This warning is never made at the expense of the *issei*. Neither are the *nisei* blamed for failing to understand completely. Generally, the stories are told from the viewpoint of a *nisei* narrator who sees the *issei* as through a glass darkly, without ever fully comprehending the feelings and actions of the older persons. The understanding is incomplete partly because of communication difficulties, but also because of the self-absorption of the *nisei*, who are intent upon conquering other worlds. Yamamoto demonstrates the impossibility of anyone's ever fully understanding the motivations and experiences of others, but she is not pessimistic. What the *issei* have lived through is in danger of being lost to their children, but if the *nisei* make a conscious effort to learn from what the *issei* have experienced, the *nisei* may also learn to understand themselves.

In "The Brown House," the imperfect communication and cultural differences between *issei* and *nisei* is seen in the interchange between the immigrant and his American-bred teenage nephew:

This nephew, who was about seventeen at the time, had started smoking cigars when he was thirteen. He liked to wear his amorphous hat on the back of his head, exposing a coiffure neatly parted in the middle which looked less like hair than like a painted wig, so unstintingly applied was the pomade which held it together. He kept his hands in his pockets, straddled the ground, and let his cigarette dangle to one side of his mouth as he said to Mr. Hattori, "Your wife's taken a powder."

The world actually turned black for an instant for Mr. Hattori as he searched giddily in his mind for another possible interpretation of this announcement. "Poison?" he queried, a tremor in his knees.

The nephew cackled with restraint, "Nope, you dope," he said. "That mean's she's leaving your bed and board."

"Talk Japanese," Mr. Hattori ordered, "and quit trying to be so smart!"

Abashed, the nephew took his hands out of his pockets and assisted his meager Japanese with nervous gestures. . . .

"Tell her to go jump in the lake," Mr. Hattori said in English, and in Japanese, "Tell her if she wants the boys, to come back and make a home for them."[67]

The humor in the passage is not derived from Hattori's inability to speak colloquial English but from the role reversal later in the passage. The *nisei* who cackled "nope, you dope," is transformed into a bumbling fool whose broken Japanese needs to be assisted by "nervous gestures." Hattori gives a final flourish to the conversation with a quip of his own in American slang. Both the *nisei* and the *issei* know what it is to have two different identities based on two different language abilities.

The language gap between first- and second-generation Japanese Americans is only one sign of the differences in cultural orientation, whether slight or vast, that impede mutual understanding. Yamamoto portrays the situation with succinct humor in "Seventeen Syllables," when Rosie's mother tries to read her *haiku*:

"Yes, yes, I understand. How utterly lovely," Rosie said, and her mother, either satisfied or seeing through the deception and resigned, went back to composing.

The truth was that Rosie was lazy; English lay ready on the tongue but Japanese had to be searched for and examined and even then put forth tentatively (probably to meet with laughter). It was so much easier to say yes, yes, even when one meant no, no. Besides, this was what was in her mind to say: I was looking through one of your magazines from Japan last night, Mother, and towards the back I found some *haiku* in English that delighted me. There was one that made me giggle off and on until I fell asleep:

It is morning and lo
I lie awake, comme il faut
sighing for some dough.

Now, how to reach her mother, how to communicate the melancholy song? Rosie knew formal Japanese by fits and starts, her mother had even less English, no French. It was much more possible to say yes, yes.[68]

The juxtaposition of *issei* and *nisei* provides the basis for much of the subtle humor in Yamamoto's stories, a gentle humor that is never derived at the expense of either generation. In "Las Vegas Charley," Noriyuki and Alice telephone their old *issei* father long distance every month to find out whether he is "still alive and kicking." The five *nisei* girls in "Seventeen Syllables" are busy swallowing peach slices without chewing them while their parents are visiting politely in the living room. And, in the same story, Rosie decides to sneak off to the fields to meet Jesus, the Chicano farmhand, while she is bowing her aunt and uncle welcome. In "The Legend of Miss Sasagawara," the internment camp Christmas party is a "gay, if odd celebration." The first performance is by an old *issei*, who delivers a speech in an exaggerated Hiroshima dialect. In the next, a young *nisei* imitates Frank Sinatra while the girls in the audience scream and pretend to faint. Then the *issei* sings old Japanese songs and perform the *dojo-suki*, a Japanese comic folk dance, while the *nisei* sing quartets or do hula dances, wearing grass skirts and brassieres. Besides humorous contrast, the juxtaposition of the *nisei* narrator's observations of the *issei* performances gives poignance to the imperfectness of her perceptions: she knows less than the readers about what is really going on in the lives of the elders.[69]

Superficially, everything seems as "normal" and wholesome as it seems to the innocent narrator. But beneath the surface are violent undercurrents, situations fraught with dangers and potential sorrows of which the narrator is only vaguely aware. The reader has premonitions that eventually the callow *nisei* will come to know those sorrows first-hand.

Yamamoto's stories are consummately women's stories. What accomplished Asian American male writers like Louis Chu, John Okada, and Carlos Bulosan could only imagine, Yamamoto presents fully. "Yoneko's Earthquake" and "Seventeen Syllables" are stories of *issei* mothers told through the oblique visions of their *nisei* daughters. In the former, the violence and tragedy of the mother's experience and the daughter's ingenuousness and self-absorption are sharply contrasted. In the course of the story, the mother falls in love with the hired man, conceives a child by him, gets an abortion, and loses the lover. Her youngest child dies suddenly, and she is condemned to a life of toil beside a husband rendered impotent during an earthquake. We know, as Yoneko does not, that her mother's life is scarred by heartaches and toil. Yoneko does not understand, as the reader does, the significance of the ring, the earthquake, or the sudden departure of Marpo, the Filipino farmhand. Yoneko understands these events only in relation to her own superstition and decision to become a "freethinker."

Yoneko has a little girl's "crush" on Marpo, whose colorful presence on the farm brings excitement to farm life for her. From Marpo, Yoneko learns about Jesus, Heaven, and Hell. She adorns her beliefs with "additional color to round out her mental images" in the way childish imaginations comfortably integrate the literal with the abstract. She wants to know:

[Who] was God's favorite movie star? . . . and did Marpo suppose that God's sense of humor would have appreciated the delicious chant she had learned from friends at school today:

There ain't no bugs on us,
There ain't no bugs on us,
There may be bugs on the rest of you mugs,
But there ain't no bugs on us?[70]

When God does not answer her call during the earthquake and Marpo leaves the farm unexpectedly, Yoneko stops "believing."

The merging of wish and reality in the child's mind, as well as the child's confusion of anger and guilt, are depicted in "Seventeen Syllables":

> Rosie . . . felt a rush of hate for both, for her mother for begging, for her father for denying her mother. I wish this old Ford would crash, right now, she thought, then immediately no, no, I wish my father would laugh, but it was too late; already the vision had passed through her mind of the green pick-up crumpled in the dark against one of the mighty eucalyptus trees they were just riding past, of the three contorted, bleeding bodies, one of them hers.[71]

The same skill used in portraying a little girl's psychology is brought to the depiction of female adolescence. Rosie notes without much thought that her mother cooks, washes, cleans house, and does the farmwork in the fields by day and then becomes a poetess by night. Her more prosaic father dislikes his wife's hobby and loses his temper when she wins a prize for her *haiku*. She never completely understands why her mother writes poetry or why the father stops her, although we are made to feel that someday she might. Rosie's candid adolescent charm and wholesomeness, especially in her world "so various, so beautiful, so new" with the attentions of an adolescent farmhand, Jesus, are starkly contrasted with the sordid secret her mother burdens her with at the end of the story.

Rosie is half-child, half-woman. She jokes and plays with her friends, but she is confused by the strange emotions awakened when Jesus kisses her. She is both elated and perturbed. In her excitement, she holds imaginary conversations with him in the fields, but she hides from his sight when he actually appears, peering at him from between cracks in the privy walls. Rosie is brought to the threshold of adulthood, frightened and apprehensive, when her mother talks to her as woman to woman. She weeps like the child she is, after recalling how Jesus had touched her like the woman she will become. Her life and her mother's life cross at the moment when the mother makes Rosie promise she will never marry at the very moment she is attracted to a man for the first time.

In both "Yoneko's Earthquake" and "Seventeen Syllables," there is a foreboding sense that the cheerful narrators' worlds will be transformed, eventually, into something not quite "so various, so beautiful, so new." There is a warning that they might inherit the worlds of their mothers, stifled and circumscribed, condemned to lives of drudgery devoid of romance or beauty with only their strength and quiet endurance to keep their spirits alive.

In "The Legend of Miss Sasagawara," the "normal," psychologically healthy young narrator and her friend are in the internment camps, dreaming of finishing college, finding "good jobs," and marrying "two nice, clean young men, preferably handsome, preferably rich, who would cherish us forever and a day." Like Rosie and Yoneko, however, these two girls will eventually face the same realities that confront Mari Sasagawara, who responds to her loveless life by going insane. How the younger girls will respond has something to do with the extent to which they can derive lessons from Mari Sasagawara's experience.

In Yamamoto's stories, men and women both seek ways to transcend their frustration and difficulties. Hattori in "The Brown House" and Matsumoto in "Las Vegas Charley" turn to gambling. In "The Legend of Miss Sasagawara," Reverend Sasagawara seeks escape through spiritual transcendence. The men are afflicted either by weakness or by callousness. In "Yoneko's Earthquake" and "Seventeen Syllables," the husbands are hard-working and serious but unable to tolerate their wives' efforts to create beauty and poetry. They ultimately crush their wives and shackle them to a life of endless toil beside them, not necessarily because they are evil, but because they cannot tolerate independence of any kind in their wives. Yamamoto's women, on the other hand, possess strength that arises from a combination of madness and a thirst for beauty and meaning in their lives. Most of them are unable to resist oppression without losing their spirit and their sanity. In this lies the kernel of the mothers' warning to their daughters.

Something of Yamamoto's attitudes towards women can be seen in a comment she made in a 1953 book review:

> It has been said that women are organically incapable of genius, and with this I agree, since I am unable to think of a single name to squelch the rhetorical question, "Has there ever been a woman philosopher?" (At the same time, I am rather puzzled as to what has been added to the world by all these male geniuses with their intricate and conflicting systems of thought).

In "Seventeen Syllables," the *nisei* narrator is warned by her mother not to let herself be dominated when she grows up. As the woman watches her husband burn the poetry prize she has won, she turns to her daughter:

> Suddenly, her mother knelt on the floor and took her by the wrists. "Rosie," she said urgently, "Promise me you will never marry!"

Shocked more by the request than by the revelation [that her mother had married her father not out of love but out of desperation], Rosie stared at her mother's face. . . . She tried to pull free. Promise, her mother whispered fiercely, promise. Yes, yes, I promise, Rosie said. But for an instant she turned away, and her mother, hearing the familiar glib agreement, released her. Oh, you, you, you, her eyes and twisted mouth said, you fool. Rosie, covering her face, began at last to cry, the embrace and consoling hand came much later than she expected.[72]

There is here a warning to *nisei* to catch the "basic truths" without being trapped by the particulars, which differ from person to person and generation to generation. The mother has been subdued, and the legacy of the mother will be passed on to the daughter. But there is still the chance that the daughter might come to comprehend the meaning of her mother's experience in time to benefit from it.

### Toshio Mori: Nisei Universalist

Yamamoto's "tender regard for Toshio Mori as a person" and her "admiration for his work" are derived in part from the similarities between the two *nisei* writers. They share a certain reverence for the *issei* in general and for the *issei* woman in particular. Both writers are concerned with presenting a balanced portrait of Japanese American community life from inside, a portrait in which the main characters are the *issei* and *nisei* themselves, but both use that portrait-making to make statements that are at once unique and universal, that transcend the particularities of a particular group at a particular point in time.

Toshio Mori had been a voracious reader of popular novels from the age of seven or eight, devouring between five hundred and one thousand library books each year.[73] When he came across the serialized versions of Marquand's *Mr. Moto* and Kyne's *The Pride of Palomar* in the library, he became acutely aware of the prevalent stereotypes of Japanese in American fiction. Because it is generally easier to create and sell caricatures than to present reality consistently, he said, he worried about these stereotypes and felt that there should be genuine portrayals of Japanese American life that would "break down the pre-conceived caricatures."[74] Mori addressed himself to the white reading public in an attempt to explain these realities.

Mori lived all his life in the East Bay Japanese American community, except for his sojourns at Tanforan Assembly Center and at Topaz Relocation Center during the war. Like Yamamoto, Mori's first language was Japanese, which his parents spoke exclusively. Constrained and dissatisfied with the limitations of his immediate experience, Mori dreamed first of becoming a professional baseball player and later, after having studied comparative relgions and philosophy, of being a monk. It was his mother who encouraged him to become a writer; Mori began writing after she told him that he was reading too much and not writing enough.

Mori describes his mother as a strong-willed, illiterate woman of immense intelligence and imagination. Mori was inspired by the stories his mother told him every evening until he was in his late teens while she prepared meals after the farmwork was done: "She told me of the past and the present, all subjects, human nature, faith, greed, how to live, with frank examples from her own or someone else's life, good or bad." From the beginning, Mori felt a profound affinity for his mother and for the Japanese-speaking *issei* in general, whom he felt had experienced and survived many hardships and life changes without bending and whose stories he urgently believed should be recorded and preserved.

> I used to sit and listen as *issei* friends would take me around and confide in me. I had affinity with these older *issei* because I was able to talk with them. I wanted to know more about them so that I might someday write about them, about how they came here and what they experienced. I knew an *issei* who immigrated here as a student and became a Hollywood masseur for Douglas Fairbanks and Charlie Chaplin. There was an old *bonsai* hobbyist who used to invite me to join him in the Sierras in search of natural dwarf trees. He had been from a *samurai* family and had become a socialist member of the IWW. As a whole I thought that *issei* were more interesting, stronger characters than the *nisei*. *Nisei* as a whole didn't associate much with the *issei*. They were struggling to become good obedient American citizens so that they could be accepted as part of American life. Someday I'd like to write a novel about the old *issei* bachelor life, about how it was when they first came to America, based on the stories the old men tell me.[75]

In *Yokohama, California* (1949), an anthology of short stories written during the 1930s and 1940s, and *The Chauvinist and Other Stories* (1979), Mori takes his readers into the parlors and kitchens of Japanese American homes, into the Oakland Japanese American ghetto, and finally into the assembly centers and war relocation camps. We witness births, deaths, marriages, catching glimpses of family life and relationships between the young and old. We overhear snatches of conversations in flowershops and at small town soda fountains. There are few white characters in the stories, just as there was little interaction between the Japanese American community and the white world circumbscribing and containing it, "calling the shots" from a distance, as Yamamoto has said.[76] We come to understand how the members of this community sustain themselves within the shelter provided them by their ethnic enclave, which makes possible a certain serenity and integrity among those for whom race discrimination was an indisputable fact of life. There is an implicit sense of order and purpose in this community. Mori's unerringly benevolent eye catches its members in the act of living.

What is most striking about Mori's portraits of Japanese American life, however, is the resilience of the individual human spirit that sustains the community through trivia and adversity, emerging always undaunted, tenacious, and almost divine. The plight of the lonely *issei* bachelors is poignantly revealed in "Operator, Operator" (1938), whose protagonist, Gunsuke Iwamura, an aging gardener too old and infirm to find work, continues to wait for the calls that never come. The striking contrast between the fading *issei* and the ebullient young *nisei* is movingly rendered in "Miss Butterfly" (1939), where two teenage *nisei* girls reluctantly don their kimonos to perform a traditional Japanese dance for their father's friend, before rushing off in their white gowns to a high school dance with their boyfriends. To Sachi and Yuki, the *odori* means little, but for lonely old Hamada-San, it stirs memories of old Japan, of cherry blossoms and pine-studded hills, the taste of Japanese fruits and fish and rice cakes, and the thought of his long-lost ancestors.

Mori touches even bitterness and frustration with understanding. The troubled minds beneath the *nisei*'s seemingly carefree attitude are revealed in the bitter conversation in "The Sweet Potato" (1941):

[L]ook at those people going back and forth. Wandering forever. . . . that's what we're all doing. Searching for something, searching for the real thing . . . every one of us. Look at them going in circles. . . . We're not getting anywhere. We haven't a chance. . . . We'll fall into our parents' routine life and end there. We'll have our own clique and never get out of it.

In "The Man with the Bulging Pockets" (1944), which takes place at the Tanforan Assembly Center, a jealous old *issei* tries to compete for the attention and affection that the children render to another old man, even though men "belong to one big circle [and] should join hands and rejoice in the heart of a child."[77]

In almost all Mori's writing, beneath the disappointments and difficulties of external life the abiding reality is the inherent resilience and integrity of the human heart. The protagonist of "The Chauvinist" (1935) pretends to be a deaf mute so that he can transcend the grey prison life that has entombed him. He wants to create "new tones, new scales, new instrument," and to taste "everyday immortality":

Lucky guy. Stone deaf. Doesn't have to plug cotton in his ears when to bed he goes with little wifey. Doesn't need to pick up little issues of a family circle. The innocent among the snoopy gossipers and savages of dirty insults. The babe in the gusty screechy roar of modern mads—the genius of the community due to an accidental lack of sense.

The "chauvinist" smiles at the ceiling while his wife's friends engage in small talk. He watches them, wondering if the words on their lips actually reflect their minds and hearts as they speak "in the same tone, same gestures, same subject," unconscious of the loneliness and triviality they are expressing, unaware that each human being has the potential to assume a myriad of roles within a single day, not knowing that "it isn't a man's possessions or capabilities [but] his possibilities that count." Although he is pitied and scorned as a useless fool, the "chauvinist" emerges as a triumphant and solemn hero in deliberate disguise. He has rejected conventional blindness and deafness to life:

> I endorse myself, my life, to the young mind. . . . I address to the suppressed, the futile, the jobless, the woman's husband, the lonely hearts. I also address the romanticist—here is something in your line. I am deaf. This is untruth but I'm not lying. . . . I have become deaf to survive the living. . . . By representing truth in untruth and untruth in truth I may become someone I want to be. . . . While I'm still alive, I shall smile and laugh, and in spirit grab the grits of life, scraping for crumbs while cooking up the great feast of life.[78]

The protagonists of many of Mori's stories are fools in appearance and heroes in reality because their tenacious spirit helps them transcend apparent adversities. They never lose touch with the "possibilities that count." They are courageous dreamers. In "Eggs of the World" (1949), Sessue Matoi, a drunkard philosopher who urges the people around him to liberate themselves from the "inner shells" that imprison them, exhorts all who will listen to use as he has the "natural warmth of their inner selves" to release an emerging new life. Although he has uncovered "a mess" inside, at least he is free, he says:

> You see me as I am. I am not hidden beneath a shell and I am not enclosed in one either. I am walking on this earth with my good feet and also I am drinking and enjoying but am sad on seeing so many eggs in the world, unbroken, untasted, and rotten.

In "Tomorrow and Today" (1949), Hatsuye's lively and romantic imagination allows her to transcend the routine of her monotonous internment behind barbed wire. There are no fences within her as she fantasizes about Clark Gable while attending to her routine of cooking and washing and Saturday night baths, achieving a "breath-taking suspense that is a love and enormous." Even when a companion reminds Hatsuye coldly that she is ugly, she recovers, cleaving to "a dim hope that something might happen some day" and it is this hope that makes her a courageous heroine:

> The interesting part of Hatsuye is that she is hopeful in spite of the fact that she is hopeless. She knows that she is no beauty but she is hopeful that she is not all ugliness to others. That is something. And when she has but dim hope of future or of Clark Gable, she is still in possession of something alive to work with and that is something. . . . Although her hope may be unfilled there is no reason why she cannot be a lover of Clark Gable.[79]

For some of Mori's protagonists, it is art that provides this "something." In "The Distant Call of the Deer" (1937), Togo Satoshima believes firmly in himself and his call to art, continuing to play the only *shakuhachi* piece he knows despite people's attempts to discourage him. In "Japanese Hamlet" (1939), a young *nisei* wants more than anything to become a Shakespearian actor, although his relatives and friends do their best to dissuade him from what they see as an impossible ambition; the narrator himself warns him not to waste his life in this "mock play that this life was," but is unable to forget the young man's "simple persistence" and his ability to dream. In "The Seventh Street Philosopher" (1949), Motoji Tsunoda delivers a verbose lecture to an empty auditorium, trying "to reveal [to the tiny audience] the beautiful world he could see and marvel at, but which we could not see." The eccentric old man might be seen by some as a pathetic fool, a comical old wind-bag, but the narrator finds in him and his effort to stand up and express himself something brave and almost divine: "even though his words are unintelligible, there is in his voice, his gestures, his sadness, his patheticness, his bravery, which are of common lot and something the people, [something] the inhabitants of the earth could understand, sympathize and remember for a while."[80] The aspiring writer who is the protagonist of "Akira Yano" (1949) is undaunted by the rejection slips and the community's dismissal of him as an impossible dreamer. The narrator admires him and wishes him well, although we know as he does that Yano has only his own optimism to keep him alive.

These and other stories can be construed as an apology for the writer's own life, for Mori too refused to give up his own dreams despite the odds he faced. Mori decided to become a writer at the age of twenty-two, and by the time of his death early in 1980 had written five novels and hundreds of short stories, most of which are set in the rural Japanese American communities of northern California during the 1930s and 1940s. Before the war, he worked in the family's San Leandro nursery for ten or twelve hours each day and disciplined himself to write for four hours every day, whether he produced anything or not, for almost twenty years:

> Since I had to get up at dawn every morning to prepare flowers for the market, I slept only a few hours. During the day, I thought about characters and themes for stories. I used to work so hard I thought I would fall by the wayside. I had to make it or break myself trying. It was six years and many rejection slips later when my first story was finally accepted for publication.[81]

Mori sold two stories to *Coast* magazine in 1938. By 1941, he had been published in the *Clipper, Common Ground, Writer's Forum, Matrix,* and the *Iconograph,* although he says he collected enough rejection slips to "paper a room." Mori's stories captured the attention of William Saroyan, who praised him as a "natural-born writer" and encouraged him to continue his efforts. Mori's collection of short stories, *Yokohama, California,* was scheduled for publication in the spring of 1942, but Pearl Harbor and the internment intervened, and the printers suspended the publication of the book for almost eight years. *Yokohama, California* did not sell well, although it was hailed especially by Anglo reviewers and critics as a fine work. Ironically, the book was attacked by a Japanese American writer, Albert Saijo, in a Japanese American weekly, *Crossroads.*[82] Saijo condemned all *nisei* writing as muddled, sentimental, and poorly crafted, although he did begrudgingly grant a "certain vigor and charm" to some of Mori's stories and admitted that Mori's portrayal of the *issei* had a certain authenticity.

Mori continued to write during his imprisonment at Tanforan and later at Topaz, but when he returned to San Leandro after the war, he found that almost two hundred of the stories he had left stored in a barn there had been destroyed by bookworms. For almost thirty years he remained unrecognized and obscure. Still he did not let himself become discouraged. Many years later, when the younger generation of Japanese Americans rediscovered in his stories a valuable record of the buried heritage that Saijo and other older *nisei* had not deemed important, Mori was honored at Asian American Writers' Conferences in Oakland in 1975, in Seattle in 1976, and in Honolulu in 1978. The UCLA Asian American Studies Center initiated an anthology of about two dozen selctions from among his one hundred previously published and unpublished stories under the title *The Chauvinist and Other Stories* in 1979; in 1978, Isthmus Press published an edition of one of his novels, *Woman from Hiroshima,* which he had written years before. Although in his last years Mori was afflicted by debilitating illness, he was planning to write about Japanese in Hawaii and about the early *issei* bachelor experience until the day he died.

It is fortunate that Mori was "rediscovered," even if only shortly before his death, but one imagines that he would have persevered even if he had remained obscure. In "Confessions of an Unknown Writer," the narrator admits that he feels "like a deadbeat, a man alone in the world, I couldn't be a writer and I was one":

> Sometimes I kick myself inwardly for being a fool. My friends who came out of the school in the same year have become substantial citizens in their community. George Matsuo has a good-sized bank account and is single. What has a guy like that got to worry about unless he has crazy ideas? Tadashi Nozato is a good salaried salesman plus bonus and commission. Averages two hundred a month or more, owns a home, and has a beautiful wife.

But the narrator does not want to die without leaving something behind, without trying to confront his own possibilities, because he believes in his potential and the multifaceted possiblities of every individual human life:

> Do you know what capabilities man has? . . . Sometimes I am capable of murder; sometimes I can love; or I am a fanatic or the suppressed or a dreamer or the listless or a coward or any other traits of a being. It is this capability of man which is so natural to occur that I am taking myself as the story and firmly believe its worth. I believe in this capability of man; thus, a saint is no different from a dissipator. . . . [A]n unpublished and an immortal are writers from the same heart. I believe in man and also disbelieve, and there is no harm.[83]

A sensitive observer of the people and events of his community, Mori searches for significance and beauty in the ordinary, for the general and universal within the particular: "Every little observation, every little banal talk or laughing matter springs from the sadness of the earth that is reality; every meeting between individuals, every meeting of society, every meeting of a gathering, or gaiety or sorrow, springs from sadness that is the bed of earth and truth." Writing itself transforms the commonplace events of human life and preserves these ephemeral moments in time, bringing permanence to a world of flux. Mori wants to record the story of his uncle for this reason: "Perhaps his life is not colorful enough and in time he will be buried under the many millions of deaths. But his life deserves more than a space in the obituary notice." To publish his poetry would be to "do our bit to resurrect immortality, not merely for the sake of my uncle but for the likes of him."[84]

It is the artist who can best preserve the beauty and significance of the present, who can distill to its essence the awesome nature of human courage in everyday life, who can capture and communicate people's variegated flavors. In "The Woman Who Makes Swell Donuts," those who eat the donuts are partaking of their maker's essence, just as the readers of the story are tasting the flavor of both the cook and the writer who preserves her in his art. Mori writes the story so that "people from all parts of the earth may drop in and taste the flavor, her flavor, which is everyone's and all flavors" and then carry away with them forever "what is alive in her, on earth, and in men, expressly myself." Mori's materials, gathered from his immediate environment and gleaned from the lips of the immigrant generation, were Japanese American materials. But what he consciously attempted to do was to present universals in particular forms: "I try to depict human beings, no matter what, living out their days as best they can, facing their human problems. Humanity transcends race; at a certain point, national background becomes incidental and humaness is much more essential." Mori believed that white readers might take the time and have the patience to "interpret Japanese thought and approach through English words" and to recognize the humanity of his Japanese American characters through the universality of their concerns: "I wanted to do everything, I wanted to know women, I wanted to know the white people, the minds of my generation and people, the Nisei, the nature of our parents, the Issei, the culture of Japan, the culture of America, of life as a whole."[85]

Mori's universalist view is reflected in his characterization of his mother, the protagonist of his novel *Woman from Hiroshima*, the woman who continually stressed that the parts and the whole were one. The "America in her heart" was everywhere, a part of her self:

> My face and hands are wrinkled, my hair grey. My teeth are gone; my figure is bent. These are of America. I still cannot speak English too well, but I live among all kinds of people and come and go like the seasons, the bees, and the flowers. Ah, San Francisco. My dream city. My San Francisco is everywhere. I like the dirty brown hills, the black soil and the sandy beaches. I like the tall buidings, the bridges, the parks, and the roar of city traffic. They are of me.

Even when Mori's mother sees the guards at the Assembly Center, guns pointed at her, she feels that she is part of humanity and part of America because her son is a soldier also. At the train station, she feels a sense of belonging, since "the Japanese faces were now lost in the crowd as they should be," in the shared experience of bidding farewell to the sons going off to war:

> Looking about the crowd, I felt at home. I belonged. The *issei* grandmother tells her grandchildren to face the hardships and triumphs of life without giving up hope because all history is but a

part of you. . . . You don't have to die in order to become brave. You are brave when you try to live.

She warns them never to become victims of life, but to try instead to make improvements while they are alive, since life continually begins anew with each triumph and tragedy and since each person is responsible for himself and thus "makes himself": "Every mood is of you; every act represents you. Each understanding belongs to you, and are the parcel of every mystery." Even adversity has its advantages. When she learns that her son has returned from the battlefront paralyzed, she tells herself: "If nothing besets you any more you will be settling down for some dull days. Now, old woman, you have something to live for a little longer. . . . I was willing to see many bad days in order to have a few short hours of blessing."[86]

Blessing in adversity, heroism within apparent foolishness, beauty in the commonplace, humanity within ethnicity, immortality within flux—Mori's stories are sketched of unity in apparent opposition. In "Four Bits" (1953), a young *nisei* is disillusioned to find that one of his high school classmates has become a night-club stripper, until his friend reminds him that although "the old Evelyn is dead, . . . the world is full of new Evelyns."[87] In "The Sweet Potato," a bitter *nisei* meets an old white woman who treats him kindly because she had once been kindly treated by Japanese.

What emerges through all Mori's writing is a celebration of the uniqueness of each human being, which is what joins every individual to humankind, whatever his condition or ethnicity. Although the individual's secret vision cannot be transferred, it can be shared by those who are alive and filled with a desire to "listen, to give, to know, and to remember," who love life even though it brings tragedy and uncertainty.[88]

But fulfillment is very individual and personal. In "The Trees" (1949), Fukushima wants to know the secret of Hashimoto's serenity, which he understands is somehow related to what he can see in the pine trees. But because Fukushima is blinded by his own selfishness and indifference, he cannot know his friend's inner peace. In "Abalone, Abalone" (1937), the narrator discovers why old Abe collects abalone shells. In the shells, Abe sees at once what is varied and eternal. The shells, like human beings, are "very much alike and very much different." The discovery allows the narrator to feel akin to Abe and to "the collectors of shells and otherwise" in the world.[89] Although he is alone and individual, his personal discovery has brought him into the harmonious whole. It is what joins individuals and their community, Japanese Americans and others, *nisei* and *issei*, men and women.

There is great variety in the perspectives of the Japanese American family and community offered by the *nisei* writers surveyed here. What is essential to all of them is a dual impulse, towards the freedom and autonomy of the individual and towards harmony and wholeness at the same time. It cannot be denied that many older *nisei* were motivated by a desire to be assimilated into American society, even if that assimilation meant denial of their Japanese heritage. But the ethnic community somehow emerges as the strongest sustaining force for its individual members. Even in Murayama's *All I Asking for Is My Body*, it is the community context that gives meaning to the lives of all the characters.

It has often been pointed out that traditional Asian societies demand the subordination of the individual to the family and community, while the individual is supreme in modern Western societies. Asian American literature expresses the need for balance between these two emphases. Carlos Bulosan desperately searched for a place in American society, but his most meaningful experiences were among fellow Filipinos in the labor union movement, and the Filipino community in the United States, together with memories of his family in the Philippines, were a continual source of inspiration for him. Louis Chu's protagonists need to escape from the tyranny of New York Chinatown community and family life, but in the end they must re-establish their ties with their fathers in another Chinese American community. Even John Okada's Ichiro rejects the notion of leaving his community; he must reconcile himself with that community in order to become a complete human being. And while the Japanese American community as depicted in Yamamoto's and Mori's short stories is riddled with flaws and dark secrets, it is the concrete measure of universal human life. Even the debilitating effects of the internment experience might have contributed, as Wakako Yamauchi suggests, to the spiritual strength of the *nisei*:

> [W]hen we do see those old photographs of the mass evacuation, we search the faces of our brothers and sisters, and in that backward look, in those old faces, young faces, we can see the mirror of our tragedy. Few of us can hold back the tears that most often smack of self-pity, but maybe somewhere behind those tears we know that this is the event that changed the course of our lives, and though there were those among us who had more insight, more courage, whatever path we chose, we have survived—whole. . . . The fact of our survival is proof of our valor. And that is enough.[90]

# 6

# Chinatown Cowboys and Warrior Women

## Searching for a New Self-Image

For many Asian Americans, the era of the Vietnam war and the civil rights movement in the United States was an era of increased awareness of racial and cultural identity built on their need to clarify and establish their uniquely American identity. The new awareness that it was possible and desirable to be both American and nonwhite resulted in Asian American literary efforts to assert an ethnic American identity and to challenge old myths and stereotypes. Young writers attempted to "claim America" for Asian Americans by demonstrating Asian roots in American society and culture. In some cases, this meant rejecting the ethnic community as subject matter, since some writers felt that it limited them and only perpetuated the relegation of Asian Americans to marginal status. They turned their interest away from community portraiture and towards questions of individual Asian American identity within the context of the larger society.

In the early 1970s, four young Californians who had been writers and college literature teachers presented a manifesto for a new direction in Asian American culture. Taking as a symbol of their effort Kwan Kung, Chinese god of art and war, Frank Chin, Jeffery Paul Chan, Lawson Fusao Inada, and Shawn Hsu Wong edited an anthology of Asian American literature that, they asserted, expressed the genuine spirit of Asian American history and culture and not the old stereotypes that had held sway for so long. The anthology features selections from the works of Louis Chu, John Okada, Carlos Bulosan, Hisaye Yamamoto, and others and newer works by the editors and other younger writers. The editors argued that the volume of published Asian American writing had been small not because of lack of Asian American creativity, productivity, and talent but because publishers had deliberately rejected Asian American writing that contradicted popular racist views:

> Americans' stereotypes of "Orientals" were sacrosanct and no one, especially a "Chink" or a "Jap," was going to tell them that America, not Asia, was their home, that English was their language, and that the stereotype of the Oriental good or bad, was offensive. What America published was, with rare exception, not only offensive to Chinese and Japanese America but was *actively inoffensive* to white sensibilities.[1]

Frank Chin notes that a critic of his own play, "Chickencoop China-man" (1972), which focuses on a Chinese American's search for a viable identity in a racially divided society, complained that the play's protago-nist "doesn't talk or dress or act like an Oriental."[2] Even the publishing company that had issued *Flower Drum Song* and *The Hatchet Men* in handsome paperback editions rejected the new anthology, which indi-cated to the anthology editors that, while there had been no lack of readership for literature about Asians and Asian Americans from a "racist perspective," there was little interest in genuine Asian American self-expression. Some publishing companies rejected the book because it was "too ethnic," advising the editors to become better acquainted with white ethnic writers' attempts to "mold . . . 'difference' to enrich the society": They concluded that the publishers and critics accept exotic stereotypes of Asians or complete denial of differences between Asian Americans and whites: [T]he ethnicity of yellow writing embarrasses white publishers. . . . It seems whites can't hear anything but themselves when we're in the room." According to Chin and Wong, Afro-Americans have been "quicker to understand and appreciate the value of Asian American writing than whites," partly because they are not hampered by the racist assumption that Asian Americans cannot speak English well and there-fore cannot be writers of American literature:

> Yardbird Publishing Cooperative is the first Berkeley–San Francisco based national publication to acknowledge the presence of an Asian American cultural tradition that is not mere mimicry or exotic arti-fact. . . . The blacks were the first to take us seriously and sustained the spirit of many Asian American writers. . . . [I]t wasn't surpris-ing to us that Howard University Press understood us and set out to publish our book [*Aiiieeeee!*] with their first list. They liked our English we spoke and didn't accuse us of unwholesome literary devices.[3]

Chin, Chan, Wong, and other members of the Combined Asian Resources Project (CARP) have spearheaded the effort to find, revive, and reprint little-known works of Asian American literature that express unstereotyped aspects of the Asian American experience and that for that reason have achieved less popularity and lower sales than Fu Manchu or Charlie Chan portrayals. Members of CARP have helped convince the University of Washington Press to issue new editions of Carlos Bulosan's *America Is in the Heart* (1973), John Okada's *No-No Boy* (1976), Louis Chu's *Eat a Bowl of Tea* (1979), and Monica Sone's *Nisei Daughter* (1979). They have also been instrumental in bringing to press a new collection of predominantly old stories by Bienvenido N. Santos under the title *Scent of Apples* (1979) and Toshio Mori's novel, *Woman from Hiroshima* (1978), which had been written years before but which had never been published.

## Defining Chinese American Manhood

CARP's efforts have been addressed towards destroying what they call the myths that Asian Americans are temporary sojourners with foreign sensibilities or docile, compliant members of a "model minority." Because both of these myths contribute to what they see as a threat to Asian American manhood, the building of a new image of the Asian American man is high on their list of priorities.

Jeffery Paul Chan has said that the Chinese American identity is yet to be delineated. All we know is what it is not: it is not European, it is not Chinese, and it is not Afro-American. To assist its emergence, we must first "throw out what's Chinese and what's white and then try to get even. What's left will be Chinese American. Chinese America doesn't exist yet. As it accumulates, it will emerge."[4]

Because American racial policies regarding Asians have involved active attempts to exclude them as a minority from participation in American life, Chinese Americans have been taught, Chin says, "that we don't exist, that we have no style, no language, no literature, and no history besides the white version of our history." The only cultural identity allowed the Chinese American has been a foreign Chinese one, which Frank Chin holds has been "used to exclude us from American culture, and is imposed upon us as a substitute for participation in American culture. For this reason, even anthologies of ethnic American writing confuse Chinese from China with American-born Chinese, "conveniently ignoring the obvious cultural differences."[5]

In a series of letters to *Bridge* magazine, Chin has articulated some of the reasons he feels it is necessary to distinguish once and for all between the Chinese and the Chinese American:

There is no cultural, psychological bridge between men and the Chinese immigrants. There are social, racist pressures that connect us. These connections must be broken. The only bridge is time. The immigrants in time have kids and the kids become a part of Chinese-America good or bad. The immigrants will survive. Chinese-America might not, and the immigrants, the intellectuals who've become Americanized and gotten hip and lordly blowing the sweet racist smoke China-lovers and the stereotypes make the darling Chinabrain take up as a habit, blowing rifts from the Fifties Liberals book of crap, and lofted up to talk for Chinese America, and bark, and arf the same old shit, like the trained seals they are. They don't know what they're doing. And they can live with it. I can't talk with them.

Chin points out that whites from Europe are not linked with Americans of European descent, but Chinese are linked with Chinese Americans because skin color binds them together in a white supremacist society. Since what Chin really wants is to prevent racists from continually attempting to exclude Chinese Americans from participation in American life by relegating them to the status of foreigners, he also resents artificial attempts to link recent immigrants from Taiwan and Hong Kong to second-, third-, and fourth-generation Chinese Americans. In particular, he resents the aristocratic immigrant scholars and writers who proclaim themselves spokespeople for Chinese in America:

> I'm not fighting for my birthright by my Chinaman cultural integrity, an integrity shit on and kicked around by Chinese from China as well as whites. . . . I take it as a personal insult to be linked up with a "Chinese David Cassidy," a C.Y. Lee or Lin Yutang or any other Chinese, complete in his Chinese identity and a volunteer American. We're not interchangeable. Our sensibilities are not the same.[6]

To those who accuse him of being contemptuous of foreign-born Chinese and of rejecting Chinese culture, Chin responds: "The assertion of distinctions between Chinese and Chinese-Americans is neither a rejection of Chinese culture nor an expression of contempt for things Chinese. . . . It's calling things by their right names." Even so, in his letters to Frank Ching in *Bridge*, Chin's equation of Chinese immigrants with animals or stigmatized persons might lead one to believe otherwise: "I'm not shunning immigrants. I'm stating a fact that I am not Chinese. I am not shunning Albinos, elephants, dwarves, and midgets either. But call me one and I'll just have to set you straight."[7]

Several factors are operating in Chin's vehement attempts to dissociate Chinese Americans from Chinese. Perhaps because of the longevity of the attitude that Asians in America are all unassimilable foreigners, the confounding of these two identities in the minds of non-Asians is still recurring.[8] Chin's distinction between Chinese and Chinese American identity is a bid for acceptance of Chinese Americans as Americans. He calls himself "Chinatown Cowboy" because he wants to assert Chinese roots in the American West: Chinese are as much a part of American history and traditions as cowboys. Moreover, cowboys are thought of as manly and rugged; they are in stark contrast to the exotic stereotypes of Chinese as pigtailed heathens in silk gowns and slippers, whispering Confucian aphorisms about filial piety. Chin strives to differentiate Chinese Americans from the unmanly and un-American stereotype of Asian culture: "The Asian culture we are supposedly preserving is uniquely without masculinity; we are characterized as lacking daring, originality, aggressiveness, assertiveness, vitality, and a living art and culture." Chin wants Chinese Americans to be associated with the men who built the railroads across the United States. Chin himself sought a job as a railroad brakeman so that he could get in touch with his unheralded forefathers and claim their unsung history in this country:

> In every engine I rode there was the possibility that I would become the intelligence of its thrusting tons. . . . I carried the orders to make it go. And that meant more than just a hundred and thirty pound Chinese boy claiming the rails laid by his ancestors. I was above history. I was too big for the name of a little man, Frank Chin. No sir, I was a thing: BRAKEMAN! That's the person I remember being, the one I enjoy remembering on the railroad, the image I love.[9]

### The "Model Minority"

According to Chin *et al.*, the characterization of Asian Americans as a "model minority" or "middleman minority" is largely an attempt to rationalize the relationship between Black and white Americans, at the expense of both the Blacks and the Asians. Asians have been compared favorably to Blacks as more industrious, docile, and compliant.[10] By the end of World War II, Asian Americans had become "conditionally acceptable" in white society.[11] As a "model minority," Asians are supposed to be restrained, humble, and well-mannered, a people who respect law, love education, work hard, and have close-knit, well-disciplined families. Above all, they are praised for not complaining about or protesting against difficulties: they may have problems, but they really do not mind these, and they "take care of their own" instead of burdening "Americans" with their needs by seeking government aid and welfare assistance. Most important, they do not "take themselves too seriously."[12]

The new "favorable" image of Asian Americans was emphasized during the 1960s, when militant demands for social equality were being voiced by American racial minorities, led by American Blacks. At the height of the civil rights movement, a *U.S. News and World Report* article held up the Chinese as example for Blacks and other "troublesome" minority groups to follow. Although their past "hardships" would "shock those now complaining about the hardships endured by today's negroes," they are succeeding "on their own" now:

> At a time when it is being proposed that hundreds of billions be spent to uplift Negroes and other minorities, the nation's 300,000 Chinese are moving ahead on their own . . . with no help from anyone else. Still being taught in Chinatown is the old idea that people should depend on their own efforts . . . not a welfare check . . . in order to reach America's "promised land."

The article hails Chinatown as a "haven of law and order," an "island of peace and stability," the "safest place" in New York City, where inhabitants attend school regularly, "stay out of trouble," and "overcome their handicaps quietly." No mention is made of the fact that part of the reason why Chinese in America have not turned to the U.S. government for assistance might stem from the government's traditionally hostile stance towards their legal status and rights. Nor is there any acknowledgement of the problems of poverty, suicide, and tuberculosis in Chinatown communities.[13]

According to Frank Chin, the characterization of Asians by whites as preferable to other minorities because they require less "white energy" to suppress has caused some trouble in the relationship between Asians and other minorities:

> "Why can't you boys, you negroes and Mexicans," the visiting cop said, all creases, jingling metals, and hair on his knuckles, setting every chinaman boy of us up for an afternoon of fights, ". . . stay out of trouble like the Chinese? Mind your folks? Study hard? Obey the laws?" And there we chinamen were, in Lincoln Elementary School, Oakland, California, in a world where manliness counts for everything, surrounded by bad blacks and bad Mexican kids . . . suddenly stripped and shaved bare by this cop with no manly style of my own, unless it was sissiness.[14]

In an essay titled "Racist Love" (1972), Chan and Chin assert that the stereotype of Asians as docile and compliant "good minorities" is the product of "racist love."[15] Stereotypes based on "racist hate" are masculine, and include Black studs, bellicose Indians, and Mexican bandits. Racial villains of this type are hated because they cannot be controlled by whites; even so, they command respect and are superior in many ways to the buffoons, servants, and loyal sidekicks like the Stepin Fetchits, Tontos, Panchos, and Charlie Chans that are the products of racist love. Chinese Americans, according to Chan and Chin, have been more subject to racist love than racist hate, particularly in recent years, and the result has been the loss of Chinese American "manhood" through castrating paternalism.

What seems to anger Chan and Chin the most is that "white America is . . . securely indifferent about us as men" and that Chinese American men have become "the white male's dream minority . . . patient, submissive, esthetic, passive, accommodating, essentially feminine in character," a race without "sinful manhood":

> [T]he evil of the evil Dr. Fu Manchu was not sexual, but homosexual. The sexual "evil" offered by Fu Manchu to the white race is nothing less than satisfaction of the white male fantasy of white balls being irresistable. Instead of threatening white goddess blond bigtits with sexual assault, Dr. Fu swishes in to threaten all-Joe American with his beautiful nymphomaniac daughter. . . . Fu Manchu and [Charlie] Chan are visions of the same mythic being, brewed up in the subconscious regions of the white Christian's racial wetdream. Devil and angel, the Chinese is a sexual joke glorifying white power. Dr. Fu, a man wearing a long dress, batting his eyelashes, surrounded by muscular black servants in loin cloths, and with his bad habit of caressingly touching white men on the leg, wrist, and face with his long fingernails is not so much a threat as he is a frivolous offense to white manhood. Chan's gestures are the same, except he doesn't touch, and instead of being graceful like Fu in flowing robes, he is awkward in a baggy suit and clumsy. His sexuality is the source of a joke running through all of the forty seven Chan films. The large family of the bovine detective isn't the product of sex, but animal husbandry. . . . [He does] not smoke, drink, or womanize. . . . He never gets into violent things.[16]

By accepting their status as "honorary whites," say Chin and Chan, Chinese Americans have made themeselves into a "dutiful race of sissies," the "Uncle Toms" of the nonwhite people, like the elevator boy in Richard Wright's *Black Boy* who plans to go north to pass for Chinese and offers white men his ass to kick for a quarter: "We are . . . a race of yellow white supremacists, yellow white racists. We're hated by the blacks because the whites love us for being everyting the blacks are not. Blacks are a problem: badass. Chinese-Americans are not a problem: kissass." Chin urges Chinese Americans to reject their status as "honorary whites": "[I]t is clear that our acceptability, the affection and reknown we supposedly enjoy, is not based on actual achievements or contributions we have made, but on what we have not done. We have not been black.

We have not caused trouble. We have not been men." Chin views Chinese American history as a wholesale and systematic attempt to emasculate the Chinese American male. Racist laws "warred against us . . . to deny our manhood, to drive us out of the country, to kill us. . . . [T]wenty to thirty men for every woman. . . . Chinese-America was rigged to be a race of males going extinct without women." Chinese Americans were deprived of a knowledge of their history, according to Chin and the other editors of *Aiiieeeee!*, and forbidden a "legitimate mother tongue" because they were viewed as foreigners who cannot speak English:

> Only Asian-Americans are driven out of their tongues and expected to be at home in a language they never use and a culture they encounter only in books written in English. This piracy of our native tongues by white culture amounts to the eradication of a recognizable Asian-American culture here.

"The deprivation of language," is part of the castration process:

> [It has] contributed to the lack of a recognized Asian-American cultural integrity . . . and the lack of a recognized style of Asian-American manhood. . . . Language is the medium of culture and the people's sensibility, including the style of manhood. . . . Stunt the tongue and you have lopped off the culture and sensibility. On the simplest level, a man in any culture speaks for himself. Without a language of his own, he is no longer a man.[17]

### Frank Chin

The castration that Chin says Asian American males have suffered through history is also reflected, he contends, in culture, so that Chinese American males have not been permitted to speak in American literature: "Our white-dream identity being feminine, the carriers of our strength, the power of the race belongs to our women. The dream women of this dream minority naturally prefer white men to our own. . . . Four of the five American-born Chinese Americans to publish serious literary efforts are women." Chin criticizes Jade Snow Wong, Betty Lee Sung, and Virginia Lee for accommodating the stereotypes of an exoticized Chinese heritage and of the Chinese as a model minority. But he also asserts that the fact that there are more published Chinese American women than men writers emasculates Chinese American men because literary creativity is the proper domain of men: "[I]n this culture [manliness means] aggressiveness, creativity, individuality, just being taken seriously."[18]

In "Song of the Monogram Warner Bros. Chink: News To Raise the Dead" (1971), the first step in reclaiming the manhood of the Chinese

American is to gang-rape Joy, who represents the indifferent white majority:

> I've been yellow on the lawn of your keep off the grass grass
> Small and stooped, stupid and small tearing your daisies apart
> Standing around, yelling yellow stillness all over your green grass
>     lawn.
> You yawned in the morning, Joy, bobbed a boob, made my bird fly,
> Called me our Japanese gardener and shut me up.
>
> Because I feared losing my hardon and wanted to please.

The narrator takes revenge for this castrating indifference on behalf of the "twenty thousand bleeding fingerbones" of his yellow forefathers, who carved through granite and ice in the desert darkness to build the American railroad. Those silent men were

> . . . men not I, nor my father,
> Nor you, especially you, dear gollygosh you,
> Ever heard sing of the railroad, of the winds that killed them,
> Of the trains they never rode.
>
> My faceless grandfathers, men we never heard sing,
> All gone, with their laughable names, all gone.
> The Chinese American is vindicated when
> A hundred years of Chinamen
> In public
> Took turns
> At a piece of
> White ass.[19]

The new Asian American identity, according to Chin, must be built around the Asian American man's being accepted as American. To gain this acceptance, it is necessary to challenge the stereotype of quaint foreigners, to reject the notion of the passive, quiet Asian American, and to move away from the stultifying limitations of the glittering Chinatown ghetto. Three of Chin's pieces of short fiction, "Food for All His Dead" (1962), "Yes Young Daddy" (1970), and "Goong Hai Fot Choy" (1970), from an unpublished manuscript title *A Chinese Lady Dies*, are organized around the theme of Chinatown as decaying beneath an exotic facade. The central character of each work is a young Chinese American male who must come to terms with the absence of a suitable Chinese American male legacy and the stifling decay and futility of life in the Chinese American community. Ultimately, to survive and try to affirm his own manhood, he must leave Chinatown and everything it stands for behind.

The central characters of the three stories are essentially the same:

Johnny and Fred, of the former two stories, are sensitive young artists who are outgrowing their familes, Chinatown, and particularly Chinese American women. But they are not sure they can survive outside the Chinese American community. In the last story, Johnny and Fred have evolved into the character Dirigible, who is frozen into inaction as he waits for his mother, and by extension Chinatown, to die so that he can be free. Ultimately, Dirigible is developed into the main figure in the play "Chickencoop Chinaman," Tampax Lum, the Chinese American who searches for a new identity beyond the narrow confines of the Chinatown world from which he has recently escaped.

Chin's Chinatown is a barren, corrupt, and declining place where mothers and fathers are dying of wasting diseases, and their children are crippled, weary, and stifled by boredom. The Chinese people are portrayed as bugs, spiders, frogs, tipped-over mechanical toys, and oily fish gasping on dry land. The community itself is likened to a funeral parlor, an obsolete carnival, or a pathetic minstrel show.

In "Food for All His Dead," Johnny shares a "terrible secret" with his father—that the old man is dying of comsumption. The secret is more terrible to the son, since he seems to be the only person in Chinatown smart enough to know that Chinatown itself is dying: "Everyone is dying here," he tells his uncomprehending girlfriend. Johnny can no longer communicate with his father or the people of Chinatown, now that he alone knows "the secret"; he fears the "surges of nervous life" in his father and in the dying community. The terrible knowledge of impending death imposes on him the necessity of "lies and waiting." The father he used to admire has become "no longer like this father or a man," but like some ghastly creature, "no longer real as a life but a parody of live things, grinning," something that probably should be crushed to a quicker death: "The man was a fish dying and shrinking inside its skin on the sand, crazy, mimicking swimming, Johnny thought, but a fish could be lifted and slapped against a stone, thrown to cats."[20]

In "Goong Hai Fot Choy," Dirigible's mother, like Johnny's father, is dying slowly. But Dirigible's mother, emblematic now of Chinatown, is despicable, not to be regretted when she passes, a playfully senile living corpse, "a cadaver acting charming and sexy." Like her, Chinatown is expiring beneath a glittering mask, a ritual face. When Dirigible walks alone in Chinatown at dawn, he sees a deserted wasteland among the empty display windows and dry fish tanks. The streets are obsolete, "kin to the idly creaking ferris wheel and the dead merry-go-round." Chinatown is a cheap and boring carnival that has been closed. Everything is useless, deserted, frozen, dead, cold, or sleeping, as Dirigible gazes into the empty shop windows:

> The wildcats were frozen in fierce expressions, looking into a pool which used to contain water and display fish. The inside of the

window was dirty. Dead flies and moths spotted the dust at the bottom of the dry pool. He heard the voices of the crowd that wasn't shouting through all the streets after him. He saw the windows their voices weren't echoing off of. He saw all the space no one was occupying.[21]

Chin's attempt to present an unexoticized picture of Chinatown has resulted in a depiction of it as repulsive, decaying, and filled with subhuman creatures. In "Goong Hai Fot Choy," the people of Chinatown are like mechanical wind-up toys. There is a strange anonymity there, where life is likened to a dead ferris wheel, where words and expressions are "inorganically emotional," where faces turn on emotions "like a Christmas tree lighting up." People are akin to lonely, outdated machines. Chinatown events are a series of funerals, attended by overheated old ladies among Oriental rugs, lace doilies, and "mildewed memories." The people of Chinatown are buried and preserved beneath ivory masks: each time they watch the funeral processions pass by from the sidewalks, there is a shrinking away from the warm surfaces of their skins until they are mere remnants of themselves, until they seem to be frozen behind death masks.

In "Food for all His Dead," the people of Chinatown are also depicted as subhuman. The crowds in Portsmouth Square remind Johnny of "oily things and bugs floating on a tide"; they stand in "puddles of each other." Groups of old Chinese women "round-backed in their black overcoats" look like "clumps of huge beetles with white faces," and Chinese music emerging from grease- and urine-stained hallways sounds like "birds being strangled." Johnny's girlfriend, Sharon, wears an expression like a "wide frog's stare," her hand is "dry feeling, cold and dry like skin of tissue-paper covered flesh,"and her eyelashes make him think of shrunken, twitching insect legs.[22]

Chin's sympathies are clearly with the protagonists, who feel vastly superior to Chinatown's people. Johnny has already lost touch; Chinatown is too narrow for him now:

> I'd like to get outta here so quick, Sharon; I wish I had something to do! What do I do here? What does anybody do here? I'm bored! My mother's a respected woman because she can tell how much monosodium glutamate is in a dish by smelling it, and because she knows how to use a spitoon in a restaurant. Everybody's Chinese here, Sharon.

No one in Chinatown is equipped to understand Johhny's complex thoughts or his identity crisis. His father does not understand English well, and Sharon cannot comprehend the literal meaning of his words. She tells him, "You talk so nice," and he corrects her usage:

"I'll walk for you dan, okay?" She smiled and reached a hand down for him.
"You'll walk with me, not for me. You're not a dog."[23]

Johnny's self-conscious anguish is beyond Sharon's realm of experience, but he talks anyway, practicing his verbal virtuosity on her, feeling comfortably superior, even though she does not understand what he is talking about. "He enjoyed the girl; she listened to him; he did not care if she understood what he said or knew what he wanted to say. She listened to him." The dialogue is masterfully asymptotic:

"I knew more then than I do now."
"What d'ya mean? You smart now! You didn't know how to coun' or spall, or nothin', now you in colleger."
"I had something then, you know? I didn't have to ask about anything; it was all there; I didn't have questions, I knew who I was responsible to, who I should love, who I was afraid of, all my dogs were smart."
"You lucky, you had a dog!" The girl smiled.[24]

To Johnny, the Chinese community has become restrictive and repugnant because he has been made aware of the worlds that can be experienced outside Chinatown. Now he cannot decide as easily as others seem to what being "Chinese" in America is. Johnny asks the newsboy on the street, who has always remained in Chinatown and whose sense of identity has never been a question to him, "Are you really Chinese?"

"What're you ting, I'm a Negro soy sauce chicken?"
"Don't you know there's so such thing as a real Chinaman in all of America? That all we are are American Indians cashing in on a fad?"
"Fad? don' call me fad. You fad yourselv."
"No, you're not Chinese, don't you understand? You see it all started when a bunch of Indians wanted to quit being Indians and fighting the cavalry and all, so they left the reservation, see?"
"In'ian?"
"And they saw that there was this big kick about Chinamen, so they braided their hair into queues and opened up laundries and restaurants and started reading Margaret Mead and Confucius and Pearl Buck and became respectable Chinamen and gained some self-respect."
"Chinamong! You battah not say Chinamong."[25]

Ultimately, Johnny has to leave his family and his community, which is now too narrow and decadent for him. After his father's death, the world outside seems green and young.

In "Yes Young Daddy," the protagonist, Freddy, has left Chinatown for college. Freddy is young, verbal, and striving for new sophistication. When his young cousin, who is bored and lonely in Chinatown, begins writing to him, he temporarily assumes the role of her "young daddy." He corrects her grammar, tries to prepare her for eventual flight from Chinatown, and even makes a trip back to Chinatown to visit her. But even this temporary return reinforces his feeling that he belongs away from Chinatown:

> The vague familiarity, almost nostalgia, he found in the apartment house, the shadows in the corners, the worn rug with the pattern more walked out of it made Fred realize the long time he had been away. At one time he had known everybody in the house. . . . But he had left all that, and this part of his family. He did not regret leaving, for like the boy that was like all the boys that were in this house, everything was the same, familiar beyond recognition, stagnant. That was why he had left and forgotten his cousin, all part of the family. . . . "No," he thought, reaching the second flight of stairs. "It's not comfortable at all to be back, even to be nice."

Fred now turns his back on his past. He cannot do anything for Lena. He cannot be her "young daddy," or replace her dead father. He does not want to be a hero for the young Chinese Americans he left behind. He has his own identity to worry about: 'No more worrying about anybody but number one for me!' he thought, all to himself, not looking back to the house as he left, walking down the hill toward the light of Chinatown and the nearest bus home." "Home" is somewhere far away from Chinatown.[26]

Just as Fred is unable to accept responsibility for the death of Chinatown or the future of its other children, and Johnny must leave Chinatown behind for the sake of his future, Dirigible in "Goong Hai Fot Choy" awaits his mother's death in the hope that he may be saved from the petrification he sees gradually taking place all around him. Now that he has realized that he is tending a dying mother—and his "mother culture"—like a gigolo, for a price, he feels self-contemptuous and must break away lest he become a fossil like the dead things around him. Dirigible feels little besides "weariness . . . shifting monotony. . . . An elaborate, ornate impotence." As he shaves his face, he feels it becoming a mask of lather over festering sores. But he also realizes that his presence there makes the rest of Chinatown more dead:

Standing there unseen, alone with pigeons and riderless wood horses, watching everything, tensely doing nothing, nothing happening, was pointless. His being there to see in dead grey warming morning, to ignore the signs and fluttering beckoning flags, was to make everything this place and these were dead.[27]

Johnny, Fred, and Dirigible are too good for Chinatown and also too powerless to do anything but watch it die. They detest the self-deception of the people of Chinatown, who unlike them cannot see or refuse to see the dying. Johnny's father continues to rant about the Chinese Revolution of 1911, Aunt Dee insists on powdering her face into a mask and thinking dirty thoughts, and Dirigible's mother observes the Chinese New Year even as she is falling into crumbling decay. Chin's young male protagonists must leave Chinatown because there are no examples of "manhood" there for them to follow. Johnny's father is immersed in an impossible self-deception, knowing less, Johnny thinks, than his son does; Dirigible participated in deceiving his father with his mother when he was a boy. Besides the ineffectual fathers, there are only the shopkeepers, grinning and nodding over the produce in Chinatown vegetable stores.

All three protagonists are embodied in Tampax Lum, the main character in the play "Chickencoop Chinaman," which is a forum for Chin's ideas on Chinese American culture, identity, and manhood. The play contains a series of lessons for Chinese Americans: that Asian American culture can be found neither by imitating whites nor by imitating Blacks; that Asian Americans should not be forced into either an "American" or a "Chinese" mold; that Asian Americans should not allow themselves to be used as a "model minority." Chin's opinions, as expressed elsewhere in essays, are presented through the characters and situations in the play. But instead of building a new manhood and a new culture to replace the bankrupt Chinatown culture through his imaginative writing, Chin creates an overriding sense of the utter futility of the male protagonist's efforts to redefine himself.

In "Chickencoop Chinaman," Chinese American identity has been manufactured in a chickencoop by racism: it is "nylon and acrylic. . . . A miracle synthetic! Drip dry and machine washable." Chinese Americans are "children of the dead," their language the "talk of orphans." The legacy of Chinese American manhood is recalled only in vague references to a "Chinatown Kid" who used to frequent boxing matches and whose name no one can quite remember. Tam and his best friend, Blackjap Kenji, get together to sing a song imitating Helen Keller, who symbolizes Asian Americans, since she overcame her "birth defects" and can now see, hear, and speak no evil.

At first, when Tam speaks aggressively and with wit, it seems that he will be the embodiment of the new Chinese American man. But the play ends with Tam, "like a mad elephant, blowing his nose in the dark," chopping green onions with a Chinese cleaver. He has rejected the "petrified cheerios," the Aunt Jemima pancakes, and the "Chun King chopped phooey" of race stereotyping. He has also rejected the myth that Asians could be like Blacks, but he has as yet found nothing to replace the stereotypes and false directions. There are no new mythical heroes; the Chinatown Kid is not his father but a nameless dishwasher who was afraid of old white ladies peeking at him through keyholes.

Tam, the central character who might have embodied a new Asian American male identity, backs down when the half-Chinese girl attacks him, saying, "Everything you say is right. I'm a good loser. I give up." When he tries to fight, he misses the punch and falls flat on his face: "I'm the Chickencoop Chinaman. My punch won't crack an egg, but I'll never fall down." Until he can regain his true heritage, his identity, and his masculinity, he is good mostly for talk, which he hopes to inject with "some flow, some pop, some rhythm." He tries to seduce the Hong Kong Girl with his talk:

> *Hong Kong Dream Girl*: You sure have a way with words, but I'd like it better if you'd speak the mother tongue.
> *Tam*: I speak nothing but the mother tongue. . . . But I got a tongue for you baby. And maybe you could handmake my bone China.

But she giggles and runs off. When the half-Chinese girl attacks him, he retorts the only way he can, answering, "Wanna fuck?" The play ends with Tam as a midget like Dirigible—a frozen, hopeful midget, but a midget all the same. Although he is eager to find his own history, style, language, and masculine identity now that he has shed self-deception and false heroes, he is not complete. He is still experimenting.[28]

Chin calls Lum a "comic embodiment of Asian-American manhood." Although Chin contends that Tam Lum is a comic figure and the play a comedy, beneath the wit of his verbal jousts peer some of the images of death, decay, and impotence of the earlier stories, in scenes totally devoid of beauty or the possibility of love. The worlds Chin has created are peopled by repulsive cripples and synthetic orphans. One is never quite sure whether or not to laugh at the "comic manifestations of Asian-American manhood"; we are carried forward on clever metaphors and images until we are faced with the Asian American male protagonist squirming helplessly, pinpointed by his own verbal barbs.

Chin says that he wants to promote the creation of an Asian American mythology and language that is not alien or hostile to the Asian American sensibility. The task of the Asian American writer, he asserts, is "to legitimize the language, style, and syntax of his people's experience, to codify the experiences common to his people into symbols, cliches, linguistic mannerisms, and a sense of humor that emerges from an organic familiarity with the experience."[29]

But Chin's protagonists are alienated characters. Their language is often witty and ornate but it is seldom the "backtalking, muscular, singing stomping full-blooded language" Chin believes should express the "Asian American sensibility." Tam Lum's "backtalk" emerges as "outtalk." His characters are used as mouthpieces for thinly disguised lectures on Chinese American history, identity, and manhood, as in the following unbalanced dialogue:

> *Tam*: I mean, we grow up bustin our asses to be white anyway. . . . [W]hat made the folks happiest was for some asshole, some white off the wall J. C. Penney's clerk type with his crispy suit to say I spoke English well—
>
> *Lee*: You're talking too fast for me. I can't . . .
>
> *Tam*: (Continuing through Lee's interruption). And praisin me for being "Americanized" and no juvenile delinquency. "The strong Chinese family . . . Chinese culture." And the folks just smiled. The reason there was no juvenile delinquency was because there were no kids! The laws didn't let our women in . . .
>
> *Lee*: What's this got to do with anything?
>
> *Tam*: . . . and our women born here lost their citizenship if they married a man from China. And all our men here, no women, stayed here, burned all their diaries, their letters, everything with their names on it . . . threw the ashes into the sea . . . hoping that that much of themselves could find someplace friendly. I asked an old man if that was so. He told me it wasn't good for me to know such things, to let all that stuff die with the old.
>
> *Lee*: You taking me to school?
>
> *Tam*: He told me to forget it . . . to get along with "Americans." Well, they're all dead now. We laugh at 'em with the "Americans," talk about them saying "Buck Buck bagaw" instead of "giddyup" to their horses and get along real nice here now, don't we?
>
> *Lee*: Oh, Tam, I don't know.

In "Food for All His Dead," Johnny suspects the problem: "I hear myself talking all this stupid stuff, it's sort of great, you know? Because I have to listen to what I'm saying or I'll miss it." In "Goong Hai Fot Choy," Dirigible says, "I'm constantly surprised at what I have to say when no one is listening to me in the same room," and Tam Lum in "Chickencoop Chinaman" keeps talking, even though he is tired of talking, because "everytime I stop it's so goddamned awful!"[30]

The Chinese American identity Chin forges through the language and characterization of Fred, Dirigible, Johnny, and Tampax Lum is incomplete. The characters are alienated adolescents, incapacitated by the sense of their own impotence. But they are the only characters in Chin's stories and plays that emerge clearly. All the other characters are mere types. Johnny's parents are not developed; Dirigible's mother is a symbol; in fact, the women in Chin's writings belong to one of two types—dumb broads or castrators. In "Chickencoop Chinaman," the half-Chinese woman is a castrating bitch and the "Hong Kong dream girl" in her "super no-knock, rust-proof, tit-stiffening bra" and bouffant hairdo is simply a stereotype.

Frank Chin has delineated some of the factors that have suppressed the Asian American male, but a new identity has yet to be forged. It seems obvious that as long as the Asian American male is depicted as a victim of his community, his family, and women in general, the portrayal will be imcomplete. Chin's basic contempt for his characters, a contempt that is mixed with compassion for Tampax Lum and his kindred heroes, leaves the reader with the impression of futility and bored misanthropy. Chin flails out at the emasculating effects of oppression, but he accepts his oppressors' definition of "masculinity." The result is unresolved tension between contempt and desire to fight for his Asian American characters.

The battle against this oppression is individualized in the stories and plays; that the main characters are afflicted with metaphysical *angst* and elitist fantasies is no wonder, since they are drawn large and detailed compared to the mechanical toys and insects that people their world. Chin's preoccupation with death and decay, his sexism, cynicism, and sense of alienation have prevented him from creating protagonists who can overcome the devastating effects of racism on Chinese American men.

### Jeffery Paul Chan

In three short stories, Jeffery Paul Chan also grapples with the problem of identity for the young Chinese American male. In "Jackrabbit" (1974), young Frankie struggles to establish his masculine identity by pretending to be Indian instead of Chinese and by seeking out white whores in the adjacent town. He works in a diner with Old Pete, an aging Chinese bachelor whose life in America has been "like a fearful amnesia, filled with the feeling of hunger and despair and the loneliness he discovered in the human zoo" of Chinatown. America has been an "immigrant's prison" to old Pete. He recalls the life he shared with other Chinese bachelors,

> huddled with their legs drawn to their tight scrotums, talking of women, imaging the idylls of an afternoon spent under the warm quilt of a perfumed sing-song girl, imagining enough for the months

and years spent in America. All the little grunts and squeals they remembered, a kind of helpless awe at their own strength, each alone, taking a long piss in the wind.

Pete had seen a young Chinese hang himself shortly after arriving in America because he refused the life of celibacy and forced bachelorhood that was the lot of his fellow immigrants:

> "I think he had a wife in China and someone told him that only merchants can bring their wives here."
> "How can that be?"
> "It's true. I helped clean the cell, He was still hard and he had a big one too. He died with his hand wrapped around his cock. It's true. I saw it."

Pete had survived, but he had not flourished here, where Chinese were relegated to ghettos like buffaloes confined to small cages, "standing in their own shit, in the zoo at Angel Island or the big zoo of Chinese in San Francisco." After young Frankie comes to work at the store, Pete feels the urge to father the boy, to teach him something. But he is incapable of being a father to Frankie, since his own life has been stunted and incomplete. All he can offer is the impossible dream of their going to China together, or perhaps of visiting San Francisco Chinatown on a day off. He wants to instill in the boy a sense of his "Chinese identity," urging him to visit Chinese whores instead of white ones. But the Chinese male identity Old Pete holds forth is not viable for Frankie:

> "Nobody claims me, Pete. Not all my life. Mebbe next year I'm going to be an Indian around here. Hunt rabbits and scalp the Chinese. Mebbe raise mustangs in Las Vegas."
> "You Chinese, boy."
> "Come on, Pete. You said your own self, Chinese are in a zoo here. You want me to start a tong war? Eat cats? Grow a tail?"

In the end, Old Pete contributes to the boy's death because of his own cowardice and inability to act. When a white man bullies the boy, Pete exacerbates the situation by insisting that Frankie is Chinese instead of Indian, which only makes the white man more eager to harm him. Old Pete stands fearfully by, avoiding Frankie's eyes, while the white man beats the boy. Afterwards, he is still unable to understand why Frankie resisted the man:

> "You stupid boy."
> "Naaw, Pete."
> "Yeah, You stupid aw-right. That guy would have killed you."

"He stuck his fingers in my dinner."

"Jackrabbit."

"Don't matter." He cried out in pain. "It was mine."

The two Chinese American men are like the pair of jackrabbits in the cooking pot: tough, foul, and useless. When Frankie is killed, Pete thinks he is an Indian sleeping in the road. The young Chinese American is unable to establish his own identity because of the failure of the old, who refuse to give up the illusions that have limited their own lives.[31]

Jeffery Paul Chan emphasizes the futility of fantasies about China orientation. He is also concerned with smashing the myth of an exotic Chinatown, which he sees as an impediment to the assertion of a new identity for young Chinese Americans. In "Auntie Tsia Lays Dying" (1972), the narrator recalls scenes from his childhood as he watches his old aunt on her deathbed. Auntie Tsia had told him stories of China, but he is unable to make sense of her past, her present, and her Chinese identity because she confuses dream with memory and stereotypes herself. Her memories of kite-flying in China are combined in his mind with visions of hungry Chinese hordes. He somehow infers that "all of China stood expectant and hungry just beyond the bamboo ramparts, in a phalanx one mile wide and often deep." Now, as he gazes at her in the ward for the dying, he suspects that her "Peh River fishing song" was a fraud and "somehow, slightly ridiculous," like the phoney Chinese satires she fed to eagerly expectant Chinatown tourists:

> "That is Pagoda, the telephone for all the Chinese people in Chinatown. You see the many roofs," she wheezes. "That is because the many roofs keep the building cool in summer and warm in winter."
>
> They listen. There must be more. . . . "But why does the roof curl up like that, at the corners?"
>
> Auntie Tsia's face splits and divides, an ancient lacquer mask of lines, a map, and her entire expression, which seems fenced and gated by her tiny wire-frame glasses, leaps out to them: like a child, a pure and trusting sensibility shapes her quaint accent to their ears. She lowers her voice, and her raspy explanation touches their hearts, and she tells them, "When the eaves curl up, the building is happy and laughing like Ho Tai. . . . For children there is so much sadness when the mouth is straight or drooping. It is for them that the emperor of China many, many years ago told his builders that "everything must smile for my people, just as my people must smile for every occasion and be very happy." *Velly hoppy.*[32]

Chinatown and Auntie Tsia are like her fish store, dusty, dimly lit, and harboring "kept and secret selves." And Chinatown is like the "glass bound world" of the fish she keeps in tanks overcrowded with ordinary fish that tourists hope have some exotic identity. But like the Chinatown telephone booth, the fish store is a practical item: Auntie Tsia operates the store to make a living. In the end, she grows tired of the tourists and the fish, and she gives up trying to satisfy the tourists' demands for exotic stories:

> "Is this a fish market? What kind of fish is that?"
> "A small goldfish," she would vaguely reply.
> "And that one, there, what is that?"
> "That one is a large goldfish."
> "Well, isn't that wonderful. Oh, but what is that big one, the yellow orange fish with the snail on its back? Just look at it!"
> "It's dead."[33]

To the people of Chinatown, the community is a home, where off-duty waiters groom their hair with peanut oil and retired herbalists and off-duty amahs watch children at play in the park. To them, the clusters of tourists they must step around are "a jabbering swarm of monkeys, . . . tall, white-faced trees with straw hats" pointing eagerly at tawdry marketplace stalls laid out with

> a jumble of Hong Kong miscellany, tumbling blocks, rattan finger traps, commercial pranks—rubber flowers that spit a stream of water, magnetic dogs—and sugared coconut, dry fortune cookies, almond cookies, sesame seed cookies, dried litchi nuts, and a thousand other things, pickled, glazed, roasted, or embalmed, all tempting.[34]

To the narrator, Chinatown is a place of death, where listless celibacy and sterile imcompleteness are thinly covered by a cheap facade. Auntie Tsia's death is like the death of Chinatown: "Clearly, there is something to this Chinese dying, and the nonsense of Ho Tai, and the colors: silver, red, yellow . . . her brownness. The fish kites. Her dying is endless." As Auntie Tsia lies dying, she struggles to remember everything through dreams, but her memories remain incomplete. She has floated through an unreal world, and the narrator's attempt to understand the significance of her life and death is his attempt to understand Chinatown and the Chinese American experience. He feels "lost" and "guilty" because he alone must describe her life and death as well as explain himself through the description. Oppressed by the misconceptions of himself and of Chinatown, he wants to communicate beyond the veneer of exotic Chinatown, although he is only able to set forth what he is not: "I think I may not be deserving. I feel very guilty. So let me try very hard to speak clearly, sparingly, so that anyone I talk to may realize that I am a little less than what my appearance suggests—but more, however, than I am willing ever to reveal."[35]

The young Chinese American man is less "Chinese" than he may appear. We discover more about what he is not than what he is in "Auntie Tsia Lays Dying." In "The Chinese in Haifa" (1974), Chan moves further towards delineating a new identity for the Chinese American man. He is American, not Chinese: the main character, Bill Wong, is a Chinese American teacher who lives in the suburbs, smokes marijuana, and likes blintzes. To him, Chinese heritage is like the grimy, cracking, flaking antique Chinese furnishings he half-dreams his Chinese American wife is taking with her as she leaves him. He calls his sister-in-law's house in Chinatown "The Chickencoop," where Chinese Americans live like barnyard animals. His wife and sister-in-law plan to send his children to Hong Kong so that they can learn Chinese and "keep their Chinese heritage," perhaps even write their father letters in Chinese. To Wong, Chinese education amounts to "prefrontal lobotomy" of "Chinese torture"; he will be unable to read letters written in Chinese. After his wife and children are gone, having taken everything, even the towels, with them, Wong feels unburdened and looks forward to spending the winter in his newly vacant house having an affair with his Jewish neighbor's green-eyed, blond-haired wife.

Frank Chin and, to a lesser extent, Jeffery Paul Chan seem pessimistic about the possibility of a positive identity for the Asian American man. Chin's own vituperative condemnation of the foreign-born Chinese and of women who share to a great degree the problems of racism and discrimination suffered by Asian men places him in uneasy alliance with their mutual oppressors, who might gladly join him in his gloomy predictions for the future for Asian Americans:

> There is no doubt in my mind that the Asian American is on the doorstep of extinction. There's so much out-marriage now that all that is going to survive are the stereotypes. White culture has not acknowledged Asian-American art. Either you're foreign in this country, or you're an honorary white. I hope we can create work that will add to the human estate, but then I think we'll die out.[36]

When Chin left San Francisco for Seattle in the mid-1970s, he said he was leaving "for his health." Seattle, he says, has been special in Chinese American history: "The ghosts of cooks come here to cook specialties and leave them in the kitchen. Killers came here to die. Some are still dying." Chin even deems his work as a "cultural warrior" attempting to restore and perpetuate a Chinese American sensibility as doomed to failure. What he seems to be concentrating on is an ornately expressive, though premature, epitaph:

> [W]hen we're all gone, the greatness that was Asian America will be seen in the works and stories and art of the Japanese and Chinese Americans who happened here, in Seattle. San Francisco has already forgotten we were ever there. . . . San Francisco is where I fight. But I know Seattle is where I'll come to die in the presence of yellow familiars.[37]

### Shawn Hsu Wong

Chin's gloom and pessimism is counterbalanced in Shawn Hsu Wong's short novel, *Homebase* (1979). *Homebase* is about a Chinese American's journey to search for and claim roots in American soil. The book emerges as a triumphant reaffirmation of the Chinese American heritage and ends with a reconciliation between father and son, who are linked by their American roots.

The book opens with a reference from a garden book to the Chinese tree planted a century ago in California gold country. Beautiful and unwanted, the tree has flourished under the most difficult conditions:

> Inconspicuous greenish flowers are usually followed by handsome clusters of red-brown, winged fruits in late summer and fall. . . . Often condemned as a weed tree because it suckers profusely, . . . it must be praised for its ability to create beauty and shade under adverse conditions—drought, hot winds, and every type of difficult soil.

The Chinese American narrator, Rainsford, is haunted by the ghosts of the men of his great-grandfather's generation, men who built the railroads over the High Sierras. He imagines letters his great-grandfather might have written home to China, letters in which his desire to trade his wanderer's life for a permanent home in America are expressed:

> [W]hen the railroad is finished, I do not want the seasons to run over my back, letting the days and night, the weather ride me, break me. I will find a piece of land to work where I can remain in one place and watch the seasons ease on that place, root down in this difficult soil, and nurture my land.[38]

But the Chinese were "motherless and wifeless . . . in a country that hated us." The railroad builders worked their way from the hinterland to the ocean's edge. Rainsford imagines that they tried to swim home to China, and that the desert sands and the white surf are made of their broken bones, bleached by sea and sun. He is haunted by the presence of the ghosts of these unnamed ancestors. Now he must travel as they did, running through the night, his heart burning like the red iron engine of the trains they laid track for, driving, running, searching for his roots, moving across America "picking up ghosts":

> I run through a thick night, that night of black soot mixing with my sweat to drip like tears from my face; my heart is the engine's red iron and if I stop running I will be burned. Now the night driver is in me. The old night train filled with Chinamen, my grandfathers, fathers, all without lovers, without women, struggling against black iron with hands splintered from coarse cross ties. I am driving my car, moving out of a narrow side road at ninety onto a highway. With my father's spirit I am driving at night. No music. No more dreams. There is only the blur of the white line, the white guard rail at the edges of my sight as I outrun the yellow glare of lights, an ache at the temples and a pulse in the whites of my palms, knowing what is in front of me.

Beside him races the night train, built by his ancestors. The heart of America lies beneath, "in immovable granite mountains." The roots his forefathers laid down in the land are like "the roots of giant trees, . . . sharp talons in the earth of my country," clinging close to the heart of the land.[39]

Rainsford has been an orphan, living on the fringes of America, speaking Chinese or English like a ventriloquist's dummy through a grimace of clenched teeth. He dreams of traveling across the country "to straighten out America" with a patronizing, whining, "cheerleader-teaser" white teenage girl, "the shadow, the white ghost of all my love life; . . . the true dream of my capture of America":

> She is America. She tells me things about me that I am not. America patronizes me and loves me and tells me that I am the product of the richest and oldest culture in the history of the world. She credits me with all the inventions of modern life, when in fact I have nothing of my own in America.

But the girl does not understand him, does not listen to him; she thinks he is speaking Chinese. When Rainsford finally rejects her "love," she becomes irritated and tells him to go back to where he came from: "You people are not polite, you should be more like . . ." She never finished the statement. She couldn't figure out whom we should be more like. Finally, she said, "Just go back home."

Rainsford knows that he is "already at home." He drives on alone in the night terrified that he will not be able to be like his father, who had known where his home "stood rooted." He is seeking his home, his legacy, and his indentity. He sees his grandfather in the mountain fog and smells his clothes in the redwood trees as he travels through the canyons and cascades where his forefathers once worked and were buried. He dreams of walking with his father through a forest, talking like him, laughing like him, smelling like him. When he reconciles his life with his father's he finds his strength and his roots in American soil: "I knew then that I was only my father's son, that he was grandfather's son and grandfather was great-grandfather's son and that night we were all the same man.[40]

An American Indian tells Rainsford that he must find out where his people have been, see the town he is named after, so that he can claim his home, his history, and the legacy of his forefathers. Rainsford memorizes the names of towns that have been part of the Chinese American past: "[E]ach town is a day in a journal, an entry in a diary, a letter, a prayer." He feels the spirits of his ancestors rising to greet him everywhere, and he senses his father's presence in every canyon.

> This chronicling of my life should be given the name of a place. A place for friends, family, and lovers. A place I can see all the way home. A clearing full of sun. A stronghold that doesn't keep me in but pushes me away from it and makes me survive. And today, after 125 years of our life here, I do not want just a home that time allowed me to have. America must give me legends with spirit.

By claiming America as his own and by reaffirming the love that connects his life to the lives of his father and forefathers, Rainsford can affirm his American identity: "[I]dentity is a word full of home. Identity is a word that whispers, not whispers, but *gets* you to say, "ever, ever yours. . . ." Dear Father, I say, I write, I sing, I give you my love, this is a letter, whispering those words, "ever, ever yours.""[41]

When his father died, Rainsford could not comfort his mother because he could not understand and somehow feared her love for the dead man. He thought she had failed him by dying, that she had no longer wanted to stand beside him, leaving behind only the cold and hollow night sound of her jade bracelet knocking against the house. What remains to Rainsford is a future reconciliation with the Chinese American women, whom he will one day find again:

> [W]hen I dwell on my own grief for an instant, I like to think I'm on a road heading out to Wisconsin where I loved a woman, where she now lives. Her own grandfather lit out from China, sailed over the Pacific, and fled from the West Coast to Wisconsin and set roots

there. She gave me part of her life back there early one summer when I was still dreaming about grandfathers, trying to pull all of my past together. . . . But she is only the myth of the perfect day until I do get back to her home, she is the summit I must return to in the end.[42]

## Maxine Hong Kingston

Aside from Toshio Mori, few Asian American male writers have attempted multidimensional portrayals of Asian American women. They have been primarily concerned with defining themselves as men and with defining their status as members of the Asian American minority. Carlos Bulosan's *America Is in the Heart*, for example, reflects the conditions faced by Filipino men in the United States during the 1930s, when the ratio of Filipino men to women in some cities was as high as forty-seven to one. With the exception of the mother in the Philippines, Bulosan's women are mostly either prostitutes or idealized white women who symbolize the America to which the narrator so ardently seeks to belong. The Chinese woman in Louis Chu's *Eat A Bowl of Tea* is part seductress and part child. Mei Oi's intrusion into the narrow confines of the male-dominated Chinatown ghetto of the late 1940s is profoundly disruptive, but the novel is about the men, and Mei Oi exists primarily as an insistent reminder to them of their failure as husbands and fathers. She is a measure of the men's state of being, but as a character she lacks the dimensions of the male characters: she is unable to understand, let alone consciously influence, the forces that shape her life and theirs. In John Okada's *No-No Boy*, as in Bulosan and Chu, the identities of the characters as males are inextricably tied to their status as Asians in American society. Okada's women, on the other hand, are stick figures. We are not privy to why Ichiro's mother has allowed herself to become demented by her illusions, nor do we gain much insight into the emptiness that causes Emi to seek solace in the arms of men. The women in Okada's novel are appendages of the male characters around whom the book revolves.

Although his portrayals of the women are unidimensional, Okada is not anti-female. Among some contemporary Asian American male writers, however, a strident anti-female attitude can be discerned. As we have seen, the effects of racism on Asian American manhood are a critical issue in the works selected by Chin, Chan, Inada, and Wong for their anthology. In their view, the Asian American experience is unique from that of other racial minorities in the United States because of white racist attempts to exclude Asian Americans not only from American culture and society but also from "the realm of manliness"; reaffirmation of Asian American cultural integrity necessarily requires the assertion of a "recognized style of Asian-American manhood in a society where a manly style is prerequisite to respectability and notice." Chin, Chan, and others have concluded that manliness means "aggressiveness, creativity, individuality, just being taken seriously," while femininity means "lacking daring, originality, aggressiveness, assertiveness, vitality."[43]

Nor are most contemporary Asian American male writers concerned with Asian American women except as stereotypes. Chin's women are mothers who suffocate their sons, vapid girls who are unable to appreciate the complexity and sensitivity of their boyfriends, and arrogant assimilationists who operate in complicity with white racists, scorning the young man's search for self-respect and recognition. In Eugene Hum Chang's "Hypnogenocide," an Asian man is filled with rage at the sight of a white man walking with an Asian woman:

> How can I quench this hate, forget the past
> In a land where
> I am a victim
> And my women occupied

The Asian man in the poem cannot decide whom to strike first—the white man, who is the "murderer," or the Asian woman, who is the "traitor."[44]

Frank Chin has even argued, as we have seen, that the masculinity of Asian American men is threatened by the comparatively large number of Asian American women writers. Nonetheless, Chin and Jeffery Paul Chan appreciate writers like Noriko Sawada, Emily Cachapero, Wakako Yamauchi, Eleanor Wong Telemaque, and Hisaye Yamamoto, who have demonstrated a profound sympathy for an understanding of their men and whose efforts complement the efforts of male writers to correct distortions and omissions about Asian American men. But they have objected vehemently to Maxine Hong Kingston's attempts to delineate her experiences from the point of view of a Chinese American woman. Chin and Chan allege that Kingston's primary concern is the marketplace, the Kingston's *The Woman Warrior* (1975, 1976) represents her attempts to "cash in" on a "feminist fad." Chinese American psychologist and writer Ben Tong accuses Kingston of "selling out . . . her own people" by addressing herself to a predominantly white readership and gift-boxing old cliches about China and Chinese Americans, thereby obscuring the fact that Chinese Americans are not exotic foreigners but have deep roots in American life. Tong classifies Kingston's work as "white-pleasing autobiography passing for pop cultural anthropology." He even contends that in order to sell books, she depicts Chinese American women as superior to the men, indeed as victims of "perpetual torment at the hands of awful yellow men" who do not "perpetuate

Cantonese culture and traditions as their long-suffering female counterparts do.[45]

These and other criticisms of Kingston's perspectives suggest that the critics are suffering from anti-female biases. Even if Kingston did contend that Asian women are superior to men, which she clearly does not, is it not true that her critics often portray the Asian American male as hero and the female as villainess? Why should not the tables be turned when a women's viewpoint is offered? Is a woman's perspective necessarily anti-male? Should a man's perspective be anti-female?

A comprehensive look at *The Woman Warrior* and at *China Men* (1980) reveals that Kingston is never anti-male. Moreover, it can be seen that she shares the fundamental concerns expressed in literature by Asian American men: *The Woman Warrior* is an attempt to sort out what being a Chinese American means, and *China Men* lays claim to America for Chinese Americans, thereby permanently reconciling the immigrant and American-born Chinese. Both books are built around the themes of righteous vengeance and assertion: the author and the characters clearly belong to the tradition of Asian American literature that includes not only Bulosan, Chu, and Okada but also Chin and Chan.[46] Nor does the fact that Kingston is addressing common concerns from a woman's vantage point separate her from them, since to them and to her sexual identity, racial identity, and national identity come together when the claim is laid on America: the place that Frank Chin's male protagonists seek in American society will be based on acceptance of them as men; the place *The Woman Warrior's* narrator seeks will be based on acceptance of her as a woman. Kingston shares more with Chin than he would probably care to admit.

### *The Woman Warrior*: Sorting Out A Chinese American Identity

Although Kingston has said that sexism has been the "primary question in her own consciousness,"[47] *The Woman Warrior* is also a landscape of the consciousness and experience of the contemporary American-born daughter of Chinese immigrant parents. *The Woman Warrior* is about women, but it is primarily about the Chinese American's attempt to sort fact from fantasy in order to come to terms with the paradoxes that shape her life as a member of a racial minority group in America.

The narrator of *The Woman Warrior* "sees double" almost all the time: she has two vantage points, and the images are blurred. Continually confronted with dualities, contradictions, and paradoxes, she struggles to discern "what is real" from what is illusory by asking questions, trying to name the unnamed, and "speaking the unspeakable." First, she needs to know what is her Chinese heritage and what is simply externally imposed stereotype or individual idiosyncrasy:

Chinese Americans, when you try to understand what things in you are Chinese, how do you separate what is peculiar to childhood, to poverty, insanities, one family, your mother who marked your growing with stories, from what is Chinese? What is Chinese tradition and what is the movies?[48]

The subtitle of the book is "Memoirs of a Girlhood among the Ghosts." A number of white reviewers of the book focus a great deal more attention on Kingston's passing references to some whites as "Meter-Reader Ghosts" or "Five-and-Dime Ghosts" than Kingston herself does, perhaps because they are continually searching for their own counterparts in an unfamiliar Chinese American world.[49] Kingston herself has said, however, that the "ghosts" in the subtitle are not simply white people but "shadowy figures from the past" or unanswered questions about unexplained actions of Chinese, whites, and Chinese in America.

In *The Woman Warrior*, secrecy among the Chinese in America has been made necessary by harsh and racially discriminatory immigration policies. Chinese immigrants changed their names and lied about their ages and ports of entry, sometimes making their lives unintelligible to their American-born children: "There were secrets never to be said in front of the ghosts, immigration secrets whose telling could get us sent back to China. . . . 'Don't tell,' said my parents, though we couldn't tell if we wanted to because we didn't know." In many Asian immigrant families, culture is lived, not explained. Practices become confusing when customs are observed outside their original context, in a new social environment where they may seem inappropriate. In *The Woman Warrior*, the Chinese immigrant parents do not explain their behavior and practices to their children, who find themselves forced to learn about Chinese village practices by trial and error. The American-born Chinese children lose interest in understanding Chinese traditions when their parents "get mad, evasive, and shut up if you ask." They begin to conclude that the immigrant Chinese "make up their customs as they go along."[50] A jumbled collage of contradictory mental pictures of China results from the parents' not explaining enough on the one hand and funneling vivid stories of Chinese village life into their consciousnesses on the other. The American-born Chinese is left with feeling familiar with and at the same time uninformed about China. What she commands is a view of China as she pieces it together from what her parents and other immigrants tell or fail to tell her.

To the narrator, China is a place her parents call "home," where Han people are seen everywhere, where time passes more slowly than in America, and where flowers smell fresh and real. Each night, the mother explains how the children might find the village house, to which the parents intend to take them eventually. But the narrator does not want to "return" to China, where she has never been. To her, China is the distant end of the world:

> As a child I feared the size of the world. The farther away the sound of howling dogs, the farther away the sound of the trains, the tighter I curled myself under the quilt. The trains sounded deeper and deeper into the night. They had not reached the end of the world before I stopped hearing them, the last long moan diminishing toward China.[51]

The Chinese American's mental picture of China is a composite gathered from American movies and books and shreds from Chinese letters and legends. In China, a female is condemned to suffer eternally, even after death, because she has given birth to an illegitimate child. Also in China, Chinese Americans are told, the improverished and oppressed peasants are avenged by a legendary woman warrior disguised as a man. The Chinese Communists, they hear, are thieves and murderers, but they have also liberated the Chinese woman in modern times: "I've seen Communist pictures showing a contented woman sitting on her bunk sewing. . . . The woman looks very pleased. The Revolution put an end to prostitution by giving women what they wanted: a job and a room of their own."[52] The Chinese American finds that her own relatives in China are not the poor to be championed, but, due to remittances from America, have become barons who must be eliminated by the same Communists who have saved Chinese women from exploitation and despair.

To resolve these contradictions, the Chinese American will have to go to China to find out "who's lying—the Communists who say they have food and jobs for everybody or the relatives who write that they have not the money to buy salt." Until then, she will have to expect to inherit the task of sending money to these unknown relatives herself: "I'll send the relatives money, and they'll write me stories about their hunger. . . . I've been making money; I guess it's my turn. . . . It would be good if the Communists were taking care of themselves; then I could buy a color TV."[53]

One of the most critical contradictions facing the Chinese American woman in *The Woman Warrior* is the relationship between her perceptions of her Chinese heritage and American realities. This contradiction is explored primarily through the question of the women's status and role in both only obliquely understood societies.

Brave Orchid, the mother, is a woman of such fiery fortitude that she almost overpowers the narrator with her strength and vitality. After immigrating to America late in life to labor beside her husband in a laundry, she bears six children; at the age of eighty, she is still queueing up with Mexicans, Filipinos, and San Francisco winos to demand a day's work in the California tomato fields.[54] Two of the mother's stories of women are etched indelibly in the daughter's mind. The roles of these two women are paradoxical and dualistic, setting the tone for the entire book. The first is the unnamed aunt, the No-Name Woman who seems at first to be a victim but later emerges almost as an avenger. Having drowned herself in the drinking water, she might have been a "spite suicide." Despite the fact that she is supposed to be remembered only as a lesson in virtue to the females of the scandalized family, her spirit haunts the narrator. The counterpart of the No-Name Woman is Fa Mu Lan, the legendary woman warrior who avenges the wrongs perpetrated by land-owners and warlords against the peasants of China and who eventually becomes a model of filial piety and female docility.

The Chinese American daughter is forbidden to ask about "Father's-drowned-in-the-well-sister" who has no name, but years later and thousands of miles away, she remains tormented by unanswered questions: Did the baby's father participate in the rampage of the indig-nant villagers? Had the aunt been in love with him—did an urge for romance inspire her adultery, or had she been seduced or raped? What had passed through her mind as she gave birth in the pigsty and as she prepared to die? If the baby had been male—and the narrator assumes that the double suicide was only possible because it was not—would the outrage have abated? In times of plenty, would the villagers have acted differently?

The Chinese American feels strangely akin to her Chinese predeces-sor: like her, she is "like a tribal person, alone." She might even be a "substitute" in another life. The narrator's desperate desire to know what threads connect her to this mysterious ancestor turns her unwittingly into an avenger: her first task is to defy those who mean to obliterate the aunt—and the Chinese American descendants—with their silence. The Chinese American wants to know what else there was and is always trying to get things straight, always trying to name the unspeakable. Even though she is warned never to tell on the No-Name Woman, she begins her narration with the entire forbidden story.

The aunt's tragedy forces the Chinese American woman to examine the culture that produced and attempted to destroy her. Is China really a place where daughters are sold into slavery, promised to cretinous hus-bands for money, driven to suicide, stoned to death? Even Brave Orchid implies her complicity with such practices, telling her daughter that in China girls are given away free instead of costing money as they do in America. Had not Brave Orchid herself, a midwife in China, told her daughter stories of girl babies being quietly smothered at birth in heaps of ashes provided by midwives attending the birth beds? Brave Orchid had never said that she smothered the girl babies herself, but had she not been guilty by implication? Had not the Chinese Amercian narrator participated in her aunt's punishment just because she too is Chinese? Are not anti-female attitudes expressed among the Chinese immigrants in America in jokes, sayings, curses, and proverbs indications that women's enslavement is approved of among Chinese in America?

The Chinese American girls in *The Woman Warrior* notice quickly that the birth of boys is joyfully celebrated while the birth of girls passes by unnoticed. Everyone seems to complain that girls are useless and "undeserving of the food." "Feeding girls is feeding cowbirds," they agree. "Better to raise geese than girls." When the narrator, her sisters, and her girl cousins are eating, their great-grandfather looks around at them and shouts, "Maggots! Where are my grandsons? I want grandsons!" "Chinese smeared bad daughters-in-law with honey and tied them naked on top of ant nests. . . . A husband may kill a wife who disobeys him," the narrator's father is heard saying.[55] But at the same time, we see that his own wife, Brave Orchid, is aggressively independent, a survivor to be admired rather than pitied. While anti-female adages about the necessity of wifely servitude and obedience and about the uselessness of girls abound in the Chinese immigrant culture, actual subjugation of women exists only in the stories, in Chinese operas, in jokes and aphorisms, and in the imaginings of the narrator, not in real life among the immigrants.

For the Chinese American girl, the maddening paradox is that the same culture that has produced the No-Name Woman and Moon Orchid has also produced Fa Mu Lan and Brave Orchid. The mother tells the daughter that she will be "a wife and a slave" while firing her imagination with stories of the woman warrior. The Chinese American woman imagines herself as Fa Mu Lan in the same heroic tradition, leading the soldiers in battle against the oppressors of her people, avenging the wrongs that her parents have carved into her back. Unlike the cowering, simpering women who scurry from her path with shrill insect cries, blinking weakly "like pheasants that have been raised in the dark for soft meat," Fa Mu Lan is fearless and strong.[56] The narrator resolves that she will grow up to be a warrior woman, a heroine, and a swordswoman.

The question is whether or not her Chinese heritage—and the tradition of Fa Mu Lan—can serve her in America. She must address the issue of what being a Chinese American woman means. Would a Chinese American woman warrior have to "storm across China to take back our farm from the Communists, . . . to rage across the U.S."[57] to take back the laundries in New York and California that had been swallowed up by urban renewal? Can Chinese heroism serve the Chinese American?

The indomitable woman who vanquished the Sitting Ghost in China and who colors her daughter's life with her stories has an American life that consists of sorting mountains of socks in a Chinese American laundry while shielding herself from the fumes and germs emanating

from piles of dirty clothing by burning candles and holding handkerchiefs over her mouth. "You have no idea how much I have fallen coming
to America," Brave Orchid says. Her only revenge now is private:

> "No tickee, no washee, mama-san?" a ghost would say, so
> embarrassing.
> "Noisy, Red-Mouth Ghost," she'd write on its package, naming
> it, marking its clothes with its name.[58]

To the daughter, American life has not been glorious, like the tale of
Fa Mu Lan, but "slum grubby." The Chinese immigrants can indentify
with the legendary romances and a heritage that is seen only darkly by
their daughters: "Living among one's own emigrant villagers can give a
good Chinese far from China glory and a place. "That old busboy is a
swordsman," we whisper when he goes by, "He's a swordsman who's
killed fifty. He has a tong ax in his closet.'" But all the Chinese American
girl can do in America, it seems, is get straight A's and become a clerk-
typist.[59]

In comparison with the multicolored fusion of fact and fantasy
about her Chinese heritage, American life seems prosaic, almost banal.
There are fewer ambiguities and mysteries, less color and sound. The
Chinese American girl is transformed by the American schooling experience from a quiet girl with a "zero IQ" to an "American-normal" personality. The process is painful and difficult. While secrecy might prevail
among Chinese immigrants, quietness does not. "Normal Chinese
women's voices are strong and bossy," and Chinese immigrants talk all at
once with "big arm gestures, spit flying," laughing and "hollering" at
each other during Chinese operas and Chopin violin recitals performed
by their children. Chinese Americans, on the other hand, have been
silenced by a combination of Chinese American influences. Besides their
parents' refusal or inability to explain things to their children, there is the
secrecy with which they must defend themselves against American laws
that discriminate against them. The narrator hates in turn the whites for
"not letting us talk" and the Chinese for their "secrecy." American-born
Chinese are also inhibited by the difficult task of explaining what they do
not understand completely to themselves or to anyone else. Often they
feel that only they understand completely how ignorant their Chinese
parents and the "Americans" are of each other. The Chinese American
narrator is mortified by the task of demanding "reparation candy" from
the local druggist at her mother's insistence. She knows that her mother
will never understand how the druggist will view her and that the
druggist will never comprehend her mother's anger about medicine
being mistakenly delivered to her house. As a result, the Chinese American go-between is reduced to hopeless inarticulateness:

"Mymotherseztagimmesomecandy," I said to the druggist. Be cute and small. No one hurts the cute and small.

"What? Speak up. Speak English," he said, big in his white druggist coat.

". . . My mother said you have to give us candy. She said that is the way the Chinese do it."

"What?"

"That is the way the Chinese do it."

"Do what?"

"Do things." I felt the weight and immensity of things impossible to explain.

Chinese American quietude, then, comes in part from the hope that "no one will hurt the cute and small": "Some of us gave up, shook our heads, and said nothing, not one word. Some of us could not even shake our heads. At times shaking my head no is more self-assertion than I can manage."[60]

Despite all attempts, Chinese and American, to silence her, the woman warrior's spirit surges within the Chinese American narrator. She attacks her anti-self, an alter-ego, another Chinese American girl who represents the fragility and softness of the victim as opposed to the survivor. Aggravated by the girl's neatness, her papery fingers and powder-dry pink cheeks, her pastel clothing and her tiny white teeth, she longs to be the opposite: a loud, brassy girl with big yellow teeth, wearing all black clothing. A sixth-grader "arrogant with talk, not knowing there was going to be high school dances and college seminars to set me back," the narrator imagines herself stomping on the other girl's imagined bound feet with iron shoes, forcing her to speak.[61]

The narrator finally leaves home, thinking that she has chosen the avenue which will allow her to be a woman warrior in America. She pours out a list of grievances accumulated during years of silence and confusion and unanswered questions. What seems at first to be a desire to melt into the colorless "American-normal" world is really her need to first make sense of her experiences from a safe distance.

I don't want to listen to any more of your stories: they have no logic. They scramble me up. You lie with stories. You won't tell me a story and then say, "This is a true story," or, "This is just a story." I can't tell the difference. I don't even know what your real names are. I can't tell what's real and what you make up.[62]

The narrator wants to "wrap her American successes around her like a private shawl" to prove that she is "worthy of eating the food" even though she is female. Her parents, however, contribute to her unending confusion by accusing her of not being able to "tell a joke from real life," of being stupid enough to believe talk-story, and of not understanding that Chinese "like to say the opposite."[63] It is as if the narrator had imagined everything: even the lumpish boy with the obscene magazines disappears the day after her outburst, and she wonders if she had imagined him too.

The "American-normal" world she escapes to is specific, simpler, and "ghost-free."

> I had to leave home in order to see the world logically, logic the new way of seeing. I learned to think that mysteries are for explanation. I enjoy the simplicity. Concrete pours out of my mouth to cover the forests with freeways and sidewalks. Give me plastics, periodical tables, TV dinners with vegetables no more complex than peas mixed with diced carrots. Shine floodlights into dark corners: no ghosts.

But this new, antiseptic world and this "new way of seeing" have also diminished her: "[C]olors are gentler and fewer: smells are antiseptic. Now when I peek in the basement window where the villagers say they see a girl dancing like a bottle imp, I can no longer see a spirit in a skirt made of light."[64]

The Chinese American girl must leave the immigrant community "to get out of hating range," but it is from this vibrant community, that she has drawn the sustenance of her spirit. It is not the colorless world she seeks refuge in that has taught her to see who the "enemies" are. The "stupid racists" and the "tyrants who for whatever reason can deny my family food and work" are easily recognizable to her no matter what their disguise: "Business-suited in their modern American executive guises, each boss two feet taller than I am and impossible to meet eye to eye. . . . If I took the sword, which my hate must surely have forged out of the air, and gutted [him], I would put color and wrinkles into his shirt."[65]

Although she has left the immigrant community, she longs to return: "The swordswoman and I are not so dissimilar. May my people understand the resemblance soon so that I can return to them. What we have in common are the words at our backs. . . . And I have so many words—"chink" words and "gook" words too—that they do not fit on my skin."[66] She must discern now whether she can be a Chinese American woman warrior in America. If she succeeds, it will be through her Chinese heritage, the curse and blessing of her life. The question is, will the myth of Fa Mu Lan, who fought oppression and injustice, be valid here? Will that heritage that shaped her consciousness maintain its strength-giving properties? Will it serve the Chinese American, or will it die here on foreign soil?

The sword of the Chinese American female avenger will be forged of words: "The reporting is the vengeance—not the beheading, not the gutting, but the words."[67] The Chinese American woman warrior must respond to the continual throat pain that returns unless she speaks what she thinks is the truth, to report crimes and to talk story herself. Because the American-born Chinese must confront dualities and contradiction, she is blessed with a special gift: "I learned to make my mind large, as the universe is large, so that there is room for paradoxes."[68]

*The Woman Warrior* is about a Chinese American's attempt to come to terms with the paradoxes that shape and often enrich her life and to find a uniquely Chinese American voice to serve as a weapon for her life. The attempt does not simply involve sorting what is "Chinese" from what is "Chinese American" of "American." Thus Moon Orchid, Brave Orchid and her daughter, the pink-cheeked Chinese American girl, Fa Mu Lan, and No-Name Woman are defined according to their relative strength and weakness rather than according to whether they are Chinese or Chinese American. The sorting process has to do with the narrator's identity, not only as a female, but also as an American-born Chinese. At the end of the book, the process has yet to be completed: "I continue to sort out what's just my childhood, just my imagination, just my family, just the village, just the movies, just living."[69]

### *China Men*: Claiming America

Kingston says that she wrote *The Woman Warrior* and *China Men* together, having conceived of them as an interlocking story about the lives of men and women. But the women's stories "fell into place," and she feared that the men's were anti-female and would undercut the feminist viewpoint.[70] So she collected and published the women's stories in *The Woman Warrior* first, although the men's experiences are no less important and moving to her:

> When I was working on "The Woman Warrior" . . . I thought that there would be a big difference between the men and the women. I thought that in the process of writing the new book I would learn something new about how men think. I feel that I've gone as deeply into men's psyches as I can, and I don't find them that different. I care about men . . . as much as I care about women.[71]

Kingston has said that "given the present state of affairs, perhaps men's and women's experiences have to be dealt with separately for now, until more auspicious times are with us," although she would like the two books to be boxed together as two parts of a whole to be read together until integration is more possible.[72]

In *China Men*, the narrator, who is again the daughter, is less involved with the characters and far less concerned with relating how she feels about them; Kingston says that *The Woman Warrior* was a "selfish book" in that she was always "imposing my viewpoint in the stories" through the narrator. In *China Men*, on the other hand, "the person who "talks story" is not so intrusive. I bring myself in and out of the stories, but in effect, I'm more distant."[73]

Like *The Woman Warrior*, *China Men* expresses the Chinese American experience through family history combined with talk-story, memory, legend, and imaginative projection. But while *The Woman Warrior* portrays the paradoxical nature of the Chinese American experience through the eyes of an American-born Chinese, *China Men* is a chronicle of Chinese American history less particular and less personal. The distance between the narrator and the characters in *China Men* might be attributed to the fact that Kingston heard the men's stories from women's talk-story: "[W]ithout the female storyteller, I couldn't have gotten into some of the stories. . . . [M]any of the men's stories were ones I originally heard from women."[74]

In *The Woman Warrior*, two powerful women, the mother and the daughter, contend over who will talk-story in the end. The daughter prevails because it is she who can transplant the mother's talk-story in the American environment. In *China Men*, the relationship between the father and daughter does not emerge clearly. The daughter knows the father less well: he is the Chinese scholar who toils, silent and grim-faced, in the laundry, never speaking, never talking-story, but screaming "wordless male screams that jolted the house upright and staring in the middle of the night." The daughter is distressed by the anti-female curses that he mutters under his breath as he works: "[U]sually you did not play. You were angry. You scared us. Every day we listened to you swear, 'Dog vomit. Your mother's cunt. Your mother's smelly cunt.' You slammed the iron on the shirt while muttering, 'Stink pig. Mother's cunt.'" The daughter wishes that he would reassure her that these curses do not refer to her, to her mother or sisters or to women in general, but that they are simply old Chinese sayings that have no meaning at all.[75]

But the narrator's feelings about the male characters are not often brought forth in *China Men*. She feels it necessary to step aside in order to allow them to become protagonists. In attempting to depict them, she says, "I began to see a loving way to present a character, the way he would see himself. I'm not judging all the time. . . . I have really learned to present a character from his own viewpoint. I don't have to overlay that with the narrator."[76] The male characters are presented in a gallery of diverse and general possibilities as several archetypal Chinese grandfathers and fathers, and their relationship to the narrator is almost abstract. The father appears in various guises: he could be any Chinese

American's father. He immigrates to America in five different ways, by way of Cuba, Angel Island, or Ellis Island, depending on which of the versions is real. He is called at one point "the legal father" and at another "the illegal father." He could have entered the country legally, or he could have come as a paper son or by some other avenue. He is both "the father from China" and "the American father." All of the grandfathers could have been the narrator's grandfather—not only Bak Goong, who labored and dreamed in the "Sandalwood Mountains," but also the Chinese men who carved railroad trails through the granite of the High Sierras. Ah Goong who "built a railroad out of sweat" and had an American child "out of longing" when he brought a paper son from China after the San Francisco earthquake, or even "China Joe," the generalized Chinese who is spared whenever the white men drive the rest of the Chinese from their towns—all of these could have been the narrator's grandfather.

What the China men have in common is that, unlike the mother in *The Woman Warrior*, their main objective is to "claim America." Kingston has indicated:

> What I am doing in this new book is claiming America. . . . That seems to be the common strain that runs through all the characters. In story after story Chinese American people are claiming America, which goes all the way from one character saying that a Chinese explorer found this place before Lief Ericsson did to another one buying a house here. Buying that house is a way of saying that America—and not China—is his country.[77]

The men are condemned at first to a life of loneliness, without women "to hug and comfort them in their warmth" during fearful nights. When some of the railroad workers fear that they might die in the wilderness, however, Ah Goong reminds them, "We're marking the land now. The track sections are numbered, and your family will know where we leave you." Despite all attempts to prevent them from setting down roots in America, they are leaving their mark. The narrator imagines a grandfather as a railroad worker with other single young men far from their families and their women: "He took out his penis under his blanket or bared it in the woods. . . . He also just looked at it, wondering what it was that it was for, what a man was for, what he had to have a penis for." The grandfather ejaculates into space from the mountaintop, calling out that he is "fucking the whole world."[78]

Kingston's men are victimized and kept womanless, but they are never emasculated victims. Self-assured, resilient, and vocal, the Chinese railroad strikers of 1869, of whom Ah Goong is one, are described as semi-mythical heroes: they are bare-chested and brown, muscular, "perfect young gods reclining against rocks—long torsos with lean stomachs, . . . ten thousand heroes." The Cantonese of *China Men* had always been "revolutionaries, nonconformists, people with fabulous imaginations, people who invented the Gold Mountains, . . . people who knew immensity."[79] The narrator's imaginary father is one of these, facing the blinking, bored faces of the squirming children as a teacher in the village classroom. He shoots them with an imaginary pistol, stabs them with an imaginary knife. He envisions himself flying out of the classroom into the broad expanse of sky, leaving them curious as to how he had done it.

The grandfather who immigrates to Hawaii to work in the sugar cane fields carries with him the indomitable spirit and expressiveness of the Cantonese. Although he is worked like an animal, his soul seethes with rebellion and a burning desire to break the silence imposed by the labor foremen. He complains, curses, and sings

> . . . about the black mountains reddening and how mighty was the sun that shone on him in this enchanted forest and on his family in China. . . . [H]e sang to his fellow workers. "If that demon whips me, I'll catch the whip and yank him off his horse, crack his head like a coconut. In an emergency a human being can do miracles—fly, swim, lift mountains, throw them. Oh, a man is capable of great feats of speed and strength."[80]

Even after he is whipped and punished by the plantation foremen, the grandfather cannot be silenced. He camouflages his talk in coughing curses at his oppressors. Like his descendant, the grandfather is a "talk addict." He needs to "cast his voice out to catch ideas," to marvel and to sing, and also to avenge himself with a sword forged of words.

Like *The Woman Warrior*, *China Men* is a celebration of strength and a rejection of sentimentality and self-pity. Brave Orchid and her daughter are both "tough [and] end up defeating the women who are weak."[81] Even after they are threatened with lynching, reduced to laundry labor and dodging immigration officials, cheated by lying gypsies, and taunted by racists, the spirit of the men is never broken. By "banding the nation north and south, east and west" with the transcontinental railroad, they have established their legitimacy as the "binding and building ancestors of this place."[82] Even after they are subjected to "the driving-out," they remain, planting trees that take years to bear fruit. The ghosts of Third and Fourth Grandfathers are said to haunt the stables of the farm where they once lived, and their descendants still revere the vacant lot in Stockton that they call "the ancestral ground" even after generations have passed.

Each China man claims America in his own way: although Mad Sao must venture back to China to placate his mother's ghost, he brings his wife and children to settle in America. Old "uncle" Kau Goong decides to stay in California after the "gapping, gaping spaces" of the years had "put a planet" between him and his old wife in China, to whom he finally writes, "This is my home. I belong here." The narrator's "American father" has "the power of going places where nobody else went, and making places belong to him."[83] He claims America by donning Fred Astaire clothing and admiring himself in department store windows and hubcap reflections along Fifth Avenue in New York City.

Those China men who do not "claim America" are fools and weaklings. Uncle Bun, who leaves for China immediately after the 1949 Revolution, is eventually forgotten.

*China Men* attempts to recover history from deceit and lies by telling that history from a Chinese American point of view. Kingston says she chose the title exactly because it expresses the difference between the way Chinese immigrant men viewed themselves and the way they were viewed in a racist society. They called themselves *tang jen*, or China men, while the racist called them "Chinamen." In the book, we catch glimpses of the China men's view of American society from different vantage points. They resist the missionary women's attempts to force Christianity upon them with their "grisly Jesus pictures" and their pious attempts to make them say "thank God" instead of "your mother's cunt." The China men think the missionaries must have "asses as tight as their mouths." To the Chinese, English is an illogical language: "The little H's looked like chairs, the E's like lidded eyes, but the words were not CHAIR and EYE. . . . The words had no crags, windows, or hooks to grasp. No pictures. The same A, B, C's for everything. She couldn't make out ducks, cats, and mice in American cartoons either."[84] Unlike the racists, who view them as being all alike, the Chinese in America marvel that they have traveled far enough to meet "foreign and barbarous looking China Men" from districts beyond their own villages. Contrary to the popular view of them, they care deeply for each other. They entertain each other during their incarceration at immigration stations with skits, puppet shows, operas, juggling acts, and stories. They write messages to each other on the walls of Angel Island: "This island is not angelic." "It's not true about the gold."[85] They hide and feed one another when harassed by white vandals. When one dies in a railroad accident, the others pray over his grave that his ghost will ride the train home. Once, when Ah Goong watches a worker killed, he is overwhelmed first by the desire to have an arm long enough to reach out and catch him and finally by the wish that the conscious man fall faster so that his agony might end quickly.

Even though she sees them through the eyes of an American-born Chinese woman, Maxine Hong Kingston has given voice to the immigrant Chinese men. *The Woman Warrior* begins with the story of a Chinese woman and ends with the Chinese American woman's sad and angry song. *China Men* begins with the Chinese man's lament and ends with the narrator watching "the young men who listen."[86]

The Chinese American brother, Kingston has said, is the least Chinese culturally of the men in *China Men*. As an enlisted man during the war in Vietnam, he might have been any other American. But what links him to his immigrant forbears is their Chinese heritage, their refusal to be victimized, and their mutual claim on America. The brother claims America by being in the U.S. Navy. But he is haunted by terrifying nightmares of himself as a soldier in the rescuing army walking among enemy corpses who become indistinguishable from his blood relatives in the Chinese American laundry:

> Laundry tubs drain beneath the bodies. The live women and children on the ironing tables, the last captured, are being dissected. . . . He takes up the sword and hacks into the enemy, slicing them; they come apart in rings and rolls. . . . When he stops, he finds that he has cut up the victims too, who were his own relatives. The faces of the strung-up people are also those of his own family. Chinese faces, Chinese eyes, noses, and cheekbones. He woke terrified.[87]

The Chinese American brother refuses to accept a chance to go to the army's language training school, even though it would mean being able to return home, because he thinks he will be assigned to spy on or interrogate Vietnamese, whom he finds disturbingly similar to Chinese:

> The Vietnamese call their parents Ba and Ma; *phuoc* means "happiness," "contentment," "bliss," the same as Chinese. . . . *Study, university, love*—the important words are the same in Chinese and Vietnamese. Talking Chinese and Vietnamese and also French, he'd be a persuasive interrogator-torturer. He would fork the Vietnamese—force a mother to choose between her baby with a gun at its belly and her husband hiding behind a thatch, to which she silently points with her chin. "No," he told his Commanding Officer. He had been given a choice and he said No. "No, thank you."

Despite what some Chinese American male critics of Kingston have alleged, *China Men* is not anti-male; on the contrary, it is the portrait of men of diverse generations and experiences, heroes who lay claim on America for Chinese Americans and who refuse to be silenced or victimized. They are strong and vocal men who love and care for each other. *China Men* is also about the reconciliation of the contemporary Chinese American and his immigrant forefathers, nourished by their common roots, strong and deep, in American soil. Kingston's men and women are survivors. The reconciliation between the sexes is not complete, but Kingston demonstrates that Asian American writers can depict with compassion and skill the experiences of both sexes. The men and women of *China Men* and *The Woman Warrior* are vivid and concrete refutations of racist and sexist stereotypes. The complexity and diversity of the Chinese American experience as presented in these books make continued acceptance of unidimensional views of Chinese Americans difficult: for every No-Name Woman, there is a Fa Mu Lan; for every Great Grandfather of the Sandalwood Mountains, there is a Brother in Vietnam. And for each perspective set forth by Maxine Hong Kingston, there is a myriad of other Chinese American viewpoints.

# 7

# Multiple Mirrors and Many Images
## New Directions in Asian American Literature

The Asian American population in the United States has grown and diversified in recent decades. Four generations of Japanese Americans are now scattered in cities and suburbs, mostly in Hawaii and California, while new immigrants from Hong Kong, Taiwan, South Korea, the Philippines, and Southeast Asia are making their homes in new and already established Asian American communities, adding new dimensions to the needs and interests of the already existing populations. Contemporary Asian American literature reflects increasingly diverse perspectives among the people of these changing groups. There has been a new confidence inspired by the increased use of freer forms and language since the 1960s and by Asian Americans' increased appreciation of cultural pluralism in American society, which has encouraged them to express their own personal experiences in literature and to see them as part of a larger cultural tradition.

Among many contemporary Asian American writers, there is a deliberate effort to make literature as accessible to as broad an audience as possible. Present-day Asian American writers are experimenting with colloquial language that expresses their unique sensibilities with combinations of genre forms that blend drama with poetry, prose with poetry, fiction with nonfiction, and literature with history. Music and dance as well as visual arts are being brought together with oral literature. Poetry presentations and dramatic readings in community forums have increased, as have theatre and dance workshops, and film groups have been experimenting with dramatizations of Asian American literature and docudramas, which are fictional portrayals of Asian American history. New publishing outlets are being sought by writers' collectives, and small presses and ethnic publishing companies as well as Asian American studies program facilities have been publishing new Asian American writing. Work by primary and secondary school as well as college students is being solicited, collected, and printed in journals of many kinds.[1]

The late Filipino American poet Serafin Malay Syquia used to travel around the San Francisco public school district, reading poetry to primary school children and encouraging them to express themselves in poetry. Syquia's objective was

> not to teach poetry but to expose
> then guide the flow
> making sure it runs its
> course not to get
> damned before the
> process
> to witness emergence
> the metamorphosis in
> the classroom from tight-lipped
> backrow embarrassment to the
> openness of knowing you are a
> part of the whole
> not to get bogged down in the
> same ruts conditioned from the
> first grade of constant repetition
> for the sake of impression
> > a rose is a rose is a rose
> > isn't[2]

Both Syquia and Japanese American poet Janice Mirikitani say that they began writing poetry that was imitative of various English and Anglo-American poets. Mirikitani says that she used to imitate Robert Frost, Dylan Thomas, and even some Japanese poets:

> My writing was not me until I learned . . . that I didn't have to express myself according to the standards of the "dominant" culture, because there was no "dominant" culture. There were just whites trying to suppress or kill whatever contradicted them, including the culture of nonwhites. I had no place in American life until the "ethnic identity" movement. I was just a shadow, an imitation with no soul of my own.[3]

Like Mirikitani, Syquia was inspired by the writing of American minority artists, who spoke directly to his own experiences and sensibilities by addressing a collective consciousness and by focusing on questions of social justice that seemed profoundly relevant to him as an Asian American. Syquia moved away from writing poetry meant to be read and heard by no one but himself, poetry that was turned inward, poetry in which accessibility was incidental:

> My first poem . . . was a poem other people understood more than I did. It was an irony of words. Something to do with within and without; over and under; tomorrow and yesterday. I continued writing . . . long excuses for loneliness . . . closed notebook poetry that only I could understand or that other people never saw. I played with words, loving the intricacies, ambiguities of them.
> . . . so much has changed so
> much
> since my first
> poem.[4]

Syquia and Mirikitani eagerly sought out other minority writers who had moved away from "closet poetry" and who wanted to forge art into a sword against social injustice. Even their concern about the question of the Asian American's individual identity was a social question that invariably had to do with race and racism.

The focus away from solitary, metaphysical soul-searching in Asian American writing is expressed in Shawn Hsu Wong's "Letter to Kay Boyle" (1972):

> If my generation of poets are the type
> that sit on their hands, stare at themselves
> in mirrors and constantly remind themselves
> that they are poets,
> I'll be a poet in exile.[5]

Similarly, in "Boot-Licking Art" (1979), Doug Yamamoto rejects the conventional esoteric inaccessibility he finds in much contemporary American art, preferring instead the spirit and energy expressed in community street murals, which belong to everyone, particularly to "the working folks, the ones with real imagination":

> I don't want to wrap toilet paper
> around poles,
> or make a movie of myself
> nailing doors shut
> and call myself an Artist

. . . Give me the Chinatown murals
of James Dong. . . .

. . . They breathe and move
reflecting the daily life
of schoolyards and orchards,
railroads and farms,
of heritage and survival.
The murals become not so much his
as a part of the community.[6]

Maxine Hong Kingston has asserted that talking and writing are forms of
"revenge," weapons against injustice. Frank Chin frequently alludes to
Kwan Kung, the Chinese folk god of poetry and war. James Mitsui
equates poetry to weaponry in "Samurai" (1978):

The same hand
that pauses in the autumn sky
to paint wind
whispering through bamboo,
joins the other hand
on the long hilt of a naked sword
& cuts a man in half
at the thighs,
leaving behind a pair of bloody wheels:
skin, flesh, bone & marrow.[7]

Contemporary Asian American literature is characterized by new
styles and fresh language as well as new combinations of genres and
forms. Maxine Hong Kingston has attempted to express the Chinese
American language by rendering in English the rhythms and images of
the Chinese talk-story she was "born talking." Filipino American poets
Presco Tabios and Alfred Robles approximate the Filipino accent in English to achieve new effects. In "A Manong's Language" (1976), Robles
poses a militant defense of nonstandard English as the expression of "a
brown soul":

a manong's language
is made up of
"dis" and "dat"
puckyoo sunn-obbaa-bit
muderrpuckerrrr

a manong's language
is not a textbook
bound by rules
or grammatical erections[8]

These "grammatical erections" caused Jeffery Paul Chan's editors to insist that the title of his story, "Auntie Tsia Lays Dying" be "corrected." Chan replies that he will not allow grammarians to rob the Chinese American writer of the language that expresses his own sensibility and experience:

> The object of our writing is no different from that of any other writer. We mean to inject our sensibility into the culture and make it work there. That means we are the teachers. People should ask what dictionary or other sources authorize what we say, how we talk. That's a part of learning to read.[9]

In Milton's Murayama's *All I Asking for Is My Body* (1975), the pidgin is carefully and deliberately crafted to express the bicultural realities of the Japanese American characters. Murayama's *nisei* characters speak four dialects: standard and pidgin English and standard and pidgin Japanese. The pidgin English is contained in their dialogues. Criticized for awkward translations of colloquial Japanese into English, Murayama defends these renderings as an intentional effort to authenticate his characters:

> Both brothers think in English and pidgin, and their Japanese is limited and awkward. . . . Japanese is a status-conscious language. Colloquial Japanese can exist only among peers. . . . When Kiyo speaks to his father or the language school teacher, he is still and formal. . . . When Tosh and Kiyo talk to each other, they sprinkle Japanese . . . moral words [that in] Japanese [are] colloquial and light; [in] English, heavy. A literal translation of them would have these kids spouting mouth-breaking words amidst their short pidgin words.[10]

Murayama decided to print the book himself with the help of a linotype setter from Hawaii, largely because he felt that the commercial editors would "correct the English and kill the pidgin."

*Sansei* poet Ron Tanaka introduces simple Japanese words and phrases, especially as spoken by *issei* personae, into his poems, when the Japanese word has no direct equivalent. Tanaka's poems are often linguistically mixed, reflecting the world of the American-born Japanese:

baa-chan,* if you still don't understand
doomosumimasen, doomo sumimasen.† but
maybe someday i'll do something so that
you'll see that though one thing may pass away,
what you have done, what jii-chan‡ has done,
what everyone who has helped me has done,
still lives on in the world. maybe it isn't
very serene, very holy, maybe
it's still too selfish and maybe i'll always
be chooto okashii,§ just like my Japanese.[11]

The diverse rhythms of Japanese American speech, incorporating as it does pidgin, Black English, and Japanese idioms, are rendered in Garrett Kaoru Hongo's "Gardena, Los Angeles" (1977):

I went in & spun on,
slopping a tune
over my tongue
set bacon and coffee on
the stove,
said, "Hey, bro,
play me that Santana one."

WHAT SAY!'
HOW BOUT!
HEAD ON!
GET DOWN
DO IT TO IT!
DO IT ON!

. . . "Hey braddah!
How you stay?"
   We come from
   volcano side
   Beeg Eyelan.
"Go cook rice!
I tellin you!"

*Grandmother.
†I'm very sorry.
‡Grandfather.
§A little strange.

. . . I can do
the boogaloo.
I can do
the skate.
I can do
the hole-in-the-wall,
twine, duck, &
I can do
the funky chicken.

Boogie wa dekirum [*sic*] da kedo.
Odori wa zen zen dekihen.*[12]

Contemporary Asian American writers are experimenting with new language usages and new combinations of forms and genres that they say best express their particular perspectives and experiences. Maxine Hong Kingston's *The Woman Warrior* fuses fiction with nonfiction, a fusion Kingston has said is necessary to portray the Chinese American experience as she knows it. *China Men* combines historical fact with fictional interpretation, and no one generic form dominates the book. Janice Mirikitani's short stories combine prose with poetry. Bienvenido N. Santos' *You Lovely People* (1965) combines the novel and short story forms. The book is a collection of short, self-contained episodes that comprise something like a novel through the continuity of two narrative voices who represent various facets of the Filipino identity. This form is particularly appropriate to the portrayal of the Filipino American community, according to N. V. M. Gonzalez:

> I have read these stories many times over, and I have been bothered by them. Why did not the author weave these things into a novel? . . . But, then, I was soon to discover something else, a unity which the tightness of the short-story or the discipline of the novel would have destroyed. With one convention thrown by the board, the book acquired its own. . . . In a tone and vision of his own, Santos found his fiction hard enough to bring together; it hit back at him, I imagine, finally found the method.[13]

Certain images and characters do recur in contemporary Asian American literature: Chinese American writing is filled with images of trains and journeys, images that express the Chinese American heritage of railroad building and of searching for a place in American society. In Japanese American literature, images of the desert recur, usually when the internment experience is depicted. Women who rebel against the

---

*I can boogie, but I can't do the Japanese *odori* (dance).

strictures of racism and sexism are frequent, as are the grim and resilient old men whose silent strength is expressed in their lean and spare dialogue.

Contemporary Asian American literature reflects diverse themes and tendencies. Although certain patterns can be discerned, the impression that remains is one of diversity and variation. One recurrent theme with many variations is the theme of Asian American racial and social identity, especially in relationship to the Vietnam War, American racism, and relationships with other minority groups. Also recurrent is the theme of restoring the foundations of the Asian American past and finding links between the generations and across various nationalities. Literature expressing the Asian American woman's perspective and the experiences of recent Asian immigrants is also beginning to emerge.

## The Vietnam War

Because they had been viewed historically more as members of the yellow race and, as such, perpetual foreigners than as Americans, it was difficult for some Asian Americans not to respond to the racial character of American involvement in Southeast Asia. Stunned by television news footage and photographs of war-torn hamlets, some Asian Americans said they saw the faces of their friends and relatives in the visages of the Vietnamese peasants. They were susceptible to the argument that U.S. foreign policy in Asia had always been racist and genocidal for Asians, that profits had been more important than Asian lives. They perceived the parallels between the war in Vietnam and the conquest of the Philippine resistance during the Spanish American War, in which one-sixth of the Filipino population had been killed.[14] To some, it seemed that the use of the atomic bomb on Japanese civilians during World War II was evidence of racist attitudes on the part of military decision-makers and U.S. government officials towards the members of the yellow race.

Many works of contemporary Asian American literature express intense empathy with the people of Vietnam. This empathy is frequently racial rather than overtly political, because many Asian Americans viewed racism as a political issue and because of the emotionally charged appeal of this dimension of the art form. Sometimes empathy is aroused by a sense of the similarity between languages, histories, and traditions of peasant life in Vietnam as compared with the Asian American writer's ancestral land.

In *The New Anak* (1975), Filipino immigrant writer and filmmaker Sam Tagatac writes of the Filipino American soldier in Vietnam who thinks of his native land and his countrymen when he sees the tropical sun and rains, the distant hills, and the peasants with their ploughs and water buffaloes as they are strafed by American bombers:

I remember the light of that lagoon, the mythical sound of the flying dragon, spitting fire, one pass, one strafing gun across water for what is water from the sight of the gods, the crosshair splitting in the forming of a real image, so distant the face of . . . your face, my face.[15]

Similarly, the symbolic brother in Maxine Hong Kingston's *China Men*, as we have seen, is subject to nightmares that reveal fierce anti-war sentiments, which are both general and intensely personal and Chinese American. He dreads the thought that he might be assigned to interrogate Vietnamese "enemies," because he finds them so similar to Chinese.

Identification with the people of Vietnam among Asian American writers extends beyond racial and cultural similarities to the question of shared oppression. The contradictions were particularly keen for some Japanese Americans, who could reflect upon the bombing of Hiroshima and Nagasaki during World War II as well as on internment. To some, it seemed clear that it was primarily the dark-skinned people of the world who were threatened with destruction at the hands of American foreign-policymakers and military leaders. Mirikitani, a third-generation Japanese American, dedicates poems to dead heroes of Latin America and Africa, such as Pablo Neruda and Orlando Letelier of Chile and Steve Biko of South Africa. In one love poem, Africa and Asia are joined in a struggle against destruction ("Loving from Vietnam to Zimbabwe"). In "Japs" (1978), she warns:

> if you're too dark
> they will kill you
> if you're too swift
> they will buy you.
> if you're too beautiful
> they will rape you
>
> Watch with eyes open
> speak darkly
> turn your head like the owl
> behind you.
> They are coming
> to nail you to boxes.

In "Attack the Water" (1972), Mirikitani juxtaposes two war photographs and news flashes, one about an old grandmother at the Tule Lake Relocation Center and one about an elderly Vietnamese woman thirty years later. In "We, The Dangerous" (1978), she draws parallels between attempts to destroy the Japanese at Hiroshima and Tule Lake with American offensives in Vietnam decades later:

We, the dangerous.
Dwelling in the ocean.
Akin to the jungle.
Close to the earth.

Hiroshima.
Vietnam.
Tule Lake.[16]

What the Chinese American Vietnam veteran in Ashley Sheun Dunn's "No Man's Land" (1978) discovers is the similarity between the Vietnam village and the Chinatown of his childhood, between the people of those villages and the members of his own family and community, all through the eyes of the racists and killers and cheaters, the "honkies [who] can do whatever they wanna do . . . [while] we don't have a choice." In Vietnam, Stuart befriends another Chinese American soldier, whom he thinks of at first in the comical and derogatory way American-born Chinese often classify their immigrant peers:

I swear to god if I ever met a dumber Chinaman. You know, he's the type with the horn-rimmed glasses, buck teeth. When he stood up it always looked like he was about to bow or something. It was embarrassing sometimes. And the way he talked. . . !" Stuart let his face droop and went into his fresh-off-the-boat imitation. . . . "He looks a lot like our cousins, with that rat face and the skinny eyes.

Both Stuart and Sam, as Chinese Americans, are alienated from their fellow American combat soldiers, who put Vietnamese peasants' clothes with bullet-holes in them on their bunks at night. They are drawn instead to the Vietnamese shopkeepers and peasants, visiting the villages and giving away goods stolen from the army base. Stuart is moved by the Vietnamese villagers, but he detests them at the same time, perhaps for putting him into the position of being an "ugly American."[17]

When he finally returns to Chinatown, he is continually reminded by sights, sounds, smells, by people's faces, of Vietnam. Even the people of Chinatown appear to him now as helpless victims, like victims of war: [E]verytime I look around here I can see the same thing: old people walking up those streets with a look on their faces like they were god-damned fish floating in those tanks at the butchers. Stuart turns on his uncomprehending relatives because they somehow remind him of Vietnamese peasants. One night, he attacks an old uncle who has been sitting in his family's kitchen waiting for Stuart's mother to prepare some food for him:

If I find you anywhere, begging for anything, I'll cut your head off! Don't ever come here again! I can't stand all you god-damned peasant chinks crawling up Jackson Street like a bunch of slaves! . . . Sometimes I wish there'd be this huge accident . . . and it would kill off all those old people and all those people who couldn't mumble a word of English. . . . Then it would be over.

Stuart cannot overcome his grief over Sam's death. Although he had detested Sam for his clumsiness and generosity in a cutthroat world of racists and opportunists, he had loved him as well. His grief is for Sam, for the Vietnamese, for the people of Chinatown, and for himself, because he is just like those "old peasants struggling up Jackson Street," and "in a lot of ways me and Sam were the same":

I knew Sam better than anyone else, but I wanted to so bad one night wake him up and yell in his face, "You shit, why the hell don't you die!" and then I'd just kill him right there and save him the trouble of killing himself off. . . . But you know what's the worst part of it all? . . . I miss him . . . and it's the funniest thing, I start to miss myself. Sometimes I almost cry just thinking, "Poor old Stuart. He ain't never coming back."[18]

## Racism and Assimilation

Malcolm X had objected to Black men being sent to Vietnam "to fight the Yellow Man for the White Man."[19] The anguished battle cry of many racial minorities against racism was a rejection of the notion of assimilation into what they viewed as the spiritual bankruptcy, cultural sterility, imperialism, materialism, and racial self-denial of the Anglo-American ideal, which are characterized in Lawson Inada's "Report from the New Country" (1971):

Say the city is not
stale pastry:

if you know the stack of pies
at the counter's elbow—
panel of meringue, coconut coating—

you know what I mean.

. . . Ecclesiastes, the Greek
used to yell "Vanity! Vanity!
like a dirty old man.

We knew what he wanted.

Now the kids chant "Community! Community!"
on their way to the five-and-ten
His daughter drives a Buick named Electra.
They've come a ways since then.

In Inada's "Firebirds" (1971), the "white life," especially as it is imposed upon or threatens the survival of nonwhites, is angrily rejected:

We live in
Stampville
S & H.
At night, white
creepers
spray the street
like the Great
Extinguisher.

He jives
with matches.
His ass
is in ashes.

All over this world
the sirens are
singing—
Burn Baby Burn.[20]

In the poetry of Filipino American Jessica Tarahata Hagedorn, America is portrayed as a country of loneliness, sterility, and paranoia, where members of racial minorities can die a "natural death," held by the neck "on a diamond-studded leash" by "the white bandit." Meanwhile, white Americans "go to sleep / in their apartments and freeways / and bungalows and ranches / and condominiums / and waterbeds," fearful of the "amorphous lies" dictated by their televisions, seduced by the blind desire for material gain, and strangely tempted by the color and vibrant music of people of color. Moreover, America can be a dangerous place for the Asian woman:

there are rapists
out there.

some of them
don't like Asian women
they stab them
and run off to lake tahoe
in search of more pussy
in casino parking lots

. . . there are sad men
out there
some of them
don't like me
they like to talk
about corpses and dirt
and how life used to be
so good
when they were young
in the war

. . . there are killers
out there
some of them
smile at me.[21]

One of the most powerful effects of white supremacism on Asian
Americans, according to many Asian American writers, has been their
acceptance of the view of themselves presented by their detractors. In
"After the War" (1979), Karen Ishizuka describes a Japanese American
schoolboy's desire to be accepted in American society. The boy sneaks
into the bathroom to eat his Japanese *misubi* lunch, only to discover a
Chicano boy hiding there with his taco. The next day, both boys bring
sandwiches to school, which they eat proudly in front of the other
children. Even so, they share a moment of "silent pity" for each other.
The Japanese American boy wonders what is wrong with him and what
he can ever be:

I remember
passing a boy in the mirror
and stopping to look in.
I studied his face
and he studied mine.
I didn't feel how he looked.
He looked all wrong.
No that couldn't be me.
I looked past his features
and into his eyes.
What went wrong?
What's wrong with me?
What shall I do?
What shall I be?
But he just looked back at me
without saying a word.[22]

Contemporary Asian American writers inherited the social limitations faced by their precursors. Before World War II, Asians had been generally segregated from and excluded from participation in the mainstream of American life. Between the war era and the civil rights movement of the 1960s, Asian Americans were encouraged to value the ideal of racial assimilation into a hypothetical "melting pot." There were few other viable options. Jade Snow Wong and other Chinese American writers had discovered that certain aspects of their Chinese cultural heritage could serve as their "point of distinction," as long as none of these were threatening to white society. Exotic euphemization of Chinese culture and Chinese American life could enhance the acceptability of the Chinese American and provide harmless entertainment for the non-Chinese. Monica Sone and other Japanese Americans, on the other hand, were faced with the impossible choice between a Japanese and a white American identity. Japanese American heritage was ruled out as a viable option for the *nisei* seeking acceptance in American society, the prerequisite of which was the relinquishing of all vestiges of loyalty to one's Japanese racial and ethnic heritage, except perhaps as a joke or an exotic stereotype.

The Asian American could either laugh at himself along with the racists or, if he felt unable to accept their stereotypes, "go back" to Asia. Chinese American poet Nellie Wong looks at contemporary racist humor in her poem, "We Can Always" (1977):

A television comedian says:
"Women are no longer bobbing
their hair because
they are slanting
their eyes"

and people laugh

A television comedian says:
"Hi! I'm Ruru,
fry me
to Frorida"

and people laugh

A disc jockey says:
"You should know better
than to rob
a Chinese grocer
If you do
you will want to rob
again in another hour"

and people laugh

A newspaper columnist says:
"How come them heathen Chinee
are always observing New Year's
a month late? When they gonna
get up to date?"

and if we can't laugh
at ourselves, we can always
go back.[23]

In recent years, Chinese and Japanese Americans have expressed intense resentment that they had been encouraged to emulate Anglo-Americans as their superiors or to objectify their racial heritages into exotic jokes for the benefit of Anglo-American ethnocentrism. In particular, the Wakayama Group of Vancouver, British Columbia, asserts that the "acceptance" of the Asian Canadian or Asian American into white society has been only an illusion, contending that the option of "assimilation" is in fact "cultural genocide" because it threatens to rob Asian Americans of their true past while preventing them at the same time from full and equal participation in the present.

Every people has a cultural past that sustains their spirit, the writers contend; the individual white artist from Dante to Chaucer to Melville has never had to deny his roots in order to be accepted as an artist. Instead, he has affirmed these roots in his "universal" writing. The Asian American, on the other hand, has had to bid for acceptance in white society by turning his back on his past until "he evaporates into some plastic heaven where he is only a 'person,' i.e., a white man without a white past." The Asian American or Asian Canadian can never claim more than "conditional membership" in white society: he will have to "learn how to be white," to "deserve" the privilege of belonging, a privilege white persons view as their natural and inalienable right. As long as he follows the path towards "assimilation," according to the Wakayama Group, the Asian American will have given up what is his for a cultural past and traditions he can never really claim:

> A white man is a white man, connected to the Anglo-Saxon (or Western European) tradition by birth; an Asian is an Asian until he proves himself white by his actions. He cannot, therefore, ever say "we" and mean the people who produced Chaucer, Shakespeare and Milton or even Bob Dylan and the Beatles. He cannot get up in front of his white friends and say "*We* have much to be proud of."[24]

Becoming an "honorary white person" entails self-deprecation and denigration of one's cultural background and even one's racial characteristics. As one Chinese American youth writes, he had learned as an elementary school pupil that crying or becoming angry never won acceptance from the other children, while self-denigration did: "I discovered a way to get the kids off my back and to make allies. . . . [I]f you laugh and start to come down on yourself they let up real soon. I quickly became the school clown by cutting myself and my race down."[25]

Another way some Asian Americans found to win acceptance from whites was to appeal to their interest in "exotic" Asian foods and customs or artifacts, which were non-threatening, quaint objects of curiosity. In "Not from the Food" (1977), Nellie Wong writes of organizing a Chinese dinner for her office friends and taking them on a tour of Chinatown "masked, playing Oriental, inscrutable, wise." Now, recalling that time makes her feel sick and ashamed of herself. In "Drowning in the Yellow River" (1978), Janice Mirikitani writes of a young Japanese American girl who wonders while "necking in back seats / of convertibles with white boys" who she really is:

look at me—

buddhaheads

chinamen who stand
on one side of the room
and don't mess with girls

who else am i?[26]

The extent to which Asian Americans, and the Japanese American *sansei* in particular, had accepted Anglo-American standards of value and beauty, became a source of alarm to some Asian American writers. *Sansei* poet Ron Tanaka asserts that the *sansei* were fast losing their identity as Japanese Americans, becoming instead simply "non-Anglo":

[T]here is a very good chance that we Japanese Americans may literally cease to exist as a separate American minority. We are, for the most part, no longer a community in the sense of a group of people who live, work, and play together. We have our communities to join the mainstream. We are intermarrying at a faster rate than even some less visible minorities like Jews. In fifty years, there will be nothing left of us but a few pictures in someone's family album and an NBC documentary or two. It is rather passe to say that we have been ruined by success. That we have "out-whited" the whites and hence ceased to be what we are.

According to Tanaka, Japanese American assimilation has been bought at the price of "the destruction of the culture":

[W]e have lost the spiritual legacy of our Issei forbears . . . a sense of balance, of perspective. At least they knew in their hearts that life wasn't supposed to be consumed by the pursuit of wealth, power, and leisure. . . . [W]hat do we have to offer to our children? Nothing. Nothing they couldn't get elsewhere. . . , a plastic identity that costs $1.98 in a Japantown department store.[27]

Japanese American assimilation, according to Tanaka, is thinly disguised self-hatred, a response to race discrimination. In his poem, "I Hate My Wife" (1971), the Japanese American man hates his wife's "flat yellow face / and her fat cucumber legs, but mostly / for [her] lack of elegance compared to judith gluck," who has access to all the sophistication of white culture, from Bob Dylan to Andy Warhol. Perhaps the desire to disappear into the white society was inspired in large part by the experience of internment. In "Appendix to Executive Order" (1976), Tanaka traces the path of Japanese Americans from internment to assimilation:

> the people who put out that book,
> i guess they won a lot of awards.
> it was a very photogenic period
> of california history, especially
> if you were a white photographer
> with compassion for helpless people.
>
> but the book would have been better,
> i think, or more complete, if they
> had put in my picture and yours, with
> our hakujin* wives, our long hair and
> the little signs that say, "what? me
> speak japanese?" and "self-determination
> for everyone but us." and then maybe
> on the very last page, a picture of
> our kids. They don't even look like
> japanese. mo sunda ne⁺ after thirty
> years, the picture is now complete.[28]

Intermarriage between whites and Asians has been seen in recent times by some Asian Americans as evidence of racial conquest and cultural genocide rather than social acceptance and success for the Asian minority. In Eugene Hum Chang's "Hypnogenocide," an Asian Amer-

---

*White person.
⁺It's all over, isn't it? That's it, isn't it?

ican man is overcome by hatred and resentment at the sight of an Asian
woman walking with her white lover:

> Walking down Telegraph
> What's this I see?
> An Asian woman
> With a white man
> Or should I say
> A white man with
> His Asian woman
>
> . . . Deep inside something is released
> It rushes upwards, growing
> Pain spread through my body
> I hurt, I hate, I hurt
>
> . . . I am catapulted into the past
> Ugly visions machine-gunning through my mind
> . . . White men killing Vietnamese, Koreans, Japanese
> White men killing men like me
> White men killing me
>
> We are very close now
> She clinging to him
> With puppy dog eyes
> He, a hyena with his own women
> But now a lion with this woman
>
> Should I strike
> First her, then him?
> Traitor, traitor
> Murderer, murderer[29]

Many contemporary Asian American writers, armed with a new-
found consciousness of the implications of American racism, exhort their
readers not to allow themselves to be swallowed up by "white lies" and
the urge toward assimilation according to an Anglo-American standard.
In "To Amerika" (1972), Diane Mark warns Asian Americans, whose
forefathers had built the American railroads only to be relegated to
blighted ghettoes or internment camps, not to be caught "singing another
man's song":

> do we hide our hurt by
> squaring our shoulders
> and trying harder to
> get back on the merrygoround?

. . . all the white lies have added up:
and the white lies
and the
white lies
and
the white
lies

Diana Lin's "Father" (1972) is addressed to an abstraction that represents paternalism and white racism. "White cement walls" entomb "this yellow body / and other-than-yellow mind / bred from your generous seed" because the "white lips" of the "father" teach the Asian Americans to "live a white lie," depriving him of his heritage and culture while toasting his victories with "white wine." In "Rapping with One Million Carabaos in the Dark" (1974), Filipino American poet Alfred Robles urges fellow Filipino Americans:

Put down your white mind
with your eyes behind brown skin
brown = brown = brown = brown = brown =
fallen coconuts on a cold
    cold winter day.

. . . Ah, Filipinos
if you only know how brown you are
you would slide down
    from the highest
        mountain top
you would whip out your lava tongue
    & burn up all that white shit
that's keeping your people down.[30]

## Self-Definition: A Third World Identity

The late Filipino American poet Serafin Syquia expresses the feelings of many young Asian Americans who felt that they could and should define themselves rather than let themselves be defined by those who might destroy them. After the Asian immigrant parents worked "like diminuitive tontos to help / set tables / wash dishes / pick produce / and clean up after the waste makers," their children

. . . have grown up
    silently
    unobtrusive & patient

we have been educated
  by white washed schools
  and embittered by
  the concrete streets
taught how the pilgrims
  civilized the pagan indians
  and how the cavalry
  brought justice to the west

and we accepted it as the turth
  until we awoke
  and realized that the dream
    was their dream
    and not ours.

The realization that "the dream was their dream and not ours" was accompanied by much questioning by Asian Americans of many beliefs and assumptions that had been accepted heretofore. Was it right, after all, for Asian Americans to be "quiet . . . / unassuming and so agreeable," to work hard for a pat on the head and the title of "model minority"? Were the Anglo-American ideals so much aspired to by Asian Americans a self-serving and vicious lie after all? In "i can relate to tonto" (1972), Syquia questions the basic premises of white racial supremacy by sliding with Tonto instead of the white hero:

i can relate to tonto

he was a patient dude

all that dust from
silver's hoofs

riding a pinto
down mainstream

usa

he doesn't need a mask
or a silver bullet

tonto is no tonto

he picks up his unemployment
check in line 7 window j at

3 everyday tuesday while thumbin

thru bury my heart at wounded

knee[31]

Many Asian Americans have felt a deep sense of affinity with members of other American racial minority groups, with whom they shared the experience of white racism. This affiinity has been particularly strong among the writers. Al Robles writes what seems at first to be a nature poem about a pristine American northwestern scene. Suddenly, he asks:

> where are the indians?
>    dead in the ground?
> no blacks seen around here
> licking white cotton
> no chicanos or pilipinos
> in the valleys or fields
> not even one chinaman drying
> sea-weed or catching fish
> not even one japanese farmer
> seen turning the soil[32]

Robles is aware that the largest concentration of Native Americans was once in the Pacific Northwest, where hunters and fishermen flourished before the advent of the white man. Chinese fishing villages once dotted the coast and Chicano and Filipino farmworkers followed the crops from Baja California to the Pacific Northwest. Now, because of racist legislation and genocidal policies, the people of these racial groups seem to have vanished without a trace.

In an untitled poem, Alfred Robles equates white supremacism to a chilling suffocating blanket of snow that covers the multicolored earth. But like the snow, white supremacy must eventually melt, and the potential vitality of nonwhite people will burst forth like new life in the spring:

> Soon the white snow
>    will melt
> & the cold, dark nightmares
>    will die
> & bellies will be full
> & the mind will be clear
>    like a winter stream
> & we will find our peace together
> Soon when the white snow melts away
> the brown, black, yellow earth
>    will come to life.[33]

It should not be surprising that many Asian Americans, particularly those who had been farthest removed from their Asian roots, feel close to

Afro-Americans, who were demanding equality without self-negating assimilation, who could be American and nonwhite at the same time. At times, Asian Ameicans felt drawn to Afro-Americans because of what they thought was their shared experience of white racism.

Asian American singers Chris Ijima and Joanne Miyamoto characterized Asian American children as "secretly rooting for the other side."[34] In Momoko Iko's "And There Are Stories, There Are Stories," the bonds between Black and Japanese Americans as adversaries of white racism are explored. The narrator's aged father marches for Martin Luther King. The narrator herself falls out of love with a blond Texan when she discovers that he is prejudiced against Blacks:

> You know, I still feel kind of funny around kuronbos. . . .*
> [A]rmchair liberal, I guess . . . but I remember, back when I went to the Tivoli Theatre, they were showing *From Here to Eternity* . . . and when the Japs bombed Pearl Harbor, everybody in the place started hooting and hollering, for the Japs to get the Americans. . . . Go For Broke, someone yelled. . . . [G]uess some of them had seen that pineapple movie, huh. And I thought to myself, how come, black people are cheering the bad guys . . . you know . . . kurochans, maybe, they experience something like us buddhaheads.[35]

Asian Americans, like many Native Americans and Afro-Americans, chose or were forced to adopt Anglo names. In "On Names" (1975), George Leong reflects upon the Anglo naming of the Chinese and Afro-American:

> You ever wondered where you name
> come from . . . sister?
> why . . . don't nobody named Charlene
> nor George in Africa nor
> Asia. . . .
> but don't they know—whatever name
> they give us—jes make us feel like
> one big family—so big you never pin a
> clan down. Say what you name again
> i have a hard time with names so
> > to me you jes beautiful
> > sister
> > sister.[36]

Although some of his own relatives even expected him to write Japanese *haiku* in English, Lawson Inada says that he deliberately avoided

*Afro-Americans: Blacks.

traditional Japanese literary forms, observing that "of the few Asian American writers he knew those he had read he considered inferior for trying to sound acceptable 'Oriental'": "No doubt a quaint collection of cricket haikus would have been cause to praise my Oriental sensitivity." Since his experience has been an American not a Japanese one, Inada writes, trying to use Japanese poetic forms would have been an exoticization, an affectation that would not express his reality as an Asian American. Instead, he chooses jazz rhythms. Inada's rhythms and images are a rejection of both Asian and Anglo-American conventions. In "Plucking Out a Rhythm," the Japanese American poet wears the disguise of a Harlem jazz musician:

> Start with a simple room—
> a dullish color—
> and draw the one shade down.
> Hot plate. Bed
>
> Put in a single figure—
> medium weight and height—
> but oversize, as a child might.
>
> The features must be Japanese.
>
> Then stack a black pompadour on,
> and let the eyes
> slide behind a night of glass.
>
> The figure is in disguise:
>
> slim green suit
> for posturing on a bandstand,
> and turned-up shoes of Harlem. . . .
>
> Then start the music playing—
> thick jazz, strong jazz—
>
> and notice that the figure
> comes to life.
>
> sweating, growling
> over an imaginary bass—
> plucking out a rhythm—
> as the music rises and the room is full,
> exuding with that rhythm. . . .
>
> Then have the shade flap up
> and daylight catch him
> frozen in that pose
>
> as it starts to snow—
> thick snow, strong snow—

blowing in the window
while the music quiets,
the room is slowly covered,

and the figure is completely
out of sight[37]

Because the Asian American experience has been shaped in large
part by poverty and discrimination, the affinity felt by many Asian
American writers towards Afro-American writers is easy to understand.
Filipino American poet Alfred Robles writes about San Francisco Manilatown and the Filipino *manong* (elder brother), but he also writes about the
San Francisco Black ghetto. In "Fillmore Black Ghetto" (1975), we are
taken through the Black community to the adjacent Japanese American
community. We are told that "jivin' whores / hustlers / drivin' pimps /
 hip & slick hog snout / hot water / corn bread / blackeye peas / ain't all
there is":

soulsville
baby
what is is
starvin'
black children

jingle jangle

thru dark alleys
young bloods
poor blacks
reachin' & crawlin'
screamin' & hollerin'
at the white lies & promises
of holy men & politicians[38]

The contradictions between the awesome wealth displayed in the
financial district of San Francisco and the desperate poverty of the adjacent Chinatown and Manilatown districts that lie in its towering shadows
are explored in Robles' "Poor Man's Bridge" (1975), which describes the
overpass connecting Chinatown's Portsmouth Square, where the impoverished elderly Chinese and Filipinos pass away their twilight years
in the park, and the glittering, multistoried tourist hotel, the Holiday Inn,
across the street:

Poor man's bridge
    Portsmouth Square
The sun is buried underneath
The cold cement

Far gone is the laughter
That grows tall in Spring
Far gone are the old chinese women
With ancient cracked-white
Porcelain faces
Chattering in the long day sun
Far gone is spring

Poor man's bridge
    Portsmouth Square
Six steel girder-branches
Blossoms half-a-block long
Stretching nowhere[39]

In "Have's and Have-not's" (1975), Filipino immigrant poet Oscar Peñaranda juxtaposes the English word, "boating," with the Filipino word, "Boting-ting," which means swinging a long stick, as a laborer does, to point up the distance between the bejewelled billionaires "fishing for stray dreams" to fill their empty lives and the dirty tenement children gloating over pictures and television ads:

Boating?
Yea, man. Bo-ting. Bo-ting tayo
Boting-tinan ng. titi.
You know, you bo my ting. I bo your ting-bo-ting.
. . . you got your troubles
i got mine.[40]

Serafin Syquia's portrayal of the contemporary urban Filipino American youth, existing as he does in a racially divided world where style is everything, is completely unromanticized. In "chickaboom chickaboom" (1975), cars full of "stoned flips" cruise through the streets, radios blaring, looking for young girls and thinking of good times. In Syquia's "March 1/73," "highstepping / teenyboppin / badass kung fu watcher" Santo "beats up white dudes / with his third world / gang" but unconsciously wonders:

. . . what of the fear grandfather
is it real will i overcome it?

there is harmony in the rainbow
each color is part of the whole

The world of the school, the city, and the society itself are bankrupt and unable to answer Santo's unarticulated questions:

where is the love grandfather is it
. . . in the empty homes the silent
invisible parents
the channels of despair
the commercials of a system surviving
on a reputation

. . . there is a siren wailing
a red light revolving

What is needed is revolutionary change, according to Syquia, In
"Stereotype" (1975), the Filipino youths party and dance, thinking only
of good times, according to the popular stereotype:

filipinos love to dance the
tinikling the shingaling the
boogaloo penguin cold and hot
duck fandango sa funky chicken

to soul music
to rock music
to pop music
latin and jazz music

to no music

they pop their fingers
and nod their heads
to what's going on

But all the while, the partying Filipinos are "revolutionaries / thinking
about the good times ahead."[41]

The similarities between urban Filipino Americans and members of
other urban minority groups are depicted in Jessica Tarahata Hagedorn's
"Smokey's Getting Old," in which a Filipina moves from the Philippines
to various American rural and urban ghettoes. She now relates to Afro-
American music and culture, as does her son:

Nellie,
you sleep without dreams
and remember the barrios
and now it's all the same

Manila,
the Mission,
Chinatown,
East L.A., Harlem, Fillmore Street,

and you're getting kinda far
and Smokey Robinson's getting old

but our son
has learned to jive
to the Jackson Five[42]

In a racially sensitive environment, Asian Americans felt they had
no distinct cultural identity and often found that they had to choose
between identifying with either Afro-Americans or with whites, especially if they were unable to speak an Asian language fluently and did not
feel comfortable with people who were culturally and linguistically
Asian.

Some Asian Americans chose to identify with whites, who represented power and privilege. But many others aligned themselves with
Afro-Americans. As one young Chinese American college student explained, even in his primary school

> There are only two groups of people in the world,
> Blacks and Whites, and if you're gonna make it in
> this world you'd better be part of one or the
> other. . . . I soon found out that fitting into the
> group is to feel and act Black. I found out that
> being a tough bastard with the vulgar and profane
> mouth and ideas, I was more accepted because I
> was not the classic Chinaman anymore.

All went well until a young Asian American woman confronted him,
saying that since he was not Black, he should not pretend to be: "[Y]ou
can act and play all the parts of something or someone else, but you'll
never truly be that something or someone else."[43]

Confusion caused by the racial polarization between Black and
white in America is the subject of Takako Endo's "I'm Asking" (1979):

> Neither black nor white
>     Minority or majority
> Suspended between
>     To balance out power?

The manipulation of stereotypes of Asian Americans as a buffer minority
between Black and white is also obliquely addressed:

> Deceitful, disloyal
>     Industrious, model citizen,
> Category changes
>     With each new moon.

Now,
will the winds of centuries
Stir the sands of time
To color my baby
Purple?[44]

Fluctuating between Black and white, between Asian and American, many Asian Americans felt a desperate need to forge and assert their unique identities as Asian Americans:

change change
like a chameleon do
from white to black
from brown to blue

just as to say:
that clothes are not the skin of the man
just as
skin is not the essence

shed that skin
it ain't a part of you

change change
like a chameleon do
from white to black
from brown to blue[45]

One reason some Asian Americans identified with Afro-Americans stems from a desire to reject assimilation according to white racist standards. In "For My Stylin' Brothers" (1975), Reyes writes that this can also be done through the recognition of a Filipino American identity:

It's cool
We're Brothers
And we found out that we have a revolution to fight
And we didn't need none of that bureaucratic honky jive
. . . we have a heritage, you know—
And it wasn't meant to have
A black
    and beautiful
        tongue.[46]

Frank Chin writes that Asian Americans, caught between Black and white without "something rightly ours," were "hungry, all the time hungry . . . chameleons looking for color, trying on tongues and clothes and hairdos, taking on everyone else's, with none of our own, and no habitat."[47]

In an untitled poem, Patricia Mizuhara traces an Asian-American teenager's discovery of her own unique cultural and racial identity. "Used to just take someone to steal my wallet for me to lose my I.D.," she writes. The Asian American girl tries to fit into the "hippie scene . . . / of dream drugs / peace songs / hitch-hiking . . . crunchy granola / [and] . . . white boys / lanky, lean, levi-legged / electric-guitar playing / ivory-assed white boys" who liked her for her exotic appeal:

> . . . they liked me for my waist-length black hair
> because i ate with chopsticks which were outasite
> for my guaranteed shock value
> they dug me even more when
> john lennon married yoko ono

After the assassination of Martin Luther King, the Asian American girl began to

> hang out with blacks
> talked like a black person, walked like a black person
> was treated like one

Finally, she realizes that she is straddling two worlds, neither of which she fully belongs to, because she fears that she has nothing of her own:

> i realized i was only play-acting
> in a dichotomous world
> where one had to be either black or white
> neither of which category i could fit into
> afraid to be caught with any one of my numerous masks off
> for fear there'd by *nothing* underneath[48]

The Asian American search for ways to articulate the emerging Asian American identity involved trying to identify with Asian cultures. The result, for the most part, has been confusion and disappointment of the same kind experienced by American-born Asians of the previous generations who tried to live in China or Japan. As one Berkeley High School student wrote in a student magazine, asserting a Japanese American identity can become a contest between people desperate to define themselves: adolescents goad each other about how "Japanese" they are, according to how frequently they eat *sashimi*, wear *zoris*, or eat with chopsticks. In "Shinjuku Struttin" (1975), Yuri Sasaki writes that trying to pass for Japanese in Japantown makes a *sansei* feel fine until he has to speak, "and them Amerikan-Japanese words fall out" and "the cover is blown."[49]

What it means to be Chinese American on the East Coast is explored by Wing Tek Lum in poems that capture moments and sentiments not celebrated in Anglo-American literature, although familiar enough to many Asian Americans. In "Going Home" (1974), the young Chinese American is baffled and pained by his inability to meet the needs of a lost, elderly Chinese man who could have been his own father:

Ngoh m'sick gong tong hua—
besides the usual menu words,
the only phrase I really know.
I say it loudly
but he is not listening.

He keeps on talking with a smile
staring, it would seem, past me
into the night without a moon.

He's lost, presumably,
But I don't know what he's saying.
He is an old man, wearing a hat,
and the kind of overcoat
my father wears:
the super-padded shoulders.

Just then,
two young fellows approach
carrying a chair; one look
and I can tell
that they will oblige him.

I sigh, and point them out,
and hastily cross the street,
escaping.

Other familiar moments are found in a series of short poems titled "Grateful Here." In the first poem, the Chinese American "follows his Chinese nose" to Chinatown "like a salmon returning to its spawning ground." In the second poem, he visits his Chinese ancestors' graves and sings in a choir at Easter church services on the same day, participating as many Asian Americans do in two vastly differing cultural worlds. In the third poem, he walks with a white girl past "teenage hangout / overhearing insults" and experiences being stereotyped as unmanly in a racist society:

. . . They would always pick on the girl,
as though she was a lesbian.

In the penultimate poem, the relationship between race and sex is explored further, as the Chinese American traces the experience of being treated as an outlandish oddity. He begins to understand "half-enviously" the two flamboyant gay Negroes he sees "strutting regally in their high-heeled boots":

. . . I was in rural Pennsylvania,
and found housewives at the grocer's brought
their children with small, craning necks to
whisper about me.

In the final poem, the Chinese American is made aware that since he is regarded as a foreigner who can always "go back" if he has any complaints, he has no right to voice protests about injustice in American society.[50]

Wing Tek Lum traces the topography and landscape of a set of uniquely Chinese American experiences. Similarly, Lawson Fusao Inada attempts to define the Asian American. He does this by challenging stereotypes directly and by naming concrete persons and places in his poetry. In *West Side Songs* (1972), he defines the Asian American by using the forbidden terminologies invented by the racists, which he turns on their heads. We are Chinks, not Chinese, and Japs, not Japanese. Chinese are the people who do what racists want them to—they work hard, revere education, and hate Japanese. Japanese are the people who imitate whites and "hate themselves / on the sly." Better to be a Chink or a Jap than a Chinese or a Japanese:

CHINKS

Ching Chong Chinaman
sitting on a fence
trying to make a dollar
chop-chop all day

"Eju-kei-shung! Eju-kei-shung!"*
that's what they say.

When the War came
they said, "We Chinese!"

*Education.

When we went away
they made sukiyaki
saying, "Yellow all same."

When the war closed,
they stoned the Japs' homes.

Grandma would say:
"Marry a Mexican,
a Nigger, just don't
marry no Chinese."

JAPS

are great
imitators—
they stole
the Greeks'
skewers,
used them
on themselves.
Their sutras
are Face
and Hide.
They hate
everyone else,
on the sly.

They play
Dr. Charley's
games—bowling,
raking,
growing forks
on lapels.
Their tongues
are yellow
with "r's"
with "l's."

They hate
themselves
on the sly. I
used to be
Japanese[51]

Inada is responding to the need to smash myths and self-deception,
to reject racist definitions of Asian Americans and the desire to accommo-

date oneself to pressures towards assimilation that simply "didn't take" in "Amache Gate" (1975):

> . . . everything was cool, you know,
> and the rule was "Instructions: no Japanese ancestry
> allowed to show"
> and this includes Chinks, Flips, & Gooks,
>
> So we went to school with
> Spanish-Merkans and Colored Folks
> and maybe an occasional Injun
> when the moon was full,
>
> and we was a-trying our darndest ta talk
>     proper-like
> & keep our shirt-tails tucked in
> but I mean, you know, man, it just didn't take

In "Aiiieeeee!," one of the poems in Inada's "Four Songs for Asian America" (1973), it was the "drag anthropologists / and actual anthropologists" who had tried to define the Asian American out of his cultural integrity, only to discover that that integrity had survived all attempts to destroy it:

> Having concluded
> that we had achieved our goal,
> that we were truly assimilated,
> with statistics to prove it,
>
> the drag anthropologists
> and actual apologists
> set out on a celebrating stroll
> along the Grant Avenues
>
> and were amazed to discover
> in the blazing ruins,
> hatchets of extinction
> breaking open their skulls.[52]

In "Michael, in the Year of the Ox" (1973), Inada celebrates his cousin who, having defied the racist pressures to destroy him, has chosen the path of civil disobedience even if it means imprisonment:

> You became the insanely inscrutable
> Godzilla

with all the wrong convictions
and all the wrong degrees—
Bachelor of Fresno Ghettoes;
Master of Social Madness
at Tehachipi

. . . You could have
scotch-taped
your face* & suffocated
a real credit to your race;

you have
died in Vietnam
killing Yellow Men
for the Red Man's country,

you could have
totalled a Kawasaki
on a funky vineyard road

& been a story for the old.

Instead, you've become
a legend for the young.

busting locks
a rock's throw
from Chinese Camp & Manzanar†

where we laid
Mother Lode & violated
Daddy Stanford's gravel bed
for kicks & sedition . . .

All that is part of our tradition.
All of us finding

Michael in the television.
Michael behind the mirror,
Michael spiraling
out of the sounds we make & hear;

Michael, Blood Cousin, Rock
Samurai of the People fighting

locks on all of us.[53]

*It is said that some Asian Americans tried to make their eyes seem larger by scotch-taping them at night.
†Chinese Camp: a now deserted town where Chinese miners once lived. Manzanar: a relocation center for Japanese during World War II.

The rage of contemporary Asian American poets against racism and oppression emerges not only as a rejection of old stereotypes but also as a celebration of a new, self-determined identity, of new heroes and heroines whose first task is to speak the unspeakable, to reverse attempts to destroy Asian American culture and identity, both by fighting injustice now recognized and admitted and by reaching out to one another in love and communion. The anger expressed in the new Asian American literature is not the anger of alienation: it is a fierce urge towards affirmation, unity, and community, for artists, like true revolutionaries, can achieve greatness through love for humanity as manifested in hatred for injustice.

The sudden recognition of the common bonds shared by Asian Americans is the theme of Sam Tagatac's "A Chance Meeting between Huts" (1975). Whereas before, they had seen each other as they were viewed by racists—as abstractions and stereotypes—they now see each other with new eyes:

I saw her just a little
ways
a think light of shadow against morning
the light hedge
separating what is grass
and gravel

across these and the walled huts no
longer a mere
abstraction a brush
stroke but a girl
woman fleeting
tight collar
softly hard

browning as the sun
held her
   asian-asian
   filipino
eyes what is it in
the act
of recognition
blood which flows flowed all
the tribal cries

*Kayumanguingkaligatankayumanguing*
*Kaligatan*
*Kayumanguingkaligatanrizal*
*said it too**

*Brown beauty/health/brown is beautiful.

i smiled
  hello
fell the light from
  her eyes
  my light too

our blood and the passing of that empty
room
    here are the walls
where we are seen as painted
brush strokes.[54]

## Asian American Women's Writing

Except among Japanese Americans, Asian immigrant communities were predominantly male until recent years: the ratio of men to women in the Chinese American communities, for example, was as high as twenty-seven to one in 1880, and the sex imbalance did not begin to be corrected until after World War II. Nine of ten early Korean immigrants to Hawaii and the American mainland were laboring men. In 1930, Filipino men outnumbered women in the United States by fourteen to one. The presence of women, however small, was critical to the economic and social development of Asian American communties: when men had wives and children to work beside them on farms and in cities, they were better able to reclaim land and establish labor-intensive farms and to operate and develop small-scale independent businesses, such as laundries, lunch counters and restaurants, shoe repair shops, and boarding houses, setting down roots in their adopted land. Women brought stability into the bachelor societies, holding families together, building community networks, and maintaining the cultural traditions of the old country in their homes.

Asian women who chose to immigrate to the United States as wives and picture brides were probably more adventuresome than average. Some, perhaps, were eager to escape from a shadowy past. Others undoubtedly wished to escape the social strictures of their village lives. One Korean picture bride recalls her burning desire to immigrate to America near the turn of the century:

> "Ah,marriage!" then I could get to America! that land of freedom.
> . . . Since I became ten, I've [sic] been forbidden to step outside our
> gates, just like all the rest of the girls of my days. . . . [B]ecoming a
> picture bride, whatever that was, would be my answer and release.[55]

Asian immigrant women labored long and hard under often adverse and difficult conditions. They found themselves targets of racial hostility, impoverished strangers in a new land. One Japanese picture bride relates that she had resolved, on her way to America, that her heart would have to be "as beautiful as Mount Fuji" in order for her to survive: "I resolved that the heart of a Japanese woman had to be sublime, like that soaring, majestic figure, eternally constant through wind and rain, heat and cold. Thereafter, I never forgot that resolution on the ship, enabling me to overcome sadness and suffering."[56]

Although some Chinese and Japanese women were brought to America as prostitutes during the last part of the nineteenth and the early part of the twentieth centuries, and although women had occupied an absolutely inferior social status for several centuries in China, Korea, and Japan, Asian immigrant women in America were frequently highly valued by their communities and their men because of their relative scarcity and because of the needed contributions they were able to make to the economic and social well-being of their families and communities. Furthermore, in an immigrant society dominated by single men, even girl children came to be prized.

But no matter how improved their social status compared to what it would have been in their homelands at the time, Asian women in America faced race discrimination with their men. Although sexism has been an issue in Asian American communities, racism has usually been pinpointed as the more important barrier to social and economic equality for Asian American women. Even today, when Asian American women are beginning to organize around women's issues, distinctions between the goals and objectives of the white women's movement and Asian American women's needs can be clearly discerned. The links between white superracism and the oppression and exploitation of nonwhite people are explored in Janice Mirikitani's "Ms." (1972), where a clear line of demarcation is drawn between the white woman and the woman of color:

> I got into a thing
> with someone
> because I called her
> miss ann/kennedy/rockerfeller/[sic]/hughes
> instead of ms.
>
> I said
> it was a waste of time
> to worry about it.
>
> her cool blue eyes
> iced me—a victim of sexism.
>
> I wanted to accommodate her
> and call her what
> she deserved,

but knowing that would please her
instead
I said,

> white lace & satin was never soiled by sexism
> sheltered as you were by mansions
> built on Indian land
> your diamonds shipped with slaves from Africa
> your underwear washed by Chinese laundries
> your house cleaned by *my* grandmother

so do not push me any further.

and when you quit
killing us for democracy
and stop calling ME *gook*

I will call you
whatever you like.[57]

Historically, the white American women's movement has been both racist and nativist. In the mid-nineteenth century, suffragists argued that it was "degrading" for educated Anglo-Saxon women to remain voteless while "two million ignorant men are being ushered into the legislative halls. . . . What can we hope for at the hands of the Chinese, Indians, and Africans?" In the 1890s, anti-immigrant suffragists argued that enfranchised women could counteract the "ignorant foreign vote."[58] Even in contemporary times, the American women's movement addresses itself to the problems accompanying the entry of significant numbers of women into the labor force after World War II, while Asian women in America had been working for decades already and continue to participate in the labor force at a higher rate than white women. Moreover, many Asian American women find it difficult to view themselves as being at odds with Asian American men, who have experienced common problems caused by white racism.

It is clear that Asian American women are faced with both racism and sexism. Sex discrimination might account for the growing earnings gap between American men and women: on the average, American women earned only 59 cents for every dollar earned by men in 1979, a decline since 1955, when women's median income was almost 64 percent of men's.[59] But Asian American women, whose labor force participation rate and median years of schooling completed are higher than white females', earn significantly less than both white men and white women: "Asian women are clearly underrepresented in the upper echelon professional and managerial ranks, compared to either white women or white men. . . . Asian women are underrepresented in virtually every occupational category, if one looks at what the occupational distribution would be in the absence of both sex and race discrimination."[60] Where Asian American women are not underrepresented are in the jobs that have been traditionally stereotyped as women's jobs—in clerical fields—and in the so-called "Asian" jobs—in laundry work, garment factory work, food services, personal services, and paid domestic labor.[61]

Many contemporary Asian American women writers address themselves directly to affirming both their racial and their gender identities. In addition, although most Asian American male writers have not depicted the Asian American woman with much sympathy or understanding, Asian American women writers have demonstrated profound empathy for their men. In "Papa Takes a Bride" (1980), Noriko Sawada describes an *issei* man's years of toil and loneliness in America and his persistent efforts to bring a wife from Japan. When, after many unsuccessful attempts, he is finally able to sponsor a woman to marry him, he is confronted by her confession that she had been an unwed mother in Japan. Instead of condemning her as she had expected, he is touched by her tragedy and courage. Seeing her relief and gratitude, he has to struggle to hold back his own tears. In an untitled poem (1972), Filipino American poetess Emily Cachapero portrays the effects of racism on Filipino men in America, who spend their weekends drinking, smoking cigars, and "miming Muhammad Ali" by "sparring in shadows" to vent their frustrations and anger. Although she acknowledges that their response to their difficulties is a "safe . . . bloodless struggle," she also knows that their manhood has been threatened because they have been relegated to perpetual "boyhood" working as servants and menial laborers for white men in America. Wakako Yamauchi's short story "That Was All" (1980) is about a young *nisei* girl living in a remote rural area on the edge of a desert before the war. Suzuki-san, like many other *issei* bachelors of the period, lives alone, and the girl falls in love with his laughing eyes and slim brown body, moved by the mysterious needs she perceives in him. But although she is haunted by his image all her life, he eludes her except in dreams that come to her many years later, when she is herself an old woman with her own sorrow and loneliness.[62]

In Eleanor Wong Telamaque's *It's Crazy to Stay Chinese in Minnesota* (1978), Ching is most influenced by her father, who cannot be bought at any price, and Bingo, the Chinese youth at her parents' restaurant, whose slim body is like "quicksilver lightning, a thin warrior's sword." Fired by his desire to fight against injustice and oppression, Bingo teaches Ching about China and the history of Chinese in America but in the end he, like Ching's father, avoids challenging the forces that limit him in American society by deciding to return to China, leaving Ching behind to battle her racial identity problems alone.[63]

The desire to establish bonds with Asian American men is expressed in Juanita Tamayo's untitled poem (1972), in which she addresses the Filipino man who ignores her challenge to seek the love of a white woman instead:

Hey, brown man,
    with your slight, bronze back turned to me
. . . Twilight falls and you fall
Resting on her full white breasts
. . . Hey, brown man,
Turn around
    Make love to me.[64]

The links Asian American women cannot establish with their men they seek with one another. Motivated by the sense that there exist few adequate portrayals of Asian American women in American literature, Asian American women writers have been attempting to depict the uniqueness and diversity of that experience as an integral part of the American and Asian American tradition. In public performances of poetry, monologues, dialogues, and plays, women's writers' groups address themselves to themes that bring men and women together and that bring Asian American women together, always in an effort to shatter myths and stereotypes through self-expression so that Asian American women will emerge in positive self-affirmation:

We are unbinding our feet
We are women who write
We are women who work
We are women who love
Our presence in this world[65]

According to Maxine Hong Kingston, it is important for Asian Americans to recognize themselves as warriors instead of victims. Janice Mirikitani has said that although she might be "angry," she is not bitter. Allowing herself to feel like a victim would render her helpless to fight: "I'd rather be a shrew than a piece of dough." Poetess Nellie Wong has said that she wants her writing to help complete the unfinished picture of Asian American women as people who are simply "run over by a truck, abused, used as decorations." "Crazy ladies" and "wasted women" hold particular appeal to some Asian American women writers because they are often strong and creative women who are both rebels and seers, despite the fact that they are not appreciated fully by those around them.

Some Japanese American women participate willingly in their own nega-
tion, like the mother who accepts her internment without rage in Janice
Mirikitani's "Lullabye":

> She won't discuss
> the dying/her own
> as she left her self
> with the stored belongings.
>
> She wrapped her shell
> in kimono leaves
> and stamped it third class
> delivery to Tule Lake.

But Mirikitani's "Crazy Alice" is the one person in the family who really
feels the effects of the internment:

> She came to the
> wedding
> in a tattered coat
> called us all by
> the wrong names
>
> Yukio/Mizume/Kyoko
>
> No, crazy Alice
> We died in the camps
>
> > remembering/remembering
> > Alice/back then
>
> and the relatives
> laughed behind
> her back/crazy Alice
>
> > the bride is beautiful
> > who is she?
>
> crazy Alice
> it is your daughter
>
> > *okashi ne*
> > *jinsei wa okashi*
> >
> > life's so strange
> > before the war
> > i had a name[66]

The "crazy ladies" in Asian American women's writing are often
maligned and misunderstood by the ordinary people of the community,

and yet it is the memory of them that lingers on to challenge the smug complacency of those who consider themselves normal. Hisaye Yamamoto's Miss Sasagawara, the mysterious half-insane and love-starved spinster in "The Legend of Miss Sasagawara," is depicted in stark contrast to the young narrator and her friend, who wile away the monotonous days in their internment camp either discussing Miss Sasagawara's eccentricities or dreaming about "nice, clean young men, preferably handsome, preferably rich, who would cherish us forever and a day." The narrator in Wakako Yamauchi's "And The Soul Shall Dance" is haunted by the memory of Mrs. Oka, who scandalizes her rural Japanese American neighbors by drinking and smoking cigarettes and forgetting to serve tea to guests. The narrator is unable to forget the sight of Mrs. Oka, bruised and beaten by her husband, gazing into the distance with her great moist eyes while she dances alone in the desert.[67]

It is the "crazy woman" dancing in her dress of tiny mirror pieces in her mother's tales that the narrator in Maxine Hong Kingston's *The Woman Warrior* identifies herself with:

> I thought every house had to have its crazy woman or crazy girl, every village its idiot. Who would it be at our house? Probably me. . . . I was messy, my hair tangled and dusty. My dirty hands broke things: . . . And there were adventurous people inside my head to whom I talked whenever I was frivolous, violent, orphaned.[68]

The narrator in *The Woman Warrior* struggles to comprehend the legacy of craziness and conventionality, of curses and blessings, bequeathed her by her mother, who is at once a vessel of traditional culture and a courageous fighter in a harsh environment. The daughter, fearful that she has "no stories of equal pain,"[69] avoids becoming merely the transmitter of her mother's stories: although *The Woman Warrior* begins with the mother's stories, it ends with the daughter's.

In Jessica Tarahata Hagedorn's "Cristina," the grandeur and rage of the mother is a mystery at once frightening and inspiring to the daughter:

> never admitting her love/my mother's anger
> is her real strength/like an aging tigress
> still beautiful/in the afternoon light
> i could never tell her how much i want to touch her
> sometimes
> i've lost my appetite/for love/many times
> but it's my mother/i still think of/as all women
> a common occurrence
> but still frightening
> when i'm alone[70]

In Genny Lim's "On Weaning in America" (1979), the strength and resilience of the mother, whose life experiences the daughter can only imagine, makes the daughter feel worthless in comparison, since the mother's struggles seem ever more real. The daughter tries to imagine the mother as a young immigrant from Kwangtung province, wondering "who you might have been besides / a seamstress / besides a mother of seven / besides a green card holder":

> Yellow woman
> Moon chanter
> Spinner of dynasties
> Wisdom and magic
> Silent sorceress
> Herb healer
> Mother of Pearl
> Stone of Heaven
> Wings of Dragon
> Claws of Tiger
> Ocean goddess

In Nellie Wong's "From a Heart of Rice Straw," the daughter regrets that she had once been ashamed of her mother. Now she recalls the courage the old woman showed when her husband was shot by a cousin one day:

> I expected you to fly into the clouds, wail
> at Papa's side, but you chased cousin instead.
> like cops and robbers on the afternoon radio.
> It didn't matter that Papa lay bleeding.
> . . . You ran, kicking
> your silk slippers on the street, chasing
> cousin till you caught him, gun still in hand
> . . . My heart, once bent and cracked, once
> ashamed of your China ways.
> Ma, hear me now, tell me your story
> again and again.[71]

## Restoring the Foundations

It should not be surprising that many writers in developing nations have addressed themselves to the task that Ibo writer Chinua Achebe has called "repairing the foundations" to pave the way toward redefinition and regeneration after colonization. Achebe has characterized himself as "a sort of ancestor worshipper" whose primary responsibility as a writer is to help his people regain their strength and dignity by recreating their past through African eyes, "not only for the enlightenment of our detractors but even more for our own education":

> African people did not hear of culture for the first time from Europeans. . . . [T]heir societies were not mindless but frequently had a philosophy of great depth and value and beauty. . . . [T]hey had poetry, and above all they had dignity. . . . [T]he worst thing that can happen to any people is the loss of their dignity and self-respect. The writer's duty is to help them regain it by showing them in human terms what happened to them, what they lost.[72]

Achebe's celebrated first novel, *Things Fall Apart* (1958), paints a picture of traditional Ibo society on the eve of colonization. We are shown how the society was organized and how people functioned within it. The protagonist, Okonkwo, is a strong and great leader whose fatal flaw is his rigidity and resistance to the internal forces of change that cause all societies to evolve. Achebe demonstrates how the Ibo people questioned the relative efficacy and justice of their own social practices, changing them gradually as their society evolved. For example, the traditional practice of killing twins shortly after birth is being questioned by the people themselves and seems on the verge of abolition. The sudden appearance of European colonizers at the end of the novel destroys the delicate dialectical balance between tradition and change: the Ibo political leaders are captured and imprisoned, discredited in the eyes of their own people, and missionaries disrupt the society by proselytizing among outcasts. When the novel ends, the structures that had sustained the Ibos is crumbling, and there is nothing but colonization to replace it.

Similarly, contemporary Asian American writers have contended that Asian American history has been distorted and misunderstood because it has been told by racists. According to Wakayama Group, Japanese in the West have been deprived of their real past and forced instead to accept "conditional membership" in a Western European cultural tradition that denies his cultural integrity:

> The power, energy, and universal significance [of the Japanese writer in the West] will be derived from our roots—the Issei and Nisei experience as it really was. Over the years, our history has been molded into a perverted myth. . . . [T]he first obligation of the Sansei, and in particular the Sansei artist, is to regain his true past. Japanese life was rich and full with all the joys, hardships and complexity of a living people. Unless we preserve the essence of that life, it will be lost forever. . . . [W]e need to understand [the past] before we can have a realistic sense of the future.[73]

The Asian American attempt to restore the historical foundations of Asian American culture has involved the search for previously little-known authors like Carlos Bulosan, John Okada, Louis Chu, and Toshio Mori, who was the only writer among the four who lived to see several of his unpublished works brought to press through the efforts of his young Asian American admirers. It has also involved attempts to locate and translate literature written about the American experience by immigrants in their native languages.

One of the projects of the Chinese Culture Foundation in San Francisco, a community-based and foundation-supported organization comprised primarily of Chinese Americans, has been the publication of *Island: Poetry and History of Chinese Immigrants on Angel Island, 1910–1940* (1980), a selected anthology of translations of poetry written on the barracks walls at the Angel Island detention center, where Chinese immigrants were detained for exhaustive questioning during the period of Chinese exclusion between 1910 and 1940. According to the editors and translators, Him Mark Lai, Judy Yung, and Genny Lim, the poems are concrete illustrations of how ill-suited the stereotype of Chinese has been to their own realities as they expressed them. The poems have "a vitality and indomitability never before identified with Chinese Americans. The stereotypic image of a passive, complacent race of lotus-eaters will hardly find substantiation" in these poems.[74]

Some of the poems express profound anguish at the weakness of the Chinese nation, which not only necessitated emigration and exile but also permitted harsh discriminatory treatment of the Chinese in America:

Lin, upon arriving in America,
Was arrested, put in a wooden building,
And made a prisoner.
I was here for one autumn.
The Americans did not allow me to land.
I was ordered deported.
When the news was told,
I was frightened and troubled about returning to my country.
We Chinese of a weak nation
Can only sigh at the lack of freedom.
        (Written by a Taoist from the Town of Iron)

The fierce spirit of the immigrants is expressed by one unknown poet:

It's a pity heroes have no way of exercising their prowess.
I can only await the word so that I can snap Zu's whip.

The warrior's spirit and his desire for retribution for injustice is expressed in another poem:

For what reason must I sit in jail?
It is only because my country is weak and my family poor.
. . . How many people ever return from battles?
. . . Leaving behind my writing brush and removing my sword, I came to America.
Who was to know two streams of tears would flow upon arriving here?
If there comes a day when I will have attained my ambition and become successful,
I will certainly behead the barbarians and spare not a single blade of grass.

Another poem reveals the immigrants' attitude towards America:

Don't say that everything within is Western styled.
Even if it is built of jade, it has turned into a cage.[75]

The significance of the poems, which constitute "a vivid fragment of Chinese American history and a mirror capturing the image of the past" is described by the translator as follows:

The poems occupy a unique place in the literary cultures of Asian America. These immigrant poets unconsciously introduced a new sensibility, a Chinese American sensibility, using China as the source and America as a bridge to spawn a new cultural perspective. Their poetry is a legacy to Chinese Americans who would not be here today were it not for these predecessors' pioneering spirit.[76]

By penetrating and occupying the consciousness of his shadowy forbears, Chinese American writer Lawrence Yep contributes to the effort to repair the foundations of the Asian American heritage in *Dragonwings* (1975), a historical novel about the nineteenth-century Chinese in America who invented a biplane. Yep calls the book a "historical fantasy created from a newspaper account of Fung Joe Guey's 1909 flight." Since he was unable to discern from the newspaper accounts such details as why Fung had tried to build a biplane, who he was, where he was from, or whether he had a wife and family, Yep adheres as faithfully as possible to historical accuracies about the period, about the 1909 San Francisco earthquake and the details of the Chinese laundries of the period, and fills in the details that humanize the characters of the novel with his imagination:

Of the hundreds of thousands of Chinese who flocked to these shores we know next to nothing. They remain a dull, faceless mass:

statistical fodder to be fed to the sociologists, or lifeless abstractions to be manipulated by historians. And yet these Chinese were human beings—with fears and hopes, joys and sorrows like the rest of us. In the adventures of the various members of the Company of the Peach Orchard Vow, I have tried to make some of these dry historical facts become living experiences.

Yep's Chinese are drawn, he says, from composites of all the elderly Chinese men he knows. He traces the Chinese efforts to fight injustice, their group spirit, their courageous efforts to help the injured after the earthquake, and their persistent pursuit of their dreams. The father, Windrider, a courageous and spirited man seen through the eyes of his eight-year-old son, Moon Shadow, follows his dream of flying despite poverty, racist hostility towards him and his group, and his longing for the wife he had to leave behind. Yep has made a deliberate effort to counterbalance the hegemony of racist stereotypes of the Chinese in American culture by presenting the Chinese as human beings, as the people he imagines they really must have been:

> [I]t has been my aim to counter various stereotypes as presented in the media. Dr. Fu Manchu and his yellow hordes, Charlie Chan and his fortune-cookie wisdom, the laundryman and cook of the movie and television Westerns, and the houseboys of various comedies present an image of Chinese not as they really are but as they exist in the mind of white America. I wanted to show that Chinese-Americans are human beings upon whom America has had a unique effect. I have tried to do this by seeing America through the eyes of a recently arrived Chinese boy, and by presenting the struggles of his father in following his dream.[77]

For many Japanese Americans, the most critical period of the American experience was the period of internment during World War II. Lawson Inada's poetry anthology is titled *Before the War* (1971) because many Japanese Americans marked their lives around the relocation experience. Although *issei* wrote poetry in the traditional *tanka*, *haiku*, and *senryu* forms about the internment experience, much of this work has yet to be translated into English. Through the 1930s and 1940s, *nisei* writers wrote in English in their own literary journals. But the first novel about the relocation experience was published by a non-Japanese, Karen Kehoe. According to Frank Chin *et al.*:

> The appearance of *City of the Sun* in 1947 led the *Pacific Citizen* (a Japanese American community newspaper) to wonder why a

Japanese-American had not written a work of fiction or nonfiction about the camp experience. The editors then went on to speculate that perhaps the experience had been too traumatic.[78]

While it is true that many *issei* and *nisei* preferred not to discuss the experience, orally or in writing, what was written was not published outside the Japanese American community. Chin and others attribute this to the unwillingness of non-Japanese to accept a Japanese American view of internment, a view that might contain a challenge to the racist assumptions that made it possible in the first place.

Contemporary *nisei* and *sansei* writers have focused a great deal of attention on the camp experience. Many years after her own release, poet Mitsuye Yamada tries to recall what the internment meant to her as a young adult in poems collected under the title *Camp Notes*, recognizing how "What your mother tells you now / in time / you will come to know." *Kibei* Edward Miyakawa, who was a youthful inmate of the camps, recreates the experience in fiction based on historical research in *Tule Lake* (1979). Jeanne Wakatsuki Houston, who was a child at the time of incarceration, too young to recall the experience clearly, relied heavily on these historical sources for *Farewell to Manzanar* (1973). *Nisei* writer Momoko Iko traces the dramatic effects of discrimination leading up to internment on the lives of individual members of a Japanese American family in rural California in *The Gold Watch* (1974).[79]

Many of the *nisei* writing about internment many years later were attempting to recreate a past that was governed by *issei* elders, the standard-bearers of Japanese American cultural integrity whose role was understood only after they had begun to decline and pass away. *Nisei* writers Wakako Yamauchi and Hisaye Yamamoto reveal the *issei* world through the childish eyes of young *nisei* narrators and observers.

If the *nisei* saw the *issei*-dominated world as through a glass darkly, that world has been even less accessible to the third- and fourth-generation Japanese American *sansei* and *yonsei*, most of whom speak little Japanese. To them, the *issei* are old and have always been old, vestiges of a dim past that bears little resemblance to the contemporary world they wish to participate in. And yet there is a longing on the part of the *sansei* and *yonsei* to claim that dim past, to know the answers to unexplained questions, and to redefine links between the generations.

Although they were either very young or not even born at the time of internment, *sansei* and *yonsei* writers also focus their attention on the symbolic significance of the camp experience, recreating historical fantasies based on their imagination projections. In his poem, "Family Album for Charlotte Davis," Lonnie Kaneko recreates the journey to Minidoka in 1942:

The locomotive steams over names like Puyallup,
Boise, Twin Falls and Burley; it heads
where men throw nails and two-by-fours
into desert air. They fall into long lines.
Soldiers empty the cars of names
like Naganawa, Namba, Hiroshige
and proud faces named George, Linc, or Naomi
into rooms furnished with sawdust and sage.

The sign says MINIDOKA.
Nobody knows what it means.

Even today, the bitterness of the incarceration experience remains in the hearts of the *sansei* and *yonsei* who search through a library reference book to find out what "minidoka" means only to discover the irony that the years in the desert had been spent in a camp whose name signifies water: "Yesterday Charlotte asked, 'You mean there is still a bitterness?' Something wormed its way through my blood. Snake. Water. Earth. 'It is a thirst,' I say."[80]

Kaneko's short story "The Shoyu Kid" (1976) is set in an internment camp and focuses on the debilitating effects of incarceration on little boys, whose wild and decadent life makes them cruel and ruthless. We discover, in the course of the story, that the object of their scorn, another Japanese American boy, is being victimized by a white soldier. Thus the environment of the camps is framed in the symbolic oppression of the inmates by the soldiers, who represent the white racism that caused them to be imprisoned in the first place.[81]

Asian Americans' effort to reconstruct the lost past also involves the attempt to comprehend the half-buried mysteries of their parents' and grandparents' experiences. This effort is almost a compulsion in Nellie Wong's "Day of the Dead" (1977):

. . . if I worship the dead,
it is because
I hear my parents whispering
through the marrow of my bones
asking to be fed.[82]

Maxine Hong Kingston's *The Woman Warrior* and *China Men* are attempts to trace the topography of those generations, not only to uncover the identity of the contemporary Chinese American but also to destroy the myths that have prevented the past from being fully accessible to the present generation. The contemporary Asian American writer is often forced to try to piece together and sort out the meaning of the past from shreds of stories heard in childhood or from faded photographs that have never been explained.

In Wing Tek Lum's "A Picture of My Mother's Family" (1974), the poet searches for the significance of each detail from an old photograph of his grandfather and the family. He must try to put together the story of his half-forgotten ancestors and make it relevant to himself. He tries to trace resemblances between the young faces in the photograph and clouded memories of aging relatives, now long dead. The white-bonneted baby in the photograph he recalls as a sickly spinster aunt who died when he was a schoolboy. His grandfather's slender hands were "gnarled, pale roots" by the time the poet saw them as a child.

Like many American-born Asians, the poet does not even know his relatives' names, where his parents were born, or anything about their childhood in a distant land, all of which aspects of his heritage had not been relevant to his American experience. The photograph is tantalizingly unrevealing. The poet must guess, support, and assume whether his grandmother's feet were bound, what occasioned the portrait, and who the relatives in the picture really are. Like Kingston, he must rely on his own imaginative projections: his questions will remain unanswered except by his own conjectures:

> . . . It is perhaps morning, the coolness
> captured now in such clear light: they seem
> somehow illuminated by beams reflected from the moon.
> . . . My grandfather . . .
> looks on . . .
> toward his right faraway. I imagine a dark rose
> has caught his proud eye, though I do not know
> if such flowers have ever grown there.[83]

The need to understand and appreciate their heritage has prompted some Asian American writers to focus their attention on the immigrant elderly, whom they portray with a sense of urgency, sensitive to the certainty that the oldtimers and their life experiences might vanish before they can be understood and appreciated:

> My grandmother
> is dying . . .
> Ba-chan with black parasol, oil
> clothed to keep us dry,
> waiting in mud,
> slanted rain everywhere.
> . . . you slipped through my life,
> Your no-answered voice
> woven with TV sounds
> till you were beige
> like our walls.

The links between the immigrant *issei* and his *sansei* grandson is a treasure to both in Lane Nishikawa's "Grandfather" (1976):

I look at my grandfather
First generation
proud old issei man
His English is bad
Movements
Very slow and sure
His mind
Full of the world

He looks at me
Third generation
proud young sansei
His Japanese is bad
He is so quick
Too sure of himself
So much to learn

In him
I can see my heritage
My soul

In me
He can see his youth
His life.[84]

Filipino American poets Alfred Robles and Presco Tabios have devoted years to collecting the life stories and oral histories of the Filipino elderly in San Francisco. Men like Carlos Bulosan, who migrated to America as youths and spent their adult lives laboring in fields and canneries while being subjected to every form of social and economic discrimination, these *manongs* symbolize the sorrows and triumphs of life among early Filipino immigrants in America. Now, in the twilight of their lives, they live out their final days without wives or children in poverty-stricken urban ghettoes, unsung heroes of American labor, like the Filipino boxer spotlighted by Serafin Malay Syquia in "Shadowboxing" (1975):

In this corner
weighing less than he should
wearing stained trunks
aching from that cavity
unfilled
from that money wasted on paid love

styling monkey suits
blinding spotlights
trusting crooked managers and
fur-lined blondes
in this corner
scarred by years of
left jabs and right crosses of
unfilled flushes and snake eyes
staring at closed doors and no
help wanted signs
in this corner
leather fingers jabbing rice in
thin Chinese diners in
  his corner
  he sits a
  story
  aching
  to be told.[85]

Through the *manongs*, the contemporary Filipino American can trace the threads of his own history. In "These Are the Forgotten Manong," Prisco (Presco Tabios) writes of the proud-eyed Filipino elderly "glistening" in the sordid "false paradises" of bars and billiard halls on the fringes of San Francisco Chinatown, living "in youthful / memories / yesterdays promises / and todays deceptions . . . / their labor / wit and hope . . . documented / on once a month social security checks":

. . . through lonely memories of years
Manong the untold fears and hopes
are our histories
. . . Our manongs dreams are ours to be told[86]

According to Alfred Robles, the preservation of the oldtimers' tales is important to the contemporary Filipino American because through the "transmission of grief from father to son we realize that it is the son who is singing and leading the dance in the end."

The theme of the immigrant as permanent exile has held a special fascination for Filipino immigrant writer Bienvenido N. Santos, whose short stories set in the Filipino immigrant community in America are attempts to give voice to the exile in Asian American literature. Santos is writing as one of them. He had come to this country as a cultural envoy immediately prior to World War II. Forced to extend his sojourn because of the war, Santos traveled widely in America. During this time, he says, he was profoundly moved by the lives of his Filipino compatriots here.

Although he was supposed to work towards cultural understanding between the Philippines and the United States and to study English and American literature, he "studied instead the Filipino heart." When he returned to the Philippines after the war, Santos was "sad and disheartened . . . but full of stories about his lonely and lost fellow exiles in America."[87]

"In memory of the Pinoys* whose lives I shared, "Santos published a collection of short stories, *You Lovely People*,[88] in the Philippines in 1965. Santos' portrait of Filipino American life in the 1940s is a tale of men wandering, sometimes lost, in a hostile and sterile climate. It is a journey from bouyant innocence to degraded experience, which can only be endured because the exile still cherishes his memories of home.

An oldtimer helps the narrator of the stories, Ben, understand how the degradation of Filipinos in America has taken place: "I have seen many a child . . . lost in a thousand fogs of the big and small cities of the country. Those are stories for you, Ben, but they are all sad stories. All our stories are sad." Ben learns the story of Nanoy, who dies alone in a vermin-infested basement room; of Delfin, whose blonde wife keeps him waiting on the front steps of their apartment building while she seduces other men inside; of Pete, whose white wife drowns their sons in the bathtub when driven to distraction by their neighbors' racial taunts; and of Tan, whose white wife becomes an alcoholic after she is rejected by her friends and family for marrying a Filipino: "Lord, the things Filipinos do in this country. The things we say. What keeps us living on like this from day to day, from loveless kiss to loveless kiss, from venomed touch to venomed touch. . . . [T]hey are blessed ones like Nanoy, though it took him too long to die."[89]

The transformation of innocent, hopeful young Filipino immigrants eager for a life of freedom and happiness into a community of lonely exiles is gradual and irreversible. As the years pass, their glowing letters filled with "bright hopes for the future and tales of the glitter of life in the new country" cease, even while their aging parents continue to wait for the few dollars they hope to receive, "weaving bright dreams of the future." Meanwhile, the son drifts from one menial job to another and is eventually engulfed by the depravity that surrounds him:

> Soon he was gambling himself, laughing with the men when they laughed about vulgar things he himself now knew. . . . Now the drifting from one city to another. Here would be new faces. Here would be a new lease on life. But it was the same brown face everywhere, the same shortcomings, the same pitfalls. And, the

*Filipino men in America.

things he saw, the things he knew, the things he heard from the
drunken lips of whores. Who was good, was there any good face,
any good heart that remained so in this crowd?

The promise of America ultimately becomes a song repeated by cynical
bellhops in their rooming houses for laughs. The monument to Lincoln,
the poor boy who became president, becomes the background for souve-
nir photographs of Filipino men with their white girlfriends. The Gettys-
burg Address, which they had diligently memorized as school children in
the Philippines, becomes, like the "landmarks of American history . . .
meaningless . . . meaningless."[90]

The illusion of America is replaced by a fleeting dream of the
homeland, pastoral, lyrical, and no longer accessible to them. For Ben, it
is the memory of bamboo groves and the fragrance of lime in his mother's
hair. For some men it is the dream of carrying huge bags filled with silver
dollars home to their families. For others it is the memory of their now
dead wives' dark and trusting eyes. For one man, it is a faded, much-
fingered photograph of an unknown Filipino girl, who has come to
represent home to him. When Fabia asks Ben if the Filipina has changed
during his twenty years of exile in America, Ben is careful with his answer
because he knows that "all these years, he must have held on to certain
ideals, certain beliefs, even illusions peculiar to exile." Since there were
so few Filipino women in America, years might pass during which a
Filipino never saw a Filipino woman. Once, when Ambo is hospitalized,
a Filipino nurse attends him. Just seeing her makes him want to live:
"[T]hrough his fevered mind, she was his sister, she was his mother, she
was his sweetheart, she was his wife, ministering to him, talking to him
with love and he was home again."[91]

The burden of the exile is the fear of dying alone in a hostile land.
Kang had felt it keenly, and the terrible fear of dying among strangers far
from home loomed ominously before him. What had kept Ambo from
suicide in moments of profound despair and loneliness was the hope that
he was remembered at home, more than "a named mentioned now and
then, casually, always without love," more than "a blurred face in a
picture fast yellowing with the years":

> I've gone hungry for days and days in the Loop, looking vacantly at
> stores; in vermin-infested little rooms among the shiftless and un-
> washed; and I didn't care at all if I went to bed and woke up no more.
> . . . I thought of hurling myself into the river, but now I wanted to
> live; I mean, if I died, I wanted to die not here, please not here, in the
> faraway land, but somewhere in the islands where it is possible
> someone yet lives who loves me.

Even those who have lost real contact with their homes are gripped with a common anxiety when the fighting in the Philippines threatens even their distant illusions:

> Little brown men with sad, oily faces, lines deep under the eyes and around the mouth; frightened eyes, like those of a hunted deer; yellow figures and rough, hardened with labor, chafed from steaming water and the touch of hot plates and glasses. We have known of hunger away from home, ten years, twenty, thirty, a lifetime. What place will be bombed next, we ask, what do you think? My hometown?

In the end, the Filipino in America survives the loss of his innocence and illusions because of his ability to accept reality. Ambo gives up pretending someone is waiting for him in the islands: perhaps the answer lies in "wanting to remain here forever, not wanting to go home no more. Six feet of sod's six feet of sod—anywhere—and worms look pretty much the same in any climate, under any flag."[92]

The central contradiction of Filipino immigrant life during this period has been described as alienation or feelings of displacement among those who have left a traditional society where community, kinship, and mutual support are the basis of individual mental health:

> Filipinos . . . traditionally have enjoyed a highly developed sense of community (*bayanihan*) dependent on face-to-face (*damay*) relations. They have drawn their identity from extended family lines. . . . [In America, they faced] both physical distances between themselves and their motherland [which was evolving in their absence into a place to which they could no longer easily return], and the psychological distances between the Pinoys and earlier migrants from Europe and East Asia. . . . The Pinoy's expectation of *belonging* to others and not just to himself somehow had to be satisfied.[93]

Finally, Ambo recognizes that his folk loyalty and community is the community of exiles to which he does in fact belong. This fraternity of shared suffering and common understanding is the most meaningful aspect of their lives; together they are the "homeless waifs . . . the forgotten children of long lost mothers and fathers, as grown up men without childhood, bastards in an indifferent country." But they are as kin to one another:

> The Filipino members of the orchestra were looking at Leo and Val; the boys acknowledged their glances and smiles passed through music. The glances said, Filipino? Yes. And the smiles said, coun-

tryman, do I know you, or have we met before, or shall we meet perhaps, it's a familiar face, Countryman; this music is for you; my steps are easy, happy moving steps because the music is for you, Countryman.[94]

The themes in *You Lovely People* are brought together in one story that Santos wrote in 1966. "The Day the Dancers Came," which won the *Philippines Free Press* annual short story contest that year, is a concise and unified expression of the conditions of Filipino exiles in America and their fleeting confrontation with the ideal that has sustained them through their years of exile. Filipino Acayan, retired special post office policeman, former hospital, hotel, and factory worker, waiter, cook, gardener, and bearer of "several jobs that born no names," had "never looked young." His life, emblematic of the lives of thousands of other Filipino men who came to the land of golden opportunity to eke out a living on its fringes, unable to make enough money to return to their native lands but prevented by anti-miscegenation laws from marrying and starting families, has passed him by unaware like an aborted foetus. Fil has not been permitted to develop a full life, and he suddenly finds himself an old man: "In the beginning, the words he often heard were: too young, too young; but all of a sudden, too young became too old, too late. What had happened in between? A weariness, a mist covering all things." Fil had worked as a menial in a Cook County hospital, tending a row of bottles on a shelf:

> [E]ach bottle containing a stage of the human embryo in preservatives, from the lizard-like foetus of a few days, through the newly-born infant, with the position unchanged, cold and cowering and afraid. Sometimes in his sleep, Fil dreamed of preserving the stages after infancy, but somewhere he drew a blank like the many years between too young and too old.[95]

Fil Acayan's marginal existence has made his life a shadow, a recording to be played back on a portable tape recorder, which he calls his "magic sound mirror." In his isolation he has learned to make the lonely world around him meaningful through fantasy: staring at the ceiling over many years, he begins to see landscapes, and rivers in the stains and cobwebs. He imagines civilizations waxing and waning as the ceiling is changed by soot and age. Staring at the ceiling becomes a game he can play by himself while forgetting the passage of time.

When the dancers from Manila come to Chicago, he hopes to taste his lost youth and his homeland through them. He wants to invite them, his *paisanos*, to his apartment for *adobo*, to take them sightseeing in "his" Chicago. From the point of view of the dancers, it would be senseless to eat *adobo* with some old Filipino exile in Chicago. The decades Fil has lost between youth and old age divide them permanently. Fil, like many Meiji Japanese, Ch'ing Chinese, and Yi Dynasty Koreans, has been cut off from his homeland by the years between their arrival in America and today. Even his dialect, which he speaks in "florid, sentimental, poetic" style into the tape recorder, is the language of a past not known to the dancers and strange to their modern ears. Fil demands the impossible of them: he wants to relive through them the lost period between his infancy and old age, the period that spans his life in America. So the "beautiful people" reject his awkward, diffident advances, brushing past him, laughing and chatting at the hotel, their hair pomaded and exuding the fragrance of "long forgotten essence of *camia, ilang-ilang, dama de noche.*" Rebuffed, Fil fantasizes that, if they had accepted his invitation, they would have returned to the islands to tell their countrymen of the kind, amusing old Filipino who took them into his apartment:

> They would tell their folks: We met a kind, old man, who took us to his apartment. It was not much of a place. It was old—like him. When we sat on the sofa in the living room, the bottom sank heavily, the broken springs touching the floor. But what a cook that man was! And how kind! We never thought that rice and *adobo* could be that delicious. And the chicken *relleno!* When someone asked him what the stuffing was—we had never tasted anything like it—he smiled, saying, 'From heaven's supermarket,' touching his head and pressing his heart like a clown.[96]

Since the moment that would have served him as a memory of his relived lost youth remains only a fantasy, Fil records the dancers' performance on his tape recorder. He can then play back the performance, experiencing the clapping bamboo poles, the dancers' bare brown legs, "the sounds of life and death in the old country," the Igorots, the lovers, the gongs, and the feasts of his mislaid youth and distant homeland over and over again in the narrow confines of his apartment.[97] Fil knows that he will never go back to the Philippines.

The only meaningful reality in Fil's life is his friendship with his roommate, a retired porter. Tony is Fil's only family; like *manong* Fil, he was brought to America for menial labor and then relegated to a life of poverty and isolation. The two men share their exile huddling together in their loneliness, suspended between a dimly recalled homeland and the inaccessible fringes of American society. Fil is the dreamer; Tony is the realist. Tony knows that they will die in America, alone and discarded, while Fil dreams of the islands. Tony does not even attend the dancers' performance.

Fil's fantasies are abruptly interrupted by his realization that Tony is really dying, that he may lose the only family and friend in his life, the only one who has shared his floating life, "stranded without help" in the middle of a shoreless and indifferent sea.[98]

The intended audience for the stories is less the American reader than the intellectual in the Philippines, whose idealization of American life and culture and aristocratic dissociation from the low-born Pinoy Santos challenges in stories of the shared suffering and alienation of Filipinos of all social classes. There is an undertone of reproach in the portrayal of the contrast between the Filipino exile in America, who has sustained himself on dreams of the homeland, and the "beautiful people" of contemporary Manila, who little resemble the ideal cherished by the exile. In "The Long Way Home," rich Filipinos in posh coffee shops and bayside rivieras discuss in fluent Castilian or in "psuedo-Yankee twang" their plans to leave their war-torn mother country for Europe or America, "where everything can be bought for money." Santos is particularly concerned with the contrast between the Filipinos who are desperate to come to America and become completely assimilated into American life and the "oldtimers" who "did not want to become American citizens because they planned to return home to the Philippines, living the remainder of their days in the old villages, where their roots are." The irony is that most of the oldtimers never made it home again.[99]

Although Santos has not devoted his literary attention exclusively to the Filipino American experience, the life of the exile has continued to haunt him. He made three more trips to America, at first as a Rockefeller and Guggenheim fellow and later as an Exchange Fulbright Professor. In 1972, he and his family were preparing to leave for the Philippines when martial law was declared. The novel that he had scheduled for publication was disapproved and canceled; and although he had been slated to teach in the fall semester, the schools had been closed. And so Santos himself has become an unwilling exile, living in America indefinitely, suspended between the same two worlds of the oldtimers about which he had so poignantly written.

For a time, he tried to write about the recent city-bred and middle-class Filipino immigrants, who have been settling in the United States according to the new Immigration and Naturalization preferences established in 1965. Santos tried a "funny novel," *What the Hell for You Left Your Heart in San Francisco*, about "the new breed of Filipino immigrants, professionals and businessmen who lived in mansions on hills above the babel of the narrow streets, or in the exclusive residential sections away from the smell of the harbor and the fish markets." But there is something prosaic and distasteful about this "new breed," who according to Santos are "independent, luckier, . . . smart," and callous:

They know all the answers or seem to, anyhow; they glow with confidence, a beautiful people. . . . No loneliness for them. Loneliness is a disease, a terminal disease, they say in so many words, and they talk a lot. They hold glittering parties around their swimming pools, the diamonds on the fingers outshining the light in their eyes. No nostalgia for the new breed. The talk closest to home revolved around the current peso-dollar exchange, tax exemptions, loopholes in the tax laws and proven ways of circumventing [*sic*] them. Investments. New car models. At the last party I attended, they were comparing the relative power and clarity of their C.B. radios and how to keep them from being stolen.

Among the new immigrants, Santos says he feels like an "oldtimer" and wonders if his presence makes them think of their old parents back home. Consistently, he returns to his interest in the older, laboring exile:

I could not forget the smell of decay and death in the apartments of the old-timers among my countrymen who sat out the evening of their lives before television sets in condemned buildings in downtown San Francisco. Then the grin in both story and writer kept getting twisted in a grimace of pain close to tears.

Santos cannot resist focusing on the old exiles, because "now I realize that perhaps I have also been writing about myself.[100]

## Recent Immigrant Literature

Foreign-born Filipinos, Chinese, Japanese, and Koreans were ineligible for American citizenship until only a few decades ago. Changes in the regulations governing naturalization, together with the liberalization of immigration quotas in 1965, have resulted in profound changes in the demographic configurations of the Asian populations in the United States in recent years.[101] Although there are certainly many parallels between the attitudes and experiences of recent and those of earlier Asian immigrants, it is quite possible that the recent immigrant perspective will be portrayed in literature written in English because of the existence of larger numbers of bilingual young people who are imbued with a new awareness of the value of the multicultural perspective in American society, an awareness that has made them deliberately seek out their elders and forbears in their attempt to express the richness and complexity of the Asian American experience in literature. Their familiarity with the American environment in which the recent immigrant struggles to survive and sustain his foolish and courageous intentions sometimes inspires social criticism or satirical treatment of the immigrant, whose understanding of his new environment is ever less than perfect.

In a satirical story titled "The Blossoming of Bongbong" (1975), Jessica Tarahara Hagedorn, who immigrated herself from the Philippines at an early age, traces the experiences of a young Filipino immigrant in a new American environment that is not entirely hospitable to him. Unable to find a job in San Francisco, he lives with his relatives for a while, visiting bookshops and meeting brazen young girls in singles bars, where he is mistaken for a transvestite. Bongbong is confused and bewildered by American society:

> He went into the bathroom and stared at the bottles of perfume near the sink, the underarm deodorant, the foot deodorant, the cinnamon-flavored mouthwash, and the vaginal spray. They use Colgate brand toothpaste. Dove soap. Zee toilet paper. A Snoopy poster hung behind the toilet. It filled him with despair.

Bongbong writes home:

> Why do people like to look like cripples? Yesterday I saw a fat young woman wearing platform shoes that made her feet look like boats. Her dress was too short on her fat body and you could see her cellulite wobbling in her forest green pantyhose. Cellulite is the new fad in America.

Unable to tolerate the contradictions he cannot comprehend, Bongbong fears he will lose his sanity if he stays in America, and in the end he finally forgets who he is.[102]

In Hagedorn's poems, America is a land of blandness and boredom, where friendships are shallow and people's rage is hidden in glittering consumerism. Urban America is characterized by paranoia and sterility:

> television dictates amorphous lies
> to my unborn children
> telling me that
> murderers have mobilized
> into the suburbs
> and are wiping out americans
> in their grocery stores
> and living rooms

In "Song for My Father," the narrator is caught between America and the land of her father, the islands of music and tropical fruits and flowers where "life is cheap" under martial law:

i am trapped
by overripe mangoes
i am trapped
by the beautiful sadness of women
i am trapped
by priests & nuns
whispering my name
in confession boxes
i am trapped
by antiques & the music
of the future

And leaving you
again & again
for america,
the loneliest of countries

In America, the nonwhite immigrant can die a "natural death," encased in Saran Wrap on the beach. In such a setting being crazy is desirable:

. . . when you're crazy
it seems like you should sing about it
All the time: but
. . . who can stay crazy
under all this pressure?
. . . let us stay crazy
under pressure
let us stay crazy
under pressure
let us stay crazy
under pressure
(i gotta sing
    about it
all the time)

In Hagedorn's poetry, strange colors, smells, sounds, and feelings awaken racists to their own loneliness, making them want to possess or destroy the beauty of nonwhite people, which creates magic and music that draws the racist like voodoo incantations. In contrast to the sterility and paranoia of the American suburbs, the nonwhite people celebrate their lives and dispel their sorrow in the joyful music they create together:

dancing
the spirit shaking everyone

your faces are flowers of darkness
. . . children of the jungle
calling me to sing
forget my nightmares
mangoes staining my lips

Something about you
all of us
with songs inside
knifing the air of sorrow
   with our dance
   a carnival of spirits
   shredded blossoms
   in the water[103]

It should not be surprising that there has been relatively little literature written by recent immigrants themselves, pressed as they are by
problems of economic survival, language barriers, and cultural adjustments. But it can be expected that new forms of creative effort will soon
emerge from members of these groups, expressing a vital new experience. In stories they have both titled "Homecoming," Taiwan immigrant
writer Lin Hwai Min and Korean immigrant writer Kichung Kim are
concerned with the view of the homeland held by contemporary Asian
immigrants in America.

In Lin's "Homecoming" (1971), Chen Chi-hou pays a final visit to
his great-uncle in the village where his family had its roots. Chen is
haunted by a strange nostalgia for an old purity that has ceased to exist
even in the distant village, where now the flashing neon lights of wine
houses make the town seem a pathetic imitation of Taipei. The family
home is decaying and neglected, a house full of death and old junk. The
ancestral tablets lie in ruins, for there are few left in the village to tend
them. Chen's great-uncle laments:

"What a time it is! Every young man with feet is leaving. To Taipei,
Taiwan. . . . No one stays home to farm. We didn't have enough rice
reapers last month. And, more than thirty persons from New Port
have gone to America and none has returned. Five members of your
family have gone to America. And now you, the eldest grandson,
are leaving too.

Young Chen is only the latest link in a chain migration process that has
drained the vitality of the village families, leaving only the aged to tend
the home that has now become a decaying graveyard. Chen tells himself

that no one will ever return to the old home; he himself has lost the key. Now he will go to America, which "is so big you don't even meet your cousins there."[104]

Like the old *manong* whose "rituals of survival and lifelong intentions have gone awry," many recent Asian immigrants say they suffer from a feeling of homelessness, of not belonging anywhere or to anyone. Like the pre-war *issei*, they say they do not feel that they are real participants in American life, yet they know that they would be unable to resume the life they left behind them. Some immigrants are riddled with feelings of guilt for having left in the first place, and are prevented from full participation in American life in part by their sense that they are but guests in their new country.

> I've been living here for fifteen years now. I guess I always had it in the back of my mind to return to Korea one day. But when I visited there last year, it was such a bittersweet experience . . . seeing my old mother and my schoolmates and marking the distance that time had cast between us, measuring how everything had changed. . . . Even the food didn't taste the same. At one moment, I would say to myself, "I can, I can live here." At the next, I knew I could not. I am always fluctuating like that, suspended between two worlds that probably exist only in my imagination.
>
> Just when I am beginning to feel that this is my home, I will be walking along a road and a car full of white teenagers will yell out their windows as they pass by, "Stupid Chink!" and I must remember that this will never be my home.
>
> When I finally decided to become an American citizen, it was like crossing an icy river. I had to admit to myself that America, where I have lived for twelve years now, is my country. But on the day I was sworn in, I saw the other new citizens, mostly Mexicans, embracing each other and weeping for joy. I felt as if I were watching the ceremony like someone at a funeral, an outsider even in this. I had no feelings at all. Only emptiness.[105]

In Kichung Kim's "A Homecoming" (1972), Namshin returns to Korea after many years' absence to visit his aging parents, for whom he no longer has any real feelings.

> [H]e'd finally returned, after more than ten years, the only child who had gone off to America promising to come back after just four short years, and then two more and another two and so on until after the eighth or ninth year he had stopped talking about returning, and then he'd taken a job and taken out citizenship papers. But

now he was back, if only for a month during summer vacation. He didn't know what he felt at that moment, certainly neither joy nor indifference, only a sort of numbness.

For Namshin, returning to Korea is like "traveling back in time." He lies to his parents about having to stay in a downtown Seoul hotel because of some American research grant. In fact, he cannot bear the thought of staying with them in their "cramped, one-roomed hovel swarming with flies, without running water." He is unable to eat the poor fare his mother prepares for him. He is distracted by the flies and by his father's noisy chewing and swallowing. He feels comfortable only with an uncle who had lived for thirty years in America and had married an American woman. Although the uncle "had never been anything but an alien . . . [in America], never for instance becoming familiar enough with the language to understand the jokes on television," Namshin finds it easiest to talk to him because the older man knows about America and because they could "always drift into English."[106]

Although he wants to be associated with America, the land of prosperity and modern conveniences, Namshin is nevertheless annoyed when the skillful eyes of the black marketeers identify him easily as one who has returned from America. In the Western-style hotel coffee shop, he orders the beer that sounds "more Korean" to his ears, and he feels slightly superior to the Koreans who are trying to impress each other there with their familiarity with Western food. Namshin does not want to acknowledge that he is still Korean: although it is impossible for him to be accepted by the Koreans as an American, he wants to view Korea and Koreans as an American might. His only moment of peace comes when he sits down on the flush-toilet at the hotel. He wonders momentarily where the toilet muck goes, since there is no sewage system in Seoul, but he dismisses the problem as not his responsibility.

Kichung Kim paints a grim picture of the immigrant exile, suspended between two worlds and lacerated by feelings of guilt and inferiority. He also paints, in the background, a dark picture of the paradox of the larger U.S.-Korea relationship that makes a life like Namshin's possible. Namshin misses, for a fleeting moment, the shade-tree-lined streets and ox-drawn wooden-wheeled farm carts that have now been replaced by foul-smelling cars of all sizes and shapes and the ugly, hurriedly erected concrete and steel highrises that loom above the black-tiled Korean-style roofs "like begrimed corpses of some comicbook giants riddled with square, uniformly spaced bullet-holes." But he is unaware of the grim significance of the sinister scene in the streets below his hotel window, where military police patrol the streets in their jeeps after curfew, passing by the Seoul branches of American banks, "their mounted guns glinting beneath the street lamps."[107]

Disheartened by repeated rejections from publishers, who claim that his work lacks general appeal, Kichung Kim has turned away from imaginative writing about the Korean American experience and towards translating and interpreting Korean language literature. History has taught us to regret the relative paucity of published literature in English that expresses the Asian American culture and experience: hence, today's feverish attempts to collect oral histories from among rapidly vanishing oldtimers and to restore our foundations through contemporary writing about an almost-forgotten past.

Today's Asian American communities are coming to understand the importance of affirming a uniquely Asian American culture. It is clear that we must support our cultural warriors who, like Kichung Kim, can capture as few others can the living experience of Asian American people, to the everlasting benefit of our future generations.

In former years, Asian American writers expressed an intense desire to belong to and to participate fully in the main currents of American life and culture. Today's writers are still concerned with defining their identity and roots in American society. But their increased awareness of the value and legitimacy of the multicultural, multiracial elements that combine to comprise American society has given rise to many new and hopeful voices as well as diverse tendencies that reflect a wide range of concerns. As a consequence of their new sense of integration, Asian American writers are ever more comfortable expressing their dissatisfactions within American society while continuing their search for identity, beauty, and meaning through literature. Although there are many fluctuations in the recent literature between self-contempt and self-affirmation, between outrage and expressions of love, the theme that underscores the contemporary body of Asian American literature is the need for community. It is difficult to discern what shapes and patterns will emerge in the future, but at the present time Asian American writers are attempting to build bridges that span generations and nationalities, between men and women, connecting Asian Americans to each other, to other minority groups, to American society and beyond. And the hegemony of racist writing about Asians and Asian Americans is being challenged each time Asian American voices emerge in an effort to define and express the unique and ever-evolving Asian American experience.

Asian American literature is our voice to the rest of the world. It encourages our humanity and our interconnections. It helps us define our identity, culture, and community, our unity and our diversity. As such it has the potential to contribute to our sovereignty and the preservation of our cultural integrity, far from segregating Asian Americans from the rest of American society, provide a base on which positive participation in and contributions to that society can be built, for diversity and uniqueness can and should be encouraged rather than used as a justification for inequality. In some future time, there may no longer be a need to "set the record straight," and at that time perhaps we will all enjoy without limitation being equal though not alike.

Contemporary Asian American writers are in the process of challenging old myths and stereotypes by defining Asian American humanity as part of the composite identity of the American people, which, like the Asian American identity, is still being shaped and defined.

# Notes

## Preface

1. During World War II, when Japan was an enemy nation and China an ally, an article titled "How To Tell Your Friends from the Japs" appeared in *Time* magazine (Dec. 22, 1941), offering readers "a few rules of thumb" that were "not always reliable" since "there is no infallible way of telling them apart." According to the article, virtually all Japanese are short and thin, tending to "dry up . . . as they age," while Chinese are tall and better built. Japanese can be distinguished by their hard-heeled, stiffly erect gait and their hesitancy and nervousness in conversation as well as by their loud laughter at inappropriate times. But the key difference between Chinese and Japanese, the writer contends, is in facial expression: the Chinese expression is "more placid, kindly, open," while the Japanese is "dogmatic, arrogant."
2. See, for example, Ronald Tanaka, "On the Metaphysical Foundations of Sansei Poetics," *Journal of Ethnic Studies* 7, no. 2 (summer 1979): 1–36; Bruce Iwasaki, "Response and Change for the Asian in America," *Roots: An Asian American Reader*, ed. Amy Tachiki *et al.* (Los Angeles: UCLA Asian American Studies Center, 1971), and "Introduction: Asian American Literature," *Counterpoint: Perspectives on Asian America*, ed. Emma Gee (Los Angeles: UCLA Asian American Studies Center, 1976).
3. Kai-yu Hsu and Helen Palubinskas, eds., *Asian American Authors* (Boston: Houghton Mifflin Co., 1972); Frank Chin, Jeffery Paul Chan, Lawson Fusao Inada, and Shawn Hsu Wong, eds., *Aiiieeeee! An Anthology of Asian-American Writers* (Washington, D.C.: Howard University Press, 1974).
4. On *A Daughter of the Samurai*, see New York *Tribune*, Nov. 22, 1925, p. 10; on *East Goes West*, Ladie Hosie, "A Voice from Korea," *Saturday Review of Literature*, April 4, 1931, p. 707; on *Father and Glorious Descendant*, *Library Journal* 68, no. 7 (April 1, 1943): 287; on *American in Disguise*, Phoebe Adams, "Short Reviews: Books," *Atlantic Monthly* 227, no. 4 (April 1971): 104; on *Farewell to*

281

*Manzanar*, *Saturday Review World*, Nov. 6, 1973, p. 34, and *Library Journal*, Nov. 1, 1973, p. 3257.

5. *Publisher's Weekly* 212 (Sept. 1976): 72.
6. Maxine Hong Kingston, *The Woman Warrior* (New York: Vintage Books, 1977), p. 108.
7. Jane Kramer, "On Being Chinese in China and America," New York *Times Book Review*, Nov. 7, 1976, p. 19; Michael T. Malloy, "'The Woman Warrior': On Growing Up Chinese, Female, and Bitter," *National Observer*, Oct. 9, 1976, p. 25.
8. Malloy, "'The Woman Warrior,'" p. 25.
9. Kramer, "On Being Chinese," p. 1.
10. Timothy Pfaff, "Talk with Mrs. Kingston," New York *Times Book Review*, June 18, 1980, p. 26.
11. *Ibid.*
12. *Ibid.*

# Chapter 1

1. Gertrude Atherton, "Japan or 'Main Street,'" New York *Times Book Review and Magazine*, Jan. 16, 1921, p. 7.
2. Stephen Birmingham, *The Late John Marquand* (Philadelphia: J. P. Lippincott Co., 1972), p. 120.
3. Cay Van Ash and Elizabeth Sax Rohmer, *Master of Villainy: A Biography of Sax Rohmer* (Bowling Green, Ohio: Bowling Green University Popular Press, 1972), p. 215.
4. Daniel O'Connell, "Song of the Tartar Horde," quoted in William Purviance Fenn, *Ah Sin and His Brethren in American Literature* (Peking: College of Chinese Studies, 1933), pp. 18–19; Atwell Whitney, *Almond-Eyed: The Great Agitator; A Story of the Day* (San Francisco: Bancroft, 1878), p. 168.
5. Wallace Irwin, *Seed of the Sun* (rpt.; New York: Arno Press, 1978), p. 128. The novel was serialized in the *Saturday Evening Post* before being published in book form.
6. Gene Stratton-Porter, *Her Father's Daughter* (Garden City, N.Y.: Doubleday, Page & Co., 1921).
7. Irwin, *Seed of the Sun*, p. 112; Van Wyck Mason, *The Shanghai Bund Murders* (New York: Doubleday & Co., 1933), p. 271.
8. Irwin, *Seed of the Sun*, p. 233; Edgar Rice Burroughs, *The Mucker* (New York: Canaveral Press, 1963), pp. 130–131; Jack London, *The Star Rover* (New York: Macmillan Co., 1915), p. 175.
9. Jack London, *Dutch Courage and Other Stories* (New York: Macmillan Co., 1922), p. 127.
10. Jack London, "The Inevitable White Man," *South Sea Tales* (New York: Macmillan Co., 1911), pp. 235–255; Jack London, *Daughter of the Snows* (New York: Macmillan Co., 1904), p. 83; Jack London, *When God Laughs* (New York: Macmillan Co., 1911).
11. Will Irwin (text) and Arnold Genthe (photographs), *Old Chinatown* (New York: Mitchell Kennerley, 1913), p. 113; Jack London, "The Yellow Peril," *Revolution and Other Essays* (New York: Macmillan Co., 1910), pp. 284–285.

12. Sax Rohmer, *The Trail of Fu Manchu* (London: Allan Wingate, 1978; orig. pub. c. 1934), p. 49; Sax Rohmer, *The Island of Fu Manchu* (New York: Doubleday & Co., 1940).
13. Wallace Irwin, *Chinatown Ballads* (New York: Duffield & Co., 1906), p. 16.
14. Margaret MacKay, *Like Water Flowing* (London: George C. Farrar & Co., 1938); Achmed Abdullah, "A Simple Act of Piety," *The Honuorable Gentleman and Other Stories* (New York: Knickerbocker Press, 1919), p. 219. Wallace Irwin, *Seed of the Sun*, p. 51. The literature written by writers of mixed ancestry provides a startling contrast to the portrayals of the Eurasian in Anglo-American literature. Diana Chang and Han Suyin, who grew up in China, integrate the critical struggles that occupied the people of China with the Eurasian protagonists' search for identity in *Frontiers of Love* (New York: Random House, 1956) and *A Many-Splendored Thing* (Boston: Little, Brown & Co., 1952) respectively. In Chang's novel, the three Eurasian characters have complex and differing responses to their situation: One develops an intense hatred for foreign imperialism in China. Another, seduced and abandoned by an unprincipled white man, becomes a drifter, prey to other potential seducers. Both want desperately to win acceptance, but their lives and thoughts are much more complex than the one-dimensional portraits painted by Anglo-American writers about mixed-blood characters ever allow. The third character, the narrator, weighs the responses of the other two.

Like *Frontiers of Love*, Han Suyin's novels are quasi-historical. Not until near the end of *A Many-Splendored Thing* does the writer reveal that the protagonist, who considers herself Chinese, is part white. Han comments that Eurasians, while discriminated against in China by the British, are accepted by Chinese if they are culturally and linguistically Chinese, because to the Chinese biology and race are less important than culture. In contrast to the popular Anglo-American notion of Eurasian self-hatred, Chang's and Han's novels depict protagonists who do not regard their Asian heritage as a handicap. They are not particularly restless; they neither wish to be dead nor white; and they are not ashamed of China or the Chinese. No wars are waged in their veins of the type described in Anglo-American literature, although the part-Chinese protagonists are depicted as ashamed of non-Chinese who are bigoted.

Sui Sin Far, or Edith Eaton (1867–1914), and Sadakichi Hartmann (1869–1944) lived most of their lives in Europe or America. Sui was born of an English father and a Chinese mother. Having grown up amidst British middle-class families at the turn of the century, she experienced various forms of British bigotry against nonwhite people. In "Leaves from the Mental Portfolio of an Eurasian," she recounts some of these experiences of growing up among "covert smiles and sneers" and her responses to them: "I have come from a race on my mother's side which is said to be the most stolid and insensible to feeling of all races, yet I look back over the years and see myself so keenly alive to every shade of sorrow and suffering that it is almost a pain to live. . . . Why is my mother's race despised? I look into the faces of my father and mother. Is she not every bit as dear and good as he? Why? Why?" (*Independent* 66, no. 3136 [Jan. 7, 1909]: 127–128).

Sui Sin Far's short stories of Chinatown and Chinese American life, written after her immigration to the United States as a young girl, often portray the Chinese as morally superior to whites. Many of these stories are collected in a volume titled *Mrs. Spring Fragrance* (Chicago: A. C. McClurg & Co., 1912). Sui remained fiercely proud of her Chinese heritage and unwilling to attempt to "pass" for white or to let an insult to the Chinese go unchallenged. She recounts her refusal to accommodate exoticization of her Chinese heritage for the sake of acceptance by whites:

"I . . . meet some funny people who advise me to 'trade' upon my nationality. They tell me that if I wish to succeed in literature in America I should dress in Chinese costume, carry a fan in my hand, wear a pair of scarlet slippers. . . . Instead of making myself familiar with the Chinese-Americans around me, I should discourse on my spirit acquaintance with Chinese ancestors and quote in between the 'good-mornings' and 'How d'ye dos' of editors.

"'Confucius, Confucius, how great is Confucius. Before Confucius there never was Confucius,' etc. etc. etc. or something like that, both illuminating and obscuring, don't you know. They forget, or perhaps they are not aware that the old Chinese sage taught 'The way of sincerity is the way of Heaven'" ("Leaves from the Mental Portfolio of an Eurasian," p. 132).

Playwright, poet, and art critic Sadakichi Hartmann was born in Japan of a Japanese mother and a German father. Brought by his father to the United States when he was still a boy, Hartmann was looked upon as an exotic and eccentric artist in avant-garde literary and art circles here. Near the end of his life, he was "subjected to continual pressures of harassment and insults from white neighbors" (David Hsin-Fu Wand, *Asian American Heritage* [New York: Simon & Schuster, 1974], p. 127); Hartmann's white neighbors suspected him of being a Japanese spy. Hartmann's acute awareness of racism and colonialism is revealed in his prose writings: "Anyone familiar with colonization . . . should feel ashamed to belong to the white race. There is no reason to single out a special nation for an example. They are all alike. They come as raiders with missionaries and a little later with armed forces, and almost incredible to believe, wild free men become slaves, to work at blast furnaces and in mines, just for profit, control, and annual dividends, for some monster like Leopold II" (*White Chrysanthemum: Literary Fragments and Pronouncements*, ed. George Knox and Harry Lawton [New York: Herder & Herder, 1971], p. 117).

15. Rex Beach, *Son of the Gods* (New York: Harper & Brothers, 1929), p. 78.
16. Louise Jordan Miln, *Mr. and Mrs. Sên* (New York: A. L. Burt Co., 1923), p. 239.
17. Jack London, *The House of Pride* (New York: Macmillan Co., 1912), p. 172.
18. Charles G. Leland, *Pidgin English Sing-Song* (London: Kegan Paul, Trench, Trubner & Co., 1903), p. 28.
19. Hwuy-Ung, *A Chinaman's Opinion of Us and of His Own People* (New York: Frederick A. Stokes Co., 1927), "letters" to Theodore Tourrier as "translated" by a Canton Methodist missionary.
20. Chester B. Fernald, *The Cat and the Cherub and Other Stories* (New York: Century Co., 1896), p. 128.
21. Wallace Irwin, *Mr. Togo, Maid of All Work* (New York: Duffield & Co., 1921), p. 5.
22. Stuart W. Hyde, "The Chinese Stereotype in American Melodrama," *Califor-*

*nia Historical Society Quarterly* 34, no. 4 (Dec. 1955): 357, 360; Gouverneur Morris, *Yellow Men and Gold* (New York: Dodd, Mead & Co., 1911), p. 153.

23. Hubert Howe Bancroft, *Essays and Miscellany* (San Francisco: History Publishing Co., 1890), p. 309; "The Chinaman," *Putnam's* 9 (1857): 337.

24. Robert McClellan, *The Heathen Chinee* (Columbus: Ohio State University Press, 1971), p. 49.

25. Quoted in Fenn, *Ah Sin and His Brethren*, pp. 47, 55.

26. Mark Twain, *Roughing It*, vol. 2 (New York: Gabriel P. Wells, 1922).

27. Fenn, *Ah Sin and His Brethren*, p. 64.

28. Reginald W. Wheeler, Henry H. King, and Alexander B. Davidson, *The Foreign Student in America* (New York: Association Press, 1925), pp. 144, 201.

29. Charles R. Shepherd, *The Ways of Ah Sin* (New York: Fleming H. Revell, 1923), frontis.

30. London, *The Star Rover*, p. 188; Rohmer, *The Trail of Fu Manchu*, p. 126.

31. Paul Morand, *The Living Buddha* (New York: Henry Holt & Co., 1928), pp. 249, 251.

32. Dorothy B. Jones, *The Portrayal of China and India on the American Screen, 1896–1955* (Cambridge: Massachusetts Institute of Technology, 1955), p. 38.

33. Jerome Charyn, *American Scrapbook* (New York: Viking Press, 1969), p. 27; Hatsuye Egami, "Wartime Diary," *All Aboard* (Topaz Relocation Center), spring 1944.

34. John J. Epsey, "No Man Can Serve Two Masters," *New Yorker*, Feb. 3, 1945, pp. 30–33.

35. W. Somerset Maugham, *On a Chinese Screen* (New York: George H. Doran Co., 1922), pp. 233–234.

36. Asian American literature is defined here as literature written in English about the American experience by writers of Chinese, Japanese, Korean, and Filipino descent.

# Chapter 2

1. For a concise discussion of anti-Chinese activities, see Stanford M. Lyman, *Chinese Americans* (New York: Random House, 1974). Anti-Japanese activities are discussed in Roger C. Daniels, *The Politics of Prejudice: The Anti-Japanese Movement in California and the Struggle for Japanese Exclusion* (New York: Atheneum, 1972). Anti-Filipino activities are described in Bruno Lasker, *Filipino Immigration to the Continental United States and to Hawaii* (Chicago: University of Chicago Press, 1931), and Carey McWilliams, *Brothers under the Skin* (Boston: Little Brown & Co., 1942) and *Factories in the Field: The Study of Migratory Farm Labor in California* (Salt Lake City, Utah: Peregrine Publishers, 1971).

2. For a recently translated anthology of the poems carved into the walls of Angel Island, see *Island* by Him Mark Lai, Genny Lim, and Judy Yung (San Francisco: Chinese Culture Foundation, Hoc Doi Project, 1980). *Island: Poetry and History of Chinese Immigrants on Angel Island, 1910–1940* represents the efforts of contemporary Chinese Americans to document and preserve the Chinese immigrant voice in American history and culture. Similarly, writing by first-generation Japanese immigrants has been collected and translated in

*Ayumi: A Japanese American Anthology* (ed. Janice Mirikitani [San Francisco: The Japanese American Anthology Committee, 1980]), which contains autobiographical essays, poetry, and short stories written in Japanese and previously unavailable to the English-speaking reader. These writings were deliberately sought by contemporary Japanese Americans because they provided rare insights into the Japanese immigrant perspective on the American experience.

3. "The Life Story of a Japanese Servant" and "The Life Story of a Chinaman," in Hamilton Holt, ed., *The Life Stories of Undistinguished Americans* (New York: James Pott & Co., 1906).

4. See Kazuo Ito, *Issei: A History of Japanese Immigrants in North America*, trans. Shinichiro Nakamura and Jean S. Girard (Seattle: Executive Committee for Publication of *Issei*, 1973).

5. Lee Yan Phou, *When I Was a Boy in China* (Boston: D. Lothrop Co., 1887), p. 41.

6. Chiang Yee, *A Chinese Childhood* (New York: John Day Co., 1952), p. 303.

7. Etsu Inagaki Sugimoto, *A Daughter of the Samurai* (New York: Doubleday, Page & Co., 1925), p. 76.

8. *Ibid.*, pp. 154, 140, 239, 155–156. The term "feudal" is used loosely here, since there were many differences between European feudalism and earlier Asian modes of production.

9. New York *Times*, Jan. 10, 1926; New York *Tribune*, Nov. 22, 1925, p. 10.

10. Lin's portrayal of the Chinese experience in America in *Chinatown Family* (New York: John Day Co., 1948) will be discussed in Chapter 4.

11. Chan Wing-Tsit, "Lin Yutang, Critic and Interpreter," *College English* 8, no. 4 (Jan. 1947): 163–164; *Wilson Bulletin* 11, no. 5 (Jan. 1937): 298; William DuBois, "In and Out of Books," New York *Times Book Review*, Aug. 22, 1954.

12. Lin Yutang, *My Country and My People* (New York: John Day Co., 1935), pp. 82–84; Lin Yutang, *The Importance of Living* (New York: John Day Co., 1937), p. 155; Lin Yutang, *The Vigil of a Nation* (New York: John Day Co., 1944), p. 90; Lin, *My Country and My People*, p. 39; Lin, *The Importance of Living*, p. 110; Lin, *My Country and My People*, p. 70.

13. Evelyn Lowenstein *et al.*, *The Picture Book of Famous Immigrants* (New York: Sterling Publishing Co., 1962), p. 61.

14. Lin, *My Country and My People*, p. 83, and *The Importance of Living*, p. 110.

15. Chan, "Lin Yutang," p. 165; Lowenstein *et al.*, *Picture Book*, p. 61.

16. Henry Pearson Gratson, ed., *As a Chinaman Saw Us* (New York: D. Appleton & Co., 1916), p. vi.

17. Wu Tingfang, *America through the Spectacles of an Oriental Diplomat* (New York: Frederick A. Stokes, 1914), preface, pp. x, 142–143.

18. Huie Kin, *Reminiscences* (Peiping, San Yu Press, 1932), p. 28; Betty Lee Sung, *Mountain of Gold* (New York: Macmillan Co., 1967), pp. 261, 184.

19. Chiang Yee, *The Silent Traveler in New York* (London: Methuen & Co., 1950), p. 198.

20. Younghill Kang, *The Grass Roof* (New York: Charles Scribner's Sons, 1931), p. 303. Kang came to the United States as an immigrant from Korea in 1921 at the age of eighteen. He studied at Boston and Harvard universities and worked for *Encyclopedia Britannica* and the Metropolitan Museum of Art in New York. He taught English composition part-time at New York University,

where he was befriended by writer Thomas Wolfe. Wolfe introduced Kang to a publisher who gave Kang an advance upon inspecting some of Kang's manuscripts. *The Grass Roof* was published in 1931, followed by *The Happy Grove* in 1933 and *East Goes West* in 1937. Kang was living in Satellite Beach, Florida, when he died in 1972. He is survived by his widow, Frances Keeley Kang, their three children, and their two grandchildren.

21. Stanley J. Kunitz, ed., *Twentieth Century Authors* (1st supp.; New York: H. W. Wilson Co., 1955), p. 744.
22. New York *Times*, Dec. 14, 1972, p. 50.
23. Lady Hosie, "A Voice from Korea," *Saturday Review of Literature*, April 4, 1931, p. 707; *New Yorker*, 13, no. 31 (Sept. 18, 1937): 74.
24. Kunitz, ed., *Twentieth Century Authors*, p. 744.
25. Kang, *The Grass Roof*, pp. 339, 245.
26. Kang, *East Goes West*, p. 16.
27. *Ibid.*, pp. 4, 326.
28. Kang, *The Grass Roof*, pp. 362, 366.
29. Younghill Kang, *East Goes West* (New York: Charles Scribner's Sons, 1937), pp. 58–59.
30. See Linda Shin, "Koreans in America, 1903–1945," *Amerasia Journal* 1, no. 3 (Nov. 1971): 32–39. One is tempted to conclude that Kang was merely more selfish and opportunistic than his fellow exiles. But it is well to recall that many Chinese and Filipinos in America turned to fervent independence work because of the impossibility of American life for them. Experiences with exclusion laws, repatriation attempts, anti-miscegenation rulings, housing discrimination, school segregation, mob violence, and lynchings had made it clear to them that they were not welcome as permanent settlers in America. Some independence fighters, recognizing that their only chance for more than a subhuman life in America and in the world lay in a strengthened motherland, chose to devote their lives' energies to Asia.
31. Kang, *The Grass Roof*, p. 259.
32. Kang, *East Goes West*, pp. 203, 228, 318, 349.
33. *Ibid.*, p. 399.
34. *Ibid.*, p. 234. That Kang thought Kim's character and experience were highly significant is evidenced by the fact that the book was originally titled *Death of an Exile*—the exile being Kim.
35. Kang, *East Goes West*, p. 270.
36. *Ibid.*, pp. 32–33.
37. *Ibid.*, pp. 203, 328.
38. *Ibid.*, pp. 28, 66, 19–20.
39. *Ibid.*, p. 126.
40. *Ibid.*, p. 318.
41. *Ibid.*, p. 341.
42. *Ibid.*, p. 337.
43. *Ibid.*, pp. 348, 349.
44. *Ibid.*, pp. 13, 400–401.
45. Carlos Bulosan, *America Is in the Heart* (Seattle: University of Washington Press, 1973), p. 265. Carlos Bulosan (1913–1956) was born of a peasant family in Mangusmana village near Binalonan in Pangasinan Province. Bulosan's

published writings include *Letter From America* (1942), *The Voice of Bataan* (1943), *The Laughter of My Father* (1944), *The Dark People* (1944), and *America Is in the Heart* (1946) and numerous poems and short stories.

46. Kunitz, ed., *Twentieth Century Authors*, p. 26.
47. Bulosan, *America Is in the Heart*, pp. 252, 188–189.
48. *Ibid.*, p. xiv.
49. "Letters of Carlos Bulosan, 1937–1955," *Amerasia Journal* 6, no. 1 (May 1979): 144.
50. For example, Bulosan was attacked in the Philippine *Free Press* by Theodor Locsine.
51. Dolores S. Feria, ed., *Sound of Falling Light: Letters in Exile* (Quezon City: University of the Philippines: 1960), p. 79; John Fante, "Introduction," *America Is in the Heart*, p. xviii.
52. Feria, ed., *Sound of Falling Light*, p. 48.
53. P. C. Morantte, "The Problem Facing the Filipino Author," *Philippines* 1, no. 5 (June 1941): 24. It should be recalled that America's cultural hegemony in the Philippines resulted in many Filipino writers imitating Western European and American literary styles and forms and many writers addressing themselves to an American audience. Not only had the American education system been established in the islands; English had been the official language of public school education since 1900. For more than three decades, thousands of American teachers came to the islands, armed with thousands of tons of surplus American and British books. These teachers introduced English and American literature and values to the Philippines. Probably the best-known Filipino poet is Jose Garcia Villa, who exiled himself to the United States in 1929, where he continued to participate in a movement for literary experimentation. His work has little to identify it as the work of anyone other than an avant-garde American writer:

I, was, all,
Mirrors: I, was, all,
Over, and, under, beside, and around,
Inspecting, me, I, found, God's,
Unbearable beauty.
(*Poems*, vol. 2 [New York: New Directions, 1949]

It should be noted that not all literature about the Filipino American experience has been in English, despite the orientation among many Filipino writers towards an American audience. In "Recent Ilokano Fiction in Hawaii" (*Bulletin of the American Historical Collection* 6, no. 4 [1978]), Marcellano A. Foronda introduces literature written between 1924 and the present in Ilocano about the Filipino experience in Hawaii. According to Foronda, most of the early Ilocano writers concentrate on love novels (Marcos Aguinon, *Sungoo Ni Ayat* [Sincerity of Love]; Francisco Farinas, *Sudi Ni Ayat* [Tenderness of Love]). Recent fiction usually concerns itself with love relationships also, and particularly with interracial love. Foronda asserts that these works are valuable as social documents.

54. Norman Jayo's interview with P. C. Morantte, La Puente, Calif., July 3, 1980.

Another Filipino writer who turned to "goodwill autobiographies" addressed to an American audience in the hopes of winning better treatment of Filipinos in the United States was Manuel Buaken. Buaken's *I Have Lived with the American People* (Caldwell, Idaho: Caxton Printers, 1948) is the best example of this kind of writing among Filipinos. Buaken states: "Here is the life of the Filipino in your midst. This is why he is here. These are his problems and the way he has answered their challenge . . . [and] here are the American people as the Filipino sees them." Buaken begins by presenting how America is viewed from the islands as a land of freedom and justice. He describes his experiences with race discrimination, harassment by prostitutes and the police, and labor exploitation in his work as a dishwasher, a houseboy, and a migrant laborer. The book ends with an attempt to demonstrate the similarities between Americans and Filipinos and a chronicle of Filipino customs and life stories of successful or famous Filipinos like Jose Rizal. There is an appendix containing Filipino proverbs and legends.

55. Max Gissen, "The Darker Brothers," *New Republic* 114, no. 12 (March 25, 1946): 146; *U.S. Quarterly Book List* 2, no. 2 (June 1946): 96; *Christian Science Monitor* 38, no. 91 (March 14, 1946): 20.

56. Quoted in Christopher Chow, "A Brother Reflects: An Interview with Aurelio Bulosan," *Amerasia Journal* 6, no. 1 (May 1979): 158–159.

57. Carlos Bulosan, "The Thief," *Amerasia Journal* 6, no. 1 (May 1979): 84.

58. Ruben R. Alcantra, review, *Amerasia Journal* 4, no. 1 (1977): 172; Epifanio San Juan, "Introduction," *Amerasia Journal* 6, no. 1 (May 1979): 27; Carey McWilliams, "Introduction," in Bulosan, *America Is in the Heart*, p. vii.

59. Feria, ed., *Sound of Falling Light*, pp. 5, 191–192.

60. Bulosan, *America Is in the Heart*, pp. 113, 119.

61. *Ibid.*, pp. 136, 109, 121, 112, 216.

62. *Ibid.*, p. 327.

63. Feria, ed., *Sound of Falling Light*, pp. 28–29, 71. At least 93 percent of the Filipinos in California were single young men. In 1930, they outnumbered Filipino women 14 to 1. The ratio in Washington state was 33:1 and in New York state 47:1. Most Filipino social problems were related to the absence of stable family life. The scarcity of Filipino women also caused increased interest in women of other races.

64. Carlos Bulosan, "Silence," *Amerasia Journal* 6, no. 1 (May 1979): 58–59; Bulosan, *America Is in the Heart*, p. 112; Carlos Bulosan, "The Romance of Magno Rubio," *Amerasia Journal* 6, no. 1 (1979): 42.

65. Feria, ed., *Sound of Falling Light*, p. 5; Bulosan, *America Is in the Heart*, pp. 216, 301.

66. Bulosan, *America Is in the Heart*, pp. 173, 235.

67. Feria, ed., *Sound of Falling Light*, p. 43; Bulosan, *America Is in the Heart*, pp. 246, 228, 265; June 1953 letter, in Feria, ed., *Sound of Falling Light*; Bulosan, *America Is in the Heart*, p. 203.

68. Feria, ed., *Sound of Falling Light*, p. 52; Bulosan, *America Is in the Heart*, p. 306.

69. Carlos Bulosan, "My Education," *Amerasia Journal* 6, no. 1 (May 1979): 118.

70. Bulosan, *America Is in the Heart*, p. 293; Bulosan, "My Education," pp. 117, 116–117.

71. Bulosan, "My Education," pp. 116, 118.

72. Feria, ed., *Sound of Falling Light*, p. 69.
73. *Ibid.*, pp. 56–57; Carlos Bulosan, "I Am Not A Laughing Man," *The Writer* 59, no. 5 (May 1946): 145.
74. *Current Biography* (New York: H. W. Wilson Co., 1946), p. 83; *Wilson Library Bulletin* 20, no. 8 (April 1946): 570; Bulosan, "My Education," p. 118.
75. Bulosan, "Letters, 1937–1955," pp. 149, 151, 150.
76. Feria, ed., *Sound of Falling Light*, Jan. 6, 1947.

# Chapter 3

1. Vita S. Sommers, "Identity Conflict and Acculturation Problems in Oriental-Americans," *American Journal of Orthopsychiatry* 30, no. 3 (July 1960): 644.
2. For accounts of social segregation and employment problems of second-generation Asian Americans, see Willian Carlson Smith, *The Second Generation Oriental in America* (Honolulu: Institute of Pacific Relations, July 15–29, 1927); Willian Carlson Smith, *Americans in Process* (New York: Institute of Pacific Relations, 1927); and Edward K. Strong, *The Second-Generation Japanese Problem* (London: Oxford University Press, 1934).
3. Albert W. Palmer, *Orientals in American Life* (New York: Friendship Press, 1934), p. xi.
4. Cheng-Tsu Wu, *Chink!* (New York: World Publishing Co., 1972).
5. Frank Chin, Jeffery Paul Chan, Lawson Fusao Inada, and Shawn Hsu Wong, eds., *Aiiieeeee! An Anthology of Asian-American Writers* (Washington, D.C.: Howard University Press, 1974), p. xxii.
6. *Library Journal* 68, no. 287 (April 1, 1943): 287. Emphasis mine.
7. Jade Snow Wong, *Fifth Chinese Daughter* (New York: Harper & Row, 1950).
8. R. L. B., "The Bookshelf: Meeting of East and West," *Christian Science Monitor* 35, no. 113 (April 9, 1943): 12; *Commonwealth* 38, no. 18 (April 23, 1943); *Weekly Book Review*, April 11, 1943, p. 4.
9. Pardee Lowe, *Father and Glorious Descendant* (Boston: Little, Brown & Co., 1943), p. 321.
10. *Ibid.*, pp. 128, 175, 293.
11. *Ibid.*, p. 67.
12. *Ibid.*, pp. 139, 71, 288, 32.
13. *Ibid.*, pp. 140, 93.
14. *Ibid.*, pp. 296–297.
15. *Ibid.*, p. 308.
16. Wong, *Fifth Chinese Daughter*, pp. 157, 158.
17. *Ibid.*, pp. 125.
18. *Ibid.*, pp. 133, 173.
19. *Ibid.*, p. 234.
20. Gerald W. Haslam, *Forgotten Pages of American Literature* (Boston: Houghton Mifflin, 1970), p. 80.
21. Wong, *Fifth Chinese Daughter*, pp. 70, 71.
22. At her commencement speech, which was delivered at the community college in San Francisco in 1940, Wong said educations in China, "which needs all the talent she can muster." Such application would be "the perfect solution for the future of all thinking and conscientious young Chinese, including herself" (*Fifth Chinese Daughter*, pp. 82–83). What Wong does not note is the

absence of job opportunities in the United States for American-born Chinese; somehow Wong's "endless quest for the individual freedom," something she determines is an American concept, has resulted in her acceptance of an ironic compromise.

23. Jade Snow Wong, *No Chinese Stranger* (New York: Harper & Row, 1975), p. 365.
24. Wong, *Fifth Chinese Daughter*, pp. 165–166.
25. Chonk Moonhunter, Asian American Writers' Conference tapes, 1975.
26. *Ibid.*
27. *Bulletin of Concerned Asian Scholars*, 1972, p. 39.
28. Wong, *No Chinese Stranger*, p. 125.
29. Elements of Wong's autobiography are incorporated and extended in Virginia Chin-lan Lee's quasi-autobiographical *The House That Tai Ming Built* (New York: Macmillan Co., 1963. It is important to note, however, that the book was published long after the Chinese Revolution of 1949 had closed off the possibility of return to China for many Chinese "sojourners" in America. The shift away from a China orientation results in compromise or stalemate in the book: Bo-lin, the protagonist, gives up her idealized vision of China. But because the possibilities of integration into white society are also limited, she gives up her white lover as well and returns to the Chinatown curio shop to live out her days among Sung and Shang *objets d'art*. Like the Lowe and Wong autobiographies, Lee's novel is aimed at explaining something to non-Chinese. Lee relies on research about Chinese art for her presentation of Chinese "culture," which she insists is superior to Western "culture." For Bo-lin, China is a charming fairy tale. She is enchanted by descriptions of the house in China, with its peony-shaped door, rosewood furnishings, and goldfish pools; at times, the narrative degenerates into mini-lectures on Chinese bronzes and philosophy. When the archetypal white hero appears, tall, blond, and lithe among the Chinese bric-a-brac in the antique store, Bo-lin deserts the Chinese men for him. She explains Chinatown to him like a tour guide. The total effect of her turning him away is the final statement of what is implied through the book: that Chinese Americans can fight racism and defy rejection by individual whites by asserting their cultural superiority, even if it means a retreat into unreality where no one hears the isolated victor's "last laugh."
30. Ferris Takahashi, "Nisei! Nisei!" in Lillian Faderman and Barbara Bradshaw, ed., *Speaking for Ourselves* (Atlanta: Scott Foresman & Co., 1969).
31. For a discussion of the Japanese immigrants' attitudes towards returning to Japan, see Chapter 5.
32. According to the agreement, non-laboring Japanese could immigrate to this country. Japanese laboring men could bring "picture brides" from Japan.
33. That this was true is evidenced by the fact that 110,000 Japanese Americans, two-thirds of whom were American-born U.S. citizens, were interned in prison camps during World War II.
34. Daisuke Kitagawa, *Issei and Nisei: The Internment Years* (New York: Seabury Press, 1967), p. 38.
35. *Issei* parents stressed Japanese school more than ever after the passage of the Alien Land Acts and the exclusion legislation of 1924, which made them more keenly aware that they were not welcome in America. See Shotaro Frank

292        *Asian American Literature*

Miyamoto, "Social Solidarity among the Japanese in Seattle," *University of Washington Publications in Social Sciences* 2, no. 2 (Dec. 1939): 67.

36. Monica Sone, *Nisei Daughter* (Boston: Little, Brown & Co., 1953), pp. 24–28.
37. *Ibid.*, p. 48.
38. *Ibid.*, p. 27.
39. *Ibid.*, pp. 27, 85, 86.
40. *Ibid.*, p. 94.
41. *Ibid.*, pp. 133, 23, 131.
42. *Ibid.*, pp. 150, 158–159.
43. *Ibid.*, pp. 156, 124.
44. *Ibid.*, pp. 203–204, 219.
45. *Ibid.*, pp. 180, 238.
46. *Ibid.*, p. 237.
47. Ronald O. Haak, "Co-opting the Oppressors: The Case of Japanese Americans," *Transaction* 7, no. 23 (Oct. 31, 1970): 23–31.
48. E. H. Kim, "The Myth of Asian American Success," *Asian American Review* 2, no. 1 (1975): 123–149.
49. Daniel Inouye, *Journey to Washington* (Englewood Cliffs, N.J.: Prentice-Hall, 1967), is essentially a political biography of the Senator. Jim Yoshida and Bill Hosokawa, *The Two Worlds of Jim Yoshida* (New York: William Morrow, 1972), was no doubt written to capitalize on the appeal of a World War II war and adventure story and was created within the context of Hosokawa's expertise on Japanese American life. It is not a personal history any more than Inouye's political "autobiography" is.
50. Phoebe Adams, *Atlantic Monthly* 227, no. 104 (April 1971): 104; J. J. Conlin, *Best-Seller* 31, no. 9 (April 1, 1971).
51. *Saturday Review World*, Nov. 6, 1973, p. 34; *Library Journal*, Nov. 1, 1973, p. 3257.
52. Daniel Okimoto, *American in Disguise* (New York: Walker-Weatherhill, 1971), pp. 187–188.
53. *Ibid.*, pp. 200–201, 156.
54. *Ibid.*, pp. 188, 206.
55. *Ibid.*, p. 150.
56. James Michener, "Foreword," in Okimoto, *American in Disguise*, pp. x, xiv.
57. Telephone conversation, Aug. 21, 1975; Moonhunter, Asian American Writers' Conference tapes, 1975.
58. Telephone conversation, Aug. 21, 1975.
59. Part of the book is about the Wakatsuki family's experiences after Pearl Harbor. This part was written with the help of family members' and friends' recollections and "numerous writers and researchers whose works have been indispensable to our own perspective on that period" (Jeanne Wakatsuki Houston and James D. Houston, "Foreword," *Farewell to Manzanar* [New York: Houghton Mifflin Co., 1973], p. x).
60. Lee Ruttle, *Pacific Citizen*, Jan. 4–11, 1974, p. 5; Moonhunter, Asian American Writers' Conference tapes, 1975; telephone conversation, Aug. 21, 1975.
61. Moonhunter, Asian American Writers' Conference tapes, 1975.
62. Houston and Houston, *Farewell to Manzanar*, p. 122.
63. *Ibid.*, pp. 29, 31.

64. *Ibid.*, pp. 95, 114, 116, 115.
65. *Ibid.*, p. 123.
66. *Ibid.*, p. 117.
67. *Ibid.*, p. 129.
68. *Ibid.*, pp. x, 140.
69. Telephone conversation, Aug. 21, 1975.
70. In some cases, rebellious attitudes took the form of criminal and deviant behavior. According to Stanford Lyman, the frequently cited low juvenile delinquency rate among Chinese Americans was due more than anything else to the near absence of established families and the relatively small number of American-born Chinese in the United States before 1940 (Stanford M. Lyman, *Chinese Americans* [New York: Random House: 1974], p. 113). In 1910, American-born Chinese comprised only 20 percent of the total Chinese American population. Even so, between 1900 and 1927, 21 percent of California Chinese between the ages of fifteen and nineteen were arrested (Walter G. Beach, *Oriental Crime in California: A Study of Offences Committed by Orientals in the State, 1900–1927* [New York: AMS Press, 1971], p. 83). According to Thrasher, American-born Chinese were being hired as tong toughs in Chicago in the 1920s (Frederic M. Thrasher, *The Gang: A Study of 1,313 Gangs in Chicago* [Chicago: Phoenix Books, 1963]), and Leong Gor Yun reports the use of heroin, morphine, and cocaine among young Chinese hired by the Chinatown underworld (Leong Gor Yun, *Chinatown Inside Out* [New York: Barrows Mussey, 1936], p. 222).

Deliquency among American-born Chinese youth is attributed in part to employment discimination: "Chinese youth, few in number during the first eighty years of Chinese settlement in America, lived a hard life. They were regarded with suspicion and ambivalence in school, judged by both parents and teachers to be intelligent in their studies but unrealistic in their aspirations, and either ignored or molested by their white classmates. Often unable to find work that challenged their abilities or training and unwilling to migrate from or accept race discrimination in America, some drifted into petty crime. A few became professional mercenaries for the secret societies" (Lyman, *Chinese Americans*, pp. 114–115). According to a Vancouver report, American-born Chinese, "disdaining the menial work of their fathers and prevented by race prejudice from securing better positions," often developed a "grudge against society" and refused to find jobs at all (Norman S. Hayner, "Family Life and Criminality among Orientals," paper delivered at annual meeting of American Sociological Society, Dec. 29, 1936).

According to Isami Waugh, "crime and deviant acts were a relatively normal and tolerated part of life in the Japanese community" between 1920 and 1946, when significant numbers of American-born Japanese became adolescents and young adults. Young *nisei* hung about in pool halls and gambling rooms and became involved in the underworld network of prostitution, gambling, and extortion, enforced by threats and beatings. The jobs the gambling syndicate provided were "generally higher paying than those available in the legitimate economy; . . . runners for the lottery averaged several hundred dollars a month; contrast this to $18 a week for the produce worker" (Isami Arifuki Waugh, "Hidden Crime and Deviance in the Japanese

American Community, 1920–1946," paper delivered at the University of California–Berkeley Asian American Studies seminar series, 1978, p. 17). Youth groups were formed in every area where there was a significant concentration of Japanese, the most notorious being the "Exclusive Twenties," and vying groups fought among themselves. Gangs lent the status these young people had been denied in the broader society; they redefined honor and gave their members a source of pride and a sense of belonging.

A comparatively more socially acceptable form of rebellion against discrimination was the attempt on the part of American-born Asians to become "super-Asians," assiduously learning their parents' language and culture and planning an ultimate "return" to Asia. Conscious rejection of their American identity seemed a logical extrapolation from the rejection they suffered at the hands of white Americans. Said one Chinese American girl from Hawaii of her experiences as a college student in California: "It had never occurred to me that I am only a Chinese. . . . I found Americans staring at me as though I were a strange being. I realized very soon that I was not an American [*sic*], in spite of the fact that I had citizenship privileges. . . . At the University, I was referred to as a 'foreign student.' I objected at first; I insisted that I was an American . . . born on American soil and coming from an American country or state. But soon I learned that I was laughed at. . . . I see no place in American life for me. . . . There is more hope [in China] than there is here. . . . When I go to live in China, I shall expect to live as a Chinese and to think as a Chinese. . . . I am beginning to see the superiority of some Chinese customs and habits" (Smith, *The Second Generation Oriental in America*, p. 26).

Many immigrant parents supported their children's decisions to adopt an Asian identity, partly because they could see how Westernization might cause estrangement within the family, but more importantly because they foresaw nothing but menial work for their children in America. Japanese immigrant families sent their eldest sons to Japan to be educated whenever they could afford it. In 1929, there were over 20,000 *nisei* in Japan, studying or trying to find work (Smith, *Americans in Process*, p. 341). The emphasis on Japanese identity was particularly strong among the *kibei*, or Japan-educated Japanese Americans, during the internment years, when the future of Japanese in the United States seemed the bleakest.

Some parents hoped their children would be able to contribute their services towards the strengthening and modernization of the mother country. Chinese immigrant parents encouraged their children to participate in the China relief work during World War II. Korean immigrants, many of them intensely involved in the movements for Korean independence from Japanese colonial rule, hoped that their children's technological know-how would benefit the mother country and at the same time vindicate them for having left it in the first place.

Very few of these ambitions were realized. American-born Asians who had concurred with the white myth that color was more important than language or culture found to their disappointment and dismay that they were as much foreigners in Asia as they were in America. They were not treated as natives; they did not feel like natives. In "Three Roads, None Easy," Kazuo Kawai explains why: "Most of us were born here [in the United States], and we know no other country. This is 'our country' right here. As to having advantages over the people in Japan, we have the wonderful advantage of being quite unable to speak their langauge or read their papers, of being totally ignorant of their customs, history or traditions, of holding different ideals, of thinking in different ways. Yes, we have as much advantage over the people in Japan as a deaf mute has over a man in possession of all of his faculties. An American would have an infinitely easier time in Japan than we would, for they would excuse a foreigner if he makes mistakes, but we, with our Japanese names and faces, would have to conform to their rigid standards or else be 'queer.' . . . The trouble with us is that we have been too thoroughly Americanized. We have attended American schools, we speak English exclusively, we know practically nothing of Japan except what an average American knows; our ideals, customs, mode of thinking, our whole psychology is American. Although physically we are Japanese, culturally we are Americans" (Kazuo Kawai, "Three Roads, None Easy," *Survey Graphic*, May 1926, p. 165).

Immigration to China presented fewer problems to the American-born Chinese. Jobs were easier to find, Chinese attitudes towards assimilation were more flexible, and the lack of technological development as compared to Japan was a plus factor for the highly skilled immigrant. Moreover, Chinese Americans, especially those from the mainland, tended to be more fluent in their parents' language than American-born Japanese were with theirs. Even so, cultural adjustments were difficult, as one woman admitted after she had given up the attempt to find a new identity in China: "I gave up trying to be Chinese; for as soon as the people in China learned that I was an overseas Chinese, they remarked, 'Oh, you are a foreigner.' Some asked, 'Where did you learn to speak Chinese?' Some thought it remarkable that I spoke Chinese at all. So you see I was quite foreign to China. I wore Chinese clothes and tried to pass as Chinese, but I could not, so I gave up and admitted my foreign birth and education. I lack very much a Chinese background, Chinese culture, and Chinese manners and customs; I have neither their understanding nor their viewpoint nor their patience. Sometimes I was homesick for America. . . . America is really my country and my home" (Smith, *Americans in Process*, pp. 243–244).

71. Strong, *The Second-Generation Japanese Problem*, p. 12; Smith, *Americans in Process*, pp. 119–120; Mears, *Resident Orientals*, pp. 154–155.

# Chapter 4

1. "Uncle" is an honorific term applied by young Asians to their elders, even when they are not related by blood or marriage.
2. See Paul Jacobs and Saul Landau, *To Serve the Devil*, vol. 2 (New York: Vintage Books, 1971). New York Chinatown residents have accused tour guides and bus companies of manufacturing "dens of iniquity" for the benefit of the tourist dollar. According to Leong Gor Yun: "It is rumored in several cities that bus companies maintain opium dens as a show for their rubberneck patrons. If the Chinese could substantiate this rumor, they would tear the performers limb from limb. There is a story current among the Chinese that one of the performers, an old man, was given a permit by the city government to smoke opium on the ground that it did him no harm, but it is still suspected

the permit was procured by the bus company. Smokers and non-smokers alike are outraged by this false local color fobbed off on Chinatown by bus companies and the lies they hear being fobbed off on groups of gullible tourists" (Leong Gor Yun, *Chinatown Inside Out* [New York: Barrows Mussey, 1936], p. 217).

The attitude of New York Chinatown residents is shared by people in San Francisco Chinatown, according to an elderly resident interviewed by Victor and Brett DeBary Nee (*Longtime Californ'* [Boston: Houghton Mifflin Co., 1974]): "You read about underground tunnels in old Chinatown? I know nothing about them. I'm quite sure they don't exist at all. When I was a boy, you know, I used to follow the older boys everywhere and I knew all the dirty, secret places. When white people came to Chinatown looking for curiosities I used to tag along behind . . . but I never saw an underground tunnel. Just mahjong rooms in the basement. I know there was a man on Jackson Street who lived in a dirty house with sand and mud floors and never took a bath in all his life. 'The dirtier the better' was his motto for making money with the tourists" (pp. 71–72).

3. Robert McClellan, *The Heathen Chinee* (Columbus: Ohio State University Press, 1971), p. 31.

4. Tom Emch, "The Chinatown Murders," *California Living*, Sept. 9, 1973, pp. 8–21; California Department of Justice, "Triad: Mafia of the Far East," in "Organized Crime and Intelligence Report," mimeo., July 1973.

5. Downtown Community TV Center, "Chinatown: Immigrants in America," New York, 1978.

6. Bruno Lasker, *Race Attitudes in Children* (New York: Henry Holt & Co., 1929), pp. 140–141.

7. Paul C. P. Siu, "The Chinese Laundryman: A Study of Social Isolation," unpub. Ph.D. diss., University of Chicago, 1953, pp. 11–14.

8. The Chinese central government had outlawed emigration under penalty of death in 1712. But, whereas Chinese of other regions might have starved stoically to death rather than leave the country and their ancestral grounds, residents of Southeast China had few official links with the central government and considered their economic needs, local values and attitudes, and prior experience with emigration to Southeast Asia more valid than national edicts. Among northern Chinese, parents whose sons were absent were pitied for having raised "unfilial" offspring; on the southeastern coast of China, parents whose sons were working in Southeast Asian Chinatowns were envied for having resourceful sons who could send regular remittances home to the village and who might return one day as rich men.

9. Chinese were not prevented from marrying women of other races in Hawaii, where many of them married native Hawaiian women.

10. Stanford M. Lyman, *Chinese American* (New York: Random House, 1974), p. 88.

11. Nee and Nee, *Longtime Californ'*, p. 16.

The Chinese in America sent between $250 and $1,000 each year to their families in China, both for support and towards the purchase of land to which they hoped they could one day retire. The contributions of the overseas Chinese to the economic development of the Toishan region can be seen not only in the construction of railroads but also in the almost two dozen modern schools financed by the Chinese in America. Because of their economic contributions to the village, the overseas Chinese actually exercised distant power in village politics and in the affairs of their extended families. They were frequently asked in letters for advice and to arbitrate disputes in the villages (Siu, *The Chinese Laundryman*, p. 203).

The status of the wives of overseas Chinese men in the villages was raised when letters and money were received regularly. Husbands who neglected their families in China received frequent reminders of their responsibilities from wives who were not only in need of their financial support but who were also keenly aware of the decline in their village status. One laundryman complained that he was continually subjected to a barrage of requests for money and pressured to return to the village: "People back home seem to think that we can pick up gold on the streets: when they write, they ask for either money or man" (Siu, *The Chinese Laundryman*, p. 197).

12. Siu, *The Chinese Laundryman*, pp. 156, 150.
13. According to Leong Gor Yun in *Chinatown Inside Out*, "To make a good impression they collect trunks full of old rags, worn-out shoes, hardware and junk. The more trunks they take, the wealthier they look. . . . They tour the city for the first time as 'wealthy' men spilling money like water and exuding an I-no-care-about money atmosphere. When asked what they do, 'Oh,' they say, 'just open clothing stores (laundries in disguise) and the gold flows in.' . . . They live in luxury, usually a year or two, until the money is gone, glorifying the fame of the Golden Mountain. They . . . return to America, and take up an iron or a tray until they can go home again. . . . The black sheep or spendthrifts who have sojourned here for more than ten years have little chance of staging a grand homecoming. . . . The unfortunate old men who return homeless and penniless . . . live in a corner of the village hall, and beg in the countryside for a bowl of rice" (pp. 171–173).
14. Chinese who had been able to establish their American citizenship before 1924, perhaps because their papers had been destroyed during the 1906 San Francisco earthquake, could invite their sons or sell their right to sponsor sons to other non-citizens or ineligible Chinese. Young men sponsored under the "slot racket," as it was called, are called "paper sons."
15. Milton R. Konvitz, *The Alien and the Asiatic in America Law* (Ithaca, N.Y.: Cornell University Press, 1946), pp. 196–197.
16. Siu, *The Chinese Laundryman*, pp. 2, 24–25.
17. Leong, *Chinatown Inside Out*, pp. 166–169; Siu, *The Chinese Laundryman*, p. 266.
18. Leong, *Chinatown Inside Out*, p. 143; Siu, *The Chinese Laundryman*, pp. 158–159.
19. Siu, *The Chinese Laundryman*, p. 271.
20. *Ibid.*, p. 154.
21. *Ibid.*, pp. 302–311, 307, 330; Leong, *Chinatown Inside Out*, pp. 233, 230; Siu, *The Chinese Laundryman*, p. 323.
22. Leong, *Chinatown Inside Out*, pp. 225, 112.
23. *Ibid.*, pp. 210–211. Non-Chinese were welcomed by these establishments, which were frequented particularly by Filipinos, Japanese, and Koreans, especially when there was a shortage of women and an absence of family life in their communities.

Unless it is done to socially harmful excess, traditionally Chinese pass no moral judgments on gambling. But gambling has been considered a criminal offense in California. Lottery and gambling arrests accounted for two-thirds of 43,525 Chinese arrests in the United States in 1927 (Walter G. Beach, *Oriental Crime in California: A Study of Offenses Committed by Orientals in the State, 1900–1927* [New York: AMS Press, 1971], pp. 57–60; Lyman, *Chinese Americans*, p. 100). Narcotics arrests comprised almost 12 percent of the total. Both gambling and narcotics use, unlike the more socially aggressive acts of burglary and assault, are potentially more harmful to the victim of poverty and discrimination himself than to the society at large. Most Chinese narcotics addicts were impoverished, older, ghetto-dwelling menial laborers (Lyman, *Chinese Americans*, p. 105; John C. Ball and M. P. Lau, "The Chinese Narcotic Addict in the United States," *Social Forces* 45, no. 1 [1966]: 68–72). Lyman notes the "close affinity between homelessness and drug usage" among the Chinese in America.

24. Lyman, *Chinese Americans*, p. 99.
25. Nee and Nee, *Longtime Californ'*, p. 107.
26. Siu, *The Chinese Laundryman*, p. 176.
27. Corruption and abuse of power among the Chinatown elites was a natural outcome of social isolation and ghettoization. Chinatown control was consolidated early by the traditional Chinese merchant elite, which came to govern every aspect of community life and to profit from the control of the vice industry, to which the majority of the population was subject, as well as the tourist industry. Since most Chinese in America immigrated from one of seven Chinese districts, regional or dialect associations have played a highly significant role in Chinatown community structures across the United States. Confederated in 1858 in San Francisco and consolidated in 1901, the organization of district associations or the Chinese Consolidated Benevolent Association arbitrated disputes, established newspapers and language schools, advocated for Chinese in American society, and regulated credit and competition among Chinese enterprises in the United States from early days. From the beginning, the leadership of the Association was in the hands of successful merchants, who often profited handsomely from exploitation of Chinese immigrant laborers.

Moreover, the establishment of merchant leadership among the Chinese in America served to intensify the segregation of Chinese from the mainstream of American life. It was in the best interests of the merchants to keep immigrants' attention focused on China, since the merchants usually traded in Chinese goods and handled the sending of remittances to families in China. Further, the Chinese merchant stood to benefit from low wages for the Chinese laborer, just as he benefits from high rents and low paid, non-union labor in Chinatown today.

The power of the Consolidated Benevolent Association has been immense: the organization has had the power to control loans and debts, labor contracts and arbitration, and commerce. Business space was allocated according to a traditional Chinese property rights system controlled by the Association; financial aid and social recognition have been dispensed and withheld according to the dictates of the CCBA.

Those who were dissatisfied with merchant rule in Chinatown had little recourse in American society. Secret societies, or tongs, were non-kinship organizations consisting of persons who felt unserved by the clan associations and the CCBA. Criminals, outcasts, and persons expelled from their clans forswore their allegiances to their blood kin when they joined the secret societies or blood brotherhoods. The most notorious tong activities have had to do with Chinatown vice: gambling, drugs, and prostitution served as the economic base for tong activities, and disputes over control of these illegal goods and services resulted in "tong wars" and assassinations. At the highest point of tong activity, there were 3,000 hired tong gunmen in the United States. American law enforcers were often paid not to interfere with the Chinese underworld activities.

Less well known are the political, social, and charitable activities of the tongs. Besides mutual aid services, secret societies contributed vast sums to the Chinese independence movement and later to the Chinese resistance. Moreover, secret societies functioned as advocates of the poorest and most disenfranchised Chinese in America, especially cooks and waiters, against the merchant elite who controlled the CCBA.

In addition to the tongs, the Chinese Hand Laundry Alliance challenged the merchant leadership of the Chinatown communities. In 1933, the alliance had 3,200 members all across the country. Besides advocation for the laundrymen, the members of the Chinese Hand Laundry Alliance contributed importantly to the Chinese resistance and advocated an end to feudal ideas and practices among Chinese in America, beginning with the abolition of corruption within the community.

28. Leong, *Chinatown Inside Out*, p. 181; Lyman, *Chinese Americans*, p. 185.
29. Lin Yutang, *Chinatown Family* (New York: John Day Co., 1948), pp. 70, 149, 12.
30. *Ibid.*, p. 13.
31. After the Chinese Revolution in 1949, many upper-class, Mandarin-speaking Chinese who had been studying abroad in preparation for political, academic, and technological leadership in China remained in this country as "stranded Chinese" who, because of their social class and educational backgrounds, have remained apart from the earlier established Chinese population. According to Kuo Chia Ling "Orientals Integrated in American Suburbs," in Winston Press, ed., *Viewpoints* (Minneapolis: Winston Press, 1972), "stranded Chinese" exhibited a higher degree of structural assimilation into American life, regardless of degree of acculturation (p. 239). Chin Yang Lee shares much in common with the "stranded Chinese."
32. Chin Yang Lee, *Flower Drum Song* (New York: Farrar, Straus & Cudhay, 1957).
33. Frank Chin, Jeffery Paul Chan, Lawso Fusao Inada, and Shawn Hsu Wong, eds., *Aiiieeeee! An Anthology of Asian-American Writers* (Washington, D.C.: Howard University Press, 1974), p. xxxi; Frank Chin, "Confessions of the Chinatown Cowboy,"*Bulletin of Concerned Asian Scholars* 4, no. 3 (fall 1972): 65.
34. Chin Yang Lee, *Days of the Tong Wars* (New York: Ballantine Books, 1974), pp. 47, 52, 67.
35. H. T. Tsiang, *And China Has Hands* (New York: Robert Speller, 1937). About 1925, a visitor from China, Wen I-to, wrote a poem in Chinese in which he deplores the life of the Chinese laundrymen in America (Kai-yu Hsu, ed., *Twentieth Century Chinese Poetry* [New York: Doubleday & Co., 1963]):

Year in, year out, a drop of homesick tears;
Midnight, in the depth of the night, a laundry lamp. . . .
Menial or not, you need not bother,
Just see what is not clean, what is not smooth,
And ask the Chinaman, ask the Chinaman.

I can wash handkerchiefs wet with sad tears,
I can wash shirts soiled with sinful crimes,
The grease of greed, the dust of desire. . . .
And all the filthy things at your house,
Give them to me, I'll wash them, give them to me!

36. Chu attended schools and college in New Jersey, earning a B.A. in English. Later, he recieved an M.A. in sociology at New York University. Chu was the only Chinese American disc jockey in New York City. His radio program, "Chinese Festival," was aired four nights a week on WHOM-radio between 1951 and 1961, when he became a social worker. Chu was active in the New York Chinatown community and served as executive secretary of the Soo Yuen Benevolent Association. After World War II, he married a woman born and raised in China and raised four children. Chinese was the language spoken in their home.
37. Louis Chu, *Eat a Bowl of Tea* (New York: Lyle Stuart, 1961), pp. 128, 24.
38. *Ibid.*, p. 36.
39. *Ibid.*, p. 28.
40. *Ibid.*, pp. 23, 45.
41. *Ibid.*, p. 46.
42. *Ibid.*, p. 141.
43. *Ibid.*, pp. 52, 65.
44. *Ibid.*, p. 66.
45. *Ibid.*, p. 41.
46. *Ibid.*, pp. 148, 144.
47. *Ibid.*, p. 131.
48. *Ibid.*, pp. 233, 238, 158.
49. *Ibid.*, pp. 172, 143.
50. *Ibid.*, p. 222.
51. *Ibid.*, p. 231.
52. *Ibid.*, p. 12.
53. *Ibid.*, pp. 176, 119.
54. *Ibid.*, p. 168.
55. *Ibid.*, pp. 16–17.
56. *Ibid.*, pp. 148–149.

# Chapter 5

1. The average Japanese immigrant had at least an eighth-grade education.
2. For examples of Japanese-language guides providing information on emigration procedures, education and employment opportunities in America, and the Japanese immigrant communities in the United States, see: Amano Tora-

saburō, *To-Bei Rashin* [A compass to go to America] (Tokyo: Tokyō Kōseisha, 1904); Ijima Eitarō, *Beikoku tokō annai* [A guide to going to America] (Tokyo: Hakubunkan, 1902); Ishizuka Iozō. *Genkon to-Bei annai* [A current guide to America] (Osaka: Ishizuka Shōten, 1903); Katayama Sen, *To-Bei annai* [Guide to America] (Tokyo: Rōdō Shimbunsha, 1901); Kimura Yoshigorō and Inoue Tanefumi, *Saikin seikaku Hawai tokō annai* [Current accurate guide to Hawaii] (Tokyo: Hakubunkan, 1904); *Tobei Shimpō* [America-bound news] 1, nos. 1–4 (May–Aug. 1907); 2, nos. 1–4 (Sept.–Dec. 1907); 6, nos. 1–3 (Jan. 1908–March 1909) (Tokyo monthly); *Tobei Zasshi* [America-bound magazine] 9, nos. 7–9, 12 (July 3–Sept. 3, Dec. 3, 1905); 10, nos. 4–8, 10, 11, (April 3–Aug. 3, Oct. 1, Nov. 1, 1906) (Tokyo monthly).

3. Daisuke Kitagawa, *Issei and Nisei: The Internment Years* (New York: Seabury Press, 1967).

4. Charles Marden, "Orientals in the United States," *Minorities in American Society* (New York: American Book Co., 1952), p. 172.

5. Shotaro Frank Miyamoto, "Social Solidarity among the Japanese in Seattle," Seattle: *University of Washington Publications in the Social Sciences* 2, no. 2 (Dec. 1939): 67.

6. See Ivan H. Light, *Ethnic Enterprises in America* (Berkeley: University of California Press, 1972).

7. Emma Gee, "Issei Women," in Emma Gee, ed., *Counterpoint Perspectives on Asian America*: (Los Angeles: UCLA Asian American Studies Center, 1976), pp. 362–363.

8. Kitagawa, *Issei and Nisei*, p. 12.

9. Harry Kitano, "Japanese American Mental Illness," in Stanley Sue and Nathaniel Wagner, eds., *Asian Americans: Psychological Perspectives* (Palo Alto, Calif.: Science & Behavior Books, Inc., 1973), p. 189.

10. Kitagawa, *Issei and Nisei*, pp. 10–18.

11. Yamato Ichihashi, *The Japanese in the United States: A Critical Study of the Japanese Immigrants and Their Children* (Palo Alto, Calif.: Stanford University Press, 1932), p. 69; Bill Hosokawa, *Nisei: The Quiet Americans* (New York: William Morrow & Co., 1969), p. 39; Harry Kitano, *Japanese Americans: The Evolution of a Subculture* (Englewood Cliffs, N.J.: Prentice-Hall, 1969), p. 67; Kitano, "Japanese American Mental Illness," pp. 191–192; Kitagawa, *Issei and Nisei*, pp. 12–13.

12. Kitagawa, *Issei and Nisei*, p. 24.

13. Miyamoto, "Social Solidarity," p. 108; Kitano, *Japanese Americans*, pp. 23, 24.

14. Miyamoto, "Social Solidarity," pp. 60, 109.

Between 1930 and 1937, in nine Seattle high schools, fifteen *nisei* were either valedictorians or salutatorians in their respective classes. Studies conducted in California in 1927 comparing grades and IQ scores of Japanese and white students found that *nisei* IQ scores were at least equal to and sometimes higher than those of whites in most areas. The 985 Japanese American pupils in Los Angeles high schools during the 1927–1928 academic year received more A's and B's at every level when compared with white students, and had fewer C's, D's, and F's. The same results were found in studies of almost 2,000 Japanese American students in forty-seven high schools in Los Angeles, San Diego, San Francisco, Stockton, Sacramento, and Fresno (Ed-

ward K. Strong, *The Second-Generation Japanese Problem* [London: Oxford University Press, 1934], pp. 191–194).
15. Kitagawa, *Issei and Nisei*, p. 158.
16. William Carlson Smith, *Americans in Process* (New York: Arno Press, 1970), pp. 182–183.
17. Sidney L. Gulick, *Should Congress Enact Special Laws Affecting the Japanese? A Critical Examination of the "Hearings before the Committee on Migration and Naturalization" Held in California, July 1920* (New York: National Committee on America-Japan Relations, 1922), p. 57; Jon Shirota, *Pineapple White* (Los Angeles: Ohara Publications, 1972), pp. 15–16; Monica Sone, *Nisei Daughter* (Boston: Little, Brown & Co., 1953), pp. 50–51.
18. William Carlson Smith, *The Second Generation Oriental in America* (Honolulu: Institute of Pacific Relations, July 15–29, 1927), p. 10.
19. Shirota, *Pineapple White*, pp. 106–107.
20. Toshio Mori, *Woman from Hiroshima* (San Francisco: Isthmus Press, 1978), p. 37.
21. Hosokawa, *Nisei*, p. 176; John Modell, *The Economics and Politics of Racial Accommodation* (Urbana: University of Illinois Press, 1977), pp. 131–132; Taishi Matsumoto, "The Protest of a Professional Carrot Washer," *Kashu Mainichi*, April 4, 1937.
22. The 1913 California Alien Land Law allowed only U.S. citizens and persons eligible for U.S. citizenship to own land. Therefore, Japanese immigrants could not own land but American-born Japanese, who were citizens, could.
23. Hosokawa, *Nisei*, p. 189.
24. Toshio Yatssushiro, Iwa Ishino, and Yoshiharu Matsumoto, "The Japanese-American Looks at Resettlement," *Public Opinion Quarterly* 8 (summer 1944): 188–201.
25. Hosokawa, *Nisei*, p. 393.
26. *Ibid.*, p. 240. Businesses, homes, personal possessions from refrigerators and automobiles to commerical fishing boats were lost. Land was escheated or defaulted, much of it in areas that became valuable as centers of urban and suburban growth after the war. The conservative government estimate placed Japanese American losses at about $400 million.
27. See Michi Weglyn, *Years of Infamy: The Untold Story of America's Concentration Camps* (New York: William Morrow & Co., 1976), ch. 7. The camps were situated in Minidoka, Idaho; Manzanar, California; Tule Lake, California; Poston, Arizona; Gila River, Arizona; Granada, Colorado; Heart Mountain, Wyoming; Jerome, Arkansas; and Rohwer, Arkansas.
28. For example, in Poston, Arizona, in November 1942, fifty inmates were arrested after a *kibei* had been beaten, and the War Relocation Authority detained two *kibei* as suspects. Contending that the two had been held simply because they were *kibei*, several thousand protesters gathered to demand their release. The WRA dropped the charges against one *kibei* and sent the other to court. In December 1942, tension between *kibei* and pro-WRA *nisei* resulted in a fight in Manzanar, and the WRA arrested several *kibei*, particularly those who had been active in attempts to organize a kitchen workers' union. The arrested *kibei* were eventually removed to an isolation center, while sixty-five pro-WRA *nisei* were removed to another camp. See Weglyn, *Years of Infamy*, ch. 7.

29. In Hawaii, *nisei* were sometimes enlisted to help local officials search Japanese homes for contraband. Novelist Jon Shirota describes such an incident: "'I'll show 'em they can't listen to no Jap music from now on,' the Sergeant roared, trampling on the rest of the records, watching the agonizing expressions of the children with a hard-bitten, stony grin. After he had crushed all the records, he gave the phonograph a vicious kick, then stormed out the front door, the driver following behind. . . . Niro [the *nisei*] looked down at the broken records, over at the children, then slowly up at Mr. and Mrs. Ohashi who were eying him with utter contempt. We wanted to say something to them, anything, but couldn't find the words. Mr. Ohashi suddenly stepped up to him and spat in his face" (*Lucky Come Hawaii* [New York: Bantam Books, 1965], p. 247).

30. Kitagawa, *Issei and Nisei*, p. 92; Kitano, *Japanese Americans*, p. 26; Charles Kikuchi in John Modell, ed., *The Kikuchi Diary* (Urbana: University of Illinois Press, 1973), p. 63.

31. Hatsuye Egami, "Wartime Diary," *All Aboard* (Topaz Relocation Center), spring 1944.

32. Wakako Yamauchi, "The Poetry of the Issei on the Relocation Experience," in Ishmael Reed, ed., *CALAFIA: The California Poetry* (Berkeley, Calif.: Yardbird Books, 1979), pp. lxxi.

33. *Ibid.*, pp. lxxi–lxxviii.

34. Lucille M. Nixon and Tomoe Tama, *Sounds from the Unknown* (Denver: Alan Swallow, 1963).

35. Kazuo Ito, *Issei: A History of Japanese Immigrants in North America*, trans. Shinichiro Nakamura and Jean S. Girard (Seattle: Executive Committee for Publication of *Issei*, 1975).

36. Interview, Dec. 11, 1979.

37. *Ibid.*

38. Taro Katayama, "Haru," *Reimei*, spring 1933, pp. 8, 13, 14.

39. *Ibid.*, p. 15.

40. *Ibid.*, pp. 9, 17.

41. Milton Murayama, *All I Asking for Is My Body* (San Francisco: Supa Press, 1975), pp. 28, 35, 46, 30, 44.

42. *Ibid.*, p. 48.

43. *Ibid.*, pp. 47, 68.

44. *Ibid.*, pp. 48, 56.

45. *Ibid.*, p. 96.

46. *Ibid.*, pp. 79, 82, 90.

47. *Ibid.*, pp. 98, 102.

48. Murayama, "Letter," *Bamboo Ridge* 5 (Dec. 1979–Feb. 1980): 10; interview, Dec. 7, 1979.

49. Murayama, *All I Asking for Is My Body*, p. 94; Shelley Ayame Nishimura Ota, *Upon Their Shoulders* (New York: Exposition Press, 1951), p. 195.

50. Hisaye Yamamoto, "Introduction," in Toshio Mori, *The Chauvinist and Other Stories* (Los Angeles: UCLA Asian American Studies Center, 1979), p. 6; Toshio Mori, "The Slanted-Eyed Americans," in *Yokohama, California* (Caldwell, Idaho: Caxton Printers, 1949), p. 130; Sone, *Nisei Daughter*, p. 320.

51. John Okada (1923–1971) was raised in Seattle, Washington. He earned two B.A. degrees from the University of Washington, and later a M.A. in English

from Columbia University. He was working on an unpublished second novel about the "rapidly vanishing Issei" when he died. His widow offered his stories, papers, and the unfinished manuscript to the University of California at Los Angeles, but the papers were rejected, so she burned them shortly after his death.

A "no-no boy" was a person who answered "no" to the two critical questions on the loyalty questionnaire, thereby refusing to serve in the American armed forces and refusing to forswear allegiance to Japan and pledge loyalty to the United States.

52. John Okada, *No-No Boy* (Rutland, Vt.: Charles E. Tuttle Co., 1957), pp. 29, 44, 46–47.
53. *Ibid.*, pp. 137–138.
54. *Ibid.*, p. 201.
55. *Ibid.*, pp. 38–39, 11–12.
56. *Ibid.*, p. 121.
57. *Ibid.*, pp. 90–91.
58. *Ibid.*, pp. 34–36, 78.
59. *Ibid.*, pp. 174–175.
60. *Ibid.*, pp. 199, 208–209, 86.
61. *Ibid.*, pp. 202–203.
62. *Ibid.*, pp. 196, 308.
63. Frank Chin, Jeffery Paul Chan, Lawson Fusao Inada, and Shawn Hsu Wong, eds., *Aiiieeeee! An Anthology of Asian-American Writers* (Washington, D.C.: Howard University Press, 1974), p. xxxix.
64. Yamamoto, "Introduction," in Mori, *The Chauvinist and Other Stories*, p. 82.
65. Hisaye Yamamoto (DeSoto) was born in 1921 and raised near Redondo Beach, California. She began writing when she was fourteen and wrote articles for Japanese community newspapers. She was imprisoned at Poston, Arizona, in 1942, where she wrote for the camp newspaper, the Poston *Chronicle*. After resettling in Los Angeles, Yamamoto worked as a columnist, editor, and proofreader for the Los Angeles *Tribune*, a Black weekly. Yamamoto has written seven short stories and several articles. She is published and re-printed in *Kashu Mainichi*, *Rafu Shimpo*, *Crossroads*, *Sangyuo Nippo*, the *New Canadian*, the *New Pacific*, *Best American Short Stories of 1952*, the *Catholic Worker*, *Partisan Review*, the *Kenyon Review*, *Furioso*, and the *Arizona Quarterly*. Now the mother of five children, she lives in southern California.
66. Kai-yu Hsu and Helen Palubinskas, eds., *Asian American Authors* (Boston: Houghton Mifflin Co., 1972), p. 113.
67. Hisaye Yamamoto, "The Brown House," in Hsu and Palubinskas, eds., *Asian American Authors*, pp. 119–120.
68. Hisaye Yamamoto, "Seventeen Syllables," in Katherine Newman, ed., *Ethnic American Short Stories* (New York: Washington Square Press, 1975), p. 90.
69. Hisaye Yamamoto, "Las Vegas Charley," *Arizona Quarterly 17*, no. 4 (winter 1961): 303–322; Hisaye Yamamoto, "The Legend of Miss Sasagawara," *Kenyon Review* 12, no. 1 (winter 1950): 99–115.
70. Hisaye Yamamoto, "Yoneko's Earthquake," *Furioso* 6, no. 1 (winter 1951): 9.
71. Yamamoto, "Seventeen Syllables," p. 94.

72. Hisaye Yamamoto, "The Shakers," *Frontier* 14, no. 12 (Oct. 1953): 22; Yamamoto, "Seventeen Syllables," p. 103.
73. Toshio Mori (1910–1980) was born in Oakland, California, and grew up in San Leandro, California, where his family operated a nursery. Mori wrote hundreds of short stories and essays as well as several novels.
74. Interview, Dec. 11, 1979.
75. *Ibid.*
76. Yamamoto, "Introduction," in Mori, *The Chauvinist and Other Stories*, pp. 1–14.
77. Toshio Mori, "The Sweet Potato," in *The Chauvinist and Other Stories*, pp. 101, 136.
78. Toshio Mori, "The Chauvinist," in *The Chauvinist and Other Stories*, pp. 18, 20–24.
79. Toshio Mori, "Eggs of the World," in *Yokohama, California*, p. 104; Toshio Mori, "Tomorrow and Today," in *Yokohama, California*, pp. 165–166.
80. Toshio Mori, "The Seventh Street Philosopher," in *Yokohama, California*, p. 32.
81. Interview, Dec. 11, 1979.
82. *Crossroads*, March 29, 1949.
83. Toshio Mori, "Confessions of an Unknown Writer," in *The Chauvinist and Other Stories*, pp. 47, 49.
84. *Ibid.*, pp. 125, 90.
85. Interview, Dec. 11, 1979; Toshio Mori, "1936," in *The Chauvinist and Other Stories*, p. 25.
86. Mori, *Woman from Hiroshima*, pp. 119, 98, 107, 83, 122.
87. Toshio Mori, "Four Bits," in *The Chauvinist and Other Stories*, p. 100.
88. Interview, Dec. 11, 1979.
89. Toshio Mori, "Abalone, Abalone," in *The Chauvinist and Other Stories*, p. 33.
90. Wakako Yamauchi, "The Poetry of the Issei," p. lxxi.

# Chapter 6

1. Frank Chin, Jeffery Paul Chan, Lawson Fusao Inada, and Shawn Hsu Wong, eds., *Aiiieeeee! An Anthology of Asian-American Writers* (Washington, D.C.: Howard University Press, 1974), p. xxii. (The book was later re-issued by Doubleday.)
2. Julius Novick, "No Cheers for the Chinaman," New York *Times*, June 18, 1972.
3. Frank Chin and Shawn Hsu Wong, "Introduction to Yardbird Reader #3," in Chin and Wong, eds., *Yardbird Reader*, vol. 3 (Berkeley, Calif.: Yardbird Publishing Co., 1974), pp. viii, vi.
4. Jeffery Paul Chan, lecture at Stanford University, March 1, 1979.
5. Frank Chin, "Backtalk," *News of the American Place Theatre* 4, no. 4 (May 1972): 2; Frank Chin and Jeffery Paul Chan, "Racist Love," in Richard Kostelanetz, ed., *Seeing through Shuck* (New York: Ballantine Books, 1972), p. 78.
6. Frank Chin, in *Bridge* 2, no. 2 (Dec. 1972): 31, 30.
7. Frank Chin *et al.*, "Aiiieeeee! An Introduction to Asian-American Writing," in Al Young, ed., *Yardbird Reader*, vol. 2 (Berkeley, Calif.: Yardbird Publishing Co., 1973), p. 24; *Bridge* 2, no. 2 (Dec. 1972): 30.

8. Almost half a century ago, recalls *nisei* writer Hisaye Yamamoto, Japanese American children were often made to feel that they were to blame for Japan's aggressions in Asia: "I was around ten then, but I remember feeling that I was somehow responsible when the subject was brought up in class" ("Introduction," in Toshio Mori, *The Chauvinist and Other Stories* [Los Angeles: UCLA Asian American Studies Center, 1979], p. 6). In 1972, a young Chinese American living in Chicago wrote: "In school whenever a topic related to China was brought up in a social studies or history class, I would notice the other kids lookings in my direction—expecting me to be knowledgeable on the subject. Since I knew practically nothing of Chinese American history, culture, or language [having received the same education they had], I generally passed such moments by slumping into my seat and becoming suddenly engrossed in my books. . . . [People seemed to think] that I had access to 'inside' information" (Clarence Chan, "The Security Blanket of Racial Anonymity," *Bridge* 2, no. 2 [Dec. 1972]: 19). The messages conveyed by such incidents to Asian Americans are that their racial identities are primary and that they cannot be accepted as genuine Americans. Albert H. Yee wrote in 1973: "As a third-generation American, a Korean War GI, a Stanford graduate, I am typical of other Asian Americans who are outraged by such statements as 'How long have you been in the U.S.?' and 'You speak English very well'" ("Myopic Perceptions and Textbooks," *Journal of Social Issues* 29, no. 2 [1973]: 105).

9. Chin, "Backtalk," p. 2; Frank Chin, "Riding the Rails with Chickencoop Slim," *Greenfield Review* 6, nos. 1–2 (spring 1977): 83–84.

10. A series of books, articles, and monographs on Chinese and Japanese Americans have attempted to show that traditional attitudes and behavior brought to America from China and Japan rather than conditions existing in American society were responsible for the fate of the individual minority. According to George DeVos, William Peterson, Ivan Light, and others, Asians have "succeeded" in American society because traditional Chinese and Japanese norms and values were compatible with American middle-class values and the Puritan ethic. Meiji norms practiced within the Japanese American family— obligation, modesty, sensitivity to the wishes of superiors, adaptiveness, and advocacy of the least line of resistance—paved the way for acceptance of Japanese Americans by whites. According to this line of thinking, Chinese "Confucian" cultural values such as obedience, loyalty, and respect for authority were compatible with American values and made Chinese American adjustment to American society possible. See George DeVos, "A Quantitative Research Assessment of Maladjustment and Rigidity in Acculturating Japanese Americans," *Genetic Psychology Monograph* 52, no. 1 (Aug. 1955): 51–87; William Caudhill, "Japanese Personality and Acculturation," *Genetic Psychology Monograph* 45 (1952); William Caudhill and George DeVos, "Achievement, Culture, and Personality: The Case of the Japanese Americans," *Knowing the Disadvantaged*, ed. Staten W. Webster (San Francisco: Chandler Publishing Co., 1966); William Peterson, *Japanese Americans: Oppression and Success* (New York: Random House, 1971); and Ivan Light, *Ethnic Enterprise in America* (Berkeley: University of California Press, 1972).

Although it is true that passivity, docility, and obedience to authority on the part of racial minorities has been actively encouraged by the white establishment and that traditional Chinese and Japanese values did survive among Asian immigrant families, this notion of cultural compatibility does not address the question of why Chinese and Japanese had been viewed as unassimilable aliens until after World War II. Moreover, several other factors need to be taken into account. Asians were never slaves: they were immigrants; and American immigration policies have favored students, merchants, and diplomats over common laborers from Asia from 1924 to the present. Second, since the Asian population in America remained extremely small in proportion to the rest of the population and in comparison with other racial minority groups—never amounting to more than one half of one percent of the total until quite recently—outspoken militancy was more difficult and assimilation by intermarriage more possible. Moreover, protest against discrimination was discouraged by the fact that the majority of Asians in America were not entitled to the benefits and rights of U.S. citizenship until relatively recently: foreign-born Chinese could not become naturalized citizens until 1943; Filipinos not until after 1946; and Koreans and Japanese not until after 1952. Furthermore, unless "success" is measured only in terms of proportions of criminal arrests, Asian Americans are not yet successful: according to the 1970 census data for the San Francisco Bay Area, for example, where large numbers of Asian Americans are concentrated, Chinese men's income is only 55 percent of the white male income, while Filipino males earned 58 percent, Japanese males 81 percent, Chinese women 27 percent, Filipino women 38 percent, and Japanese women 39 percent, despite the fact that all the Asian groups had higher levels of educational achievements than white men. The implication of the "model minority" concept is that responsibility for problems or for change is placed on the individual rather than on external social factors such as race discrimination (David N. Moulton, "The Socio-Economic Status of Asian American Families in Five Major SMSAS," paper delivered at conference on Pacific and Asian American Families and HEW-Related Issues, San Francisco, March 1978).

11. In 1943, a national attitude survey showed that 73 percent of the persons surveyed thought of the Japanese as "treacherous." By 1967, a Field Research Corporation poll of 1,000 California residents revealed that 63 percent of those questioned felt that they could trust the Japanese "very much" (G. M. Gilbert, "Stereotype Persistence and Change among College Students," *Journal of Abnormal and Social Psychology*, 46 [1951]: 245–254).

12. A detailed look at the image of the Chinese as a "model minority" can be found in Carl Glick's *Shake Hands with the Dragon* (New York: Whittesley House, McGraw Hill, 1941). Glick observes that the "real Chinese" of New York are in fact no sinister laundrymen who cannot speak English but rather "quite charming persons" who are his "favorite people" because of their unique ability to "laugh at themselves." Modest, fatalistic, and polite, the Chinese "never complain," even when insulted or harassed by racists. Instead, they continue working hard, hoping that they can co-exist peacefully with others, always eager to please. Even when rebuffed, they "go back to the flatiron and the tray, they are patient and keep smiling" (p. 308).

13. *U.S. News and World Report*, Dec. 26, 1966. Chinese American psychologist Ben Tong argues that what are commonly assumed to be "Chinese" traits— docility, passivity, and obedience to authority—are in fact Chinese American

responses to conditions they faced in America society (Benjamin R. Tong, "The Ghetto of the Mind," *Amerasia Journal* 1, no. 3 [Nov. 1971]. Tong contends that Confucian virtues and culture were not the fundamental shapers of the experience of the uneducated peasants who comprise the bulk of the Chinese population in the United States. He asserts that the people of Kwangtung were tough, courageous, adventuresome, colorful people who were not by tradition meek or mild and who did not particularly respect docility and quietude. One has only to compare the liveliness of Chinatown streets with the silent inhibition demonstrated by many American-born Chinese college students to understand Tong's point, which is that China-born persons are more spontaneous and expressive than American-born Chinese because meekness and mildness have not been brought from China but have been cultivated in America as a response to white racism. In effect, says Tong, certain characteristics were selected out, so that outspoken rebels were weeded out by exclusion, deportation, murder, and other forms of negative reinforcement, while those who exhibited meek and mild behavior were rewarded.

Frank Chin attributes the historical "silence" and semblance of passivity among Chinese in America to the fear of recrimination and deportation among a people who were deprived of the rights and privileges of citizenship: "[W]e devoted our minds, and our lives, to not angering the beast at the switch. Life here became a day to day exercise in forestalling the Great Deportation: . . . standing outside the confines of the stereotype might bring the white man down hard on us and get our asses all deported" ("Backtalk," pp. 556–567).

In both *Woman Warrior* (1976) and *China Men* (1980), Maxine Hong Kingston underscores this basis for "Chinese American silence": "There were secrets never to be said in front of the ghosts, immigration secrets whose telling could get us sent back to China. . . . 'Don't tell,' said my parents, though we couldn't tell if we wanted to because we didn't know. . . . Lie to the American" (*The Woman Warrior* [New York: Vintage Books, 1977], p. 213).

While Chinese Americans were silenced by the threat of deportation, Japanese American "silence" grew out of shame about the incarceration and internment experience, which *issei* and *nisei* alike avoided talking about to their children. Richard Oyama writes:

When we were children,
you spoke Japanese
in lowered voices
between yourselves.

Once you uttered secrets
which we should not know,
were not to be heard by us.
When you spoke
of some dark secret
you would admonish us,
"Don't tell it to anyone else."
It was a suffocated vow of silence.

What we have come to know
Yet cannot tell
lingers like voiceless ghosts
wandering in our memory
as though memory is
desert bleached by
years of cruel exile.

It is the language
of silence within myself
I cannot fill with words
the sound of mournful music
distantly heard.
(*Transfer 38* [San Francisco: Community Press, 1979], p. 43)

Even the assumption that Asian Americans have meekly accepted injustice has been called into question, especially in contemporary times. Using internment documents declassified in the recent years, Michi Weglyn (*Years of Infamy* [New York: William Morrow & Co., 1976]) reveals that there was much protest activity among Japanese Americans in internment camps. Some of this activity addressed the question of constitutional rights and some of it addressed working and living conditions in the camps. We do know that Chinese, Japanese, and Korean communities in the United States spent millions of dollars contesting racially discriminatory legislation in American courts. And we know that Chinese railroad workers, Japanese sugar plantation workers, and Filipino migrant farmworkers all made arduous attempts to organize and demand equal pay and working conditions during the last one hundred years.

14. Frank Chin, "Confessions of the Chinatown Cowboy," *Bulletin of Concerned Asian Scholars*, fall 1972, p. 64.
15. Frank Chin and Jeffery Paul Chan, "Racist Love," in Richard Kostelanetz, ed., *Seeing through Shuck* (New York: Ballantine Books, 1972).
16. *Ibid.*, p. 66.
17. *Ibid.*, p. 60; Chin, "Backtalk," p. 556; Chin, "Confessions of the Chinatown Cowboy," pp. 62–67; Chin et al., eds., *Aiiieeeee! An Anthology of Asian-American Writers*, pp. xliv, xxviii, xlviii.
18. Chin, "Confessions of the Chinatown Cowboy," p. 67.
19. Jeffery Leong (Frank Chin), "Song of the Monogram Warner Bros. Chink," in Ishmael Reed, ed., *Yardbird Reader*, vol. 1 (Berkeley, Calif.: Yardbird Publishing Co., 1971), pp. 131–133.
20. Frank Chin, "Food for All His Dead," in Kai-yu Hsu and Helen Palubinskas, eds., *Asian American Authors* (Boston: Houghton Mifflin Co., 1972), pp. 56, 58.
21. Frank Chin, "Goong Hai Fot Choy," in Ishmael Reed, ed., *19 Necromancers from Now* (New York: Doubleday & Co., 1970), p. 33.
22. Frank Chin, "Food for All His Dead," pp. 56, 63, 62.
23. *Ibid.*, p. 64.
24. *Ibid.*, pp. 64, 65.
25. *Ibid.*, p. 64.

26. Frank Chin, "Yes Young Daddy," in Katherine Newman, ed., *Ethnic American Short Stories* (New York: Washington Square Press, 1975), pp. 193, 199.
27. Chin, "Goong Hai Fot Choy," p. 33.
28. Frank Chin, "Chickencoop Chinaman," act II, scene 4, in Chin and Wong, eds., *Yardbird Reader*, vol. 3, and act I, scene 2, in Chin *et al.*, eds., *Aiiieeeee! An Anthology of Asian-American Writers*.
29. Chin *et al.*, eds., *Aiiieeeee! An Anthology of Asian-American Writers*, p. xxxvii.
30. Chin, "Chickencoop Chinaman," act I, scene 2; Chin, "Food for All His Dead," p. 63; Chin, "Goong Hai Fot Choy," p. xliv.
31. Jeffery Paul Chan, "Jackrabbit," in Chin and Wong, eds., *Yardbird Reader*, vol. 3, pp. 227, 222, 225, 235.
32. Jeffery Paul Chan, "Auntie Tsia Lays Dying," in Hsu and Palubinskas, eds., *Asian American Authors*, pp. 78, 84.
33. *Ibid.*, p. 84.
34. *Ibid.*, p. 81.
35. *Ibid.*, p. 85.
36. Nikki Bridges, "Conversations and Convergences," paper delivered at Asian American Women Writers' Panel, Occidental College, Jan. 1978, p. 16.
37. Frank Chin, "Yellow Seattle," *The Weekly*, Feb. 1–7, 1978, p. 11.
38. Shawn Hsu Wong, *Homebase* (New York: I. Reed Books, 1979), p. 27.
39. *Ibid.*, pp. 29, 31.
40. *Ibid.*, pp. 78, 80, 101.
41. *Ibid.*, pp. 114, 111, 31–32.
42. *Ibid.*, p. 79.
43. Chin and Chan, "Racist Love," p. 68.
44. Eugene Hum Chang, "Hypnogenocide," in Alvin Planas and Diana Chow, eds., *Winter Blossoms* (Berkeley: University of California–Berkeley, Asian American Studies Department, 1978).
45. Benjamin R. Tong, "On the 'Recovery' of Chinese American Culture," San Francisco *Journal* 4, no. 45 (July 30, 1980): 5.
46. According to Ben Tong, the "heterodox Chinese sensibility," both a reaction against and an extension of Confucian orthodoxy, can be traced through Chinese folk literature and culture: "[E]verything a Cantonese does is tantamount to a warrior's act," which does not signify "murderous violence" in every case but is highly moral and based on aggressive loyalty (Benjamin R. Tong, "Warriors and Victims: Chinese American Sensibility and Learning Styles," in Lee Morris, Greg Sather, and Susan Scull, eds., *Extracting Learning Styles from Social/Cultural Diversity: Studies in Five American Minorities* [Norman, Okla.: University of Oklahoma Press, 1978]). For this reason, revenge is a common theme in Cantonese folk culture.
47. Interview, June 9, 1980.
48. Maxine Hong Kingston, *The Woman Warrior* (New York: Vintage Books, 1977), p. 6.
49. Jeffery Paul Chan has criticized Kingston's use of the word "ghosts," which he, like many white critics (see Walter Clemons, "East Meets West, *Newsweek* 88 [Oct. 11, 1976]), says refers to white people. According to Chan, Kingston mistranslates "gwai" as Christian missionaries do, as "devil" or "ghost,"

when it actually means "asshole," because she is catering to a "white interpretation" of Chinese ("Jeffery Paul Chan, Chairman of S.F. State Asian
American Studies, Attacks Review," San Francisco *Journal*, May 4, 1977).
50. Kingston, *The Woman Warrior*, pp. 213, 215, 216.
51. *Ibid.*, p. 116.
52. *Ibid.*, p. 73.
53. *Ibid.*, pp. 239–240.
54. Until *The Woman Warrior* was translated into Chinese, Kingston's mother
could not read the book. But when asked what her daughter should write
about next, she said "discrimination in hiring" (Nan Robertson, " 'Ghosts' of
Girlhood Lift Obscure Book to Peak of Acclaim," New York *Times*, Feb. 12,
1977, p. 26).
55. Kingston, *The Woman Warrior*, pp. 54, 222, 225.
56. *Ibid.*, pp. 52–53.
57. *Ibid.*, p. 58.
58. *Ibid.*, pp. 90, 123.
59. *Ibid.*, pp. 61, 62.
60. *Ibid.*, pp. 200, 199, 198, 200.
61. *Ibid.*, p. 202.
62. *Ibid.*, p. 235.
63. *Ibid.*, pp. 62, 235.
64. *Ibid.*, pp. 237, 238.
65. *Ibid.*, pp. 62, 58.
66. *Ibid.*, p. 63.
67. *Ibid.*, p. 63. Writing, Kingston has said, is like "having a fit" or going to war.
Besides helping release tensions, it serves her as a form of social activism, like
"going to meetings and carrying signs" to protest the draft (Timothy Pfaff,
"Talk with Mrs. Kingston," New York *Times Book Review*, June 18, 1980, p.
25).
68. Kingston, *The Woman Warrior*, p. 35.
69. *Ibid.*, p. 239.
70. Interview, Berkeley, Calif., June 9, 1980.
71. Pfaff, "Talk with Mrs. Kingston," p. 26.
72. Interview, Berkeley, Calif., June 9, 1980.
73. Pfaff, "Talk with Mrs. Kingston," p. 26.
74. *Ibid.*
75. Maxine Hong Kingston, *China Men* (New York: Alfred A. Knopf, 1980),
pp. 13, 12.
76. Leah Garchik, " 'China Men' Came from a River of Images," San Franscisco
*Chronicle & Examiner Review*, May 24, 1981, p. 4.
77. Pfaff, "Talk with Mrs. Kingston," p. 1.
78. Kingston, *China Men*, pp. 132, 138, 144.
79. *Ibid.*, pp. 141–142, 90.
80. *Ibid.*, pp. 100–101.
81. Interview, Berkeley, Calif., June 9, 1980.
82. Kingston, *China Men*, p. 146.
83. *Ibid.*, pp. 183, 184, 238.

84. *Ibid.*, pp. 93, 247.
85. *Ibid.*, p. 56.
86. *Ibid.*, p. 308.
87. *Ibid.*, pp. 291, 300–301.

# Chapter 7

1. Asian American plays are being performed by San Francisco's Asian American Theatre Company, which was established in 1973; in Los Angeles by the East West Players, which was founded in 1965; and by the relatively new Pan-Asian Repertory Theatre in New York, as well as by the American Place Theatre and the Joseph Papp Public Theatre in New York City and the Mark Taber Forum Center Theatre Group in Los Angeles. Visual Communications, which was established in Los Angeles a decade ago, has produced a docudrama on the Japanese immigrant experience, "Hito Hata" (1980), and is currently working on a film based on Carlos Bulosan's *America Is in the Heart*.

During the late 1960s, an Asian American newspaper called *Gidra* was established in Los Angeles and flourished for several years, featuring essays, articles, and literary work by Asian American writers, mostly on questions of racial identity and community activities. This newspaper was largely supported by public contributions and volunteer work. The Asian American Studies Center at the University of California at Los Angeles, founded at the end of the decade, published the first reader in Asian American Studies, *Roots: An Asian American Reader*, in 1971. This collection was followed in 1976 by another anthology of fiction and essays, *Counterpoint: Perspectives on Asian America*. The program at UCLA has also produced a scholarly journal, *Amerasia*, which began publication in 1971. The editors of *Amerasia* have actively promoted Asian American literature by sponsoring writing contests and by publishing old and new works in various volumes, some of which have been completely devoted to creative writing. The Asian American Studies Center at UCLA is also responsible for the 1979 publication of a collection of Toshio Mori's stories, *The Chauvinist*.

Two issues of *Asian American Review*, both of which contain Asian American poetry and short stories, were published by the Asian American Studies program at the University of California at Berkeley in 1975 and 1976, in addition to three volumes of student writing titled *Dwell among Our People* (1977), *Winter Blossoms* (1978), and *Hanai* (1980) and a journal of literature and essays titled *Asian Women* (1971). The Asian American Studies program at the University of California at Davis issued an anthology of literature titled *Rising Waters* (1975), while the program at California State University at Long Beach has published two volumes of a new literary magazine, *Echoes from Gold Mountain* (1978 and 1979). The editors discuss why they established the journal: "Believing that the Asian American experience is unique, diverse, and relevant, some students, staff, and faculty from Long Beach started the journal early in 1977. The title, *Echoes from Gold Mountain* itself, reminds us of our ancestors' encounters with America, the so-called 'gold mountain' of opportunity and prosperity. Too many of those angry, disillusioned voices went unrecorded or were conveniently distorted to accommodate media stereotypes and half-truths. *Echoes from Gold Mountain*, being a vehicle of creative expression of the Asian American experience, exists to encourage those writers and artists in the development of their own unique creative potential and to be a visible documentation of the many different voices from 'gold mountain' today."

Since 1970, the Basement Workshop in New York City has published the Asian American magazine *Bridge* two or three times each year. This journal features Asian American literature and essays. The Basement Workshop also supported, together with the Before Columbus Foundation and others, two volumes of Asian American poetry, *In the City of Contradictions* (1979) and *American-Born and Foreign* (1979), through the poetry magazine *Sunbury*.

Asian American writers in the Pacific Northwest have collected writings for a special Asian American literature edition of the *Greenfield Review* (1977), edited by Garrett Kaoru Hongo, who with Alan Chong Lau and Lawson Fusao Inada also published *The Buddha Bandits Down Highway 99* (1978), a poetry collection, through their Buddhahead Press, funded by the California Arts Council.

A combination of private grants and support from the Third World Communications Press of the San Francisco Glide Memorial Chruch, the Kearny Street Workshop and Jackson Street Gallery, and the Asian American Studies program at San Francisco State University made possible an impressive anthology of Filipino-American contemporary literature and art, *Liwanag: Literary and Graphic Expressions by Filipinos in America* (1975), which was edited by Emily Cachapero, the late Bayani Mariano, Luis Syquia, and others.

One of the most active solicitors of Asian American literature has been Janice Mirikitani, who edited the now-defunct Asian American literary and political magazine *Aion* in the early 1970s. Mirikitani edited *Third World Women*, an anthology of poetry and essays by Afro-American, Chicano, Native American, and Asian American women in 1972 (Third World Communications), and spearheaded another anthology of third world writers, *Time to Greez! Incantations from the Third World*, in 1975. She is editor of *Ayumi: A Japanese American Anthology*, a collection of literary and visual art by four generations of Japanese Americans.

Asian Pacific writing has appeared in journals published in Vancouver, Toronto, and Honolulu, where *Bamboo Ridge* is published. *Talk Story* (1978), the first contemporary anthology of Hawaii's local writers, was edited by Eric Chock, Darrell Lum, and others, supported by federal funds from the National Endowment for the Humanities and the Hawaii State Foundation on Culture and the Arts.

In many cases, Asian American writing, especially writing that did not address stereotypical expectations, has been rejected by publishers who say that there is no market for such materials. According to the editors of the late Monfoon Leong's *Number One Son* (1975), it was necessary for the ethnic journalism media to take up the work of publishing Leong's short stories because the existing "national literary magazines" rejected them as well written but unmarketable.

Milton Murayama established his own printing press at home so that he could publish and market *All I Asking for Is My Body* himself: "Self-publishing was an act of rebellion like Tosh's refusing to play by the rules and languages of 'inherited conventions.' Timidity and conformity to their rule of shame would have made me mute, arthritic, and bitter-bitter-bitter (I was already bitter with 35 years of writing, a pile of rejection slips, and four unpublished novels)" ("Letter," *Bamboo Ridge* 5 [Dec. 1979–Feb. 1980]: 7). Murayama says that he had been troubled by the feelings that publishers and readers might be susceptible to myths and stereotypes about the Asian American experience: "The true history of our people has been denied. . . . I want to express what has not been expressed before. . . . But I knew that if I was going to write about Japanese Americans, there were only two possibilities: cute and quaint portrayal or real portrayal. The problem with real portrayal is that the general readers and publishers have preconceived notions and don't like to have their ideas shaken up. They simply want them reinforced. I knew I couldn't do that" (Dec. 7, 1979, interview). Murayama had been discouraged by publishers who told him that there was little interest in the Asian American experience unless it could be piqued by political controversies, which might help develop a temporary market: "I had . . . *My Body* with an agent in N.Y. This was during the Senate Watergate hearings. She wrote me, 'After the Senator Inouye incident, I thought there might be a market for your story, and I sent it to. . . .'" The incident referred to was John Erlichmann's lawyer calling Senator Inouye a "Jap." Another agent . . . said: no way a commerical publisher would do since there is little interest in the mainland in the Japanese American experience or in regional writing on Hawaii" ("Letter," p. 7).

Because of what he perceived as market considerations of commercial publishers and because he feared that editors would distort his portrayals or "correct the English and kill the pidgin" he had so carefully crafted and which he deemed so important to the authenticity of his writing, Murayama decided to start his own small press in the early 1970s. *All I Asking for Is My Body* was printed by Supa Press with the help of a linotype setter from Hawaii who was familiar with pidgin. The book won an American Book Award from the Before Columbus Foundation, which was established in 1976 to promote and distribute writing by multicultural writers. The response among Japanese Americans has been favorable, particularly in Hawaii, where most of the three printings of 10,000 volumes has been sold and where, according to critic Rob Wilson, the book has become "an underground classic and campus bestseller" (Rob Wilson, "Review: All I Asking for Is My Body," *Bamboo Ridge* 5 [Dec. 1979–Feb. 1980]: 2). Murayama has received numerous letters from Asian American readers praising the book and its relevance to their own lives (Dec. 7, 1979, interview).

New Asian American writing, then, has been supported by volunteer labor, community organizations, ethnic studies programs, and a combination of private and public foundation support rather than by the traditional American publishing establishment. Much of the literary work discussed in this and subsequent chapters is contained in new Asian American journals and publications.

2. Serafin Malay Syquia, untitled mimeo., 1972.
3. Janice Mirikitani, interview, Dec. 10, 1979.

4. Syquia, 1972 mimeo.
5. Shawn Hsu Wong, "Letter to Kay Boyle," in Kai-yu Hsu and Helen Palubins-kas, eds., *Asian American Authors* (Boston: Houghton Mifflin Co., 1972), p. 87.
6. Doug Yamamoto, "Boot-Licking Art," in Asian American Student Association, California State University, Long Beach, eds., *Echoes from Gold Mountain* (Los Angeles: Peace Press, 1979), pp. 16–17. Jim Dong is a founding member of the San Francisco Chinatown Kearny Street Workshop, a loosely organized group of visual artists, photographers, and writers. The Kearny Street Workshop was established in 1972 "to serve the Asian community through the media of arts and crafts." The expressed goal of the group has been "to form a vehicle to help bring changes to the conditions that surround our people." In literature and art, the workshop promotes "the importance of literature and art, not as art for art's sake, but as works more genuine and reflective of our people and society" (*We Won't Move* [San Francisco: Kearny Street Workshop Publications, 1977], p. 3). Members of the workshop have designed and executed wall murals depicting community life. Members of the Chinatown community participated in painting the murals.
7. James Mitsui, "Samurai," *Crossing Phantom River* (Port Townsend, Wash.: Graywolf Press, 1978), p. 8.
8. Alfred Robles, "A Manong's Language," *Bridge* 4, no. 4 (Oct. 1976): 37.
9. Frank Chin and Jeffery Paul Chan, "Racist Love," in Richard Kostelanetz, ed., *Seeing through Shuck* (New York: Ballantine Books, 1972), p. 79.
10. Murayama, "Letter," pp. 9–10.
11. Ron Tanaka, "Sansei No Uta," Sacramento, Calif., 1974, mimeo. pp. 16–17.
12. Garrett Kaoru Hongo, "Gardena, Los Angeles," *Greenfield Review* 6, nos. 1–2 (spring 1977): 71–73.
13. N. V. M. Gonzalez, "Introduction," in Bienvenido N. Santos, *You Lovely People* (Manila: Benipayo Press, 1965), pp. ix–x.
14. Luzviminda Francisco, "The First Vietnam," *Letters in Exile* (Los Angeles: UCLA Asian American Studies Center, 1976).
15. Sam Tagatac, "The New Anak," in Frank Chin, Jeffery Paul Chan, Lawson Fusao Inada, and Shawn Hsu Wong, eds., *Aiiieeeee! An Anthology of Asian-American Writers* (Washington, D.C.: Howard University Press, 1974), p. 248.
16. Janice Mirikitani, "Loving from Vietnam to Zimbabwe," *Awake in the River* (San Francisco: Isthmus Press, 1978); Janice Mirikitani, "Japs," *Awake in the River*; Janice Mirikitani, "Attack the Water," Third World Communications, eds., *Third World Women* (San Francisco: Third World Communications, 1972), pp. 167–168; Janice Mirikitani, "We the Dangerous," *Awake in the River*.
17. Ashley Sheun Dunn, "No Man's Land," *Amerasia Journal* 5, no. 2 (1978): 132, 112.
18. *Ibid.*, pp. 131, 127–131, 131.
19. *The Autobiography of Malcolm X* (New York: Grove Press, 1964).
20. Lawson Fusao Inada, "Report from the New Country," *Before the War* (New York: William Morrow & Co., 1971), pp. 94–95; Lawson Fusao Inada, "Firebirds," *Before the War*, pp. 84–85.
21. Jessica Tarahata Hagedorn, "Soul/Sacrifice," *Dangerous Music* (San Francisco: Momo's Press, 1975), (unnumbered pp.); Jessica Tarahata Hagedorn, "Solea," *Dangerous Music*.

22. Asian American Student Association, eds., *Echoes from Gold Mountain* (1979), p. 21.

23. Nellie Wong, "We Can Always," *Dreams in Harrison Railroad Park* (Berkeley, Calif.: Kelsey St. Press, 1977), p. 29.

24. Wakayama Group, "Why Are There So Few Sansei Writers?" *Bridge* 2, no. 1 (Sept.–Oct. 1972): 20, 18.

25. Ron Low, "Newly-Found Asian Male," in Amy Tachiki, Buck Wong, Franklin Odo, and Eddie Wong, eds., *Roots: An Asian American Reader* (Los Angeles: UCLA Asian American Studies Center at 1971), p. 106.

26. Nellie Wong, "Not from the Food," *Dreams in Harrison Railroad Park*, p. 22; Janice Mirikitani, "Drowning in the Yellow River," *Awake in the River*.

27. Ron Tanaka, *Koreatown Weekly*, Sept. 8, 1980.

28. Ron Tanaka, "I Hate My Wife," Tachiki *et al.*, eds., *Roots: An Asian American Reader*, p. 46; Ron Tanaka, "Appendix to Executive Order," in "Sansei No Uta," pp. 12–13.

29. Eugene Hum Chang, "Hypnogenocide," in Alvin Planas and Diana Chow, eds., *Winter Blossoms* (Berkeley: University of California Asian American Studies Department, 1978), p. 34.

30. Diane Mark, "To Amerika," in Third World Communications, eds., *Third World Women*, p. 90; Diana Lin, "Father," in Third World Communications, eds., *Third World Women*, p. 151; Alfred Robles, "Rapping with One Million Carabaos in the Dark," in Frank Chin and Shawn Hsu Wong, eds., *Yardbird Reader*, vol. 3 (Berkeley, Calif.: Yardbird Publishing Co., 1974), pp. 78–79.

31. Serafin Malay Syquia, "The Silent Minority," mimeo., San Francisco, 1972; Serafin Malay Syquia, untitled poem, mimeo., San Francisco, 1972.

32. Alfred Robles, untitled poem, Emily Chachapero *et al.*, eds., *Liwanag: Literary and Graphic Expressions by Filipinos in America* (San Francisco: Liwanag Publications, 1975), p. 145.

33. Alfred Robles, untitled poem, in Janice Mirikitani, ed., *Aion* (Asian American Publications) 1, no. 2 (fall 1971): 81.

34. "Grain of Sand," Paredon Records, New York, 1973.

35. Momoko Iko, "And There Are Stories, There Are Stories," *Greenfield Review* 6, nos. 1–2 (spring 1977): 42.

36. George Leong, "On Names," in Janice Mirikitani *et al.*, eds., *Time to Greez! Incantations from the Third World* (San Francisco: Glide Publications/Third World Communications, 1975), pp. 16–17. Asian immigrants' names were often changed, reversed, or mutilated by immigration officials who could not understand or pronounce them. Others' names were changed because they had entered the country illegally, as paper sons and daughters, to circumvent the exclusion laws.

37. Bruce Iwasaki, "Response and Change for the Asian in America," in Takichi *et al.*, eds., *Roots: An Asian American Reader*, p. 96; Lawson Fusao Inada, *Before the War*, pp. 13–14.

38. Alfred Robles, "Fillmore Black Ghetto," in Chachapero *et al.*, eds., *Liwanag*, p. 159.

39. Alfred Robles, "Poor Man's Bridge," in Cachapero *et al.*, eds., *Liwanag*, p. 144.

40. Oscar Peñaranda, "Have's and Have Not's," in Cachapero *et al.*, eds., *Liwanag*, p. 108.

41. Serafin Syquia, "chickaboom, chickaboom" in Cachapero *et al.*, eds., *Liwanag*,

p. 183; Serafin Syquia, "March 1/73," in Cacapero *et al.*, eds., *Liwanag*, p. 184; Serafin Syquia, "Stereotype," in Cachapero *et al.*, eds., *Liwanag*, p. 188.
42. Jessica Tarahata Hagedorn, "Smokey's Getting Old," *Greenfield Review* 6, nos. 1–2 (spring 1977): 15.
43. Ron Low, "Newly-Found Asian Male," pp. 107, 108.
44. Takako Endo, "I'm Asking," *Bridge* 7, no. 1 (spring–summer 1979): 32.
45. Luis Syquia, "Chameleon Brown," in Cachapero *et al.*, eds., *Liwanag*, p. 163.
46. Reyes, "For My Stylin' Brothers," in Cachapero *et al.*, eds., *Liwanag*, p. 140.
47. Frank Chin, "Confessions of the Chinatown Cowboy," *Bulletin of Concerned Asian Scholars*, fall 1972, p. 59.
48. Patricia Mizuhara, untitled, unpub. poem, Berkeley, Calif., 1974.
49. "What Is Nip?" in Asian American Writers' Project, eds., *Reflections* (Berkeley, Calif.: Berkeley High School, 1977); Yuri Sasaki, "Shinjuku Struttin'," in Asian American Studies Planning Group, University of California at Santa Cruz, eds., *Rising Waters* (Santa Cruz: University of California at Santa Cruz, 1975).
50. Wing Tek Lum, "Going Home," in Chin and Wong, eds., *Yardbird Reader*, vol. 3, p. 239; Wing Tek Lum, "Grateful Here," in Chin and Wong, eds., *Yardbird Reader*, vol. 3, p. 243.
51. Lawson Fusao Inada, "West Side Songs," in Hsu and Palubinskas, eds., *Asian American Authors*, pp. 111–112.
52. Lawson Fusao Inada, "Amache Gate," in Mirikitani *et al.*, eds., *Time to Greez!*, pp. 73–74; Lawson Fusao Inada, "Four Songs for Asian America," *Bridge* 2, no. 6 (Aug. 1973): 23.
53. Lawson Fusao Inada, "Michael, in the Year of the Ox," *Bridge* 2, no. 6 (Aug. 1973): 23–24.
54. Sam Tagatac, "A Chance Meeting between Huts," in Cachapero *et al.*, eds., *Liwanag*, p. 191.
55. Harold Hakwon Sunoo and Sonia S. Sunoo, "The Heritage of the First Korean Women Immigrants in the United States, 1903–1924," paper prepared for the Tenth Annual Conference of the Association of Korean Christian Scholars of North America, Chicago, April 8–10, 1976, p. 6.
56. Emma Gee, "Issei Women," in Gee, ed., *Counterpoint: Perspectives on Asian America* (Los Angeles: UCLA Asian American Studies Center, 1976), p. 362.
57. Janice Mirikitani, "Ms." in Third World Communications, eds., *Third World Women*, p. 166.
58. Carol Hymowitz and Michaele Weissman, *A History of Women in America* (New York: Bantam Books, 1978), pp. 158, 274.
59. "Income Gulch Widens between Sexes," San Francisco *Sunday Examiner & Chronicle*, June 17, 1979, p. 15.
60. Pauline L. Fong, "Economic Status of Asian Women," paper delivered at the Advisory Council on Women's Educational Programs, San Francisco, Feb. 1976, pp. 4–5. Gloria Kumagai, in "The Asian Woman in America," *Explorations in Ethnic Studies* 1, no. 2 (July 1978): 32, gives the following figures for median wages of full-time, year-round Asian American female workers in 1970 as compared with median wages of white men and women in the United States: white men, $7,391; white women, $4,777; Filipino women, $3,513; Japanese women, $3,236; Chinese women, $2,686; Korean women, $2,741.
61. Fong, "Economic Status of Asian Women," pp. 4–5.

62. Noriko Sawada, "Papa Takes a Bride," *Harper's* 261, no. 1567 (Dec. 1980): 56–64; Emily Cachapero, untitled poem, in Third World Communications, eds., *Third World Women*, p. 175; Wakako Yamauchi, "That Was All," *Amerasia Journal* 7, no. 1 (spring 1980): 115–121.
63. Eleanor Wong Telamaque, *It's Crazy to Stay Chinese in Minnesota* (New York: Thomas Nelson, 1978), p. 106.
64. Juanita Tamayo, untitled poem, in Third World Communications, eds., *Third World Women*, p. 49.
65. "Unbound Feet," Nov. 1979 performance at the Oakland, Calif., Museum.
66. Janice Mirikitani, interview, San Francisco, Dec. 10, 1979; Nellie Wong, interview, Berkeley, Calif., Oct. 29, 1980; Janice Mirikitani, "Lullabye," in Third World Communications, eds., *Third World Women*, pp. 164–165; Janice Mirikitani, "Crazy Alice," *Awake in the River*.
67. Hisaye Yamamoto, "The Legend of Miss Sasagawara," *Kenyon Review* 12, no. 1 (winter 1950): 101; Wakako Yamauchi, "And the Soul Shall Dance," in Chin et al., eds., *Aiiieeeee! An Anthology of Asian American Writers* pp. 193–200.
68. Maxine Hong Kingston, *The Woman Warrior* (New York: Vintage Books, 1977), pp. 220–221.
69. Maxine Hong Kingston, *China Men* (New York: Alfred A. Knopf, 1980), p. 207.
70. Jessica Tarahata Hagedorn, "Cristina," *Dangerous Music*.
71. Genny Lim, "On Weaning in America," *Bridge* 7, no. 1 (spring-summer 1979): 28; Nellie Wong, "From a Heart of Rice Straw," *Dreams in Harrison Railroad Park*, p. 98.
72. Chinua Achebe, "The Role of the Writer in a New Nation," *Nigeria Magazine* 81 (June 1964): 158.
73. Wakayama Group, "Why Are There So Few Sansei Writers?" *Bridge* 2, no. 1 (Sept.–Oct. 1972): 21.
74. "Introduction," in Him Mark Lai, Genny Lim, and Judy Yung, eds., *Island: Poetry and History of Chinese Immigrants on Angel Island, 1910–1940* (San Francisco: Chinese Culture Foundation, Hoc Doi Project, 1980), p. 27. More than 135 poems have been recorded, including those copied from the walls by detainees Smiley Jann and Tet Yee in 1931 and 1932.
75. Lai et al., eds., *Island*, pp. 128–129, 134–135, 84–85, 134–135.
76. "Introduction," *ibid.*, p. 28.
77. Lawrence Yep, "Afterword," *Dragonwings* (New York: Harper & Row, 1975), pp. 247–248.
78. Chin et al., eds., *Aiiieeeee! An Anthology of Asian-American Writers*, p. xliii.
79. Mitsuye Yamada, *Camp Notes* (San Lorenzo, Calif.: Shameless Hussy Press, 1976); Edward Miyakawa, *Tule Lake* (Waldport, Ore.: House by the Sea Publishing Co., 1979); Jeanne Wakazuki Houston and James D. Houston, *Farewell to Manzanar* (San Francisco: San Francisco Book Company/Houghton Mifflin Co., 1973); Momoko Iko, "The Gold Watch," in Chin et al., eds., *Aiiieeeee! An Anthology of Asian-American Writers*.
80. Lonnie Kaneko, "Family Album for Charlotte Davis," *Amerasia Journal* 3, no. 1 (summer 1975): 134, 135.
81. Lonnie Kaneko, "The Shoyu Kid," *Amerasia Journal* 3, no. 2 (1976).
82. Nellie Wong, "Day of the Dead," *Dreams in Harrison Railroad Park*, p. 120.

83. Wing Tek Lum, "A Picture of My Mother's Family," in Chin and Wong, eds., *Yardbird Reader* vol. 3, p. 141.
84. Leslee Kimiko Inaba, "For Kima," *Third World Women*, pp. 142–143; Lane Nishikawa, "Grandfather," *Bridge* 4, no. 4 (Oct. 1976): 54.
85. Serafin Malay Syquia, "Shadowboxing," in Cachapero *et al.*, eds., *Liwanag*, p. 175.
86. Presco Tabios, "These Are the Forgotten Manong," in Cachapero *et al.*, eds., *Liwanag*, p. 132.
87. In Hsu and Palubinskas, eds., *Asian American Authors*, p. 161.
88. Santos changed the original title, *The Hurt Men*, to *You Lovely People*, a phrase he had frequently heard white girls use to describe the Pinoys.
89. Bienvenido N. Santos, *You Lovely People*, pp. 79, 88–89.
90. *Ibid.*, pp. 67, 53.
91. *Ibid.*, pp. 139, 113.
92. *Ibid.*, pp. 79, 156, 148–149, 157.
93. Leonard Caspar, "Introduction," in Bienvenido N. Santos, *Scent of Apples* (Seattle: University of Washington Press, 1979), p. xi.
94. Santos, *You Lovely People*, p. 65.
95. Bienvenido N. Santos, "The Day the Dancers Came," *The Day the Dancers Came: Selected Prose Works* (Manila: Bookmark, 1967), p. 3.
96. *Ibid.*, pp. 12, 16–17.
97. *Ibid.*, p. 19.
98. *Ibid.*, p. 15.
99. Santos, *You Lovely People*, pp. 168–169; Bienvenido N. Santos, "The Filipino as Exile," *Greenfield Review* 6, nos.1–2 (spring 1977): 55.
100. Santos, "Preface," *Scent of Apples*, p. xx; Santos, "The Filipino As Exile," pp. 52–53; Santos, "Preface," *Scent of Apples*, p. xx; Santos, "The Filipino As Exile," p. 51.
101. Today almost 275,000 immigrants are admitted to this country each year, not including certain categories, such as close relatives of American citizens, who are admitted without quota. In 1978 alone, 176,362 immigrants from Vietnam, the Phillippines, Korea, and Taiwan came to America to settle. In 1980, 168,000 Indochinese refugees made a new home in their adopted land. New immigration has affected the Asian American population in various ways. While American-born Chinese had previously outnumberd immigrants, to-day about half of all Chinese in the United States are recent immigrants. The Chinatowns of New York and San Francisco have been infused with new vitality, and old problems are now compounded by new needs. The majority of Filipinos in this country are now newcomers; unlike the single men from rural backgrounds who comprised the group during World War II, these new immigrants are predominantly urban members of the Philippine middle class, encouraged to immigrate both by the limited socioeconomic opportunities in their homeland and the professional and technical preferences established by the new American immigration quota system. The Korean American population in California increased by 559 percent between 1970 and 1980, so that today's population of half a million consists predominantly of newcomers with limited English-language skills. A few years ago, only a few thousand Koreans lived in Los Angeles, which now boasts a Koreatown community of

almost 200,000. The fastest-growing Asian immigrant group is the Indochinese population, which has had a much shorter history in this country
than Chinese, Japanese, or Filipinos. Japanese immigrants, meanwhile, are
far fewer in number, since the limitations in education and employment
opportunities afflicting the people of Taiwan, Hong Kong, South Korea, and
the Philippines are much less critical in contemporary Japan. Unlike the other
Asian groups, the Japanese American population is comprised primarily of
American-born, English-speaking persons. And while the most viable Asians
in the United States were formerly Chinese and Japanese, it has been esti-
mated that the Korean and Filipino populations here will outnumber Chinese
and Japanese in the near future, if the present immigration trends continue.

102. Jessica Tarahata Hagedorn, "The Blooming of Bongbong," *Dangerous Music*.
103. Jessica Tarahata Hagedorn, "Justifiable Homicide," *Dangerous Music*; Jessica
Tarahata Hagedorn, "Song for My Father," *Dangerous Music*; Jessica Tarahata
Hagedorn, "Easter Sunday," *Dangerous Music*; Jessica Tarahata Hagedorn,
"Canto Negro," *Dangerous Music*; Jessica Tarahata Hagedorn, "Something
About You," *Dangerous Music*.
104. Lin Hwai-Min, "Homecoming," *Bridge* 1, no. 1 (July-Aug. 1971): 33.
105. From interviews of recent immigrants at the Korean Community Center of
the East Bay, Oakland, Calif., Jan. 15, 1980.
106. Kichung Kim, "A Homecoming," *Bridge* 2, no. 6 (Aug. 1973): 28, 27, 29.
107. *Ibid.*, p. 31.

# Bibliography

## Asian American Literature

*As a Chinaman Saw Us: Passages from His Letters to a Friend at Home.* New York: D. Appleton & Co., 1916.

Asian American Student Association, California State University, Long Beach. *Echoes from Gold Mountain.* 2 vols. Los Angeles: Peace Press, 1978, 1979.

Asian American Writers Project, eds. *Reflections.* Berkeley, Calif.: Berkeley High School, 1977.

Berssenbrugge, Mei-mei. *Random Possession.* New York: I. Reed Books, 1979.

Buaken, Manuel. "Where Is the Heart of America?" *New Republic* 103 (Sept. 23, 1940): 410.

————. *I Have Lived with the American People.* Caldwell, Idaho: Caxton Printers, 1948.

Bulosan, Carlos. *The Voice of Bataan.* New York: Coward-McCann, 1943.

————. *The Laughter of My Father.* New York: Harcourt Brace & Co., 1944.

————. *America Is in the Heart.* Seattle: University of Washington Press, 1946, 1973.

————. "I Am Not a Laughing Man." *The Writer* 59, no. 5 (May 1946): 143–146.

————. *Sound of Falling Light: Letters in Exile,* ed. Delores S. Feria. Quezon City: University of the Philippines, 1960.

————. "My Education." *Amerasia Journal* 6, no. 1 (May 1979): 113–119.

————. "Selected Letters of Carlos Bulosan, 1937–1955." *Amerasia Journal* 6, no. 1 (May 1979): 143–154.

————. "Silence." *Amerasia Journal* 6, no. 1 (May 1979): 57–60.

————. "The Thief." *Amerasia Journal* 6, no. 1 (May 1979): 83–85.

————, ed. *Chorus for America.* Los Angeles: Wagon & Star, 1942.

Cachapero, Emily. Untitled poem. *Third World Women,* ed. Third World Communications, p. 175. San Francisco: Third World Communications, 1972.

Cachapero, Emily, *et al.,* eds. *Liwanag: Literary and Graphic Expressions by Filipinos in America.* San Francisco: Liwanag Publications, 1975.

Chan, Jeffery Paul. "Auntie Tsia Lays Dying." *Asian American Authors*, ed. Kai-yu Hsu and Helen Palubinskas, pp. 77–85. Boston: Houghton Mifflin Co., 1972.

————. "Jackrabbit." *Yardbird Reader*, vol. 3, ed. Frank Chin and Shawn Hsu Wong, pp. 217–238. Berkeley, Calif.: Yardbird Publishing Co., 1974.

Chang, Diana. *Frontiers of Love*. New York: Random House, 1956.

Chang, Eugene Hum. "Hypnogenocide." *Winter Blossoms*, ed. Alvin Planas and Diana Chow, p. 34. Berkeley: University of California–Berkeley, Asian American Studies Department, 1978.

Chao, Buwei Yang. *Autobiography of a Chinese Woman*. Westport, Conn.: Greenwood Press, 1970.

Char, Tin-Yuke. *The Sandalwood Mountains*. Honolulu: University of Hawaii Press, 1975.

Chennault, Anna. *A Thousand Springs: The Biography of a Marriage*. New York: Paul S. Eriksson, 1962.

Chiang, Fay. *In the City of Contradictions*. New York: Sunbury Press, 1979.

Chiang, Fay; Huie, Helen Wong; Hwang, Jason; Oyama, Richard; and Yung, Susan L. *American Born and Foreign*. New York: Sunbury Press, 1979.

Chiang, Monlin. *Tides from the West: A Chinese Autobiography*. New Haven, Conn.: Yale University Press, 1947.

Chiang Yee. *The Silent Traveler in New York*. London: Methuen & Co., 1950.

————. *A Chinese Childhood*. New York: John Day Co., 1952.

Chin, Frank. "Goong Hai Fot Choy." *19 Necromancers from Now*, ed. Ishmael Reed, pp. 31–54. New York: Doubleday & Co., 1970.

————. "Backtalk." *News of the American Place Theatre* 4, no. 4 (May 1972): 1–2.

————. "Confessions of the Chinatown Cowboy." *Bulletin of Concerned Asian Scholars*, fall 1972, pp. 58–70.

————. "Don't Pen Us Up in Chinatown." *New York Times*, Oct. 8, 1972, pp. 1, 5.

————. "Food for All His Dead." *Asian American Authors*, ed. Kai-yu Hsu and Helen Palubinskas, pp. 48–61. Boston: Houghton Mifflin Co., 1972.

————. "Chickencoop Chinaman, Act I." *Aiiieeeee! An Anthology of Asian-American Writers*, ed. Frank Chin et al., pp. 50–74. Washington, D.C.: Howard University Press, 1974.

————. "Chickencoop Chinaman, Act II." *Yardbird Reader*, vol. 3, ed. Frank Chin and Shawn Hsu Wong, pp. 259–291. Berkeley, Calif.: Yardbird Publishing Co., 1974.

————. "Yes, Young Daddy." *Ethnic American Short Stories*, ed. Katherine Newman, pp. 187–200. New York: Washington Square Press, 1975.

————. "Backtalk." *Counterpoint: Perspectives on Asian America*, ed. Emma Gee, pp. 556–557. Los Angeles: UCLA Asian American Studies Center, 1976.

————. "The Only Real Day." *Counterpoint: Perspectives on Asian America*, ed. Emma Gee, pp. 510–524. Los Angeles: UCLA Asian American Studies Center, 1976.

————. "Where I'm Coming From." *Bridge* 4, no. 3 (July 1976): 28–29.

————. "Riding the Rails with Chickencoop Slim." *Greenfield Review* 6, nos. 1–2 (spring 1977): 80–89.

————. "Yellow Seattle." *The Weekly*, Feb. 1–7, 1978, pp. 10–11.

Chin, Frank, and Chan, Jeffery Paul. "Racist Love." *Seeing through Shuck*, ed. Richard Kostelanetz, pp. 65–79. New York: Ballantine Books, 1972.

Chin, Frank; Chan, Jeffery Paul; Inada, Lawson Fusao; and Wong, Shawn Hsu, eds. *Aiiieeeee! An Anthology of Asian-American Writers.* Washington, D.C.: Howard University Press, 1974.

Chin, Frank, and Wong, Shawn Hsu, eds. *Yardbird Reader*, vol. 3. Berkeley, Calif.: Yardbird Publishing Co., 1974.

Chock, Eric. *Ten Thousand Wishes.* Honolulu: Bamboo Ridge Press, 1978.

Chock, Eric; Lum, Darrell H. Y.; Miyasaki, Gail; Robb, Dave; Stewart, Frank; and Uchida, Kathy, eds. *Talk Story: An Anthology of Hawaii's Local Writers.* Honolulu: Petronium Press, 1978.

Chou, Cynthia L. *My Life in the United States.* North Quincy, Mass.: Christopher Publishing House, 1970.

Chu, Louis. *Eat a Bowl of Tea.* New York: Lyle Stuart, 1961.

*Current Biography*, p. 83. New York: H. W. Wilson Co., 1946.

Dunn, Ashley Sheun, "No Man's Land." *Amerasia Journal* 5, no. 2 (1978): 109–133.

Egami, Hatsuye. "Wartime Diary." *All Aboard* (Topaz Relocation Center), spring 1944, n.p.

Endo, Takako, "I'm Asking." *Bridge* 7, no. 1 (spring-summer 1979): 32.

Garcia Villa, Jose. *Poems*, vol. 2. New York: New Directions, 1949.

Hagedorn, Jessica Tarahata. *Dangerous Music.* San Francisco: Momo's Press, 1975.

———. "Smokey's Getting Old." *Greenfield Review* 6, nos. 1–2 (spring 1977): 15.

Han Suyin. *A Many-Splendored Thing.* Boston: Little, Brown & Co., 1952.

Harada, Margaret N. *The Sun Shines on the Immigrant.* New York: Vantage Press, 1960.

Hartmann, Sadakichi. *Passport to Immortality.* Beaumont, Calif.: The author, 1927.

———. *Buddha, Confucius, Christ.* New York: Herder & Herder, 1971.

Hayakawa, Sessue Kintaro. *The Bandit Prince.* New York: Macaulay Co., 1926.

Higa, Lori, *et al.*, eds. *Rising Waters.* Santa Cruz: University of California at Santa Cruz, Asian American Studies Planning Group, 1975.

Holt, Hamilton, ed. *The Life Stories of Undistinguished Americans.* New York: James Pott & Co., 1906.

Hongo, Garrett Kaoru. "Gardena, Los Angeles." *Greenfield Review* 6, nos. 1–2 (spring 1977): 71–73.

———, guest ed. "Special Asian American Writers' Issue." *Greenfield Review* 6, nos. 1–2 (spring 1977).

Hongo, Garrett Kaoru; Lau, Alan Chong; and Inada, Lawson Fusao. *The Buddha Bandits Down Highway 99.* Mountain View, Calif.: Buddhahead Press, 1978.

Houston, Jeanne Wakatsuki, and Houston, James D. *Farewell to Manzanar.* San Francisco: San Francisco Book Co./Houghton Mifflin Co., 1973.

Hsu, Kai-yu, ed. *Twentieth Century Chinese Poetry.* New York: Doubleday & Co., 1963.

Hsu, Kai-yu, and Palubinskas, Helen, eds. *Asian American Authors.* Boston: Houghton Mifflin Co., 1972.

Huie, Kin. *Reminiscences.* Peiping: San Yu Press, 1932.

Iko, Momoko. "The Gold Watch." *Aiiieeeee! An Anthology of Asian-American Writers*, ed. Frank Chin *et al.*, pp. 89–114. Washington, D.C.: Howard University Press, 1974.

———. "And There Are Stories, There Are Stories." *Greenfield Review* 6, nos. 1–2 (spring 1977): 39–46.

Inaba, Leslee Kimiko. "For Kima." *Third World Women*, ed. Third World Communications, pp. 142–143. San Francisco: Third World Communications, 1972.

Inada, Lawson Fusao. *Before the War*. New York: William Morrow & Co., 1971.

————. "Amache Gate." *Time to Greez! Incantations from the Third World*, ed. Janice Mirikitani *et al.*, pp. 73–74. San Francisco: Glide Publications/Third World Communications, 1972.

————. "West Side Songs." *Asian American Authors*, ed. Kai-yu Hsu and Helen Palubinskas, pp. 111–112. Boston: Houghton Mifflin Co., 1972.

————. "Four Songs for Asian America." *Bridge* 2, no. 6 (Aug. 1973): 23–25.

————. "Michael, in the Year of the Ox." *Bridge* 2, no. 6 (Aug. 1973): 23–24.

Inouye, Daniel, with Elliot, Lawrence. *Journey to Washington*. Englewood Cliffs, N.J.: Prentice-Hall, 1967.

Kashiwagi, Hiroshi. "The Plums Can Wait." Unpub. MS, San Francisco, 1975.

Kaneko, Lonnie. "Family Album for Charlotte Davis." *Amerasia Journal* 3, no. 1 (summer 1975): 134.

————. "The Shoyu Kid." *Amerasia Journal* 3, no. 2 (1976): 1–9.

Kang, Younghill. *The Grass Roof*. New York: Charles Scribner's Sons, 1931.

————. *East Goes West*. New York: Charles Scribner's Sons, 1937.

————. "Oriental Yankee." *Common Ground* 1 (1941): 59–63.

Katayama, Taro. "Haru." *Reimei*, spring 1933, pp. 7–17.

Kearny Street Workshop. *We Won't Move*. San Francisco: Kearny Street Workshop Publications, 1977.

Kim, Kichung. "A Homecoming." *Bridge* 2, no. 6 (Aug. 1973): 27–31.

Kingston, Maxine Hong. *The Woman Warrior*. New York: Vintage Books, 1977.

————. *China Men*. New York: Alfred A. Knopf, 1980.

Kiyooka, Chiyono Sugimoto. *Chiyo's Return*. New York: Doubleday Doran & Co., 1935.

Kogawa, Joy. *A Choice of Dreams*. Toronto: Canadian Publishers, 1974.

————. *Jericho Road*. Toronto: Canadian Publishers, 1977.

Kudaka, Geraldine. *Numerous Avalanches at the Point of Intersection*. Greenfield Center, N.Y.: Greenfield Review Press, 1979.

Lai, Him Mark; Lim, Genny; and Yung, Judy. *Island*. San Francisco: Chinese Culture Foundation, Hoc Doi Project, 1980.

Lau, Alan Chong. *Songs for Jadina*. Greenfield Center, N.Y.: Greenfield Review Press, 1980.

Lee, Chin Yang. *Flower Drum Song*. New York: Farrar, Straus & Cudhay, 1957.

————. *Lover's Point*. New York: Farrar, Straus & Cudhay, 1958.

————. *Days of the Tong Wars*. New York: Ballantine Books, 1974.

Lee, Virginia Chin-lan. *The House That Tai Ming Built*. New York: Macmillan Co., 1963.

Lee Yan Phou. *When I Was a Boy in China*. Boston: D. Lothrop Co., 1887.

Leong, George. "On Names." *Time to Greez! Incantations from the Third World*, ed. Janice Mirikitani *et al.*, pp. 16–17. San Francisco: Glide Publications/Third World Communications, 1975.

————. *A Lone Bamboo Doesn't Come from Jackson St*. San Francisco: Isthmus Press, 1977.

Leong, Jeffery (Frank Chin). "Song of the Monogram Warner Bros. Chink." *Yardbird Reader*, vol. 1, ed. Ishmael Reed; pp. 131–133. Berkeley, Calif.: Yardbird Publishing Co., 1971.

Leong, Monfoon. *Number One Son.* San Francisco: East/West Publishing Co., 1975.

Li, Ling Ai. *Life Is for a Long Time.* New York: Hastings House, 1972.

Lim, Genny. "On Weaning in America." *Bridge* 7, no. 1 (spring-summer 1979): 28–29.

Lin, Adet, and Lin, Anor. *Our Family.* New York: John Day Co., 1939.

Lin, Adet; Lin, Anor; and Lin, Meimei. *Dawn over Chungking.* New York: John Day Co., 1941.

Lin, Diana. "Father." *Third World Women*, ed. Third World Communications, p. 151. San Francisco: Third World Communications, 1972.

Lin Hwai-min. "Homecoming." *Bridge* 1, no. 1 (July-Aug. 1971): 20–26.

Lin Yutang. *My Country and My People.* New York: John Day Co., 1935.

———. *The Importance of Living.* New York: John Day Co., 1937.

———. *The Vigil of a Nation.* New York: John Day Co., 1944.

———. *Chinatown Family.* New York: John Day Co., 1948.

———. *On the Wisdom of America.* New York: John Day Co., 1950.

Lowe, Pardee. *Father and Glorious Descendant.* Boston: Little, Brown & Co., 1943.

Lum, Wing Tek. "Going Home." *Yardbird Reader*, vol. 3, ed. Frank Chin and Shawn Hsu Wong, p. 239. Berkeley, Calif.: Yardbird Publishing Co., 1974.

———. "A Picture of My Mother's Family." *Yardbird Reader*, vol. 3, ed. Frank Chin and Shawn Hsu Wong, p. 141. Berkeley, Calif.: Yardbird Publishing Co., 1974.

Mark, Diane. "To Amerika." *Third World Women*, ed. Third World Communications, p. 90. San Francisco: Third World Communications, 1972.

McCunn, Ruthanne Lum. *Thousand Pieces of Gold.* San Francisco: Design Enterprises of San Francisco, 1981.

Mirikitani, Janice. "Attack the Water." *Third World Women*, ed. Third World Communicatons, pp. 167–168. San Francisco: Third World Communications, 1972.

———. "Ms." *Third World Women*, ed. Third World Communications, p. 166. San Francisco: Third World Communications, 1972.

———. *Awake in the River.* San Francisco: Isthmus Press, 1978.

———. "The Survivor." *Amerasia Journal* 7, no. 1 (spring 1980): 121–127.

———, ed. *Aion* (Asian American Publications) 1, no. 2 (fall 1971).

Mirikitani, Janice, *et al.*, eds. *Time to Greez! Incantations from the Third World.* San Francisco: Glide Publications/Third World Communications, 1975.

Mitsui, James. *Crossing Phantom River.* Port Townsend, Wash.: Graywolf Press, 1978.

Miyakawa, Edward. *Tule Lake.* Waldport, Ore.: House by the Sea Publishing Co., 1979.

Mizuhara, Patricia. Untitled poem. Unpub. MS, Berkeley, Calif., 1974.

Mori, Toshio. *Yokohama, California.* Caldwell, Idaho: Caxton Printers, 1949.

———. *Woman from Hiroshima.* San Francisco: Isthmus Press, 1978.

———. *The Chauvinist and Other Stories.* Los Angeles: UCLA Asian American Studies Center, 1979.

Murayama, Milton. *All I Asking for Is My Body.* San Francisco: Supa Press, 1975.

———. "Letter," *Bamboo Ridge* 5 (Dec. 1979–Feb. 1980): 6–7.

Nishikawa, Lane. "Grandfather." *Bridge* 4, no. 4 (Oct. 1976): 54.

Nixon, Lucille M., and Tama, Tomoe, trans. *Sounds from the Unknown.* Denver: Alan Swallow, 1963.

Okada, John. *No-No Boy.* Rutland, Vt.: Charles E. Tuttle Co., 1957.

Okimoto, Daniel. *American in Disguise.* New York: Walker-Weatherhill, 1971.

Okubo, Mine. *Citizen 13660.* New York: Columbia University Press, 1946.

Ota, Shelley Ayame Nishimura. *Upon Their Shoulders.* New York: Exposition Press, 1951.

Oyama, Richard. "Untitled." *Transfer 38,* ed. Paul Bailiff, p. 43. San Francisco: Community Press, 1979.

Pahk, Induk. *September Monkey.* New York: Harper & Bros., 1954.

Park, No-Yong. *An Oriental View of American Civilization.* Boston: Hale, Cushman, & Hunt, 1934.

_____. *Retreat of the West.* Boston: Hale, Cushman, & Flint, 1937.

Peñaranda, Oscar. "Have's and Have Not's." *Liwanag: Literary and Graphic Expressions by Filipinos in America,* ed. Emily Cachapero *et al.,* p. 108. San Francisco: Liwanag Publications, 1975.

Planas, Alvin, and Chow, Diana, eds. *Winter Blossoms.* Berkeley: University of California–Berkeley, Asian American Studies Department, 1978.

Planas, Alvin; Yuen, Kevin; Becker, Elaine; and Neal, La Schele, eds. *Hanai: An Anthology of Asian American Writings.* Berkeley: University of California–Berkeley, Asian American Studies Department, 1980.

Reyes. "For My Stylin' Brothers." *Liwanag: Literary and Graphic Expressions by Filipinos in America,* ed. Emily Cachapero *et al.,* p. 140. San Francisco: Liwanag Publications, 1975.

Robles, Alfred. Untitled poem. *Aion* (Asian American Publications) 1, no. 2 (fall 1971): 81.

_____. "Rapping with One Million Carabaos in the Dark." *Yardbird Reader,* vol. 3, ed. Frank Chin and Shawn Hsu Wong, pp. 78–79. Berkeley, Calif.: Yardbird Publishing Co., 1974.

_____. Untitled poem. *Liwanag: Literary and Graphic Expressions by Filipinos in America,* ed. Emily Cachapero *et al.,* p. 145. San Francisco: Liwanag Publications, 1975.

_____. "Fillmore Black Ghetto." *Liwanag: Literary and Graphic Expressions by Filipinos in America,* ed. Emily Cachapero *et al.,* p. 159. San Francisco: Liwanag Publications, 1975.

_____. "Poor Man's Bridge." *Liwanag: Literary and Graphic Expressions by Filipinos in America,* ed. Emily Cachapero *et al.,* p. 144. San Francisco: Liwanag Publications, 1975.

_____. "A Manong's Language." *Bridge* 4, no. 4 (Oct. 1976): 37.

Santos, Bienvenido N. *You Lovely People.* Manila: Benipayo Press, 1965.

_____. "The Day the Dancers Came." *The Day the Dancers Came: Selected Prose Works,* pp. 195–207. Manila: Bookmark, 1967.

_____. "The Filipino as Exile." *Greenfield Review* 6, nos. 1–2 (spring 1977): 47–55.

_____. *Scent of Apples.* Seattle: University of Washington Press, 1979.

Sawada, Noriko. "Memoir of a Japanese Daughter." *Ms.* 68 (April 1980): 68–76, 110.

_____. "Papa Takes a Bride." *Harpers* 261, no. 1567 (Dec. 1980): 58–64.

Shirota, Jon. *Lucky Come Hawaii.* New York: Bantam Books, 1965.

_____. *Pineapple White.* Los Angeles: Ohara Publications, 1972.

Sone, Monica. *Nisei Daughter.* Boston: Little, Brown & Co., 1953.

Sugimoto, Etsu Inagaki. *A Daughter of the Samurai.* New York: Doubleday Page & Co., 1925.

_____. *A Daughter of the Narikin.* New York: Doubleday Doran & Co., 1932.

Sui Sin Far (Edith Eaton). "Leaves from the Mental Portfolio of an Eurasian." *Independent* 66, no. 3136 (Jan. 7, 1909): 125–132.

_____. *Mrs. Spring Fragrance.* Chicago: A. C. McClurg & Co., 1912.

Sun, Patrick Pichi. *Recollections of a Floating Life.* Taipei: China Post, 1972.

Syquia, Luis. "Chameleon Brown." *Liwanag: Literary and Graphic Expressions by Filipinos in America,* ed. Emily Cachapero *et al.,* p. 163. San Francisco: Liwanag Publications, 1975.

Syquia, Serafin. "chickaboom, chickaboom." *Liwanag: Literary and Graphic Expressions by Filipinos in America,* ed. Emily Cachapero *et al.,* p. 183. San Francisco: Liwanag Publications, 1975.

_____. "March 1/73." *Liwanag: Literary and Graphic Expressions by Filipinos in America,* ed. Emily Cachapero *et al.,* p. 184. San Francisco: Liwanag Publications, 1975.

_____. "Stereotype." *Liwanag: Literary and Graphic Expressions by Filipinos in America,* ed. Emily Cachapero *et al.,* p. 188. San Francisco: Liwanag Publications, 1975.

Tabios, Presco. "These Are the Forgotten Manong." *Liwanag: Literary and Graphic Expressions by Filipinos in America,* ed. Emily Cachapero *et al.,* p. 132. San Francisco: Liwanag Publications, 1975.

Tagatac, Sam. "The New Anak." *Aiiieeeee! An Anthology of Asian-American Writers,* ed. Frank Chin *et al.,* pp. 150–168. Washington, D.C.: Howard University Press, 1974.

_____. "A Chance Meeting between Huts." *Liwanag: Literary and Graphic Expressions by Filipinos in America,* ed. Emily Cachapero *et al.,* p. 191. San Francisco: Liwanag Publications, 1975.

Takahashi, Ferris. "Nisei! Nisei!" *Speaking for Ourselves,* ed. Lillian Faderman and Barbara Bradshaw, p. 218. Atlanta: Scott Foresman & Co., 1969.

_____. "The Widower." *Speaking for Ourselves,* ed. Lillian Faderman and Barbara Bradshaw, pp. 155–161. Atlanta: Scott Foresman & Co., 1969.

Takashima, Shizuye. *A Child in Prison Camp.* New York: William Morrow & Co., 1974.

Tamagawa, Kathleen. *Holy Prayers in a Horse's Ear.* New York: Ray Long & Richard R. Smith, 1932.

Tamayo, Juanita. Untitled poem. *Third World Women,* ed. Third World Communications, p. 49. San Francisco: Third World Communications, 1972.

Tanaka, Ronald. "I Hate My Wife." *Roots: An Asian American Reader,* ed. Amy Tachiki *et al.,* p. 46. Los Angeles: UCLA Asian American Studies Center, 1971.

_____. "Sansei No Uta." Mimeo., Sacramento, Calif., 1974.

Telamaque, Eleanor Wong. *It's Crazy to Stay Chinese in Minnesota.* New York: Thomas Nelson, 1978.

Third World Communications, eds. *Third World Women.* San Francisco: Third World Communications, 1972.

Tsiang, H. T. *The Hanging on Union Square*. New York: H. T. Hsiang, 1929.
———. *And China Has Hands*. New York: Robert Speller, 1937.
Uchida, Yoshiko. *Journey to Topaz*. New York: Charles Scribner's Sons, 1971.
Wand, David Hsin-Fu, ed. *Asian American Heritage*. New York: Simon & Schuster, 1974.
Watanna, Onoto (Winnifred Eaton Babcock). *Tama*. New York: Harper & Bros., 1910.
———. *Sunny-san*. New York: George H. Doran Co., 1922.
Wen, I-To. "The Laundry Song." *Twentieth Century Chinese Poetry*, ed. Kai-yu Hsu, pp. 51–52. New York: Doubleday & Co., 1963.
Wong, Jade Snow. *Fifth Chinese Daughter*. New York: Harper & Row, 1950.
———. *No Chinese Stranger*. New York: Harper & Row, 1975.
Wong, Nellie. *Dreams in Harrison Railroad Park*. Berkeley, Calif.: Kelsey St. Press, 1977.
Wong, Shawn Hsu. "Good Luck, Happiness and Long Life." *Counterpoint: Perspectives on Asian America*, ed. Emma Gee, pp. 464–470. Los Angeles: UCLA Asian American Studies Center, 1976.
———. *Homebase*. New York: I. Reed Books, 1979.
———. "Letter to Kay Boyle." *Asian American Authors*, ed. Kai-yu Hsu and Helen Palubinskas, p. 87. Boston: Houghton Mifflin Co., 1972.
Wu Tingfang. *America through the Spectacles of an Oriental Diplomat*. New York: Frederick A. Stokes, 1914.
Yamada, Mitsuye. *Camp Notes*. San Lorenzo, Calif.: Shameless Hussy Press, 1976.
Yamamoto, Doug. "Boot-Licking Art." *Echoes from Gold Mountain*, ed. Asian American Student Association, California State University, Long Beach, pp. 16–17. Los Angeles: Peace Press, 1979.
Yamamoto, Hisaye. "The Legend of Miss Sasagawara." *Kenyon Review* 12, no. 1 (winter 1950): 99–115.
———. "Yoneko's Earthquake." *Furioso* 6, no. 1 (winter 1951): 5–16.
———. "The Shakers." *Frontier* 4, no. 12 (Oct. 1953): 22.
———. "Las Vegas Charley." *Arizona Quarterly* 17, no. 4 (winter 1961): 303–322.
———. "The Brown House." *Asian American Authors*, ed. Kai-yu Hsu and Helen Palubinskas, pp. 114–122. Boston: Houghton Mifflin Co., 1972.
———. "Seventeen Syllables." *Ethnic American Short Stories*, ed. Katherine Newman, pp. 89–103. New York: Washington Square Press, 1975.
Yamauchi, Wakako. "The Boatman of River Toneh." *Amerasia Journal* 2, no. 2 (fall 1974): 203–207.
———. "And the Soul Shall Dance." *Aiiieeeee! An Anthology of Asian-American Writers*, ed. Frank Chin et al., pp. 193–200. Washington, D.C.: Howard University Press, 1974.
———. "That Was All." *Amerasia Journal* 7, no. 1 (spring 1980): 115–120.
Yee, Carl, ed. *Dwell among Our People*. Berkeley: University of California–Berkeley, Asian American Studies Department, 1977.
Yep, Lawrence. *Dragonwings*. New York: Harper & Row, 1975.
———. *Child of the Owl*. New York: Harper & Row, 1975.
Yoshida, Jim, and Hosokawa, Bill. *The Two Worlds of Jim Yoshida*. New York: William Morrow, 1972.
Yung, Wing. *My Life in China and America*. New York: Henry Holt & Co., 1909.

# Anglo-American Portrayals of Asians and Asian Americans

Abdullah, Achmed. *The Honourable Gentleman and Other Stories.* New York: Knickerbocker Press, 1919.

Ash, Cay Van, and Rohmer, Elizabeth Sax. *Master of Villainy: A Biography of Sax Rohmer.* Bowling Green, Ohio: Bowling Green University Popular Press, 1972.

Atherton, Gertrude. *The Californians.* New York: A. Wessels, 1906.

──────. "Japan or 'Main Street.'" New York *Times Book Review and Magazine,* Jan. 16, 1921. p. 7.

Ayscough, Florence. *The Autobiography of a Chinese Dog.* New York: Houghton Mifflin Co., 1926.

Bancroft, Hubert Howe. *Essays and Miscellany.* San Francisco: History Publishing Co., 1890.

Barnes, Anna M. *The Red Miriok.* Philadelphia: American Baptist Publication Society, 1901.

Beach, Rex. *Sons of the Gods.* New York: Harper & Brothers, 1929.

Biggers, Earl Derr. *The Chinese Patriot.* Indianapolis: Bobbs-Merrill Co., 1926.

──────. *Behind That Curtain.* Indianapolis: The Bobbs-Merrill Co., 1928.

──────. *The Black Camel.* Indianapolis: Bobbs-Merrill Co., 1929.

──────. *Charlie Chan Carries On.* Indianapolis: Bobbs-Merrill Co., 1930.

Birmingham, Stephen. *The Late John Marquand.* Philadelphia: J. B. Lippincott Co., 1972.

Bishop, Claire Huchet. *The Five Chinese Brothers.* New York: Scholastic Book Services, 1962.

Black, Monica. *Moonflete.* London: Robert Hale & Co., 1972.

Blessing-Eyster, Nellie. *A Chinese Quaker.* New York: Chicago: Fleming H. Revell Co., 1902.

Bloom, Ursula. *The Secret Lover.* New York: E. P. Dutton & Co., 1931.

Bramah, Ernest. *Kai Lung Unrolls His Mat.* New York: Doubleday Doran & Co., 1928.

Buck, Pearl S. *The Good Earth,* New York: John Day Co., 1931.

──────. *Dragon Seed.* New York: John Day Co., 1942.

──────. *The Living Reed.* New York: John Day Co., 1963.

Burke, Thomas. *Limehouse Nights.* New York: Robert McBride & Co., 1917.

──────. *Nights in London.* New York: Henry Holt & Co., 1918.

──────. *More Limehouse Nights.* New York: George H. Doran Co., 1921.

──────. *A Tea-Shop in Limehouse.* Boston: Little, Brown & Co., 1931.

Burroughs, Edgar Rice. *The Mucker.* New York: Canaveral Press, 1963.

Butterworth, Hezekiah. *Little Sky-High or the Surprising Doings of Washee Washee Wong.* New York: Thomas Y. Crowell & Co., 1901.

Carpenter, Grant. *The Night Tide.* New York: H. K. Fly Co., 1920.

Charyn, Jerome. *American Scrapbook.* New York: Viking Press, 1969.

"The Chinaman." *Putnams* 9 (1857): 339–350.

Conquest, Joan. *The Street of Many Arches.* New York: MacCaulay Co., 1924.

──────. *Crumbling Walls.* New York: MacCaulay Co., 1927.

──────. *Forbidden.* New York: MacCaulay Co., 1927.

Cronin, A. J. *The Keys of the Kingdom*. Boston: Little, Brown & Co., 1941.

Cruso, Colomon. *The Last of the Japs and the Jews*. New York: Herman W. Lefkowitz, 1933.

Cummins, E. S. "An Honest Heathen, A Study." *Lippincott's Monthly Magazine* 50 (Dec. 1892): 783–792.

Cunningham, E. V. *The Case of the One-Penny Orange*. New York: Holt Reinhart & Winston, 1977.

————. *The Case of the Russian Diplomat*. New York: Harcourt Brace Javonovich, 1978.

Dean, Jeannette. "Old Men in the Square." *California Living*, May 9, 1971, p. 35.

DeBra, Lemuel. *Ways That Are Wary*. New York: Edward J. Clode, 1925.

DeMiomandre, Francis. *Orientale*. New York: Brentano's Publishers, 1929.

Dillon, Richard H. *The Hatchet Men*. New York: Ballantine Books, 1962.

Dobie, Charles Caldwell. *San Francisco Tales*. New York: Appleton Century Co., 1935.

Doyle, C. W. *The Shadow of Quong Lung*. Philadelphia: J. B. Lippincott Co., 1900.

Dressler, Albert. *California Chinese Chatter*. San Francisco: A. Dressler, 1927.

Driggs, Raymond. "Mrs. Van Brunt's Convert." *Lippincott's Magazine* 48 (Sept. 1891): 359–369.

Epsey, John J. "No Man Can Serve Two Masters." *New Yorker*, Feb. 3, 1945, pp. 20–23.

Eskelund, Karl. *My Chinese Wife*. New York: Doubleday Doran & Co., 1945.

Fernald, Chester B. *The Cat and the Cherub and Other Stories*. New York: Century Co., 1896.

————. "The Pot of Frightful Doom." *Century* 52, no. 3 (July 1896): 369–374.

Fielde, Adele M. *A Corner of Cathay*. New York: Macmillan & Co., 1894.

Ford, John. *The Tokyo Contract*. London: Angus & Robertson, 1971.

Ford, Julia Ellsworth. *Consequences*. New York: E. P. Dutton & Co., 1929.

Franklin, Mae M. *My Chinese Marriage*. London: John Lane, Bodley Head, 1912.

Fraser, Hugh Mrs. *A Maid of Japan*. New York: Henry Holt & Co., 1905.

Gale, James S. *The Vanguard*. New York: Fleming H. Revell Co., 1904.

Gelzer, Jay. *The Street of a Thousand Delights*. New York: Robert M. McBride, 1921.

Genthe, Arnold (photography), and Irwin, Will (text). *Old Chinatown*. New York: Mitchell Kennerly, 1913.

Gervais, Albert. *Madame Flowery Sentiment*. New York: Covici Friede, 1937.

Glick, Carl. *The Laughing Buddha*. New York: Lothrop, Lee & Sheppard Co., 1937.

————. *Shake Hands with the Dragon*. New York: Whittesley House, McGraw-Hill, 1941.

Glynn-Ward, Hilda. *The Writing on the Wall*. Vancouver: Sun Publishing Co., 1921.

Gowen, Vincent H. *Sun and Moon*. Boston: Little, Brown & Co., 1927.

Graham, Dorothy. *Lotus of the Dusk: A Romance of China*. New York: Frederick A. Stokes Co., 1927.

Griggs, Veta. *Chinaman's Chance: The Life Story of Elmer Wok Wai*. New York: Exposition Press, 1969.

Hackforth-Hones, Gilbert. *Yellow Peril*. London: Hodder & Stoughton, 1972.

Haining, Peter. *The Hero*. London: New English Library, 1974.

Harte, Bret. "'The Heathen Chinee" or 'Plain Language from Truthful James.'" *Overland Monthly* 5 (Sept. 1870): 287–288.

————. *Tales of the Argonauts*. Boston: Houghton Mifflin Co., 1872.

————. *In the Carquinez Woods*. New York: Houghton Mifflin Co., 1884.

Headland, Isaac Taylor. *The Chinese Boy and Girl*. New York: Fleming H. Revell Co., 1901.

Hebden, Mark (John Harris). *A Killer for the Chairman*. London: Michael Joseph, 1972.

Hekking, Johanna M. *Pig Tails*. New York: Frederick A. Stokes Co., 1937.

Hingston, Edward P. *The Genial Showman*. London: Hotten, 1870.

Hixson, Carter. *The Foreign Devil*. New York: Robert Speller, 1937.

Holland, Clive. *My Japanese Wife*. 4th ed. Westminister, Eng.: Constable, 1895.

————. *Mousmé: A Story of the West and East*. New York: Frederick A. Stokes Co., 1901.

Hosmer, M. "Mary Ann and Chyng Loo, Housekeeping in San Francisco." *Lippincott's Magazine* 6 (Oct. 1870): 354–361.

Hwuy-Ung. *A Chinaman's Opinion of Us and of His Own People*. New York: Frederick A. Stokes Co., 1927.

Irwin, Wallace. *Chinatown Ballads*. New York: Duffield & Co., 1906.

————. *Letters of a Japanese Schoolboy*. New York: Doubleday Page & Co., 1909.

————. *Mr. Togo, Maid of All Work*. New York: Duffield & Co., 1921.

————. *Seed of the Sun*. New York: Arno Press, 1978. Orig. pub. New York: George H. Doran Co., 1921.

Irwin, Will (text), and Genthe, Arnold (photographs). *Old Chinatown*. New York: Mitchell Kennerley, 1913.

Jacob, Heinrich Eduard. *Jacqueline and the Japanese*. Boston: Little, Brown & Co., 1930.

Johnson, Marjorie R. *Chinatown Stories*. New York: Dodge Publishing Co., 1900.

Jones, Idwal. *China Boy*. Los Angeles: Primavera Press, 1936.

Keith, Agnes Newton. *Beloved Exiles*. Boston: Little, Brown & Co., 1972.

Kim, Agnes Davis. *I Married a Korean*. New York: John Day Co., 1953.

Kinney, Henry Walsworth. *Broken Butterflies*. Boston: Little, Brown & Co., 1924.

Kipling, Rudyard. *From Sea to Sea: Letters of Travel*. New York: Doubleday Page & Co., 1920.

Knox, Jessie Juliet. *In the House of the Tiger*. New York: Eaton & Mains, 1911.

Kyne, Peter B. *The Pride of Palomar*. New York: Cosmopolitan Book Corp., 1921.

La Piere, Richard Tracy. *When the Living Strive*. New York: Harper & Brothers, 1941.

Lea, Homer. *The Vermilion Pencil*. New York: McClure Co., 1908.

Leland, Charles G. *Pidgin English Sing-Song*. London: Kegan Paul, Trench, Trubner & Co., 1903.

London, Jack. *Daughter of the Snows*. New York: Macmillan Co., 1904.

————. *Revolution and Other Essays*. New York: Macmillan Co., 1910.

————. *South Sea Tales*. New York: Macmillan Co., 1911.

————. *When God Laughs*. New York: Macmillan Co., 1911.

————. *The House of Pride*. New York: Macmillan Co., 1912.

————. *The Star Rover*. New York: Macmillan Co., 1915.

————. *The Valley of the Moon*. Salt Lake City: Peregrine Smith, 1915.

————. *The Human Drift*. New York: Macmillan Co., 1917.

————. *Faith of Men*. New York: Macmillan Co., 1919.

———. *On the Makaloa Mat.* New York: Macmillan Co., 1919.

——— —. *Dutch Courage and Other Stories.* New York: Macmillan Co., 1922.

Long, John Luther. *Miss Cherry-Blossom of Tokyo.* Philadelphia: J. B. Lippincott Co., 1895.

McCall, Sidney. *The Breath of the Gods.* Boston: Little, Brown & Co., 1905.

MacKay, Margaret. *Like Water Flowing.* London: George C. Farrar & Co., 1938.

Madden, Maude Whitmore. *When the East Is in the West: Pacific Coast Sketches.* New York: Fleming H. Revell Co., 1923.

Marquand, John P. *Mr. Moto's Three Aces.* Boston: Little, Brown & Co., 1936.

———. *Ming Yellow.* London: Robert Hale, 1942.

Martin, Ralph J. *Boy from Nebraska: The Story of Ben Kuroki.* New York: Harper & Brothers, 1946.

Mason, Richard. *The World of Suzie Wong.* New York: World Publishing Co., 1957.

Mason, Van Wyck. *The Shanghai Bund Murders.* New York: Doubleday & Co., 1933.

———. *The Hong Kong Airbase Murders.* Garden City, N.Y.: Crime Club, 1937.

Mathews, Frances Aymar. *A Little Tragedy at Tien-Tsin.* New York: Robert Grier Cooke, 1904.

Maugham, W. Somerset. *East and West.* New York: Literary Guild, 1921.

———. *On a Chinese Screen.* New York: George H. Doran Co., 1922.

Meagher, Maude. *White Jade.* Boston: Houghton Mifflin Co., 1930.

Michener, James A. *Hawaii.* New York: Random House, 1959.

Miller, Joaquin. "Phoebe of Sandy Gulch." *Overland Monthly* 14, no. 1 (Jan. 1875): 74–79.

Miln, Louise Jordan. *Mr. Wu.* New York: A. L. Burt Co., 1918.

———. *Mr. and Mrs. Sên.* New York: A. L. Burt Co., 1923.

———. *Ruben and Ivy Sên.* New York: Frederick A. Stokes Co., 1925.

———. *Red Lily and Chinese Jade.* New York: Frederick A. Stokes Co., 1928.

Morand, Paul. *The Living Buddha.* New York: Henry Holt & Co., 1928.

Morris, Gouverneur. *Yellow Men and Gold.* New York: Dodd, Mead & Co., 1911.

———. *The Footprint and Other Stories.* New York: Charles Scribner's Sons. 1920.

Newman, Shirlee Petkin. *Yellow Silk for May Lee.* New York: Bobbs-Merrill Co., 1961.

Norris, Frank. "Thoroughbred." *Overland Monthly* 2nd ser. 25 (Feb. 1895): 196–201.

———. "Bandy Callaghan's Girl." *The Wave* 15, no. 16 (April 18, 1896): 4–5.

———. *Moran of the Lady Letty.* New York: Doubleday & McClure, 1898.

———. *The Third Circle.* New York: John Lane, 1909.

O (Lionel James). *The Yellow War.* New York: McClure, Phillips & Co., 1905.

Oakes, Vanya. *Footprints of the Dragon.* Philadelphia: John C. Winston Co., 1949.

Packard, Frank L. *The Dragon's Jaw.* Garden City, N.Y.: Crime Club, 1937.

Parabellum (Ferdinand H. Giantoff). *Banzai.* New York: Baker & Taylor Co., 1908.

Paris, John. *Kimono.* London: Collins' Clear-Type Press, 1921.

———. *Sayonara.* New York, Boni & Liveright, 1924.

———. *Banzai.* New York: Boni & Liveright, 1926.

Pettit, Charles. *The Son of the Grand Eunuch.* New York: Boni & Liveright, 1927.

———. *Elegant Infidelities of Madame Li Pei Fou.* New York: Horace Liveright, 1928.

———. *Petal-of-the-Rose.* New York: Horace Liveright, 1930.

Poole, Ernest. *Beggars' Gold.* New York: Macmillan Co., 1921.

Porter, Hal. *Mr. Butterfry and Other Tales of New Japan*. London: Angus & Robertson, 1970.

Potter, John Dean. *Yamamoto, the Man Who Menaced America*. New York: Viking Press, 1965.

Raucat, Thomas. *The Honorable Picnic*. Tokyo: Charles E. Tuttle, 1924.

Robbe-Grillet, Alain. *The House of Assignation*. London: Calder & Boyars, 1970.

Rohmer, Sax (Arthur Sarsfield Ward). *The Insidious Dr. Fu-Manchu*, New York: McBride, Nast, 1913.

————. *The Mystery of Dr. Fu-Manchu*, London: Methuen.

————. *The Yellow Claw*. New York: McKinley, Stone & MacKenzie, 1915.

————. *The Devil Doctor*. New York: McBride, 1916.

————. *The Return of Dr. Fu-Manchu*. New York: McBride, 1916.

————. *The Hand of Fu-Manchu*. New York: McKinley, Stone & MacKenzie, 1917.

————. *The Si-Fan Mysteries*. London: Methuen, 1917.

————. *Dope*. New York: Cassell & Co., 1919.

————. *Tales of Chinatown*. Garden City, N.Y.: Doubleday Page & Co., 1922.

————. *Yellow Shadows*. Garden City, N.Y.: Doubleday Page & Co., 1926.

————. *Daughter of Fu-Manchu*. New York: Crime Club, 1931.

————. *The Mask of Fu Manchu*. New York: P. F. Collier & Son, 1932.

————. *Yu'an Hee See Laughs*. New York: Crime Club, 1932.

————. *Fu Manchu's Bride*. New York: Crime Club, 1933.

————. *Tales of East and West*. New York: Crime Club, 1933.

————. *President Fu Manchu*. New York: Crime Club, 1936.

————. *The Island of Fu Manchu*. New York: Doubleday & Co., 1940.

————. *Shadow of Fu Manchu*. New York: Crime Club, 1948.

————. *Re-Enter Fu Manchu*. Greenwich, Conn.: Fawcett Publications, 1957.

————. *Emperor Fu Manchu*. Greenwich, Conn.: Fawcett Publications, 1959.

————. *The Trail of Fu Manchu*. London: Allan Wingate, 1978, Orig. pub. c. 1934.

Seth, Ronald. *Spies At Work: A History of Espionage*. New York: Philosophical Library, 1954.

————. *A Spy Has No Friends*. New York: Library Publishers, 1954.

Shears, Sarah. *Courage to Serve*. London, Paul Elek, 1974.

Shepherd, Charles R. *The Ways of Ah Sin*. New York: Fleming H. Revel, 1923.

————. *Lim Yik Choy: The Story of a Chinese Orphan*. New York: Fleming H. Revell Co., 1932.

————. *The Story of Chung Mei*. Philadelphia: Judson Press, 1938.

Sparks, Theresa A. *China Gold*. Fresno, Calif.: Academy Library Guild, 1954.

Stevenson, F. V. "My China Boys." *Lippincott's Magazine* 27 (March 1881): 261–269.

Stickney, H. C. "Timely." *Lippincott's Magazine* 57 (June 1896): 859–864.

Stone, Grace Zaring. *The Bitter Tea of General Yen*. New York: Grosset & Dunlap, 1930.

Stratton-Porter, Gene. *Her Father's Daughter*. Garden City, N.Y.: Doubleday, Page & Co., 1921.

Strobridge, Idah Meacham. *The Land of Purple Shadows*. Los Angeles: Artemisia Bindery, 1909.

Sutherland, Howard Vigne. *Songs of a City*. San Francisco: Star Press, 1904.

Swinehart, Lois Hawks. *Sarangie, a Child of Chosen*. New York: Fleming H. Revell Co., 1926.

Taylor, Charles M. *Winning Buddha's Smile*. Boston: Gorham Press, 1919.

Teskey, Adeline M. *The Yellow Pearl*. New York: George H. Doran Co., 1911.

Twain, Mark (Samuel Clemens). *Sketches*. New York: Harper & Brothers, 1899.

———. *Roughing It*. Vol. 2., New York: Gabriel P. Wells, 1922.

Wallace, Kathleen. *I Walk Alone*. New York: Doubleday Doran & Co., 1931.

Wells, Florence. *Tama: The Diary of a Japanese School Girl*. New York: Woman's Press, 1920.

Wheat, Lu. *The Third Daughter*. Los Angeles: Oriental Publishing Co., 1906.

———. *Ah Moy: The Story of a Chinese Girl*. New York: Grafton Press, 1908.

Whitney, Atwell. *Almond-Eyed: The Great Agitator; A Story of the Day*. San Francisco: Bancroft, 1878.

Wiley, Hugh. *Jade and Other Stories*. New York: Alfred A. Knopf, 1921.

———. *Manchu Blood*. New York: Alfred A. Knopf, 1927.

———. *The Copper Mask*. New York: Alfred A. Knopf, 1932.

Woodworth, Herbert G. *In the Shadow of Lantern Street*. Boston: Small, Maynard & Co., 1920.

# General References

Achebe, Chinua. "The Role of the Writer in a New Nation." *Nigeria Magazine* 81 (June 1964): 157–160.

Adams, Phoebe. "Short Reviews: Books." *Atlantic Monthly* 227, no. 4 (April 1971): 104.

Akagi, Roy Hidemichi. "The Second Generation Problem: Some Suggestions toward Its Solution." Mimeo., Japanese Students Christian Association in North America, New York, 1926. Rare Materials Collection, Bancroft Library, University of California–Berkeley.

Alba, Jose C. "Filipinos in California." *Pacific Historian* 2 (1967): 37–41.

Allen, Henry. "Warrior's Luck." Washington *Post*, June 26, 1980. pp. D1, D4.

Amano Torasaburō. *To-Bei Rashin* (A compass to go to America). Tokyo: Tokyō Kōseisha, 1904.

Anderson, Grant K. "Deadwood's Chinatown." *South Dakota History* 5, no. 3 (summer 1975): 266–285.

Angoff, Charles. "An Oriental Views America." *American Mercury* 70, no. 1 (Aug. 1950): 241–245.

Anthony, Donald E. "Filipino Labor in Central California." *Sociology and Social Research* 16 (Sept. 1931–June 1932): 149–156.

Armentrout-Ma, L. Eve. "Chinese in California's Fishing Industry, 1850–1941." *California History* 60, no. 2 (summer 1981): 142–157.

Ball, John C., and Lau, M. P. "The Chinese Narcotic Addict in the United States." *Social Forces* 45, no. 1 (Sept. 1966): 68–72.

Ballard, Walter J. "Filipino Students in the United States." *Journal of Education* 67 (1908): 272.

Barlow, Janelle M. "The Images of the Chinese, Japanese, and Koreans in American Secondary School Textbooks, 1900–1970." Unpub. Ph.D. diss., University of California–Berkeley, 1972.

Barnett, Milton. "Alcohol and Culture: A Study of Drinking in a Chinese-

American Community." Unpub. Ph.D. diss., Cornell University, Ithaca, N.Y., 1952.

_____. "Kinship as a Factor Affecting Cantonese Economic Adjustment in the United States." *Human Organization* 19, no. 40 (0000): 40–46.

Barth, Gunther. *Bitter Strength: A History of Chinese in the United States, 1859–1870.* Cambridge, Mass.: Harvard University Press, 1964.

Beach, Walter G. *Oriental Crime in California: A Study of Offenses Committed by Orientals in the State, 1900–1927.* New York: AMS Press, 1971.

Bean, Robert Bennett. *The Races of Man.* New York: University Society, 1935.

Beck, Louis J. *New York's Chinatown.* New York: Bohemia Publishing Co., 1898.

Beja, Morris. "It Must Be Important: Negroes in American Fiction." *Antioch Review* 24, no. 3 (fall 1964): 323–336.

Blackburn, Sara. "Notes of a Chinese Daughter" (review of *The Woman Warrior*). *MS.*, Jan. 1977, pp. 39–40.

Blauner, Robert. *Racial Oppression in America.* New York: Harper & Row, 1972.

Bogardus, Emory S. *Immigration and Race Attitudes.* Boston: D. C. Heath, 1928.

_____. "The Filipino Immigrant Problem." *Sociology and Social Research* 13 (May–June 1929): 472–479.

_____. "American Attitudes towards Filipinos." *Sociology and Social Research* 29 (Sept.-Oct. 1929): 59–69.

_____. "Filipino Immigrant Attitudes." *Sociology and Social Research* 14 (May-June 1930): 469–479.

Bogle, Donald. *Toms, Coons, Mulattoes, Mammies, and Bucks.* New York: Viking Press, 1973.

Bolman, Helen P. Review of *Father and Glorious Descendant. Library Journal* 68, no. 7 (April 1, 1943): 287.

Bowler, Alida C. "Social Hygiene in Racial Problems—the Filipino." *Journal of Social Hygiene* 18 (1932): 452–456.

Bradford, Roark. *Ol' Man Adan an' His Chillun.* New York: Harper & Bros., 1928.

Braun, Joan Catherine. "'Yellow Daughters,' Culture." *Plexus*, Oct. 1980, p. 8.

Bridges, Nikki. "Conversations and Convergences." Paper delivered at the Asian American Women Writers' Panel, Occidental College, Los Angeles, Jan. 1978.

Brigham, J. C. "Ethnic Stereotypes." *Psychological Bulletin* 76 (1971): 15–38.

Brinkley-Rogers, Paul. "Outwhiting the Whites." *Pacific Citizen*, Dec. 1972, pp. 22–29.

Brown, Francis J., and Roucek, Joseph S. *One America: The History, Contributions, and Present Problems of Our Racial and National Minorities* (3rd ed.; Englewood Cliffs, N.J.: Prentice-Hall, 1952).

Brown, Sterling A. "Negro Character As Seen by White Authors." *Journal of Negro Education* 2, no. 2 (April 1933): 179–203.

_____. *Negro Poetry and Drama.* Washington, D.C.: Associates in Negro Folk Education, 1937.

_____. "A Century of Negro Portraiture in American Literature." *Massachusetts Review* 7, no. 1 (winter 1966): 73–96.

_____. *The Negro in American Fiction.* New York: Arno Press, 1969.

Buaken, Iris Brown. "My Brave New World." *Asia and the Americas* 43 (1943): 268–270.

————. "You Can't Marry a Filipino Not If You Live in California." *Commonweal* 41 (March 1945): 534–537.

Bunting, Glenn. "Is There Love after Mail-Order Marriage?" San Jose *Mercury News*, April 19, 1981, pp. 1–9.

Cabezas, Amado Y. "The Labor Force Status of Chinese Americans in the San Francisco Bay Area." Paper delivered at the Chinese American Community Forum, Oakland, Calif., Oct. 23, 1976.

————. "A View of Poor Linkages between Education, Occupation, and Earnings for Asian Americans." Paper delivered at the Third National Forum on Education and Work, San Francisco, Feb. 2–4, 1977.

————. "Evidence for the Low Mobility of Asian Americans in the Labor Market." Paper delivered at the UCLA–San Francisco State University–HEW Region IX and DOL Region IX Conference on Minorities in the Labor Market, March 31–April 1, 1977.

————. "Myths and Realities Surrounding the Socio-Economic Status of Asian and Pacific Americans." Paper delivered at the U.S. Commission on Civil Rights Consultation, Washington, D.C., May 8–9, 1979.

California Department of Justice. "Triad: Mafia of the Far East." In "Organized Crime and Criminal Intelligence Report," mimeo., July 1973.

California Fair Employment Practice Commission. *Chinese in San Francisco, 1970: Employment Problems of the Community as Presented in Testimony before the California Fair Employment Practice Commission.* San Francisco: The Commission, Dec. 1970.

Callao, Maximo Jose. "Cultural Shock—West, East, and West Again." *Personnel and Guidance Journal* 51, no. 6 (Feb. 1973): 413–416.

Cariaga, Roman, "Some Filipino Traits Transplanted." *Social Process* 2 (1936): 20–23.

Carlson, Lewis H. *In Their Place: White America Defines Her Minorities, 1850–1950.* New York: John Wiley & Sons, 1972.

Carnoy, Martin. *Education as Cultural Imperialism.* New York: David McKay Co., 1974.

Carter, Edward C. *China and Japan in Our University Curricula.* Chicago: University of Chicago Press, 1930.

Castagnozzi, Mary. "Maxine Hong Kingston Discusses Her Writing." *East/West*, May 13, 1981, p. 7.

Castro, Patria A. "Filipino Writers in America." Unpub. M.A. thesis, Columbia University, New York, 1951.

Catapusan, Benicio T. "The Filipino Labor Cycle in the United States." *Sociology and Social Research* 19 (Sept.-Oct. 1934): 61–63.

————. "Filipino Intermarriage Problems in the United States." *Sociology and Social Research* 22 (Jan.-Feb. 1938): 265–272.

————. *The Social Adjustment of Filipinos in the U.S.* Los Angeles: University of Southern California, 1940.

————. "The Filipinos and the Labor Unions." *American Federationist* 47 (1940): 173–176.

————. "Leisure-Time Problems of Filipino Immigrants." *Sociology and Social Research* 26 (Sept. 1941–Aug. 1942): 146–153.

Caudhill, William, and DeVos, George. "Achievement, Culture, and Personality:

The Case of the Japanese Americans." *The Disadvantaged Learner: Knowing, Understanding, Educating*, ed. Staten W. Webster, pp. 208–228. San Francisco: Chandler Publishing Co., 1966.

Chai, Chu. "Administration of Law among the Chinese in Chicago." *Journal of Criminal Law* 22 (1932): 806–818.

Chan, Clarence. "The Security Blanket of Racial Anonymity." *Bridge* 2, no. 2 (Dec. 1972): 19–21.

Chan, Sucheng. "Historical Notes on Racial Discrimination against Asians in America." Paper prepared for the World Conference for the Eradication of Racism and Racial Discrimination, Basle, Switzerland, May 18–21, 1978.

Chan Wing-Tsit. "Lin Yutang, Critic and Interpreter." *College English* 8, no. 4 (Jan. 1949): pp. 163–169.

Chang, Cordelia J. "Chinese-American Culture and Literature, 1943–1969: The Best of East and West?" Unpub. paper, University of California–Berkeley, Asian American Studies Library, 1969.

Chang, Francis Y. "An Accommodation Program for Second-Generation Chinese." *Sociology and Social Research* 18, no. 6. (July-Aug. 1934): 541–554.

Chen, Eugenia V. "Survey of Chinese Youth and Student Clubs in New York City." Unpub. M.A. thesis, University of Michigan, Ann Arbor, 1945.

Cheng, Fu Lung. "A Chinese Student and Western Culture." *Sociology and Social Research* 66, no. 1 (Sept.-Oct. 1931): 23–38.

Chesnaux, Jean. *The Chinese Labor Movement, 1919–1927*, trans. H. M. Wright. Stanford, Calif.: Stanford University Press, 1968.

Chin, Irving Shen Kee. "The Chinese in New York City." *Chinese Americans: School and Community Problems*, pp. 18–28. Chicago: Integrated Education Associates, 1972.

"The Chinaman." *Putnams* 9 (1857): 337.

Chinese Historical Society of America. *The Life, Influence, and the Role of the Chinese in the United States, 1776–1960*. San Francisco: The Society, 1976.

Chinn, Thomas W. *A History of Chinese in California: A Syllabus*. San Francisco: Chinese American Historical Society, 1969.

Chiu, Ping. *Chinese Labor in California, 1850–1880: An Economic Study*. Madison, Wisc.: State Historical Society of Wisconsin, for the Department of History, University of Wisconsin, 1967.

Chonk Moonhunter. Asian American Writers' Conference Tapes. San Francisco, 1975.

Chow, Christopher. "A Brother Reflects: An Interview with Aurelio Bulosan." *Amerasia Journal* 6, no. 1 (May 1979): 155–166.

Choy, Bong-Youn. *Koreans in America*. Chicago: Nelson-Hall Publishers, 1979.

Chu, George. "Chinatowns in the Delta: The Chinese in the Sacramento–San Joaquin Delta, 1870–1960." *California Historical Society Quarterly* 49 (1970): 21–38.

Chu, Limin. "The Images of China and the Chinese in the *Overland Monthly*, 1868–1875, 1883–1935." Unpub. Ph.D. diss., Duke University, Durham, N.C., 1965.

Chun, Ki-Taek. "The Myth of Asian American Success and Its Educational Ramifications." *Institute for Urban and Minority Education Bulletin* 15, nos. 1–2 (winter-spring 1980): 2–12.

Chun-hoon, Lowell. "Jade Snow Wong and the Fate of Chinese-American Identity." *Asian Americans: Psychological Perspectives*, ed. Stanley Sue and Nathaniel N. Wagner, pp. 125–135. Palo Alto, Calif.: Science & Behavior Books, 1973.

Clark, Helen F. "The Chinese of New York Contrasted with Their Foreign Neighbors." *Century Magazine* 53, no. 1 (Nov. 1897): 104–113.

Clemons, Walter. "East Meets West." *Newsweek* 88 (Oct. 11, 1976): 108–109.

Condit, Ira M. *The Chinaman As We See Him*. New York: Fleming H. Revell, 1900.

Conroy, Hilary, and Miyakawa, T. Scott. *East across the Pacific*. Santa Barbara, Calif.: American Bibliographical Center, CLIO Press, 1977.

"Contemporary Chivalry of the Samurai." New York *Times Book Review*, Jan. 10, 1926, p. 2.

Cook, Sherburne F. "The California Indian in Anglo-American Culture." *Ethnic Conflict in California History*, ed. Charles Wollenberg, pp. 23–42. Los Angeles: Tinnon-Brown, 1970.

Coolidge, Mary. *Chinese Immigration*. New York: Henry Holt, 1909.

"Coolie Cargoes." Asian Studies Inquiry Program, *China and the United States*, pp. 25–27. San Francisco: Field Educational Publications, 1969.

Council on Interracial Books for Children. "Asian Americans in Children's Books." *Interracial Books for Children Bulletin* 7, nos. 2–3 (1976).

————. *Stereotypes, Distortions, and Omissions in U.S. History Textbooks*. New York: Racism and Sexism Resource Center for Educators, 1977.

Cressey, Paul G. *The Taxi-Dance Hall*. Chicago: University of Chicago Press, 1932.

Croghan, Richard V. *The Development of Philippine Literature in English (since 1900)*. Quezon City: Alemar-Phoenix Publishing House, 1975.

Culin, Stewart. "The Gambling Games of the Chinese in America." *Publications of the University of Pennsylvania, Series in Philology, Literature, and Archaeology* 1, no. 4 (1891): 1–17.

Daniels, Roger C. "Westerners from the East: Oriental Immigrants Reappraised." Pacific Historical Review, 35, no. 4 (Nov. 1966): 373–383.

————. *The Politics of Prejudice: The Anti-Japanese Movement in California and the Struggle for Japanese Exclusion*. New York: Atheneum, 1972.

————. *The Decision to Relocate the Japanese-Americans*. Philadelphia: Lippincott Co., 1975.

Daniels, Roger C., and Olin, Spencer C., Jr. *Racism in California: A Reader in the History of Oppression*. New York: Macmillan Co., 1972.

DeVos, George. "A Quantitative Research Assessment of Maladjustment and Rigidity in Acculturating Japanese Americans." *Genetic Psychology Monograph* 52, no. 1 (Aug. 1955): 51–87.

DeWitt, Howard. *Anti-Filipino Movements in California: A History, Bibliography and Study Guide*. San Francisco: R & E Research Associates, 1976.

Didion, Joan. Review of *The Woman Warrior*. *Booklist* 73, no. 5 (Nov. 1, 1976): 385.

————. Review of *The Woman Warrior*. *Kirkus Reviews* 44, no. 14 (July 15, 1976): 826.

————. "A Book of Common Prayer" (review of *The Warrior Woman*). *California Monthly*, April-May 1977, p. 9.

Dillon, Richard H. *The Hatchet Men*. New York: Coward-McCann, 1962.

Dinnerstein, Leonard. *The Aliens*. New York: Meredith Corp., 1970.

Dobie, Charles. *San Francisco's Chinatown*. New York: Appleton-Century, 1936.

Downtown Community TV Center. "Chinatown Immigrants in America." Film, New York, 1978.

Durgnat, Raymond. "The 'Yellow Peril' Rides Again." *Film Society Review* 5, no. 2 (Oct. 1969): 36–39.

Edwards, Thomas R. "Books in Brief: Five Novels." *Harper's* 263, no. 1575 (Oct. 1976): 100.

Ellison, Ralph. *Shadow and Act.* New York: Random House, 1953.

Emch, Tom. "The Chinatown Murders." *California Living,* Sept. 9, 1973, pp. 8–21.

Endo, Russell. "Asian Americans and Higher Education." Paper delivered at the annual meeting of the Southwest Sociology Association, March 1974.

Epsey, John J. "A Filipino's Triumph of Faith and Spirit" (review of *America Is in the Heart*). New York *Herald Tribune Weekly Book Review* 19, no. 33 (April 11, 1943): 4.

Fenn, William Purviance. *Ah Sin and His Brethren in American Literature.* Peking: College of Chinese Studies, 1933.

Fiedler, Leslie A. *The Return of the Vanishing American.* New York: Stein & Day, 1968.

Fiset, Bill. "East Meets West." Oakland *Tribune,* May 2, 1979.

Fong, Kathryn M. "Woman's Review of 'Woman Warrior.'" San Francisco *Journal,* Jan. 25, 1978, p. 6.

Fong, Pauline L. "Economic Status of Asian Women." Paper delivered at the Advisory Council on Women's Educational Programs, San Francisco, Feb. 1976.

Ford, Nick Aaron. "Black Literature and the Problem of Evaluation." *College English* 32, no. 5 (Feb. 1971): 536–547.

Foronda, Marcellano A. "Recent Ilokano Fiction in Hawaii." *Bulletin of the American Historical Collection* 6, no. 4 (1978): 8–30.

Francisco, Luzviminda. "The First Vietnam." *Letters in Exile,* ed. Jesse Quinsaat, pp. 1–22. Los Angeles: UCLA Asian American Studies Center, 1976.

Franklin, John Hope. *Color and Race.* Boston: Houghton Mifflin Co., 1968.

Frazier, Thomas R. *The Underside of American History: Other Readings.* New York: Harcourt Brace Jovanovich, 1973.

Friar, Ralph E., and Friar, Natasha A. *The Only Good Indian . . . : The Hollywood Gospel.* New York: Drama Book Specialists/Publishers, 1972.

Fuchs, Lawrence H. *Hawaii Pono: A Social History.* New York: Harcourt Brace & World, 1961.

Fujimoto, Isao. "Don't Mistake the Finger Pointing at the Moon for the Moon." *Chinese-Americans: School and Community Problems,* pp. 1–7. Chicago: Integrated Education Associates, 1972.

Fujitomi, Irene, and Wong, Diane. "The New Asian-American Woman." *Asian Americans: Psychological Perspectives,* ed. Stanley Sue and Nathaniel Wagner, pp. 252–263. Palo Alto, Calif.: Science & Behavior Books, 1973.

Gallup, George. "Chinese Looking Better." San Francisco *Chronicle,* March 13, 1972, p. 15.

Garchik, Leah. "A Chinese Quest for Identity." *Asiaweek,* April 24, 1981, pp. 41–42.

_____. "'China Men' Came from a River of Images." San Francisco *Examiner & Chronicle,* May 24, 1981, pp. 4–5.

Gee, Emma. "Issei Women." *Counterpoint: Perspectives on Asian America*, ed. Emma Gee, pp. 359–364. Los Angeles: UCLA Asian American Studies Center, 1976.

———, ed. *Counterpoint: Perspectives on Asian America.* Los Angeles: UCLA Asian American Studies Center, 1976.

Gilbert, G. M. "Stereotype Persistence and Change among College Students." *Journal of Abnormal and Social Psychology* 46 (1951): 245–254.

Gissen, Max. "The Darker Brothers." *New Republic* 114, no. 12 (March 25, 1946): 420–422.

Givens, Helen L. "The Korean Community in Los Angeles." Unpub. M.A. thesis, University of Southern California, Los Angeles, 1939.

Goethe, C. M. "Filipino Immigration Viewed as a Peril." *Current History* 34 (June 1931): 353–354.

Goldberg, George. *East Meets West.* New York: Harcourt Brace Jovanovich, 1970.

Gompers, Samuel, and Gutstadt, Herman. *Meat vs. Rice: American Manhood against Asian Coolieism.* San Francisco: Asiatic Exclusion League, 1908.

Gonzalo, D. F. "Social Adjustments of Filipinos in America." *Sociology and Social Research* 14 (Nov.-Dec. 1929): 548–575.

Gordon, Milton M. *Assimilation in American Life.* New York: Oxford University Press, 1964.

Gray, Paul. "Book of Changes" (review of *The Woman Warrior*). *Time* 108, no. 23 (Dec. 1976): 91.

Grodzins, Morton. *Americans Betrayed: Politics and the Japanese Evacuation.* Chicago: University of Chicago Press, 1949.

Gulick, Sidney L. *Should Congress Enact Special Laws Affecting the Japanese? A Critical Examination of the "Hearings before the Committee on Migration and Naturalization" Held in California, July 1920.* New York: National Committee on America-Japan Relations, 1922.

H. J. S. "The Back Door to America" (review of *America Is in the Heart*). *Christian Science Monitor* 38, no. 91 (March 14, 1946): 20.

Haak, Ronald O. "Co-opting the Oppressors: The Case of the Japanese-Americans." *Transaction* 7, no. 23 (Oct. 31, 1970): 23–31.

Handley, Katherine Newkirk. *Four Case Studies in Hawaii.* Honolulu: University of Hawaii Press, 1957.

Handlin, Oscar. *The Uprooted.* Boston: Little, Brown & Co., 1952.

Hansen, Arthur A., and Hacker, David A. "The Manzanar 'Riot': An Ethnic Perspective." *Amerasia Journal* 2, no. 2 (fall 1974): 112–157.

Hartmann, Sadakichi. *White Chrysanthemums: Literary Fragments and Pronouncements*, ed. George Knox and Harry Lawton. New York: Herder & Herder, 1971.

Haslam, Gerald W. *Forgotten Pages of American Literature.* Boston: Houghton Mifflin Co., 1970.

Hayner, Norman S. "Family Life and Criminality among Orientals." Paper delivered at the annual meeting of the American Sociological Society, Dec. 29, 1936.

———. "Social Factors in Oriental Crime." *American Journal of Sociology* 43 (May 1938): 908–920.

Heizer, Robert F., and Almquist, Alan F. *The Other Californians: Prejudice and Discrimination under Spain, Mexico, and the United States to 1920*. Berkeley: University of California Press, 1971.

Hernton, Calvin C. *Sex and Racism in America*. New York: Doubleday & Co., 1965.

Higham, John. *Strangers in the Land*. New York: Atheneum, 1963.

Hori, Ami Chiyo. "Are the Sansei Avoiding Each Other?" *The Asianaian* 2, no. 1 (1979): 13–18.

Hosie, Lady. "A Voice from Korea." *Saturday Review of Literature*, April 4, 1931, p. 707.

Hosokawa, Bill. *Nisei: The Quiet American*. New York: William Morrow & Co., 1969.

Houchins, Lee, and Houchins, Chang-Su. "The Korean Experience in America." *Pacific Historical Review* 43 (1974): 548–575.

Houston, James D. "Writing a Non-Fiction Novel about the Internment of Japanese-Americans during World War II." *Solidarity* 9, no. 5 (May-June 1975): 66–72.

Hoyt, Edwin P. *Asians in the West*. New York: Thomas Nelson Publishers, 1974.

Hsu, Francis L. K. *Under the Ancestor's Shadow*. New York: Doubleday & Co., 1967.

————. *The Challenge of the American Dream: The Chinese in the United States*. Belmont, Calif.: Wadsworth, 1971.

Hsu, Kai-yu, ed. *Twentieth Century Chinese Poetry*. New York: Doubleday & Co., 1963.

Hundley, Norris. *The Asian American: The Historical Experience*. Santa Barbara, Calif.: American Bibliographical Center, CLIO Press, 1976.

Hyde, Stuart W. "The Chinese Stereotype in American Melodrama." *California Historical Society Quarterly* 34, no. 4 (Dec. 1955): 357–367.

Hymowitz, Carol, and Weissman, Michaele. *A History of Women in America*. New York: Bantam Books, 1978.

Ichihashi, Yamato. *The Japanese in the United States: A Critical Study of the Japanese Immigrants and Their Children*. Palo Alto, Calif.: Stanford University Press, 1932.

Ichioka, Yuji. *A Buried Past*. Berkeley: University of California Press, 1974.

Ignacio, Art; Kim, E. H.; Umemoto, Ann; Wang, Ling-Chi; and Wong, Sreve, eds. *Asian American Review* 2, no. 1 (1975).

Ijima Eitarō. *Beikoku tokō annai* (A guide to going to Japan). Tokyo: Hakubunkan, 1902.

"Income Gulch Widens between Sexes." San Francisco *Sunday Examiner & Chronicle*, June 17, 1979, p. 15.

Ishizuka Iozō. *Genkon to-Bei annai* (A current guide to America). Osaka: Ishizuka Shoten, 1903.

Isaacs, Harold R. *Images of Asia: The American View of China and India*. New York: Capricorn Books, 1962.

Ishigo, Estelle. *Lone Heart Mountain*. Los Angeles: Anderson, Ritchie & Simon, 1972.

Ito, Kazuo. *Issei: A History of Japanese Immigrants in North America*, trans. Shinichiro Nakamura and Jean S. Girard. Seattle: Executive Committee for Publication of *Issei*, 1973.

Iwasaki, Bruce. "Response and Change for the Asian in America." *Roots: An Asian American Reader*, ed. Amy Tachiki *et al*, pp. 89–100. Los Angeles: UCLA Asian American Studies Center, 1971.

―――. "Introduction: Asian American Literature." *Counterpoint: Perspectives on Asian America*, ed. Emma Gee, pp. 452–463. Los Angeles: UCLA Asian American Studies Center, 1976.

Jackman, Norman R. "Collective Protest in Relocation Centers." *American Journal of Sociology* 63 (1957): 264–272.

Jacobs, Paul, and Landau, Saul. *To Serve the Devil*, vol. 2. New York: Vintage Books, 1971.

Jayo, Norman. Interview with P. C. Morantte. La Puente, Calif., July 3, 1980.

"Jeffery Paul Chan, Chairman of S.F. State Asian American Studies, Attacks Review." *San Francisco Journal*, May 4, 1977, p. 6.

Johnson, Albert. "Beige Brown or Black." *Film Quarterly* 13, no. 1 (fall 1959).

Jones, Dorothy B. *The Portrayal of China and India on the American Screen, 1896–1955*. Cambridge: Massachusetts Institute of Technology, 1955.

Kagan, Leigh, and Kagan, Richard. "Oh Say Can You See? American Blinders on China." *America's Asia: Dissenting Essays on Asian-American Relations*, ed. Edward Friedman and Mark Selden, pp. 3–39. New York: Pantheon Books, 1971.

Kagiwada, George, and Fujimoto, Isao. "Asian American Studies: Implications for Education." *Personnel and Guidance Journal* 51, no. 6 (Feb. 1973): 400–405.

Kaku, Michio. "Asian Americans for a Fair Media." *Bridge* 2, no. 6 (Aug. 1973): 40–42.

―――. "Media and Racism and the Comics." *Bridge* 3, no. 1 (Feb. 1974): 82–86.

Kakugawa, Frances. "Asian-American Literature." *English Journal* 63, no. 7 (Oct. 1973): 110–111.

Kane, H. H. *Opium Smoking in America and China*. New York: G. P. Putnam, 1882.

Kane, M. B. *Minorities in Textbooks*. Chicago: Quadrangle Books, 1970.

Kang, Lynn. "Thoughts of the Times." *Korea Times*, July 16, 1972, pp. 3–4.

Katayama Sen. *To-Bei annai* (Guide to America). Tokyo: Rōdō Shimbunsha, 1901.

Katz, Bill. Review of *Before the War*. *Library Journal* 96, no. 1 (Jan. 1, 1971): 82.

Keim, Margaret Laton. "The Chinese as Portrayed in the Works of Bret Harte: A Study of Race Relations." *Sociology and Social Research* 25, no. 5 (May-June 1941): 441–450.

Keiser, Albert. *The Indian in American Literature*. New York: Oxford University Press, 1933.

Kershkhoff, Alan C., and McCormick, Thomas C. "Marginal Status and Marginal Personality." *Social Forces* 34, no. 1 (Oct. 1955): 48–55.

Kikuchi, Charles. *The Kikuchi Diary*, ed. John Modell. Urbana: University of Illinois Press, 1973.

Kim, Bernice. "Koreans in Hawaii." *Social Science* 9 (1934): 409–413.

Kim, Bok-Lim C. "Asian Americans: No Model Minority." *Social Work* 18 (May 1973): 44–53.

―――. "An Appraisal of Korean Immigrant Service Needs." *Social Casework* 57, no. 3 (1976): 139–148.

―――. *The Asian Americans: Changing Patterns, Changing Needs*. Montclair, N.J.: Association of Korean Christian Scholars in North America, 1978.

Kim, Elaine H. "The Myth of Asian American Success." *Asian American Review* 2, no. 1 (1975): 123–149.

_____. "Asian Americans and College English." *Education and Urban Society* 10, no. 3 (May 1, 1978): 321–336.

Kim, Hyung-Chan. "Some Aspects of Social Demography of Korean Americans." *International Migration Review* 8 (1974): 23–42.

_____, ed. *The Korean Diaspora.* Santa Barbara, Calif.: American Bibliographical Center, CLIO Press, 1977.

Kim, Hyung-Chan, and Patterson, Wayne. *Koreans in America, 1882–1974.* Dobbs Ferry, N.Y.: Oceana, 1974.

Kim, Warren Y. *Koreans in America.* Seoul: Po Chin Chai Printing Co., 1971.

Kimura Yoshigorō and Inoue Tanefumi. *Saikin seikaku Hawai tokō annai* (Current accurate guide to Hawaii). Tokyo: Hakubunkan, 1904.

Kinsman, Clare D., ed. *Contemporary Authors.* Detroit: Gale Research Co., Book Tower, 1974.

Kinsman, Clare D., and Tennehouse, Mary Ann. *Contemporary Authors.* Detroit: Gale Research Co., Book Tower, 1973.

Kirk, Grayson. "The Filipinos." *Annals of the American Academy of Political and Social Science* 223 (July 1942): 45–48.

Kitagawa, Daisuke. *Issei and Nisei: The Internment Years.* New York: Seabury Press, 1967.

Kitano, Harry. *Japanese Americans: The Evolution of a Subculture.* Englewood Cliffs, N.J.: Prentice-Hall, 1969.

_____. "Japanese American Mental Illness." *Asian Americans: Psychological Perspectives,* ed. Stanley Sue and Nathaniel Wagner, pp. 180–201. Palo Alto, Calif.: Science & Behavior Books, 1973.

_____. *Race Relations.* Englewood Cliffs, N.J.: Prentice-Hall, 1974.

Kitano, Harry, and Sue, Stanley. "The Model Minorities." *Journal of Social Issues* 29 (1973): 1–9.

Konvitz, Milton R. *The Alien and the Asiatic in American Law.* Ithaca, N.Y.: Cornell University Press, 1946.

Kramer, Jane. "On Being Chinese in China and America." *New York Times Book Review,* Nov. 7, 1976, pp. 1, 18–19.

Kumagai, Gloria L. "The Asian Woman in America." *Explorations in Ethnic Studies* 1, no. 2 (July 1978): 27–39.

Kung, Sien-Woo. *Chinese in America: Some Aspects of Their History, Status, Problems, and Contributions.* Seattle: University of Washington Press, 1962.

Kunitz, Stanley J. *Twentieth Century Authors,* 1st supp. New York: H. W. Wilson Co., 1955.

Kunitz, Stanley J., and Haycraft, Howard. *Twentieth Century Authors.* New York: H. W. Wilson Co., 1955.

Kuo Chia Ling. "Orientals Integrated in American Suburbs." *Viewpoints,* ed. Winston Press, pp. 233–240. Minneapolis: Winston Press, 1973.

Kuo, Helena. "Son and Illustrious Parent." *New York Times Book Review* 48, no. 15 (April 11, 1943): 19.

Kwoh, Beulah Ong. "The Occupational Status of American-born Chinese Male College Graduates." *American Journal of Sociology* 53, no. 3 (Nov. 1947): 192–200.

Lan, Dean. "Chinatown Sweatshops." *Amerasia Journal* 1, no. 3 (Nov. 1971): 40-57.

Larson, Charles K. "Heroic Ethnocentrism: The Idea of Universality in Literature." *American Scholar* 42, no. 3 (summer 1973): 463–475.

Lasker, Bruno. *Race Attitudes in Children.* New York: Henry Holt & Co., 1929.

_____. *Filipino Immigration to Continental United States and to Hawaii.* Chicago: University of Chicago Press, 1931.

_____. "In the Alaska Fish Canneries." *Mid-Pacific Magazine* 43 (1932): 335–338.

Latham, Edith F. "Japanese and Chinese in American Fiction, 1900–1938." Unpub. M.A. thesis, Columbia University, New York, 1938.

Lawrence, James R. "The American Federation of Labor and the Philippines Independence Question, 1920–1935." *Labor History* 7 (1966): 62–69.

Lederer, Richard, and Hall, Robert L. "Literature and the Minority Student." *Independent School Bulletin* 33, no. 4 (May 1974): 50–52.

Lee, Calvin. *Chinatown, U.S.A.* Garden City, N.Y.: Doubleday, 1965.

Lee, Chong Sik. *The Politics of Korean Nationalism.* Berkeley: University of California Press, 1963.

_____, ed. *Asian Immigrant Children in Schools.* Philip Jaisohn Memorial Paper no. 5. Philadelphia: Philip Jaisohn Memorial Foundation, 1979.

_____, ed. *Asian American Students Speak Out.* Philip Jaisohn Memorial Paper no. 6. Philadelphia: Philip Jaisohn Memorial Foundation, 1979.

Lee, Rose Hum. "The Social Institutions of a Rocky Mountain Chinatown." *Social Forces* 27 (Oct. 1948): 1–11.

_____. "The Decline of Chinatowns in the United States." *American Journal of Sociology* 54, no. 5 (March 1949): 422–432.

_____. *The Chinese in America.* Hong Kong: Hong Kong University Press, 1960.

Leonard, John. "She Talks to the Cantonese in Dreams." San Francisco *Sunday Examiner & Chronicle,* June 15, 1980, p. 38.

Leong, Gor Yun. *Chinatown Inside Out.* New York: Barrows Mussey, 1936.

Levy, Audrey. Review of *The Woman Warrior. Books West* 1 (April 1977): 27.

Lew, Louise. "Review of 'Woman Warrior.'" *Bridge* 5, no. 1 (April 1977): 47.

Lewis, Lewis, Henry T. *Ilocano Rice Farmers.* Honolulu: University of Hawaii Press, 1971.

Light, Ivan. *Ethnic Enterprise in America: Business and Welfare among Chinese, Japanese, and Blacks.* Berkeley: University of California Press, 1972.

_____. "The Ethnic Vice Industry, 1880–1944." *American Sociological Review* 42, no. 3 (June 1977): 464–479.

Lin Yueh-hwa. *The Golden Wing: A Sociological Study of Chinese Familism.* London: Kegan Paul, Trench, Trubner, 1948.

Lind, Andrew W. "Interracial Marriage as Affecting Divorce in Hawaii." *Sociology and Social Research* 49 (Oct. 1964–July 1965): 17–26.

_____. *Hawaii's People,* 3rd ed. Honolulu: University of Hawaii Press, 1967.

Liu, Kwang-Ching. *Americans and Chinese.* Cambridge, Mass.: Harvard University Press, 1963.

Liu, Ling. *The Chinese in North America.* Los Angeles: East-West Culture Publishing Association, 1949.

Lo, Samuel E. *Asian Who? In America.* Roseland, N.J.: East-West Who, 1971.

Lockhead, Donald G. "An Examination of the Presentation of Non-Anglo-Saxon Ethnic Groups in High School Literary Anthologies." Unpub. Ph.D. diss., University of Utah, Salt Lake City, 1971.

Loewen, James W. *The Mississippi Chinese: Between Black and White*. Cambridge, Mass.: Harvard University Press, 1971.

Lowenstein, Evelyn, *et al.*, eds. *The Picture Book of Famous Immigrants*. New York: Sterling Publishing Co., 1962.

Logan, Rayford W. *The Betrayal of the Negro*. New York: Collier Books, 1965.

Loomis, A. W. "How Our Chinamen Are Employed." *Overland Monthly*, March 1869, pp. 231–240.

Louis, Kit King. "Problems of Second Generation Chinese." *Sociology and Social Research* 16, no. 3 (Jan.-Feb. 1932): 250–258.

Lovett, Robert Morss. "East and West of Shanghai." *New Republic* 93, no. 1199 (Nov. 24, 1937): 80.

———. Review of *East Goes West*. *New Republic* 93, no. 1201 (Dec. 8, 1937): 153–154.

Low, Ron. "A Brief Biographical Sketch of a Newly-Found Asian Male." *Roots: An Asian American Reader*, ed. Amy Tachiki *et al.*, pp. 105–108. Los Angeles: UCLA Asian American Studies Center, 1971.

Lui, Garding. *Inside Los Angeles Chinatown, USA*. 1948.

Lyman, Stanford M. *The Asian in the West*. Social Science and Humanities Publication no. 4. Reno: Western Studies Center, Desert Research Institute, University of Nevada System, 1970.

———. "Red Guard on Grant Avenue: The Rise of Youthful Rebellion in Chinatown." *Asian Americans: Psychological Perspectives*, ed. Stanley Sue and Nathaniel Wagner, pp. 3–12. Palo Alto, Calif.: Science & Behavior Books, 1973.

———. *Chinese Americans*. New York: Random House, 1974.

———. *The Asian in North America*. Santa Barbara, Calif.: American Bibliographical Center, CLIO Press, 1977.

Lyman, Stanford M.; Willmott, William; and Ho, Berching. "Rules of a Chinese Secret Society in British Columbia." *Bulletin of the School of Oriental and African Studies* 27, no. 3 (1964): 530–539.

Lynch, William S. "Loyalty in Spite of All." *Saturday Review of Literature* 29, no. 10 (March 9, 1946): 7–8.

McCabe, James D., Jr. *Lights and Shadows of New York Life: Or, the Sights and Sensations of the Great City*. Philadelphia: National, 1872.

McClellan, Robert. *The Heathen Chinee*. Columbus, Ohio: Ohio State University Press, 1971.

McCullough, Norman Verrle. *The Negro in English Literature*. Devon, Eng.: Arthur H. Stockwell, 1962.

McLeod, Alexander. *Pigtails and Gold Dust*. Caldwell, Idaho: Caxton Printers, 1947.

McPherson, William. "Ghosts from the Middle Kingdom" (review of *The Woman Warrior*). Washington *Post Book World*, Oct. 10, 1976, p. E1.

McWilliams, Carey. "Exit the Filipinos." *Nation* 141 (1935): 265.

———. *Factories in the Field: The Study of Migratory Farm Labor in California*. Salt Lake City, Utah: Peregrine Publishers, 1971.

————. *Brothers under the Skin*. Boston: Little, Brown & Co., 1942.

Malloy, Michael. " 'The Woman Warrior': On Growing Up Chinese, Female, and Bitter." *National Observer*, Oct. 9, 1976, p. 25.

Manchel, Frank. "Stereotyping in Film." *Film Study: A Resource Guide*, pp. 88–122. Teaneck, N.J.: Fairleigh Dickinson University Press, 1973.

Mapp, Edward. *Blacks in American Films: Today and Yesterday*. Metuchen, N.J.: Scarecrow Press, 1972.

Marden, Charles. *Minorities in American Society*. New York: American Book Co., 1952.

Maruyama, Magoro. "Yellow Youth's Psychological Struggle." *Mental Hygiene* 55, no. 3 (July 1971): 382–390.

Matsumoto, Taishi. "The Protest of a Professional Carrot Washer." *Kashu Mainichi*, April 4, 1937.

Maykovich, Minako K. *Japanese American Identity Dilemma*. Tokyo: Waseda University Press, 1972.

Mears, Eliot Grinnell. *Resident Orientals on the American Pacific Coast*. New York: Institute of Pacific Relations, 1927.

Medwick, Lucille. "The Chinese Poet in New York." *New York Quarterly*, no. 4 (fall 1970), pp. 95–115.

Melendy, H. Brett. "California's Discrimination against Filipinos, 1927–1935." Institute of Asian Studies, *Occasional Papers*, no. 1, pp. 3–10. Quezon City: The Institute, 1967.

————. *Asians in America*. Boston: Twayne Publishers, 1977.

Meredith, G. M., and Meredith, C. G. "Acculturation and Personality among Japanese-American College Students in Hawaii." *Asian Americans: Psychological Perspectives*, ed. Stanley Sue and Nathaniel Wagner, pp. 104–110. Palo Alto, Calif.: Science & Behavior Books, 1973.

Methewson, Ruth. "Ghost Stories" (review of *The Warrior Woman*). *New Leader* 60 (June 6, 1977): 14–15.

Miller, Stuart Creighton. *The Unwelcome Immigrant: The American Image of the Chinese, 1785–1882*. Berkeley: University of California Press, 1969.

Miyamoto, Kazuo. *Hawaii: End of the Rainbow*. Rutland, Vt.: Charles E. Tuttle, 1964.

Miyamoto, Shotaro Frank. "Social Solidarity among the Japanese in Seattle." *University of Washington Publications in the Social Sciences* 11, no. 2 (Dec. 1939): 57–128.

Modell, John. "Class or Ethnic Solidarity: The Japanese Company Union." *Pacific Historical Review* 38, no. 2 (May 1969): 193–206.

————. "Tradition and Opportunity: The Japanese Immigrant in America." *Pacific Historical Review* 40, no. 2 (May 1971): 163–182.

————. *The Economics and Politics of Racial Accommodation*. Urbana: University of Illinois Press, 1977.

————, ed. *The Kikuchi Diary*. Urbana: University of Illinois Press, 1973.

Montagu, Ashley. *Race and I.W.* New York: Oxford University Press, 1975.

Morantte, P. C. "The Problem Facing the Filipino Author." *Philippines* 1, no. 5 (June 1941): 24.

Morgan, Murray. *Skid Road: An Informal Portrait of Seattle*, rev. ed. New York: Viking Press, 1960.

Moulton, David M. *The Socioeconomic Status of Asian American Families in Five Major SMSAS.* San Francisco: Asian American Service Institute for Assistance to Neighborhoods, 1978.

Munoz, Alfredo N. *The Filipinos in America.* Los Angeles: Mountainview Publishers, 1971.

Nahm, Tom Kagy. "Stop Stereotyping Me." *Newsweek,* Dec. 15, 1978, p. 15.

Namias, June. *First Generation.* Boston: Beacon Press, 1978.

Navarro, Jovina, ed. *Diwang Pilipino.* Davis: University of California at Davis, Asian American Studies, 1974.

Nee, Dale Yu. "Asian America Writers' Conference." *Bridge* 3, no. 6 (Aug. 1975): 42–48.

Nee, Victor. "The Kuomintang in Chinatown." *Bridge* 1, no. 5 (197?)· 20 24.

Nee, Victor, and de Bary, Brett. "Meanwhile, Back in Chinatown." San Francisco *Bay Guardian* 6, no. 2 (March 28, 1972): 3–7.

———. *Longtime Californ'.* Boston: Houghton Mifflin Co., 1974.

Nelson, Douglas. *Heart Mountain.* Madison: University of Wisconsin Press, 1976.

Nolen, Eleanor Weakley. "The Colored Child in Contemporary Literature." *Horn Book* 18, no. 5 (Sept. 1942): 348–355.

Norcross, John. "A Filipino's Lot in America" (review of *America Is in the Heart*). Chicago *Sun Book Weekly* 5, no. 97 (March 10, 1946): 4–5.

Novick, Julius. "No Cheers for the Chinaman." *New York Times,* June 18, 1972, p. 3D, cols. 1–4.

O'Brien, Robert W. "The Changing Role of the College Nisei during the Crisis Period, 1931–1943." Unpub. Ph.D. diss., University of Washington, Seattle, 1945.

Ogawa, Dennis. *From Japs to Japanese: The Evolution of Japanese-American Stereotypes.* Berkeley, Calif.: McCutchan, 1971.

———. "The Jap Image." *Asian Americans: Psychological Perspectives,* ed. Stanley Sue and Nathaniel Wagner, pp. 3–12. Palo Alto, Calif.: Science & Behavior Books, 1973.

Okamura, Raymond. "Schooling and Employment of Asian Americans." *Chinese Americans: School and Community Problems,* pp. 8–11. Chicago: Integrated Education Associates, 1972.

Omatsu, Glenn. "Nihonmachi Beat." *Hokubei Mainichi,* Jan. 12, 1972.

Paik, Irwin. "That Oriental Feeling." *Roots: An Asian American Reader,* ed. Amy Tachiki *et al.,* pp. 30–36. Los Angeles: UCLA Asian American Studies Center, 1971.

Palmer, Albert W. *Orientals in American Life.* New York: Friendship Press, 1934.

Park, Robert E. *Race and Culture.* New York: Free Press, 1950.

Pawlowska, Bethany Korwin. "It Takes an Orchestra to Play America." *Berkeley Monthly,* Dec. 1980, pp. 59–60.

Pearce, Roy Harvey. *Savagism and Civilization.* Baltimore: Johns Hopkins Press, 1953.

Pernia, Ernesto M. "The Question of the Brain Drain from the Philippines." *International Migration Review* 10 (1976): 63–72.

Perry, Jesse. "Viewpoint: Notes toward a Multicultural Curriculum." *English Journal* 64, no. 4 (April 1975): 8–9.

Peterson, William. *Japanese Americans: Oppression and Success.* New York: Random House, 1971.

Pfaff, Timothy. "Talk with Mrs. Kingston." New York *Times Book Review*, June 18, 1980, pp. 1, 25–27.

————. "Whispers of a Literary Explorer." *Horizon*, July 1980, pp. 58–63.

Phillips, Alan. "The Criminal Society That Dominates the Chinese in Canada." *MacLean's* 7, no. 11 (April 1962): 40–48.

Pomada, Elizabeth. "Passionate Memoir of a Girlhood among Ghosts" (review of *The Warrior Woman*). San Francisco *Sunday Examiner & Chronicle World* Oct. 17, 1976, p. 41.

————. "Paperbacks: New and Noteworthy" (review of *The Warrior Woman*). New York *Times Book Review*, Aug. 14, 1977, p. 31.

Price, John A. "The Stereotyping of North American Indians in Motion Pictures." *Ethnohistory* 20, no. 2 (spring 1973): 153–171.

————. "Lin Yutang." *Wilson Library Bulletin* 11, no. 5 (Jan. 1937): 298.

————. Review of *East Goes West*. *New Yorker* 13, no. 31 (Sept. 18, 1937): 74.

————. Review of *Father and Glorious Descendant*. *Library Journal* 68, no. 7 (April 1, 1943): 287.

————. Review of *America Is in the Heart*. *Wisconsin Library Bulletin* 42, no. 3 (March 1946): 45.

————. Review of *America Is in the Heart*. *Christian Science Monitor* 38, no. 91 (March 14, 1946): 20.

————. Review of *America Is in the Heart*. *Booklist* 42, no. 13 (March 15, 1946): 225.

————. Review of *America Is in the Heart*. *Wilson Library Bulletin* 20, no. 8 (April 1946): 570.

————. Review of *America Is in the Heart*. *United States Quarterly Book List* 2, no. 2 (June 1946): 96.

————. Review of *Before the War*. *Choice* 8, no. 8 (Oct. 1971): 1014.

————. Review of *Farewell to Manzanar*. *Library Journal*, Nov. 1, 1973, p. 3257.

————. Review of *Warrior Woman*. *Publisher's Weekly* 210, no. 6 (Aug. 9, 1976): 80.

Quinsaat, Jesse, ed. *Letters in Exile: An Introductory Reader on the History of Pilipinos in America.* Los Angeles: UCLA Asian American Studies Center, 1976.

Quinto, Delores. "Life Story of a Filipino Immigrant." *Social Process* 4 (1938): 71–78.

R. L. B. "The Bookshelf: Meeting of East and West" (review of *Father and Glorious Descendant*). *Christian Science Monitor* 35, no. 113 (April 9, 1943): 12.

Rabinowitz, Dorothy. "Books in Brief" (review of *Farewell to Manzanar*). *Saturday Review World*, Nov. 6, 1973, p. 34.

Reckless, Walter C. *Vice in Chicago.* Montclair, N.J.: Patterson Smith, 1969.

Review of *Daughter of the Samurai*. New York *Herald Tribune*, Nov. 22, 1925.

Richmond, Anthony H. *Readings in Race and Ethnic Relations.* Oxford: Pergamon Press, 1972.

Riis, Jacob. *How the Other Half Lives: Studies among the Tenements of New York.* New York: Sagamore Press, 1957.

Robertson, Nan. "'Ghosts' of Girlhood Lift Obscure Book to Peak of Acclaim." New York *Times*, Feb. 12, 1977, p. 26, cols. 1–4.

Rodecape, Lois. "Celestial Drama in the Golden Hills." *California Historical Quarterly* 23, no. 2 (June 1944): 97–116.

Rojo, Trinidad A. "Social Maladjustments among Filipinos in the United States." *Sociology and Social Research* 21 (May-June 1937): 447–457.

Ronquillo, Remigio B. "The Administration of Law among the Chinese in Chicago." *Journal of Criminal Law* 25 (July 1934): 205–224.

Rose, Arnold, and Rose, Caroline. *America Divided*. New York: Alfred A. Knopf, 1948.

———. *They and We*. New York: Random House, 1974.

Ross, Robert H., and Bogardus, Emory S. "The Second-Generation Race Relations Cycle." *Sociology and Social Research* 24, no. 4 (March-April 1940): 357–363.

Sandmeyer, Elmer Clarence. *The Anti-Chinese Movement in California*. Urbana: University of Illinois Press, 1973.

San Juan, Epifanio. *Carlos Bulosan and the Imagination of the Class Struggle*. Quezon City: University of the Philippines Press, 1972.

———. "Introduction." *Amerasia Journal* 6, no. 1 (May 1979): 3–29.

Sata, Lindbergh S. "Musings of a Hyphenated American." *Asian Americans: Psychological Perspectives*, ed. Stanley Sue and Nathaniel Wagner, pp. 150–156. Palo Alto, Calif.: Science & Behavior Books, 1973.

Sayre, Robert F. *Thoreau and the American Indians*. Princeton, N.J.: Princeton University Press, 1977.

Saxton, Alexander. *The Indispensable Enemy: Labor and the Anti-Chinese Movement in California*. Berkeley: University of California Press, 1971.

Scharrenberg, Paul. "Filipinos Demand Special Privileges." *American Federationist* 46 (1939): 1350–1353.

Schrieke, Bertram Johannes. *Alien Americans*. New York: Viking Press, 1936.

Schraufnagel, Noel. *From Apology to Protest: The Black American Novel*. Deland, Fla.: Everett/Edwards, 1973.

Schroyer, Preston. "Family Document." *Saturday Review of Literature* 26, no. 22 (May 29, 1943): 28.

Schwartz, Shepard. "Mate Selection among New York City's Chinese Males, 1931–1938." *American Journal of Sociology* 56 (May 1961): 562–568.

Shin, Linda. "Koreans in America, 1903–1945." *Amerasia Journal* 1, no. 3 (Nov. 1971): 32–39.

Sienkiwicz, Henry K. "The Chinese in California, as Reported by Henry K. Sienkiwicz," trans. Charles Morley. *California Historical Society Quarterly* 24 (Dec. 1955): 301–316.

Sigall, Harold, and Page, Richard. "Current Stereotypes: A Little Fading, a Little Faking." *Journal of Personality and Social Psychology* 18, no. 2 (May 1971): 247–255.

Simpson, George Eaton, and Milton, Ginger J. *Racial and Cultural Minorities: An Analysis of Prejudice and Discrimination*. New York: Harper & Row, 1972.

Siu, Paul C. P. "The Chinese Laundryman: A Study of Social Isolation." Unpub. Ph.D. diss., University of Chicago, 1953.

Skillin, Edward. "More Books of the Week" (review of *Father and Glorious Descendant*). *Commonweal* 38, no. 1 (April 23, 1943): 18–19.

Smith, William Carlson. *The Second Generation Oriental in America*. Honolulu: Institute of Pacific Relations, July 15–29, 1927.

———. *Americans in Process*. New York: Arno Press, 1970.

Social Science Institute. *Orientals and Their Cultural Adjustment.* Social Science Source Documents, no. 4. Nashville, Tenn.: Fisk University, 1946.

Sommers, Vita S. "Identity Conflict and Acculturation Problems in Oriental-Americans." *American Journal of Orthopsychiatry* 30, no. 3 (July 1960): 637–644.

———. "The Impact of Dual-Cultural Membership on Identity." *Psychiatry* 27, no. 4 (1964): 332–344.

Spears, Jack. "The Indian on the Screen." *Films in Review* 10, no. 1 (Jan. 1959): 18–35.

Starke, Catherine Juanita. *Black Portraiture in American Fiction.* New York: Basic Books, 1971.

"Stereotypes." *Thought and Statement,* ed. William Leary and James Steel Smith. New York: Harcourt Brace & World, 1960.

Stevens, Larry. *Chinese Americans.* Stckton, Calif.: Hammer Press, 1970.

Stonequist, Everett V. "The Problem of the Marginal Man." *American Journal of Sociology* 41, no. 1 (July 1935): 1–12.

———. *The Marginal Man.* New York: Russell & Russell, 1961.

Strong, Edward K. *The Second-Generation Japanese Problem.* London: Oxford University Press, 1934.

"Success Story of One Minority Group." *US News and World Report,* Dec. 26, 1966, pp. 49–56.

Strouse, Jean. "Dis-Oriented Men" (review of *China Men*). *Newsweek* 95, no. 24 (June 16, 1980): 88.

Stumbo, Bella. "Chinatown's New Dragon—Street Gangs." *View* (Los Angeles *Times*), Sept. 19, 1971, p. 16.

Sue, Derald Wing. "Ethnic Identity: The Impact of Two Cultures on the Psychological Development of Asians in America." *Asian Americans: Psychological Perspectives,* ed. Stanley Sue and Nathaniel Wagner, pp. 140–149. Palo Alto, Calif.: Science & Behavior Books, 1973.

———. "Understanding Asian Americans: The Neglected Minority." *Personnel and Guidance Journal* 51, no. 6 (Feb. 1973): 385–416.

Sue, Derald Wing, and Sue, Stanley. "Chinese American Personality and Mental Health." *Roots: An Asian American Reader,* ed. Amy Tachiki *et al.,* pp. 72–82. Los Angeles: UCLA Asian American Studies Center, 1971.

Sue, Stanley, and Wagner, Nathaniel, eds. *Asian Americans: Psychological Perspectives.* Palo Alto, Calif.: Science & Behavior Books, 1973.

Sung, Betty Lee. *Mountain of Gold.* New York: Macmillan Co., 1967.

———. *The Chinese in America.* New York: Macmillan Co., 1972.

Sunoo, Harold Hakwon, ed. "Koreans in America." *Korean Christian Scholars Journal* 2 (spring 1977).

Suzuki, Peter T. "Wartime *Tanka*: Issei and Kibei Contributions to a Literature East and West." *Literature East and West* 21 (1977): 242–254.

Tachiki, Amy; Wong, Buck; Odo, Franklin; and Wong, Eddie, eds. *Roots: An Asian American Reader.* Los Angeles: UCLA Asian American Studies Center, 1971.

Tagaki, Paul, and Platt, Tony. "Behind the Gilded Ghetto: An Analysis of Race, Class, and Crime in Chinatown." *Crime and Social Justice,* spring-summer 1978, pp. 2–25.

Taliaferro, Frances. "Spirited Relatives." *Harper's* 261, no. 1563 (Aug. 1980): 76–77.

Tanaka, Ronald. "On the Metaphysical Foundations of Sansei Poetics." *Journal of Ethnic Studies* 7, no. 2 (summer 1979): 1–36.

———. "Shito, or the Way of Poetry." *Journal of Ethnic Studies* 9, no. 4 (winter 1982): 1–64.

———. "The Circle of Ethnicity." *Journal of Ethnic Studies* 8, no. 3 (fall 1980): 1–64.

Taylor, Helene Scherff. Review of *America Is in the Heart*. *Library Journal* 71, no. 5 (March 1, 1946): 343–344.

TenBruek, Jacobus; Barnhard, Edward N.; and Matson, Floyd W. *Prejudice, War, and the Constitution*. Berkeley: University of California Press, 1972.

Thomas, Dorothy Swaine. *The Salvage*. Berkeley: University of California Press, 1952.

Thompson, David. "The Filipino Federation of America, Incorporated: A Study in the Natural history of a Social Institution." *Social Process* 7 (1941): 24–35.

Thrasher, Frederic M. *The Gang: A Study of 1,313 Gangs in Chicago*. Chicago: Phoenix Books, 1963.

*Tobei Shimpō* (America-bound news) 1, nos. 1–4 (May–Aug. 1907); 2, nos. 1–4 (Sept.-Dec. 1907); 6, nos. 1–12, and 7, nos. 1–3 (Jan.-March 1908).

*Tobei Zasshi* (American-bound magazine) 9, nos. 7–9 (July 3–Sept. 3, 1905; Dec. 3, 1905); 10, nos. 4–8 (April 3, 1906; Aug. 3, 1906; Oct. 1, 1906; Nov. 1, 1906).

Tong, Benjamin R. "The Ghetto of the Mind." *Amerasia Journal* 1, no. 3 (Nov. 1971): 1–31.

———. "A Living Death Defended as the Legacy of a Superior Culture." *Amerasia Journal* 2, no. 2 (fall 1974): 178–202.

———. "Critic of Admirer Sees Dumb Racist." *San Francisco Journal*, May 11, 1977, p. 6.

———. "Warriors and Victims: Chinese American Sensibility and Learning Styles." *Extracting Learning Styles from Social/Cultural Diversity*, ed. Lee Morris, Greg Sather, and Susan Scull, pp. 70–93. Washington, D.C.: Southwest Teacher Corps Network, 1978.

———. "On the 'Recovery of Chinese Culture." *San Francisco Journal* 4, no. 45 (July 30, 1980): 5–7.

Tow, Julius S. *The Real Chinese in America*. New York: Academy Press, 1923.

Ueda, Reed. "The Americanization and Education of Japanese Americans: A Psychodramatic and Dramaturgical Perspective." *Cultural Pluralism*, ed. Edgar G. Epps. Berkeley, Calif.: McCuthcan Publishing Corp., 1974.

United States Commission on Civil Rights. *Civil Rights of Asian and Pacific Americans: Myths and Realities*. Consultation proceedings, May 8–9, 1979. Washington, D.C.: The Commission, 1979.

———. "Success of Asian Americans: Fact or Fiction? *Clearinghouse Publication* no. 64 (Sept. 1980): 1–28.

United States Department of Commerce, Bureau of the Census. *General Population Characteristics: U.S. Summary*. Washington, D.C.: Government Printing Office, 1970.

Vallangca, Robert V. *Pinoy: The First Wave*. San Francisco: Strawberry Hill Press, 1977.

Vangelder, Robert. "An Interview with Doctor Lin Yutang." New York *Times Book Review* 46, no. 18 (May 4, 1941): 2, 18.

Wade, James. "Younghill Kang's Unwritten Third Act." *Korea Journal*, April 1973, pp. 57–61.

Wakayama Group. "Why Are There So Few Sansei Writers?" *Bridge* 2, no. 1 (Sept. 10, 1972): 17–21.

Walbridge, Earle F. "Carlos Bulosan" (review of *America Is in the Heart*). *Wilson Library Bulletin* 40, no. 8 (April 1946): 570.

Wang, Ling-Chi. "Chinese in the United States, 1940–1970: Historical Framework and Overview." Unpub. MS, Berkeley, Calif., 1980.

"The Warrior Woman." *Publisher's Weekly* 212 (Sept. 29, 1976): 72.

Watanabe, Colin. "Self-Expression and the Asian American Experience." *Personnel and Guidance Journal* 51, no. 6 (Feb. 1973): 390–396.

Waugh, Isami Arifuki. "Hidden Crime and Deviance in the Japanese American Community, 1920–1946." Paper delivered at the University of California–Berkeley Asian American Studies seminar, 1978.

Weglyn, Michi. *Years of Infamy: The Untold Story of America's Concentration Camps.* New York: William Morrow & Co., 1976.

Weiss, Melford. "Selective Acculturation and the Dating Process: The Pattern of Chinese-Caucasian Interracial Dating." *Journal of Marriage and the Family* 23, no. 2 (1970): 273–278.

Wheeler, Reginald W.; King, Henry H.; and Davidson, Alexander B. *The Foreign Student in America.* New York: Association Press, 1925.

Williams, Frederick. *Language and Poverty.* Chicago: Markham Publishing Co., 1970.

Wilson, Carol Green. *Chinatown Quest.* San Francisco: California Historical Society, 1931.

Wilson, Rob. "Review: 'All I Asking for Is My Body.'" *Bamboo Ridge* 5 (Dec. 1979–Feb. 1980): 2–5.

Wolfe, Tom. *Radical Chic and Mau-Mauing the Flak-Catchers.* New York: Farrar, Straus & Giroux, 1970.

Wollenberg, Charles, ed. *Ethnic Conflict in California History.* Los Angeles: Tinmon-Brown, 1970.

Wong, Eugene Franklin. *On Visual Media Racism: Asians in the American Motion Pictures.* New York: Arno Press, 1978.

Wong, Nellie. "The Woman Warrior." *Bridge* 6, no. 4 (winter 1978/79): 46–48.

Wong, Paul. "The Emergence of the Asian American Movement." *Bridge* 2 (1972): 32–39.

Wong, Sharon. Review of *The Woman Warrior*. *Library Journal* 101 (Sept. 15, 1976): 1849.

———. "Woman Warrior: Real Oppressions but No Answers." *Equality* (Asian Americans for Equality) 1, no. 3 (Jan.-Feb. 1978): 1.

Wong, Victor. "Childhood 1930s." *Ting, the Cauldron: Chinese Art and Identity in San Francisco,* ed. Elizabeth Abbott *et al.*, pp. 15–24. San Francisco: Glide Urban Center, 1970.

———. Childhood II." *Ting, the Cauldron: Chinese Art and Identity in San Francisco,* ed. Elizabeth Abbott *et al.*, pp. 69–72. San Francisco: Glide Urban Center, 1970.

Wu, Cheng-Tsu. *Chink!* New York: World Publishing Co., 1972.

Wunsch, Marie Ann. "Walls of Jade: Images of Men, Women, and Family in Second Generation Asian-American Fiction and Autobiography." Unpub. Ph.D. diss., University of Hawaii, Honolulu, 1977.

Yamada, Mitsuye. "Invisibility Is an Unnatural Disaster." *Bridge* 7, no. 1 (spring 1979): 10–13.

Yamauchi, Wakako. "The Poetry of the Issei on the Relocation Experience." *CALAFIA: The California Poetry*, ed. Ishmael Reed, pp. lxxi–lxxviii. Berkeley, Calif.: Yardbird Books, 1979.

Yatssushiro, Toshio; Ishino, Iwao; and Matsumoto, Yoshiharu. "The Japanese-American Looks at Resettlement." *Public Opinion Quarterly* 8 (summer 1944): 188–201.

Yee, Albert H. "Myopic Perceptions and Textbooks." *Journal of Social Issues* 29, no. 2 (1973): 99–113.

Yee, Harold T. "The General Level of Well-being of Asian Americans." San Francisco: Asian American Service Institute for Assistance to Neighborhoods, 1977.

Yee, Min. "Chinatown in Crisis." *Newsweek* 75 (Feb. 23, 1970): 57–58.

———. "Cracks in the Great Wall of Chinatown." *Ramparts* 2, no. 4 (1972): 34–38, 56–59.

Yoneda, Carl. "One Hundred Years of Japanese Labor in the U.S.A." *Roots: An Asian American Reader*, ed. Amy Tachiki *et al.*, pp. 150–158. Los Angeles: UCLA Asian American Studies Center, 1971.

Yoshioka, Robert B., *et al.* "Asian Americans and Public Higher Education in California." Report prepared for the California State Legislature Joint Committee on the Master Plan for Higher Education, Feb. 1973.

Yung, Judy. "Kowtows to 'Woman Warrior.'" *East/West*, April 13, 1977, p. 7.

Zo, Kil Young. *Chinese Emigration into the United States, 1850–1880*. Ann Arbor: University of Michigan Microfilms, 1971.

# Index

355

16  93